D1237293

SPEAKING THE TRUTH IN LOVE

Orthodox Christianity and Contemporary Thought

Series Editors: George Demacopoulos and Aristotle Papanikolaou

This series consists of books that seek to bring Orthodox Christianity into an engagement with contemporary forms of thought. Its goal is to promote (1) historical studies in Orthodox Christianity that are interdisciplinary, employ a variety of methods, and speak to contemporary issues; and (2) constructive theological arguments that, in conversation with patristic sources, focus on contemporary questions ranging from the traditional theological and philosophical themes of God and human identity to cultural, political, economic, and ethical concerns. The books in the series will explore both the relevancy of Orthodox Christianity to contemporary challenges and the impact of contemporary modes of thought on Orthodox self-understandings.

SPEAKING THE TRUTH IN LOVE

*Theological and Spiritual Exhortations of
Ecumenical Patriarch Bartholomew*

ECUMENICAL PATRIARCH BARTHOLOMEW

Edited and with an Introduction by
JOHN CHRYSSAVGIS

FORDHAM UNIVERSITY PRESS
New York 2011

Copyright © 2011 Fordham University Press

All rights reserved. No part of this publication may be reproduced, stored in a retrieval system, or transmitted in any form or by any means—electronic, mechanical, photocopy, recording, or any other—except for brief quotations in printed reviews, without the prior permission of the publisher.

Fordham University Press has no responsibility for the persistence or accuracy of URLs for external or third-party Internet websites referred to in this publication and does not guarantee that any content on such websites is, or will remain, accurate or appropriate.

Fordham University Press also publishes its books in a variety of electronic formats. Some content that appears in print may not be available in electronic books.

Library of Congress Cataloging-in-Publication Data

Bartholomew I, Ecumenical Patriarch of Constantinople, 1940–
    Speaking the truth in love : theological and spiritual exhortations of Ecumenical Patriarch Bartholomew / Ecumenical Patriarch Bartholomew ; edited and with an introduction by John Chryssavgis.
        p. cm.— (Orthodox Christianity and contemporary thought)
    Includes bibliographical references and index.
        ISBN 978-0-8232-3337-3 (cloth : alk. paper)—ISBN 978-0-8232-3339-7 (ebook)
        1. Theology.   2. Orthodox Eastern Church—Doctrines.   3. Spiritual life—Orthodox Eastern Church.   4. Christian union—Orthodox Eastern Church.   I. Chryssavgis, John.   II. Title.
BX395.B37A5   2011
230′.19—dc22

                                                                                2010034536

Printed in the United States of America

13   12   11   5   4   3   2   1

First edition

CONTENTS

FOREWORD

There is one aspect of the rich deposit of theological writing from His All Holiness, the Ecumenical Patriarch, that is particularly striking and valuable in our day. He shows an absolute consistency in his commitment to an understanding of Christian identity, an understanding central to the Eastern Christian tradition—though sadly not always so much in evidence in the modern Western Christian world: an understanding that insists that to be a Christian is not primarily to adhere to a set of principles and decide to be affiliated to an organization; it is to be taken into a comprehensive new reality. "Membership of the Church," he writes in his 1997 lecture at Georgetown University, "is not an act of cataloguing a person as a member of a group but the true rebirth of this person in a new reality, the world of grace." Christian identity is an "ontological" matter; as some of the best contemporary Orthodox theologians have put it, Christian faith is about the alternatives of life and death rather than of abstract good or evil. The Church is where the divine life is lived on earth by the outpouring of the Holy Spirit which creates in us the living prayer of Christ the Son of the eternal Father. To be a Christian is to participate, not just to give mental assent or emotional loyalty.

Two highly significant things follow from this. As many of the following addresses and essays make plain, faithfulness to the Church has to be distinguished from loyalty to national or cultural identities. Orthodox Christianity is not and must not become the prisoner of local or ethnic identity; not that such identities are evil, but that they are all of them to be taken into the catholic identity of the Body of Christ so that they serve each other and the good of the whole Christian community. "It is time for us to begin to reconcile nationalism and ecumenism," declares the Patriarch in his address at the British Museum in 1993; and that, as he makes plain, involves the difficult task of engaging in honest historical memory, both celebrating the heritage of a local past and its Christian culture or cultures *and* looking at it with a critical eye for what needs repentance. And, as the Patriarch explains in an especially profound and moving homily delivered in 1997 in St Peter's Basilica, this acknowledgment of failure and sin in our history is something we must learn to *share* as Christians—not something we can exploit to reproach one another, but a matter of making ourselves freely responsible for each other within the Body. In this spirit, His All Holiness has given sacrificially of his energies in furthering collaboration between the local autocephalous and autonomous churches of the Orthodox world, convinced that the Orthodox witness in our day requires a more coherent and convergent approach than ever in terms of local churches working together. Only so will the world come to know that in Christ "all the divisions of the world are overcome and the common nature of all human beings is affirmed" (from the Message of the assembled Orthodox Primates in 2008).

But this is a conviction that has its roots in the deepest insights of the theology expounded by the Patriarch. He naturally takes for granted that theology of communion, *koinonia*, which has been so important a part of what Orthodoxy has shared with the rest of the Christian world, especially in recent decades. But he adds to this a theme that has been touched on by a number of modern Orthodox writers yet has not made quite the same impact—perhaps because it reminds us of the cost of discipleship. Communion entails *kenosis*: The life-giving identification of God the Word with humanity meant a self-emptying, a refusal of isolation and safety and individual power, so that divine and human life could truly interpenetrate. "His total sharing in our humiliation is the true summit of his divine omnipotence" (from an address to the Trondheim Conference of CEC in 2003). So too our identification with one another in the Body of Christ requires of us a *kenotic* love for one another, if the flow of life within the Body of Christ is to be at its fullest. Christian relations with other Christians constitute "a spiritual communion, a kenosis that aspires to the enrichment of the other. It is not a contest aimed at scoring victory over the other, but an offering of the overflow of experience in participating in the truth of Christ. It is precisely for this reason that it is an offering that is unselfish and sacrificial." These words, from a greeting in 2002 to a delegation from the Vatican, express with great force a doctrinal perception that pervades much of the Patriarch's writing and thinking. And it is out of this insight that he can so memorably define our calling under God as "opening up to the heart; opening up to the other; and opening up to creation" (from his 2009 lecture at Fordham)—conscious of all the cost that such "opening" brings, yet seeing it as part of the gift of Christlike self-emptying that we are summoned and enabled to offer one another.

These deeply reflective and creative pieces are the evidence of a mind and heart steeped in the traditions of Orthodox theology and the disciplines of the *Philokalia* and the other great landmarks of spiritual guidance in the Eastern Church. Out of this treasury come things new and old: a reaffirmation of the essential doctrines of the Church, with a careful and pastorally sensitive defense of Orthodox discipline, but also a radical and challenging engagement with the contemporary world in all its tragic confusion and self-destructive complexity. The Patriarch is well-known for his tireless advocacy on environmental questions: Here the reader will find the full theological background for his commitments. Here too there is a serious and consistent exposition of the Christian doctrine of the glory and the vulnerability of the human person—the image of God, yet also the victim of self-inflicted tragedy. Here, above all, is a clear and compelling statement of what it means to accept the new life offered in Christ, life in communion and self-giving. The Patriarch does not avoid difficult questions, the often frustrating and saddening practicalities of living in a divided Christian world, but locates all of them in the context of a theology that is unambiguously grounded in the transforming effect of the Incarnation of the Word and the gift of the Spirit.

The Christian world is fortunate to have in this historic office a thinker and pastor of such wisdom, capable of holding the diverse problems of the day firmly within the generous bounds of classical Christian orthodoxy. This is not only a book of intellectual interest for believers; it is in its way a strong *apologetic* for orthodox Christian faith, showing how richly the Eastern tradition can illuminate the issues of our times. Christians of all confessions may well give thanks for the witness of His All Holiness to these great truths, and for his unfailing ecumenical charity and courtesy. It is a privilege to be able to welcome the publication of these essays and addresses, in the hope that they will assist in that enriching, kenotic spiritual communion that the Patriarch both describes in his words and embodies in his service to the Church.

+ Rowan Cantuar:

From Lambeth Palace,
Pentecost, 2010

PREFACE

This is the second of three volumes of Ecumenical Patriarch Bartholomew's writings. The first volume spoke to a contemporary world about human rights, religious tolerance, international peace, and environmental awareness. A third volume will follow, containing the Ecumenical Patriarch's presentations and statements on environmental degradation, global warming, and climate change. The series should be read alongside relevant chapters in another monograph by His All Holiness, entitled *Encountering the Mystery: Understanding Orthodox Christianity Today* (New York: Doubleday, 2008).

Speaking the Truth in Love contains a selection of major letters, addresses, and statements by His All Holiness Ecumenical Patriarch Bartholomew, particularly as these relate to his ecumenical vision and sincere desire "for the unity of the Churches of God" through balanced and bilateral dialogue with other Christian confessions. Whereas the first volume covered global and interfaith issues, this volume represents the inter-Christian initiatives and theological outreach of the Patriarch, covering a range of topics, such as ecumenism and theology. Moreover, it includes an anthology of significant lectures—and even certain unique addresses—on a variety of ecclesiastical and scholarly occasions, such as the historical gatherings of leaders of Orthodox Patriarchates and autocephalous churches as well as notable academic conferences and events.[1] Finally, it also encompasses a selection of pastoral letters and addresses—ecclesiastical, ecumenical, and academic in nature—by His All Holiness on a variety of occasions, such as Easter and Christmas and ceremonies accompanying his reception of honorary doctorates and academic awards.

---

1. Subtitles and footnotes throughout the introduction and the volume belong to the editor and are provided to facilitate reference and reading of the texts.

In addition to ongoing guidance received from Fordham University Press as well as the support of Dr. Aristotle Papanikolaou and Dr. George Demacopoulos, cofounding directors of the Orthodox Christian Studies Program at Fordham University, I am deeply grateful to Paul Gikas at the Ecumenical Patriarchate, whose encouragement and assistance have proved invaluable throughout this entire series—and beyond.

J.C.

Introduction

REV. DR. JOHN CHRYSSAVGIS

The Ecumenical Patriarch was trained and experienced in inter-Christian relations, having pursued studies in Roman Catholic theology at the Gregorian University of Rome, in Protestant thought at the University of Munich, and in the ecumenical movement at the World Council of Churches in Geneva. Moreover, he has lectured widely on the significance and role of Orthodox theology in contemporary society, having received honorary doctorates from esteemed academic institutions throughout the world.

Unafraid to address sensitive and even controversial issues—such as papal primacy, divisions within Christianity, and the fragility of inter-Orthodox unity—His All Holiness balances Orthodox doctrine and canon law with open-mindedness and open-heartedness. Sometimes, his remarks appear gentle and provide guidelines, revealing historical and human understanding of misconceptions or deviations. At other times, his words have the effect of rebuke and even censure; they seek to rectify errors or inform ignorance. Always, however, his statements reflect a profound and positive determination to "speak the truth in love" (Eph. 4.15) in an effort to provide a contribution to ecumenical discussion that will prove constructive in the search for Christian unity. In this regard, he is faithful to the teaching of St. Paul, who urges leaders

> to equip the saints for the work of ministry, for building up the body of Christ, until all of us come to the unity of the faith and of the knowledge of the Son of God, to maturity, to the measure of the full stature of Christ.

For we must no longer be as children, tossed to and fro and blown about by every wind of doctrine, by people's deceit or by their craftiness in schemes. But *speaking the truth in love*, we must grow up in every way into him who is the head, into Christ, from whom the whole body, joined and knit together by every ligament with which it is equipped, as each part is working properly, promotes the body's growth in building itself up in love.

Eph. 4.12–16

Moreover, as His All Holiness often confesses and acknowledges, he stands fully in the tradition of a long list of Ecumenical Patriarchs from antiquity (such as St. Gregory the Theologian in the fourth century and St. John Chrysostom in the fifth century) through contemporary times (such as Patriarchs Athenagoras and Dimitrios, his immediate predecessors).

The visits of Ecumenical Patriarch Bartholomew to Rome as the personal guest of Pope John Paul II marked the first occasion in history that an Orthodox patriarch met so regularly with the Roman Catholic pope. His invitation to Pope Benedict XVI marked the opening of the pontiff's ministry and the pontiff's first visit to a Christian minority within a Muslim nation. Over the last two decades, Bartholomew is also the first Ecumenical Patriarch to have traveled so widely throughout the world and to have convened meetings of Orthodox primates of autocephalous churches as well as assemblies of bishops directly within the Ecumenical Patriarchate. This book plainly reveals the spiritual depth and profound doctrine of the Orthodox Church from the unique perspective of a Christian leader *speaking the truth in love* (Eph. 4.15).

The first volume in this series by Fordham University Press incorporates a detailed biographical note on Ecumenical Patriarch Bartholomew. In the present volume, I have chosen instead to outline significant moments that shaped the Patriarch's ecumenical conscience and theological principles, which have enabled him to articulate "the truth in love." The timeline below is complemented by passages from three exceptional theologians—the late Professor Olivier Clément (an extraordinarily insightful and inspiring French theologian and historian, who interviewed His All Holiness in preparation for a book), His Eminence Archbishop Demetrios of America (a senior and revered hierarch and scholar of the Orthodox Church, who in his diverse roles representing His All Holiness has comprehended and embraced the vision of the Ecumenical Patriarchate), and Dr. Samuel Kobia (former general secretary of the World Council of Churches, who explicitly testified to the ecumenical openness of the Patriarchate and actively supported the ecumenical leadership of His All Holiness).

BIOGRAPHICAL TIMELINE

Key Educational and Ecumenical Milestones

STUDENT YEARS

1957–61 Following primary and secondary schooling on his island of Imvros and at the Zografeion Lyceum in Istanbul, His All Holiness studied at the Patriarchal Theological School of Halki.[1]

1963–68 His All Holiness pursued graduate studies in Europe.

1963–66 He enrolled at the Pontifical Oriental Institute of the Gregorian University in Rome. There he completed his doctoral dissertation, "The Codification of the Holy Canons and Canonical Constitutions in the Orthodox Church."[2]

During his time in Rome, Vatican II was in full swing and, as a student, His All Holiness was among the first Orthodox observers to participate in this historic council of the Roman Catholic Church.

While in Rome as a young deacon, he stayed at the Pontifical French Seminary, directed by the Holy Ghost Fathers, and performed volunteer work with the Little Sisters of Jesus (of Fr. DeFoucault). There he crossed paths with such pioneers of ecumenism as Cardinal Augutin Bea as well as Fathers Jean Daniélou, Yves Congar, Emmanuel Lanne, Christophe Dumont, Pierre Duprey, and Henri De Lubac. He also came to know Pope Paul VI personally.

In Italy, he mastered Italian, Latin, and French. He is also fluent in Greek, Turkish, and English.

---

1. See the first address in Chapter 4, "Academic Discourses," 314.

2. Published in 1970 at the Patriarchal Institute for Patristic Studies in Thessaloniki, Greece.

1966–67   He studied at the Ecumenical Institute of Bossey in Switzerland, an academic (graduate) school affiliated with the World Council of Churches. At Bossey, he came into contact and studied under the inspirational theologian Nikos Nissiotis, who served as director of the school.[3]

1967–68   At the University of Munich, he learned about Protestantism as he studied canon law and learned German.

EARLY APPOINTMENTS

1968–72   He returned to Turkey, where he served as assistant dean at the Patriarchal Theological School of Halki. In 1969, he was ordained to the priesthood by his spiritual father, Metropolitan Meliton of Chalcedon, and appointed archimandrite of the Patriarchal Court by Ecumenical Patriarch Athenagoras.[4]

His All Holiness was a founding member (serving as vice president for several terms) of the Society of Canon Law of the Oriental Churches, which is based in Vienna.

He was a member of the bilateral commission that prepared and edited the historical publication *Tomos Agapis* (Rome and Istanbul, 1971), which contains the official correspondence between the Vatican and the Phanar from 1958 through 1970.

This period also saw the first theological and ecclesiastical publications by His All Holiness in a variety of journals in Istanbul (*Stachys*), Thessaloniki (*Gregory Palamas*), and Geneva (*Episkepsis*). Most of his articles were related to canonical and spiritual matters.[5]

---

3. An outstanding and creative Greek theologian, Nissiotis (1925–86) taught philosophy and psychology of religion at the University of Athens. He was also an ecumenical visionary and permanent observer at Vatican II.

4. A senior and influential hierarch of the Ecumenical Patriarchate, Metropolitan Meliton of Chalcedon (1913–89) served during the tenures of Patriarch Athenagoras and Patriarch Dimitrios.

5. For a comprehensive list of publications by His All Holiness before his election to the Ecumenical Throne, see V. Istavridis, "Bartholomew Archontonis of Constantinople: from 1940 to 1991," *Gregory Palamas* 77, 754 (1994): 411–21.

INTERNATIONAL EXPERIENCE

1972–91   He directed the Private Patriarchal Office as the closest co-worker and advisor of Ecumenical Patriarch Dimitrios until the repose of the latter, when he was elected archbishop of Constantinople, New Rome, and Ecumenical Patriarch. He accompanied Ecumenical Patriarch Dimitrios on all his visits of love, peace, and unity as well as generally on all foreign trips, which proved to be a rich source of indispensable experience and wisdom in interchurch and interfaith relations. These journeys included visits to autocephalous and autonomous Orthodox Churches, the pope, the archbishop of Canterbury, and the World Council of Churches. In 1973, he was elected metropolitan of Philadelphia and, in 1974, a member of the Holy and Sacred Synod.

During these years, His All Holiness published a number of articles on relations with the Roman Catholic Church and the ecumenical movement as well as on the convocation of the forthcoming Holy and Great Council of the Orthodox Church and on the Orthodox "diaspora." Moreover, it is during this period that His All Holiness clearly perceived and articulated his conviction of and dedication to the ecumenical conscience and character of the Ecumenical Patriarchate.

In 1980, he was instrumental in establishing the official theological dialogue between the Roman Catholic and the Orthodox Churches, which was first announced during the official visit of Pope John Paul II to the Phanar on November 30, 1979.[6] In 1987, His All Holiness accompanied Ecumenical Patriarch Dimitrios on his official visit to the Vatican.

1990   He chaired a meeting of the Inter-Orthodox Preparatory Commission for the Holy and Great Council of the Orthodox Church, initiating discussion about the problem of multiple

---

6. This occasion marked the first time that a Roman Pope traveled to Istanbul in order to visit the Ecumenical Patriarchate.

jurisdictions in Western nations (the so-called "diaspora").[7] In his opening address as chairman of the commission, Bartholomew—then metropolitan of Chalcedon and senior metropolitan of the Holy and Sacred Synod—spoke of the pride of the Church in its "weakness" and of the treasure of the Church in its "clay vessels" (2 Cor. 4.7), thereby clearly denouncing any spirit of triumphalism.[8]

1990   He received his first honorary doctorate, from the University of Athens.[9]

He served as member (fifteen years) and as vice president (eight years, 1975–83) of the Faith and Order Commission of the World Council of Churches, the only commission in which Roman Catholics also participate. He was vice president during the development of the BEM (Baptism, Eucharist, and Ministry) document. He participated in three general assemblies of the WCC: Uppsala (1968), Vancouver (1983), and Canberra (1991). In 1991, during the Seventh General Assembly of the World Council of Churches, he was elected to the Central Committee.

ECUMENICAL PATRIARCH

1991   Bartholomew was elected on October 22 and enthroned on November 2, 1991, as 270th Archbishop of Constantinople, New Rome, and Ecumenical Patriarch.

---

7. To date, the Inter-Orthodox Preparatory Commission has met in Chambésy in 1971, 1986, 1990, 1993, and 2009. Parallel to these meetings, four preconciliar Pan-Orthodox Conferences have taken place in Chambésy in 1972, 1982, 1986, and 2009. In addition, two special congresses have convened to discuss the common celebration of Easter (1977) and the operation of local episcopal assemblies (1995).

8. See Bartholomew, Metropolitan of Chalcedon, "The Pride of the Church 'in Its Weakness,'" *Ekklesia* (Athens, 1991): 7–13 [in Greek].

9. His All Holiness also holds honorary doctorates from academic institutions throughout the world, including the United States (including Yale University, Tufts University, Georgetown University, and Fordham University), Britain (including City University, Exeter University, and Edinburgh University) Europe (including Catholic University of Louvain, Ravenna University, and Aix-en-Provence University), and Asia (Adamson University and Flinders University).

1992   He convened the first historic *Synaxis* of Primates of all auto-cephalous Orthodox churches (March 31, 1992). Five such gatherings have taken place in Istanbul (1992, 2000, and—most recently—in 2008), Patmos (1995), and Jerusalem/Bethlehem (2000). He convened the first *Synaxis* of Orthodox hierarchs of the Ecumenical Patriarchate (September 1, 1992). These gatherings have since taken place biennially in Istanbul on September 1, the opening of the church calendar.

He has annually either visited or received visits from the Church of Rome and regularly done the same with the arch-bishop of Canterbury. Archbishop George Carey of Canter-bury visited the Phanar in October 1992.

Ecumenical Patriarch Bartholomew formally visited the World Council of Churches (WCC) and the Conference of European Churches (CEC), addressing the opening of the lat-ter's Twelfth General Assembly in Trondheim, Norway, in 2003.

1993   He paid an official visit to the Lutheran Church of Sweden (on the occasion of the four hundredth anniversary of the Council of Uppsala, in commemoration of the founding of the Lutheran Church of Sweden).

1994   He resumed publication of *Orthodoxia*, the official journal of the Ecumenical Patriarchate.[10]
On Holy Friday, Ecumenical Patriarch Bartholomew was in-vited by Pope John Paul II to lead the "Via Crucis" procession at the Coliseum and to deliver the occasional meditation.[11]

1995   Ecumenical Patriarch Bartholomew was the personal guest of Pope John Paul II in the Tower of St. John at the Vatican (June 27–30), where formerly, as a student, he would visit Patriarch Athenagoras when the latter was in Rome. On that

---

10. *Orthodoxia* first appeared in 1926, but publication was interrupted in 1963 when the printing press of the Ecumenical Patriarchate was closed by the Turkish government.

11. For an English translation, see Olivier Clément, *Conversations with Ecumenical Patriarch Bartholomew I* (New York: St. Vladimir's Seminary Press, 1997), 239–61. See also the *Information Service* of the Pontifical Council for Promoting Christian Unity, no. 86 (1994), 2–3.

occasion, Patriarch Bartholomew and Pope John Paul II together recited the Nicene-Constantinopolitan Creed in the original Greek, just as Patriarch Dimitrios and Pope John Paul II had done in St. Peter's Basilica on December 6, 1987. The latter was the first time such an historical encounter had occurred in Rome between an Ecumenical Patriarch and a Roman Catholic Pope.

In 1995, His All Holiness was the official guest of the World Council of Churches, whose general secretary at the time was Dr. Konrad Raiser; he paid an official visit to the Church of Norway for the celebration of its millennium since its Christianization as well as to the Roman Catholic and Evangelical Churches of Germany to promote a spirit of reconciliation and love.

2000   During his official visit to Hungary, at the invitation of its prime minister, Ecumenical Patriarch Bartholomew announced the canonization by the Ecumenical Patriarchate of the founding king of Hungary, Stephen I (997–1038), who had already been declared a saint by the Roman Catholic Church in 1686—a profound ecumenical and spiritual gesture inasmuch as it was the first time since the Schism that a Western saint was recognized by the Orthodox Church.

2002   Ecumenical Patriarch Bartholomew met with Pope John Paul II in Assisi and at the Vatican on the occasion of the Day of Prayer for Peace (January 24–25). In the same year, Pope John Paul II joined, by satellite, the Ecumenical Patriarch during the Adriatic Symposium in order to sign the Venice Declaration on environmental awareness and ethics (June 5–10).

2004   Ecumenical Patriarch Bartholomew visited the Vatican on the occasion of the fortieth anniversary since the extraordinary and historical meeting of Ecumenical Patriarch Athenagoras and Pope Paul VI in Jerusalem in 1964. It also marked the eight hundredth anniversary since the Fourth Crusade; Pope John Paul II officially acknowledged and apologized for the tragic events of that crusade.

On this occasion, at the request of His All Holiness, Pope John Paul II, as a tangible recognition of past errors and as a significant step in the process of reconciliation between the two "sister churches," pledged that the sacred relics of St. Gregory the Theologian (329–90) and St. John Chrysostom (c. 347–407)—both predecessors of Ecumenical Patriarch Bartholomew as archbishops of Constantinople—would be returned to Constantinople and restored to the Patriarchal Church in Istanbul. On November 27, 2004, His All Holiness personally accompanied the relics from the Vatican to the Church of St. George at the Phanar, where they were first placed before the Patriarchal Throne and, finally, along the north wall of the nave.

2006 At the invitation of His All Holiness, marking the beginning of his papal ministry, Pope Benedict XVI visited the Ecumenical Patriarchate on November 29–30 on the occasion of the feast day of St. Andrew the Apostle.

2008 His All Holiness delivered the main homily at the sixtieth-anniversary celebration of the World Council of Churches, at St. Pierre Cathedral in Geneva.

2009 In October, His All Holiness delivered the keynote address at the opening plenary of the World Council of Churches' Faith and Order Commission in Crete.

Earlier, in July, His All Holiness accepted an invitation to attend the Thirteenth Assembly of the Conference of European Churches (CEC) and address the meeting on the occasion of the fiftieth-anniversary celebrations.

Olivier Clément: Conversations with Ecumenical Patriarch Bartholomew

The Memory of the Undivided Church

From *Conversations with Ecumenical Patriarch Bartholomew I*, by Olivier Clément (New York: St. Vladimir's Seminary Press, 1997). Excerpts are drawn from pages 173–91. Reprinted with kind permission.

For Bartholomew, ecumenism is not a luxury but a duty. He likes to call to mind the undivided Church, the spiritual matrix of Europe, where

East and West were united and worked together. The uniting factors—which remain our common roots—certainly consisted of Scripture, but also of the writings of the Fathers and the early monks. . . . The Fathers and monks have developed a "spiritual theology" that is inseparable from the liturgy and from contemplation, a theology which is essentially identical in both East and West, at least until the great Cistercian mystics of the twelfth century. And it was the same for art. . . .

The undivided Church by instinct organized itself according to an ecclesiology of communion, based on the Pentarchy,[12] with Rome and Constantinople as universal centers of agreement. The canons of the Council of Sardis concerning appeals to Rome and the Roman right to hear them were accepted in the East. East and West certainly did not interpret primacy in the same way, but the miracle of communion always prevailed—that communion which, said St. Ambrose, must unite the churches, that *fidelium universitas*, wrote Pope St. Leo. . . .

During his visit to Norway on June 4, 1995, for the millennium of its Christianization under the leadership of King Olaf Tryggvason, Bartholomew recalled how much the unity of the Church was then alive in Europe. Certainly, Rome and Constantinople, the two great ecclesiastical centers, did not always agree. But they were conscious of being part of one, undivided Church. Otto III, the western Emperor, was, through his mother Theophano, the nephew of Basil II, the eastern Emperor, as was Prince Vladimir of Russia, who had just been converted. This was a period in which a multitude of nations entered the Church, the one Church of Christ: the Poles in 966, the Russians in 988, the Norwegians in 995, the Hungarians in 1000. It is significant that Olaf Tryggvason was baptized in England, that he conducted negotiations in Constantinople concerning the baptism of Vladimir of Russia, and that he organized the Church of Norway with the assistance of the Archbishopric of Hamburg and Bremen. . . .

Healing Wounds, Building Bridges

The Patriarch recalls an example of truly Christian attitudes maintained under the worst of conditions, an example he raised in November 1994, in Belgium, when he visited Chevetogne, a Catholic monastery dedicated

---

12. The concept of the five ancient sees—or patriarchates—of Rome, Constantinople, Antioch, Alexandria and Jerusalem.

to dialogue with Orthodoxy: Only a few years after 1204, the second Latin Emperor of Constantinople, Henry, Count of Flanders and Hainaut, vigorously opposed the papal legate, Cardinal Pelagius, and saved the Orthodox clergy from persecution. Henry also preserved the monasteries of Mt. Athos. After his death, many Orthodox mourned him, and the monks of the Great Lavra long preserved his memory as a benefactor.[13] It is, therefore, possible to "proclaim peace" when others preach war, to call brothers those whom others see only as enemies. . . .

In the last decades, there has been enormous progress in the rapprochement between churches. Thanks to Patriarch Athenagoras and Pope Paul VI, the anathemas of 1054 have been lifted and the dialogue of love has begun. Today, relations between Rome and Constantinople are better than they were before the schism, so great were the problems in mutual understanding caused by geographic separation and differences in language.

Our churches, the Patriarch insists, must overcome the problem of Uniatism. Then we can resume the normal agenda of our dialogue. An intermediate solution is already apparent, though it has not been accepted by all the Orthodox churches (intermediate, because when unity of faith approaches, there will no longer be Uniate churches!). When the Catholic-Orthodox Joint Commission met in 1993 at Balamand, in northern Lebanon, the Catholic side condemned Uniatism as a means to restore unity. And it had already done the same earlier in Freising. The Catholic Church has undergone a change of heart and now considers as unacceptable the methods it employed for centuries. The Orthodox, on their side, have agreed to tolerate an abnormal ecclesial situation, until the Uniate churches themselves finally come to understand their own situation.

Toward an Experiential Realism of Salvation

Contemporary ecumenism, it seems, needs to abandon verbal arguments in order to base itself on an experiential realism of salvation. Systems and concepts, which are after all only markers, must be immersed in the total life of the Church, in the best of its experience. We must enter into the perspective of the "other" to discover an aspect, for us unexpected or

---

13. Founded in 963, it is the first and one of the principal monasteries on Mt. Athos.

neglected, of the face of Christ. The disfigured face of the Crucified One, endlessly scrutinized by the West, and the transfigured face of the Resurrected One, endlessly glorified by the East, are one and the same face; and even their difference reveals the immensity of God's love for us.

The Patriarch likes to cite examples of the richness of such an experiential ecumenism. Between Chalcedonian Orthodoxy and non-Chalcedonian Orthodoxy (that of the Armenians, Jacobites, Copts, Ethiopians, and certain parts of the Church of India), we have come to realize that the faith is the same. And this after so many centuries of mutual condemnation and persecution! This one faith is expressed in two conceptual systems which were long mutually opposed. For the Chalcedonians, the word *physis* (nature) represents either the divinity or the humanity, both united in the person of Christ. For the non-Chalcedonians, the same word represents the unity of Christ, his living, personal reality in which the divine and the human are united.

The issue of the *Filioque*, which divides the Christians of East and West, is another example. In the patristic era (for the *Filioque* was already formulated by St. Ambrose, and perhaps by St. Hilary of Poitiers), there were two distinct, but both legitimate, approaches to the mystery of the Holy Trinity. The West contemplated the surging and, as it were, the overflowing of divine love from the Father and the Son to the Spirit, and through the Spirit to us. With greater rigor, the East (when the West tried to be rigorous, as with St. Augustine, it got confused!)[14] saw the properly personal character of the Spirit in this procession (*ekporeusis*): The Spirit is the breath of the Father, who carries his Word, who dwells in the Word, who manifests himself through the Word. In the seventh century, St. Maximus the Confessor explains (and accepts) the *Filioque* not in the perspective of the Spirit's ultimate origin—for the Father is the only principle in the Trinity—but of his manifestation and his "economy."

The Encounter with Rome

The Patriarch has several times spoken of "our elder brother, Pope John Paul II," "Bishop of the First Rome, with whom we share a communion

---

14. For a balanced review of the theology of St. Augustine, see George Demacopoulos and Aristotle Papanikolaou, eds., *Orthodox Readings of Augustine* (New York: St. Vladimir's Seminary Press, 2008).

of love." But he always specified that we can progress toward unity only in the fear of God, with sincerity and prudence.

In Rome, he was the personal guest of the Pope in the St. John Tower, high up in the Vatican Tower. At the liturgy in St. Peter's on June 29, 1995, in his homily, the Patriarch openly raised the question of primacy, of its modes of expression. We must reflect together in order to be made worthy of the grace of a common chalice. We must reflect together on the true meaning of Peter's confession of faith in Caesarea Philippi, a text which has provoked, and continues to provoke, so much controversy.[15] Today, Bartholomew said, after much affliction and humiliation, we have reached the maturity of a truly apostolic awareness: we understand that primacy is less a question of persons than of ministries of service. These ministries are indeed urgent if we seek not to be admired by men, but to please God. The chief Christian virtue is humility, which is inseparable from repentance. It is not possible to confess, with the Byzantine liturgy, that "One is holy, one is Lord, Jesus Christ, to the glory of God the Father" and, simultaneously, to seek within the Church a power and glory other than an attitude of *kenosis* and service.[16]

The Patriarch stressed the need for self-criticism and continuous repentance, adding that to denounce the one who erred first is not the issue, or whether he erred more or less. Even the ancient philosophers held that this was an unworthy preoccupation for persons of quality. For us, he affirmed, the fundamental question is the salvation of the world. How are we to save our neighbor, our innumerable neighbors, and, uniquely through the neighbor, save ourselves? To cite the golden rule formulated by St. Paul: "Bear one another's burdens, and so fulfill the law of Christ" (Gal. 6.2). When a kenotic ethos finally prevails, then we will easily restore the unity of faith.

The Pope responded that his authority indeed has meaning only as service. He evoked Peter, but also Paul and Andrew. He cited the passage from Luke in which Christ sent the apostles out "two by two" (Luke 10.1), adding: "Perhaps this means that Christ also sends us out two by two to preach his Gospel in the West and in the East. Christ sends us

---

15. For further reading, see J. Meyendorff (editor), *The Primacy of Peter: Essays in Ecclesiology and the Early Church*, Crestwood, N.Y.: St. Vladimir's Seminary Press, 1972.

16. *Kenosis*: self-emptying. See Phil. 2.7. See also the Foreword, viii.

together so that we may bear witness to him. Thus we can no more remain separated, but we must walk together, because this is the will of the Lord."

The faithful applauded the two men long and hard, cheering them as they stood over the tomb of St. Peter. Together they came to the central loggia of the basilica to recite the *Angelus* and to bless the crowds. And when the crowd began to disperse, the Patriarch shouted out: "Courage! Let us love one another!"

Several times, and notably in Zurich on December 14, 1995, the Patriarch has stated that there is no biblical foundation for the notion that the ministry of the Pope involves governance over the entire Church. The command addressed by Christ to Simon Peter applies to each bishop, and to all bishops together, according to the conciliar principle. Certainly the Church of Rome, a church founded by the Apostles Peter and Paul, was given the responsibility of solicitude, of "presiding in love" among the local churches, but certainly not of governing over these churches. Before the schism, the Bishop of Rome was primus inter pares, in full interdependence with all bishops who were, collegially, the successors of the apostles.

In an interview given at the end of June, 1996, to the Polish weekly *Tygodnik Powszechny*, the Patriarch again criticized the developments in the papacy after the schism, to the point that it claimed a "direct and truly Episcopal," worldwide jurisdiction over all the faithful and all bishops—his jurisdiction is "a theological error," Bartholomew affirmed.

The Encounter with Protestants

The rapprochement between Rome and Constantinople must not ignore the Protestant churches, but should rather include them as well. For us, western Christianity consists of both Rome and its Reformation. Rome was unable to accept the Reform, but perhaps the Orthodox presence will enable Rome more readily to accept some of its demands. . . . Relations between Protestants and the Orthodox are ancient, dating to the early days of the Reformation.

It has often been said that if the schism between East and West had not taken place, then the upheaval of the sixteenth century would have been avoided. Perhaps the understanding of the Church as *koinonia*—that "communion" about which we hear so much today—would have counterbalanced the role of Rome. Perhaps an appreciation for the sacramental character of prophecy, of the freedom of the Spirit, could have prevented the dissociation and reification that occurred in lower Scholasticism. Who can say?

The Patriarch is not ignorant of the fact that a certain Orthodox intransigence causes problems for many Protestants. But this immobility—let them understand—can be explained as a result of historical trauma. Nearly all the Orthodox Churches in the twentieth century were for a long time churches "bearing the cross," as was said of the French Protestant communities after the revocation of the Edict of Nantes. This Orthodox immobility—liturgical, by the way, but not theological—signifies, during a long winter of history, a stubborn fidelity to that which is essential. Today, the large Protestant communities can help us greatly in awakening the pneumatological, prophetic dimension of Orthodoxy. They can help us overcome the temptation of ritualism by reminding us of the priority of the Gospel, of its revolutionary character! And the Orthodox, on their side, may well have something to say about the sacramental aspect of the Church and about prophecy, about the hermeneutics of the Fathers, about the true vocation of the ecumenical council.

As for the sects, which are today engaged in a frenzy of proselytism in Orthodox countries left helpless after the collapse of Communism, they should not be confused with the large communions issuing from the Reformation. The sects worry our faithful and arouse confessionalistic reflexes. But perhaps the sects also force us to question our practices, and sometimes our liturgical languages, or the presence of a real, living community in our parishes.

ARCHBISHOP DEMETRIOS: A MINISTRY OF UNIVERSAL RECONCILIATION

Excerpts from Archbishop Demetrios, *Ways of the Lord: Perspectives on Sharing the Gospel of Christ* (New York: Greek Orthodox Archdiocese of America, 2010), 155–71. From an address entitled "The Ecumenical Patriarchate and its Ministry of Reconciliation" by His Eminence Archbishop Demetrios, delivered at the Sacred Heart University in Fairfield Connecticut, November 9, 2005. Used with kind permission.

The ministry of the Ecumenical Patriarchate may be aptly termed a ministry of reconciliation.

The Ecumenical Patriarchate and Dialogue among Christians

The history of Christian ecumenical dialogue has long-standing origins. The Ecumenical Patriarchate has been a part of the so-called ecumenical movement since its beginnings. Its resolute and firm commitment to ecumenical dialogue is the result of its living out its beliefs in real action. It seeks to live and breathe the prayerful petition of the Divine Liturgy of St. John Chrysostom: "For the peace of the whole world, for the stability of the holy churches of God, and for the union of all, let us pray to the Lord." An even more expressive example is found in the Divine Liturgy of St. Basil the Great, which includes the petition: "Visit us with your goodness, Lord. Put an end to the schisms of the churches."

The Ecumenical Patriarchate's involvement with ecumenical dialogue dates back as early as the sixteenth century with the so-called Augsburg-Constantinople encounter. This encounter consisted of a series of short exchanges between the Lutheran theologians of Tübingen and Ecumenical Patriarch Jeremiah II. These exchanges were of considerable interest in terms of the theological doctrinal differences and similarities posed between the Lutheran reformers and the Orthodox theologians. Though we cannot call those exchanges "dialogues" in the formal sense of the term, they were, nonetheless, cordial exchanges that were indicative of greater things to come in the history of ecumenism.

The modern ecumenical movement proper may be viewed as being formally facilitated by the 1930 Lambeth Conference of Anglican Bishops in Canterbury. Though there had been several informal exchanges in the nineteenth century between the Anglican communion and the Orthodox, the 1930 Lambeth Conference represents a significant period in the activity of the Ecumenical Patriarchate in terms of sustained ecumenical dialogue, and also as showing the role of the Ecumenical Patriarch as *primus inter pares*, or first among equals, in organizing the efforts of the other autocephalous Orthodox Patriarchates in ecumenical activity. At the 1930 Lambeth conference, the Ecumenical Patriarch Photios II arranged for a delegation of the Orthodox Church to be sent to Canterbury under the leadership of the Patriarch of Alexandria. Here, Resolution 33 of the 1930 Lambeth Conference is particularly demonstrative. This resolution, in part, reads:

> The Conference heartily thanks the Œcumenical Patriarch for arranging in co-operation with the other patriarchs and the autocephalous Churches

for the sending of an important delegation of the Eastern Orthodox Church under the leadership of the Patriarch of Alexandria, and expresses its grateful appreciation of the help given to its Committee by the delegation, as well as its sense of the value of the advance made through the joint meetings in the relations of the Orthodox Church with the Anglican Communion.

Report of the Lambeth Conference, 1930

But this was certainly not the beginning of ecumenical activity with the Ecumenical Patriarchate as it concerned dialogue with other Christians. We may look to a rather prominent encyclical issued in 1920 by the Ecumenical Patriarchate addressed "Unto the Churches of Christ Everywhere," an unprecedented encyclical of global scope urging all Christian churches to take concrete actions to come closer together in their common faith. This encyclical reads, in part:

We consider . . . that above all, love should be rekindled and strengthened among the churches, so that they should no more consider one another as strangers and foreigners, but as relatives, and as being a part of the household of Christ and fellow heirs, members of the same body and partakers of the promise of God in Christ.

Ephesians 3.6

Since the issuance of that encyclical in 1920, followed by the 1930 Lambeth Conference, the Ecumenical Patriarchate has continued an active role in ecumenical dialogue among Christians. Significantly, we may note its role as a founding member of the World Council of Churches in 1948, in which it is still very active, maintaining offices today at its Geneva headquarters.

In addition to these numerous inroads to dialogue that the Ecumenical Patriarchate has made with Protestant Churches, its continuing dialogue with the Roman Catholic Church since the twentieth century has resulted in a rapprochement that continues to grow with the passing of every year. The highly visible and historic meeting of Ecumenical Patriarch Athenagoras with Pope Paul VI in 1964 resulted in some very tangible expressions of dialogue and reconciliation. First, it led to the establishment of local dialogues and exchanges between theologians in various countries throughout the world. Just one year later, in 1965, the North

American Orthodox-Catholic Theological Consultation was established. This represents one of the longest continuously running dialogues between Orthodox Christians and Roman Catholic Christians in the Western Hemisphere. The North American Consultation has consistently produced joint theological statements elaborating upon significant aspects of the Christian faith that have done much to nurture the bonds of unity between our two churches. Recent examples are the agreed statement of the Consultation issued in 1999, entitled "Baptism and 'Sacramental Economy,'" and the agreed statement issued in 2003, entitled "The *Filioque*—A Church Dividing Issue?"

Further examples of what can be characterized as the dialogue of love between the Churches of Rome and Constantinople include, among others, two very tangible expressions. The first is the exchange of visiting delegations on the patronal feasts of the churches, the Feast of Sts. Peter and Paul on June 29, for Rome; and the Feast of St. Andrew on November 30, for Constantinople, respectively. On some occasions, these exchanges have included visits from the Pope or the Patriarch himself. A second expression of the ongoing dialogue of love between the two churches was marked by the very historic occasion of the return in November of 2004 from Rome to Constantinople of the Holy Relics of two Archbishops of Constantinople, St. Gregory the Theologian and St. John Chrysostom. This return was made possible by Pope John Paul II's gracious granting of a request made by Ecumenical Patriarch Bartholomew to return the relics of his predecessors to Constantinople after having been in Rome for over 800 years. That such a request could be made and granted is a testimony to the genuine sincerity of the dialogues between the Ecumenical Patriarchate and the Roman Catholic Church, which we pray will continue under the ministry of Pope Benedict XVI. It is also a testimony to the active presence of the Holy Spirit in the ongoing process of the reconciliation of Christendom.

CONCLUDING REMARKS

In spite of overwhelming difficulties and burdens from internal governmental conflicts, the Ecumenical Patriarchate stands today as a witness of Christian martyrdom and hope. Its achievements, efforts, and genuine desire to reconcile all human beings with one another in a spirit of love, even though it operates from a position of what the world may consider weakness, is an iconic reflection of the power of the Holy Spirit. Its agonies and joys capture what St. Paul was trying to express as he was reflecting upon the Lord's encouraging example: "My grace is sufficient for you: for my power is made perfect in weakness" (2 Cor. 12.9). The Ecumenical Patriarchate is a modern, eloquent example of power made perfect in weakness.

For us also, the Ecumenical Patriarchate is an example of the reconciliation and love to which we are commonly called as Christians, who through coming together and looking in each other's eyes might find a common resolve to work toward the unity that has been the fervent prayer of the Lord Jesus Christ when He asked His Father that those who believe in Him may all be one (John 17.20–21).

Samuel Kobia: On the Ecumenical Nature of the Patriarchate and Patriarch Bartholomew

A letter from Samuel Kobia, General Secretary of the World Council of Churches, to His All Holiness Ecumenical Patriarch Bartholomew.

Letter from the World Council of Churches

Grace, mercy and peace be with you from God the Father and from the Lord Jesus Christ, the Son of the Father, in truth and love!

2 John

Warmest greetings to you from the World Council of Churches. This letter comes from the headquarters of the WCC and the Ecumenical Center in Geneva as a sign of support in a time of concern for Your All Holiness. It is an expression of the worldwide solidarity that exists among WCC member churches of every continent for the Ecumenical Patriarchate whose headquarters are in Istanbul.

We write as a result of recent developments, especially the decision of the Supreme Court of Appeals and subsequent acts by judicial authorities in Turkey which have again challenged your Patriarchate's long-established use of the title "Ecumenical." We also recall our letter of May 2007 to the Turkish ambassador in Geneva, when violence and threats against church members there included threats to your person. Please know that amid these troubles you have our firm support in the fulfillment of the Patriarchate's important religious ministries.

The term "Ecumenical" holds great significance for Christians. It is precious to all who understand the call of churches to affirm life, seek unity, and serve their neighbors. It has a unique and historic importance to the world's 300 million Orthodox believers. The title "Ecumenical" is given only to the Patriarchate of Constantinople, as "first among equals" among those entrusted with the leadership of the Orthodox world. In consequence and over many centuries, it has become the name by which the Patriarchate is known throughout the world.[17]

Your ecumenical standing was amply recognized when the moderator and officers of the World Council of Churches met in your Patriarchate in Phanar, Istanbul, in December of last year. As officers of the world's largest ecumenical organization, they especially noted the historic role of the Ecumenical Patriarchate in promoting fellowship and cooperation among Christian churches and confessional families around the world.

They noted that the Church of Constantinople's "ecumenical" commitment has been tangibly manifested in the Ecumenical Patriarchate's historic standing and its many initiatives:

A leading role since the earliest centuries of the Christian church with recognition of the title "Ecumenical" since the sixth century;

The establishment of relations by the Ecumenical Patriarch Jeremiah with Reformation theologians in Europe in the sixteenth century;

The development of relations with the Church of England in the nineteenth century;

Becoming the first church in the world to plan for an international ecumenical institution such as the WCC, with the Patriarchal Encyclical of 1920 (at the time when the modern state of Turkey was being formed);

Bringing together in the name of Christian unity, after centuries of separation, the Primates of the churches of Rome and of Constantinople, including

---

17. As Metropolitan of Philadelphia, His All Holiness delivered an address—in 1986 at the Archaeological Society of Athens—on the ecumenical nature of the Church. See Bartholomew, Metropolitan of Philadelphia, "The Ecumenical Conscience of the Church of Constantinople and the Concern for all Churches," *Ekklesia* (Athens, 1987): 5–29 [in Greek].

the visit of His Holiness Pope Benedict XVI with Your All Holiness in
Phanar, Istanbul, in 2006;

Facilitating and coordinating theological dialogues between the Orthodox
churches, other Christian churches, and confessional families, thus creating
bridges across denominational borders.

The many "ecumenical" initiatives undertaken by your Patriarchate
are not limited to promoting dialogue only among Christians. Your All
Holiness has personally become a leading figure of the contemporary ecumenical movement by continuing the long-standing tradition of the Ecumenical Patriarchate and playing an especially active role in the fields of

Interreligious dialogue and collaboration between Christians, Muslims and
Jews, including your emphasis on the multireligious character of the great
city where you live;

Reconciliation among peoples and cultures;

The protection of the natural environment, a matter that is poignantly ecumenical in the current era.

For all these we are grateful. We cherish your leadership in the global
ecumenical movement. We are also grateful for the permanent support offered to the World Council of Churches by the Ecumenical
Patriarchate.

We wish you to know of our wholehearted appreciation of the authenticity and importance of the Ecumenical Patriarchate as an institution and
of the Ecumenical Patriarch as an office within the wider church world.

By copy of this letter, member churches of the WCC are being invited
to pray for you and to offer other expressions of solidarity. Meanwhile,
we note that the Conference of European Churches has also assured you
of their support and intends to raise the present concern at the forthcoming Third European Ecumenical Assembly in Sibiu, Romania.

Finally, we note with satisfaction that, despite the current difficulties,
there is also recognition and appreciation being accorded to you and to
the Ecumenical Patriarchate from within Turkish society. These sentiments are well placed. They are a credit to the nation.

They are a reminder of the high regard in which many around the
world hold the Turkish people. We pray that such positive estimations
may be widely heard and clearly understood. We trust that these attitudes
will eventually carry the day as a true reflection of the constitution of your
country and of the outlook of its people.

1

Patriarchal Proclamations

Encylicals for Easter, Christmas, and Great Lent

EASTER ENCYCLICALS

BARTHOLOMEW
By the Grace of God,
Archbishop of Constantinople, New Rome, and Ecumenical
    Patriarch,
To all the Faithful of the Church:
Grace, mercy, and peace from Christ the Savior Risen in Glory

> The customary address and introduction of
> encyclical letters on the occasion of Easter

Holy Pascha 1993

RENEWAL OF THE SENSES

Having arrived again this year through intense prayer and fasting—and through the blessed devotional piety that they instill—at Easter, the feast of feasts and celebration of celebrations, it is natural that, despite the joyfulness of the occasion, we feel contrite because we do not have any "wedding garment" with which to enter the bridal chamber of Christ, "where there is the clear sound of those celebrating."

Neither do we have any appropriate word with which to praise the wondrous event of the Resurrection from the dead, which relates not only directly to Christ but also to all of us who believe in him: "For since we believe that Jesus died and rose again, even so, through Jesus, God will bring with Him those who have fallen asleep" (1 Thess. 4.14).

The Church does not conceal our human perplexity and poverty before the empty tomb of Christ; nor is she ashamed of it. Rather, she confesses it in celebrating the magnificent canon of Easter. Through the words of this holy hymnography, we invite and entreat, in order to announce the event of the Resurrection straightway not only to Zion but also to the entire world, not just any witnesses, who simply "heard," but in particular the women—namely, the ones who had gone to the tomb early in the morning; indeed, these women can be called "evangelists through sight."

Come, O women, evangelists through sight, and tell Zion: Receive from us the Good News of the joy of the Resurrection of Christ.

There are, therefore, witnesses "who hear" and witnesses "who see." The manner in which each faithful individual participates in the redemptive work of the Risen Lord always fluctuates between these two categories. For those who are informed merely "from what is heard" about the Resurrection, and consequently do not experience the "good change," it is impossible to envisage the "spectacle" of the transfigured world. Inasmuch as "faith comes from what is heard" (Rom 10.17), it does not remain the passive information of the mind but purifies and enlightens all the senses, opening the eyes to the "miracle," which is basically "a spectacle."

However, when speaking about "sight" in connection with matters of faith, we do not imply merely eyesight. The blessing of Christ for those "who have not seen and yet believe" (John 20.29) would otherwise be incomprehensible. Simple eyesight is a question of "inspection," which is purely a desire stemming from worldly curiosity. "Sight," on the contrary, is a higher degree of devotional piety, which allows us to dwell beyond what is visible and to see "what no eye has seen, nor ear heard, nor the heart of man conceived" (1 Cor 2.9).

Only in this way can we understand why in the sacred writings of the Church the verb "to behold" has such a decisive meaning. St. John the Evangelist bore witness to Christ saying: "We have beheld his glory, glory as of the only Son from the Father, full of grace and truth" (John 1.14). Likewise, in Orthodox worship we always traditionally confess, "Having beheld the Resurrection of Christ, we bow down to the Holy Lord, Jesus, the only sinless one."

However, while we behold the Resurrection of Christ, who as God and Man is unrivalled in holiness, dominion, and sinlessness, it is not possible for us to forget the world for which he died and has risen. When we see this world in the light of the Resurrection, it assumes another nobility, another sacredness, and, in general, another perspective. It automatically becomes the "empowered" transfigured world of God, which was created to be saved and not to perish.

For this reason, we believe in the resurrection of the body. For this reason, we do not allow the dead to be cremated. For this reason, we cannot tolerate famine and subjugation, war and captivity, as well as all their consequences, which dishonor God and humanity alike. The glory of the Risen Lord lies precisely in that He suffered for us and instead of us; therefore, He saves us from all these.

This is why in Orthodox iconography, in contrast to the sacred art of the West, depictions of the Resurrection include the scene of the descent of Christ into Hades. He descended "to the bowels of Hades" so that Hades would be powerless. "O death, where is your victory? O death, where is your sting?"[1] "Hades" and "death," however, are not mythical powers. They are tangible realities of darkness, which we confront as individuals and as societies at every step of our daily lives. Hades and death are the imprisonment within our own self-love, selfish soul, and isolation.

Christ refutes and overcomes the state of self-independence and rebellion, which was also the very essence of Adam's fall, having become "a curse for us" (Gal 3.13). Giving life as "a ransom for many" (Matt. 20.28), by His blood He establishes a society no longer hindered by racial, social, cultural, or other distinctions. It is enough for us to accept individuality in Christ in its fullness, and to love our "neighbor as our own self" (Mark 12.31).

In the bio-theories and worldviews of the world's intellectuals, who constantly invalidate each other, the faithful always resist the definitive "sight" of the entire universe reconciled in the blood of the "slaughtered Lamb." For only the One without sin could, "through the Cross, bring joy to the entire world."

---

1. From the *Catechetical Homily* of St. John Chrysostom, which is read each year at the conclusion of the Easter midnight service.

We pray that this joy of the Resurrection, which ceaselessly springs forth from the Cross, may fill the whole world abundantly. Taking this opportunity, we are pleased to announce that, in the venerable atmosphere of this ineffable joy, immediately after Holy Pascha[2] we shall begin our official visitations to the autocephalous sister Orthodox churches as well as to the heads of the non-Orthodox Churches,[3] with whom our holy Orthodox Church is engaged in a dialogue of love and truth. Christ is risen!

Holy Pascha 1995

WAR AND PEACE

With profound reverence and abundant spiritual joy, the Mother Church of Constantinople, joins with you, her beloved children throughout the oikoumene, in devout celebration and commemoration on this radiant and bright Holy Sunday. "Uncreated light has bodily risen from the tomb, and as a handsome bridegroom enhances the joy of the Resurrection."

The mystery of the glorious Resurrection from death of our Lord Jesus Christ has steadfastly remained the center of faith and worship for our Orthodox Church. The entire theology of the Christian East revolves persistently around the incomprehensible miracle of Christ's victory over death. Repeatedly the Orthodox ethos has always been Paschal: "Praised be the God and Father of our Lord Jesus Christ, He who in His great mercy gave us new birth; a birth unto hope which draws its life from the Resurrection of Jesus Christ from the dead; a birth to an imperishable inheritance, incapable of fading or defilement" (1 Peter 1.3–4).

The historical event of the Resurrection of our Lord was never perceived in the Orthodox tradition as exclusively a Christological event, as a biographical incident, which in an isolated manner refers only to the

---

2. From the Hebrew *Pesakh*, *Pascha* is the Greek word for Easter, signifying the "Passover" from death to life through the Resurrection of Jesus Christ. It is the central feast of the Orthodox Church and liturgical calendar.

3. An indication of the beginning of the Ecumenical Patriarch's formal visits to other Orthodox churches and other Christian confessions.

theanthropic nature of Christ.[4] Parallel and concurrently, His human nature, His reference to human salvation, was also extolled.

Humanity and the world have often tasted the bitterness and cruelty of death. Fifty years have passed, this Paschal season, since the end of the Second World War, the source of all manner of suffering and sorrow, a face-to-face confrontation with death. The holocaust of those who perished, the millions orphaned, the victims of genocide and racial hatred, but also the poverty and bodily and spiritual pain—these remain in the self-awareness of humanity as a horrible memory and a tragic reminder of the inhumanity and irrationality to which man is led when apart from God.

What more was the Second World War than a consequence and result of the irrationality that oppresses the soul and conscience and intellect and actions of man when, rebuking the Resurrected Lord of life, he self-reliantly makes an idol of himself: "What a wretched man I am! Who can free me from this body under the power of death?" (Rom. 7.24). No one can save man from death except the theanthropic Lord, who was resurrected from the dead and abolished "the body of death," having "smitten the bars of iron asunder and broken our bonds, bringing us out of darkness and the shadows of death." From the very depths of its being, humankind of all races and generations, throughout the ages, has rejected death. Knowingly or unknowingly, it turns to the values of life.

We especially include, among humankind's efforts to uphold the sanctity of life and establish peace, the founding of the United Nations, which was established fifty years ago. A few weeks following the end of the Second World War, this "league of nations" convened in the hope of a future bereft of a bloodstained humanity. Looking to the security of world peace and the advancement of international cooperation, this union of nations revitalized the morale of peoples worldwide and opened new horizons for humankind, who had so severely been tested in the past.

The events that will take place on the occasion of the fiftieth anniversary since the founding of this international organization will indeed give reason and opportunity for our re-baptism in the indestructible ideals for life, peace, justice, and respect for the human person. The celebrations of this jubilee, far beyond any contemporary frivolity and superficiality, must raise serious questions as we look to the future. A new beginning is

---

4. That is, divine and human.

needed in the efforts of the world community to overcome the impasse among nations and in general to humanize humanity.

The founding of this international organization unquestionably manifests and conveys the inner desire of humanity for community and fraternization. If we depend on the common experience of the human race, we will confirm that this desire has profound roots in human nature and corresponds to the very essence of the human spirit. Created as an icon of God, humanity finds itself within the desire of communion and love.

Our holy Orthodox Church experiences and promotes this communion as an uninterrupted Paschal joy, as a sincere mystery of love and glory. The incomprehensible miracle of the Resurrection imbues and enlightens our ecclesiastical life. It is revived as eucharistic participation in all of its historical vitality. The eucharistic life—as unceasing communion of true life in the Church—is evidence of and points to our victory over death. It is a profound conviction and ample proof that "through death we have become immortal." Herein, justifiably, we rejoice and give glory and thanksgiving.

In celebrating and declaring the miracle of the Resurrection from the dead of our Lord and God and Savior Jesus Christ, our holy Church, through her theology, worship, and ethos, seeks but one thing: namely, to underscore to all of her children that the divine events are offered in her and through her as a living communion and a historical presence for all the faithful. With humility and obedience, it is enough that humankind direct its path toward an evangelical life cultivated and revitalized only in the Church and through the Church. In particular, let us love "the holy Church, instituted . . . in honor of God," knowing well that "the will" of our Lord, resurrected from the dead, "is the salvation of man to which the Church has been called." Rejecting and disavowing all slander against the Church and any soul-destructive disobedience to her—these are "the fruit of the enemy and an obstacle to piety and a denial of the Kingdom"—let us "love peace, seek unity, and cultivate love for which God is pleased." "Let us cleanse our senses and witness the inaccessible light of the Resurrection." "Holding our Paschal candles, let us approach Christ who is risen from the tomb." "Let us be glorious in splendor for the festival and let us embrace one another. Let us say also to those who hate us: 'Let us forgive all things in the Resurrection' and so let us cry out: 'Christ is risen!'"

May the grace, peace, joy, and light that shattered our eternal bonds and conquered death be with you. By His Resurrection, may we also be resurrected with Christ our true God, and may our patriarchal prayer and paternal blessing be with you and all your family and loved ones. Glory and honor unto the ages of ages to the Lord of life, who is risen from the dead.

Holy Pascha 1996

FLEE WITH PETER; STAY WITH MARY; JOURNEY TO EMMAUS

From this venerable see of the Ecumenical Patriarchate, where we experience year-round the pain of Good Friday, we can genuinely announce to you the joyful message of the Matins of the first day of the week—the message of the event that constitutes the life and the hope of the universe:

> Christ is risen! And the fallen Adam is resurrected with Him. Christ is risen! And all of humankind has been resurrected. Christ is risen! And the whole universe is full of fragrance.

We thank the giver of life, because He perpetually grants us the renewal of crosses. We glorify the Savior of the world, because He has enriched us with the gifts of continuous trials and made us partakers of His unceasing comfort.

Those weeping and unjustly treated, those searching and in doubt: Despair not! Be patient, and He will come in the middle of the night as the bridegroom of life. He dawns from the last trial of the tomb as conqueror over death. We have waited to see the end, and the beginning has been revealed to us. We have reached fullness. Now everything is filled with light. We all come together as brothers and sisters in exceeding joy. Choirs of archangels and angels dance together with the humble, the humiliated, the hopeless, the dead.

Remain faithful to the end. Each of you: Move and express yourselves freely and personally. Flee along with Peter and John to the tomb and you will believe in the Risen One. Stay with Mary beside the tomb in mourning and you will encounter the Lord. Journey to Emmaus while reflecting on your problems; express your doubts; confess your hopelessness; and without recognizing Him you will find at your side the Risen One clarifying your doubts. "He interpreted to them in all the scriptures the things concerning

Himself." He will reveal to you the great mystery of life, that "Christ should suffer these things in order to enter into His glory."

The Passion is linked to the Resurrection, and Good Friday to Pascha. A seed dying in the earth is an inseparable part of the cycle of germination. Misfortunes are woven together with comfort; and the resurrection of Christ prevails. Within the joyful mourning of our holy Church, the light of joy and the abundance of goodness in the Lord are so great that every living thing of goodwill abounds in it; it intoxicates the excavated earth of the soul of man with its manifold trials and wounds; and, in turn, it sprouts there heavenly joy.

The truth of our personal pain forewarns and attests to the authenticity of the joy of the Resurrection, which is coming and has already come through the Cross to all of humanity. Live the pain of history with gratitude and faith in the Risen One. It is He who directs the destinies of the world. Suffer along with the trials and misfortunes of your personal life with confidence in the Lord of glory, and you will find Him always a companion and a defender and supporter of your life.

Continue the struggle of your work. Go down to the sea of your life and all that you have tried to do. You will see the Risen One on the seashore. And coming out of the boat with a multitude of fish in your nets, signifying all that you seek in life, you will find on the seashore nourishment ready to eat—"a piece of broiled fish and beeswax"—which will sweeten any bitterness in your mouth and sustain your heart. And nobody will ask who He is because you will be sure that He is the Risen Lord, who blesses and sanctifies the universe.

Then, discovering the hidden depths of His love and compassion, you will walk in the light of His countenance and know Him as perfect God and perfect Man, as the Alpha and the Omega of history and of your life. You will recall that once you had thought that He had abandoned you crucified on a cross of sorrows. It was precisely then that He stood closer to you in vigil, working out the mystery of your healing and salvation.

Now, as those having received the experience of the Resurrection, you are assured that the dead and the Risen Lord was, is, and will be with us every day, until the end of the ages, as the only hope and salvation for us, as well as for all men and women, to the ends of the earth. Christ is risen from the dead and life reigns! To Him be glory and dominion unto the ages.

Holy Pascha 1998

THE CATECHETICAL HOMILY OF ST. JOHN CHRYSOSTOM

> Let all partake of the banquet of faith!
> Let all enjoy the riches of goodness!

Now that we have "completed the soul-profiting fast of the forty days" and arrived at the glorious day of the Resurrection, we wanted to address you with festal words of joyful consolation. However, as we approach the *Catechetical Homily* of our predecessor, St. John Chrysostom, we are overwhelmed by the flood of his perpetual light, such as we feel when all the stars in the heavens disappear at the rising of the sun.[5]

This heavenly man and earthly angel, who celebrated the mystery of the Holy Eucharist on the sacred altar of this all-venerable see on that light-bearing night of the Resurrection of the Lord, was literally taken captive by the joy of the Resurrection and became a vessel moved by God Himself. And so it was not he who spoke, but the Spirit spoke through him. The *Catechetical Homily* is not a human artifice but an outburst of incomparable joy—that the Lord is risen—and a torrential flood of heavenly light.

"Grace shining forth from his mouth like a beacon" has set ablaze the lamp of the Great Church. It has at once enlightened the Church of Constantinople and the entire oikoumene, for his golden preaching is manifest through the ages and throughout every Church. This *Catechetical Homily* is the unique homily of the Resurrection, for all humanity and for the world. For wherever the Resurrection of the Lord is celebrated, in every Orthodox church, in every language and to every people, this inexhaustible and remarkably brief Paschal homily is heard over and over again.

It instructs our hearing. It gladdens our hearts. It surpasses our expectations. It abolishes our fears. It causes our grieving to cease. It brings joy and conveys forgiveness. It rewards those who have labored from the first

---

5. The *Catechetical Homily*, a Paschal homily of St. John Chrysostom, is recited aloud each year at the end of the Easter vigil. The entire congregation participates interactively in this classic reading, which opens with the words: "If anyone is devout and a lover of God, let them enjoy this beautiful and radiant festival." One of the great Fathers and perhaps the greatest preacher of the early Church, St. John Chrysostom (347–407) was born in Antioch and served as archbishop of Constantinople in the last decade of his life.

hour and does not scorn those who have arrived at the eleventh. Finally, it calls to all of us—those who have fasted and those who have not, the self-disciplined and the slothful alike—that we might all honor this day. He who listens attentively is amazed with the boldness and daring of this most holy Church Father, although the answer actually lies in the saint's life and conduct.

For he himself fasted, practiced ascetic discipline, and sacrificed himself for the sake of the Risen One and his brothers; for he knew—far and away above every human conception—the love of God; for he was worthy of divine grace and replete with the Holy Spirit; for he became a god by grace. He loved his brethren according to the likeness of God. He understood how much weaker brethren suffered and what they were losing through their slothfulness and negligence. For this reason, he can be bold and behaves as a wise teacher of divine things. He speaks the language of the age to come. He unveils the secret and hidden things of the love of God. And finally, surpassing every human thought and all human righteousness, he outlines relationships. He abolishes condemnation. He calls all to joy.

"Let all partake of the banquet of faith! Let all enjoy the riches of goodness." This is the faith of the Church, the openness of love, the power of the Resurrection. The *Catechetical Homily* teaches us truth and shows us love. It reveals to us that the truth of faith is the revelation of divine love and that, without the Cross of love, we cannot know the truth of the Resurrection. The divine Chrysostom speaks with such boldness because he loves. For he has seized the furthest edge of the Resurrection. And he beholds the vision of a paradise of joy and the salvation of his brethren, for whom Christ died and rose again.

For this reason, today is the principal feast of the Orthodox Church, as it is the death of Hades and the destruction of the enemy. The crowning joy in the life of the Christian is sharing in the banquet of faith with all of the saints, where the riches of divine goodness invite all of us to rejoice. However, there are many who do not partake of this universal joy. And this is not because they are not invited—for all are invited—but because they have not yet learned to love. They are not able to love, because they do not consider that the most sublime joy is to partake of the riches of God's goodness, the limitless love of the risen Lord for all humankind.

God rewards through love and reproves through love. Love created all things in the beginning. And love will judge all things at the end. The Lord's Resurrection is the manifestation of the triumph of the love of God. The *Catechetical Homily* of our father among the saints John Chrysostom, Archbishop of Constantinople, continually inspires and empowers the whole Orthodox Church like a divine gift. And it explains why the humble Phanar is a place of theology as well as why the glory of the Great Church is the Cross.

For its people are humble and contrite, people of love and people of the Cross—these are the ones who always possess the joy of the Resurrection. There have been tens of thousands of such Christians in the past in the Orthodox Church, and they continue to this day. Among those who hold this shining place are those who bear the cross of asceticism and follow the monastic way of life, especially those on the Holy Mountain of Athos. Throughout the unceasing march of the centuries, even to this very day, they keep the feast in such places as the Holy Patriarchal and Stavropegic Monastery of Xenophon, where we commemorate a thousand years of continuous spiritual life.[6] All of these people, who have served through the ages in this sacred monastery and who continue the good fight today, on the Holy Mountain and throughout the whole world, partake of the heavenly mysteries. They know the sure and fast freedom of being children of God. They partake of the banquet of faith and the riches of His goodness.

And when they commune at the sacred and spiritual altar, they receive, "unto faith unashamed, love unfeigned and full abundance of wisdom," the body and blood of the Risen One. Let us imitate their way of life through our love and our willingness to carry the Cross. For, one day, all that is will cease to be. All human achievements will pass away. The powers of heaven will be shaken. And what will remain as the light that never wanes, the salvation of all, is the event of the Resurrection, the triumph of divine love in truth.

Truly the Lord is risen! And Life is shared abundantly in heaven and throughout the earth! To Christ our God, who is risen from the dead, be glory, honor, and dominion unto the ages of ages.

---

6. Xenophontos Monastery, one of twenty communities on Mount Athos, celebrated its millennial anniversary in 1998. Great Lavra, the first monastic community established on Mount Athos, celebrated its millennium in 1963.

Holy Pascha 2002

JOY IN A WORLD OF SORROW

Christ is risen! We welcome with this joyous salutation, beloved brethren and sons and daughters in the Lord, the feast of the Resurrection of our Lord Jesus Christ. We participate this year once again in the universal celebration of the Resurrection, through which and on account of which we experience in our life the transcendence of death and all sorrow.

We bow before and express our thanks to our Lord Jesus Christ, who rose from the dead, because those of us who worship and honor Him He renders worthy to see the wondrous deeds of God, to become recipients of the supernatural light of His resurrection, which leads us to new life, and to feel this new life pulsating robustly in our hearts and vanquishing the many and great sorrows of the present life.

Standing unwaveringly on the rock of faith in the Lord's resurrection and our own, we sing joyfully along with the hymnographer and praise the sacred and all-venerable Pascha: the outward and festal Pascha but also the inner and mystical one, which is accomplished in the depths of our hearts, instilling in our spirit the life of the risen Christ and the unquenchable joy of eternal life in Christ.

We rejoice in every way, enjoying in body and spirit the gifts of Jesus Christ who loves us. And we wholeheartedly pray that all our fellow human beings would become participants of this joy and bliss, especially those downtrodden by various sorrows and tribulations and those who do not know the joy of the Resurrection or the love of the risen Christ toward us all. Faith in the Resurrection of Christ and our participation in it deflect every pain, offer hope, conquer fear of death, and grant optimism and joy.

We are not ignorant of human pain, injustice, harassment, illness, poverty, and deprivation. We do not live outside the present sorrowful universal condition. We are crucified with Christ and suffer with all our fellow human beings who are treated unjustly. Yet we know that there is a healer for all these, our Risen Lord Jesus Christ, who suffered and was crucified for us, who also granted us victory over death and, by overcoming all sorrows, the expectation of ineffable joy and the indisputable promise of eternal life.

The feast of the Resurrection of Christ is for us a turning point of joy within the vast sea of life's sorrows. It is a point of recovery through hope and of replenishment through spiritual endurance, so that we can face the complexities of contemporary life with optimism. It is from this feast that we draw courage—as the word of the Lord exhorts us, "Be of good cheer, I have overcome the world"—because the Resurrection is the greatest victory over the power of evil in the world, which is "very good" inasmuch as it was God's goodness that created it for us human beings. The Resurrection of Christ reminds us that we have the possibility and the duty through His grace to resist every fall and sin, every disappointment and pessimism, and to look to Him and to His Church for divine grace and help in every difficult circumstance.

Be of good cheer, then, beloved sons and daughters in the Lord, and make peace with one another, rejoicing in the worldwide Paschal celebration. For Christ's Resurrection is also our resurrection; and Christ's victory over evil can also be ours through His grace and our persistence in the struggle against every evil, pain, and bereavement.

This is what we wholeheartedly wish for all of you, on whom we invoke the grace, peace, and strength of the risen Christ. And we call all of you to repeat the salutation of the victory of Christ over every evil: Christ is risen!

Holy Pascha 2003

TRIUMPH OF HUMILITY OVER PRIDE

Christ is risen! "You healed the brokenness of humanity, O Lord, having restored it by your divine blood," sings St. John Damascene, addressing our Lord Jesus Christ, who was crucified, suffered, and rose from the dead.[7] And another hymnist exclaims: "You were captured, I am not ashamed; you were lashed, I do not deny; you were nailed to the Cross, I do not conceal. I boast of your Resurrection; for your death is life to me, O almighty and loving Lord; Glory to you."[8]

In the passage of history, humanity has repeatedly prepared its own brokenness. Indeed, every time it adopts the pride and mindset of

---

7. St. John of Damascus (676–749) was a great hymnographer and defender of icons.

8. *Sticheron* (hymn) of Saturday, grave (or seventh) tone.

Babel—namely, the usurpation of divine rule and substitution of human desires and ambitions for the divine law—it returns to the confusion of Babel, to discord, disagreements, conflict, and ruin. There have been many who destroyed prosperous empires in their desire to make them greater; many who became self-destructive in setting before them aims of conceited pride; many who were humiliated in raising their own stature against God's moral law; many who destroyed others in their desire to lord over and dominate them; many who realized in the end that the damage that they brought on themselves was far greater than what they caused others.

In contrast to those who—through haughtiness, pride, ambition, or any such egocentric impulse—caused the brokenness of the world, our Lord Jesus Christ accepted with extreme humility to undergo all those things that the leader of this world and his emissaries wished to impose on Him in order to turn Him into naught and secure for themselves the domination of the world. He was captured as a conspirator, though He was the peacemaker; He was flogged as an evildoer, though He was the benefactor and healer; and ultimately, He was crucified as a criminal, though He was innocent and the model of all goodness.

And what was the result? When all the opponents of humility and peace thought that the gravestone covered forever Him who preached sermons that overturned their convictions as to what was right and expedient, He rose again, incorruptible, out of the tomb, as healer of the brokenness of the world. Since then He continues to heal all the brokenness of humanity, because He has the power to reconstruct it, renew it, and to resurrect it.

There are many ruins of humanity that we encounter in our time: ruins of buildings and other works; ruins of human bodies and body parts; ruins of the natural environment; and, above all, ruins of moral values, which affect civilization. All these are destroyed by haughtiness accompanied by acquisition of power. And the only way of healing these ruins is to turn to Him who humbly received on himself human brokenness and in his humanity was made worthy of the Resurrection.

In the midst of so many new and violent deaths, the message of the resurrection sounds like the greatest paradox! And yet it is the only message that brings hope and truth. It is the greatest message, beyond any other, since life is a far greater reality than any effort to extinguish it. This is because life is the result and manifestation of the creative activity of God's love, and no deadly power that militates against life can successfully prevail over it.

Foretelling His death to His disciples, the Lord offered them this admonition: "Have courage; I have overcome the world!" He triumphed by reversing human values, by accepting humility that was hateful to many in its superiority, at a time when, like today, everybody sought after glory and honor. It is this same admonition that we too offer you today, as a father to his beloved children in the Lord. Take courage and rejoice, because Christ's victory over the world—a victory that is spiritual and unrelated to worldly domination—is offered to all who desire and accept the value of humility through which this victory is acquired.

Let all flesh that speaks contrary to this be silent. Behold, the King of Glory emerges from the grave. Christ is risen, demonstrating the infinite might of humility and peace. Nothing else can conquer death. May the risen Lord heal all brokenness of contemporary humanity, granting peace and life to all human beings, removing all hatred and bloodshed, and exchanging them for peaceful cooperation for the good of all.

Holy Pascha 2004

TRIUMPH OF LIFE OVER DEATH

Christ is risen! As we greet you, dearly beloved, with this Paschal exclamation, we reminisce about the philanthropic action of our Lord Jesus Christ—the divine Logos, through whom everything was created—in offering life to humankind. We also think of the devil's cruel pursuit, and of people misled by the devil becoming his instruments, in trying to deprive humankind of the great and sacred gift of life.

The sacred gift of life is intended by God to bring joy. The mouths of the myrrh-bearing women, says the sacred hymnist, were filled with joy as they cried, "Christ is risen." Ever since, thousands of people have continued to cry, "Christ is risen," and the hearts of innumerable devout Christians are filled with joy in repeating the announcement "Christ is risen." For all of us value life as God's greatest gifts to humanity. It is a valuable gift through which we can enjoy all other divine gifts; for, without the gift of life, we would not have any awareness of the gifts offered to us by God.

The source of life and joy is Christ, beloved brothers and children. He invites us all to become participants of His divine gifts. He invites not only us, as Orthodox Christians, but every person. Every human being is invited to partake in the fullness of a joyful life. God created human beings so that they might live joyfully; He intended for us to be adornments of the material and spiritual universe. He gave each person the opportunity to enjoy all creation. This could become possible, of course, only if people showed respect for one another, and, moreover, if they loved God and all other beings. The observance of this commandment leads to social harmony in the context of all creation in the service of humanity; and it is based on freedom as the foundation of love. Our feeling of this love, which is based on free will, reveals the ineffable beauty of the Lord's face—the most desired face, as the holy Church Fathers say—and also the face of every beloved human person. The human face reflects and depicts the divine and supreme beauty of God's face; for it was created in His image and likeness.

Every faithful Christian, and every human being, must feel the opportunity to experience and cherish life, also recognizing this right in all others. Unfortunately, however, the devil hated human life and turned murderous, implanting the idea of homicide in the human race. The devil persuaded Cain to kill his brother; this was the first fratricide. Since then, many human beings, in imitation of the devil, have hated the life of others. As a result, throughout history and to this day, myriads of human beings have been deprived of the blessings of life and joy because of murderous and invidious acts committed by other human beings.

Yet, Christ rose to offer us life and abundance of life. Therefore, it is inconceivable for a Christian—or, indeed, anyone else who loves life and respects God—to want to or actually to commit murder or to cause pain to others. The killing of people, and moreover the indiscriminate killing of innocent people, is an inhuman, condemnable, and certainly cowardly act. Moreover, every selfish deed that causes pain to some people in order to satisfy others is likewise condemnable.

As always, this year's celebration of the Resurrection of Christ involves the same predicament; it is clouded by a multitude of grave incidents. We hear about many group homicides and other hurtful acts committed by people against people. Christ, who is the way, the resurrection, and the life and who lived an earthly life of doing good and healing, shows to all people the way of love and giving, of justice and respect for the life and happiness of others, as the only way that leads humanity to true joy and fullness of life. Christ resisted His persecution and death through forgiveness, love, good deeds, sacrifice, and resurrection. He proved that the power of evil, despite its fierce aspiration to kill the leader of life, failed. And He persuades us that, in our time, the powers of evil will again be defeated by the greater power of love, which is the only way to resurrection.

And so, beloved children in the Lord, we should not be afraid in the face of evil, which seems to prevail. At the end, our Risen Lord Jesus Christ will be victorious along with those who believe in His Resurrection. Yet our victory will not be against our fellow human beings but against evil. For Christians want all people to partake in this victory so that none will be defeated by evil or lose both their earthly and, what is more important, their eternal life.

We greet all of you with the Paschal greeting "Christ is risen," and we pray that you will travel the road of this Holy Pascha in the joy of the Resurrection. We pray that through your pious life you will also contribute to the promotion of a spirit of love, inspiring others to respect the life and the joy of their fellow human beings, so that good may prevail over evil and that the leader of life, our risen Lord Jesus Christ, will reign in your hearts.

Holy Pascha 2005

TRIUMPH OF GOOD OVER EVIL

It is with great joy that we address you once again with the Resurrection greeting, "Christ is risen!" This greeting incorporates and heralds the substantive content of our Christian faith: "We celebrate death's death." This message continues to be unique and daring even in our time. For, although as many as two thousand years have elapsed since the birth of Jesus Christ, humanity has not yet advanced to the point that it respects life as Jesus Christ honored it.

Unfortunately, murderous tendencies remain widespread. People obliterate their competitors in order to prevail. Murderers kill to rob or destroy incriminating evidence. Terrorists kill to force nations and governments to accept their demands. Ideologues take lives so that their ideology might prevail. Nations clash in pursuit of racial domination, and thousands on opposing sides are killed because a spirit of reconciliation and peace is lacking. Fanatics murder those who do not share their views and ways. Believers of one faith kill others who represent a different faith. Ruthless people kill to satisfy bloodthirsty instincts. Some commit suicide because they consider the divine gift of life an unbearable burden. In general, murderous acts otherwise condemned by all humanity, yet committed (purportedly) even in the name of God, tend to become acceptable, legitimate means for accomplishing certain objectives that, wrongly, are valued more than human life.

Amid this abundance of bloodshed, there appears the leader and giver of life, who was murdered by humanity, trumpeting to all that murderous acts are not signs of success; He heralds that resurrection and judgment await us all, that life is stronger than death, and that those who build on the death of fellow human beings labor in vain. Our risen Lord Jesus Christ confirmed through His Resurrection the message that He is the way, the truth, and the life. He also confirmed that God did not create death and takes no pleasure in the loss of life (Wis. 1.13). God created everything to last eternally, but death entered the world as a result of human impiety. Yet, the love of God, unable to tolerate the predominance of death over human beings, rescues humanity and remedies the ills of human sin.

He was incarnated, assumed mortal flesh, and willingly suffered death on the cross. However, He returned to life, through His own power, stronger than death, thereby becoming the forerunner of all who want to return to life with Him. Firstborn among the dead, firstfruit of the resurrected, giver of life and of life after death, He abolished the bearer of death. Contemporary humanity is so familiar with catastrophic evil that it does not always understand the joy and depth of the Resurrection, the restitution and eternal life that our risen Lord Jesus Christ has given us. All those who foretaste and recognize the joy arising from the Resurrection experience this exultation when they say "Christ is risen." Today, then, Orthodox Christians celebrate with all people who experience this joy of the Lord's Resurrection and address one another with the victorious greeting, "Christ is risen!"

Holy Pascha 2006

FORETASTE OF THE RESURRECTION

> O life, how can you die?
> How can you dwell in a tomb?

All of creation, choirs of angels, the multitudes of humankind: All are astonished and amazed. The entire creation stands with fear and trembling in the presence of the great and unspeakable mystery of the Holy Passion and the glorious Resurrection of Christ the Savior, asking: "How is it possible that Life, true Life, Life itself, the source of Life, can die? How can a grave become the dwelling place of Life, of our Lord Jesus Christ, who said of himself, 'I am . . . the life'?" (John 14.6). The answers are revealed in the Resurrection.

Many of the questions asked in the past remain unanswered today. What happened then, once and for all, is repeated without ceasing. The mystery continues, as does our wonder. Christ remains for many in our own day "a sign that is spoken against" (Luke 2.34). He is crucified yet rises to life. The crucified one remains, "to some, a stumbling block; to others, foolishness" (1 Cor. 1.23). Some scoff at hearing of the risen one (Acts 17.32); others slander Him (Matt. 28.11–15); but He reigns in the hearts of the faithful.

We, the faithful, enjoy a foretaste of the Resurrection. We live in the Resurrection, not fearing the physical death of the body, because we believe in the Resurrection of Christ and of all human beings. We experience it as reality through fellowship in the saints who, though dead according to human understanding, in reality live on, communicating with and supporting us. However, the shrill voice of fanaticism, which rang then and has rung unceasingly ever since, continues to cry: "Crucify him, crucify him!" The powerful ones of this world, who answered such cries with cowardice and denial of responsibility, continue to reply: "Take him yourselves and crucify him" (John 19.6).

Life is risen! Christ is risen! And we bear witness to His Resurrection not only by offering rational arguments and proofs but especially by living our lives in accordance with the Resurrection. Only then does our witness become credible, when the Resurrected Christ lives within us, when our entire being radiates the joy, conviction, and peace of the Resurrection.

Certainly, our lives and the life of our natural environment remain threatened by death. We are not implying here decay and deterioration in the biological sense but rather death and destruction brought about suddenly, in cruel and violent ways that challenge our conscience, trivialize the human person, and destroy the beauty of nature.

We mean, among other things, that death that puts an end to human life before it even has the chance to see the light of the sun. We mean those countless children who lose their lives because of poverty, hunger, lack of basic medicine, and the cruelty of those who have the power to do what is necessary to save these children but do not do it. We mean as well those children whose innocence is impudently exploited and corrupted. We mean the victims of daily acts of violence—of religious, nationalistic, and racial clashes—as well as the victims of fanaticism and war. Such acts are callously and uncaringly committed by those who turn deaf ears to humanity's call for an end to hostilities and for the establishment of peace throughout the world.

Finally, we mean the plundering of the natural environment by human beings who, driven by greed and lust for profit, violently and cunningly subordinate and exploit creation. Such conduct not only distorts the beauty of creation granted by our Creator but also undermines the foundations and conditions necessary for the survival of future generations. We mean, in short, those types of life that bear the signs of death, be they spiritual or moral—the consequences of disordered passions and errors, of deprivation or greed, of the trivialization and oppression of life.

Beloved children in the Lord, we venerate once again this year the Holy Passion of our Savior Jesus Christ. We know that the teaching about His death on the Cross remains foolishness for those who remain unbelievers and follow the way of destruction. It is, however, the power of God for us who faithfully walk in the way of salvation (1 Cor. 1.18) in the brilliant light of the Resurrection. In this power and joy of the Resurrection of Christ, we respect the life of our fellow human beings. We call for an end to the killing of one another, and we denounce all violence and fanaticism that threatens life. The victory of the Resurrection must be experienced as a victory of life, of solidarity, of the future, and of hope. "Christ is risen, and life reigns. To Him be glory and dominion unto the ages of ages."

Holy Pascha 2007

DEATH NO LONGER REIGNS

Christ is risen! Once again we hear this joyful Christian greeting within our Christian communities. Yet many of us, being prosperous, disregard the question and the very real issue of death, choosing to live as though it did not exist and that the Resurrection was without meaning. However, "fearful is the mystery of death," as the sacred hymnographer reiterates and as daily reality reinforces. The fear of death, most acute in those who confront problems of health or old age, even when it is alleviated in a variety of ways, consumes our peace of mind, fills the soul with irrational anxiety, and often leads to suicide when relentless insecurity becomes unbearable.

The Resurrection of Christ put an end to this insecurity. Death is no longer the ruler of life; it is not the inevitable end of our existence. Our tombstones do not overshadow our existence forever with everlasting silence. The stone that shut the tomb of Christ was rolled away, and Christ emerged triumphant, as master over death, unscathed by its sting, the firstborn of the dead. From that moment, the door of the tomb remained open for all. The fear of death has vanished for all who wish to follow in the footsteps of Christ. All things have been filled with joy and hope. "Death, where is your sting? Hell, where is your victory?" asked our predecessor St. John Chrysostom.

To many, however, our words still sound like "an idle tale" (Luke 24.11). The Athenians at the Pnyx, on hearing the Apostle Paul speaking of resurrection of the dead, ridiculed him and left, saying sarcastically, "We'll hear you again some time!" Even the Apostles, who had heard from the Lord that He would rise on the third day, hesitated to accept the proclamation of the myrrh-bearing women that the Lord had indeed risen.

However, beloved children in the Lord, we live the ever-present death and continuous Resurrection of the Lord, not only in the sacrifice of Golgotha that we see portrayed in our churches but also in the lives of the saints, both ancient and contemporary. The Lord rose and granted life. Yet He continues to grant resurrection and life. Death is now a gate of passage to a new state of life. It has ceased to be a prison for souls, a dead end, a state without hope. The boundaries of death's stronghold were broken down, its gates shattered, and everyone who follows Christ is able to return to life with Christ.

Believe, then, and have hope! Be free from death's fear and life's anxieties; for those who believe, like you, death is no more. Only cleanse your souls and bodies, enlisting as followers of Christ, who is also your own Resurrection. Christ has risen, and you are all potentially risen! The glad and joyful message of the Resurrection is a personal message for you. It is not something foreign or irrelevant to you. Your mouths should be filled with joy when you say, "Christ has risen!" For "truly He is risen!" and we, too, are raised with Him. May His life-giving grace, "which heals what is infirm and completes what is lacking," be with you all.

Holy Pascha 2008

THE UNCONDITIONAL LOVE OF GOD

Behold, the winter has passed! [Song of Songs 2.11]

Arisen is the spring of salvation; flowers appear across the land, the sound of the turtle-dove is heard, . . . the vines are in bloom and give forth their fragrance. [Song of Songs 2.12–13]

A sacred *Pascha*—great and holy—has arisen; and it warms, lights, and makes radiant the world. "Now all things are filled with light, both heaven and earth and the nethermost regions of the earth."

Select verses from the Canon of Pascha

Christ is risen! Our God, beyond all suffering and immortal, the beautiful Bridegroom of the Church, the Lord Jesus Christ, our firstborn brother and dearest friend, "is risen from the dead, having trampled down death by death," three days after He cried out from the crest of the Cross: "It is consummated!" (John 19.30). "Hades was embittered when it encountered" (Is. 14.9) Him, because Christ destroyed his lordship. As God, He rightly emptied out his chambers of darkness, freely "bestowing life on those in the tombs." Not only this; but to all those who believe in Him from then until the consummation of the age—indeed, to all those who live in Him and hold fast to their faith and confession in Him until the end—the Lord grants everlasting life and a sure resurrection. Christ, "who has girded His loins with righteousness and clothed His sides with truth" (Is. 11.5), is risen from the tomb. "As the One who loves human-kind, He has raised up Adam, the father of us all."[9]

Behold, then, beloved brethren and children, the crown of our Great Feast and the atmosphere of springtime; in the midst of its first bloom, the Church announces the Good News to the universe. The heavy winter of death has passed away! The icy tyranny of the devil and his domination have been overcome. The frightful reign of darkness and perdition has been undone. "The Lord is King, he has clothed himself in majesty!" (Psalm 92.10).

We behold Jesus who, of His own free will, out of unconditional love, suffered on the Cross, died, and was buried for our sake and for our salvation. We have just now worshipped Him risen from the dead, and together with the Apostles and the Myrrh-Bearers we have heard from His holy mouth the words "Peace be unto you!" (John 20.20) and "Re-joice!" (Matt. 28.9). So our hearts are filled with joy. Indeed, "no one will take our joy from us" (John 16.22), because the personal death of every single human being has been abolished. This is why we, who have cruci-fied the carnal mindset of the old person "together with the passions and lusts" (Gal. 5.24) and "who have died with Christ, believe that we shall also live with Him" (Rom. 6.8). For even as "we have been buried" with Christ "through baptism" (Rom. 6.4), we have become "planted with Him"—that is, become partakers of His Resurrection (Rom. 6.5).

St. Gregory the Theologian trumpets this truth with supreme rhetori-cal skill when he says: "Yesterday I was crucified with you, O Christ; today I abound with glory. Yesterday I died with you; today I am filled with life. Yesterday I was buried with you; today I arise with you."[10] What has plagued us from ages past has once and for all been resolved by the Risen Lord. Our agony is over. "Christ is risen, and life can truly be lived!"[11] From now on, life and our Resurrection are not things to be

---

9. From the Service of the Resurrection.

10. From the *Homily on Holy Pascha* by Gregory the Theologian (330–90). One of three Church Fathers formally proclaimed as "theologians" in the Orthodox Church, St. Gregory briefly served as archbishop of Constantinople (381) before and during the Second Ecumenical Council.

11. From the *Catechetical Homily* of St. John Chrysostom.

sought—neither dream nor utopia. From here on, life exists and the Resurrection, too, exists: They are a concrete, tangible reality. A reality with a specific face and name: "a name above every name," Jesus Christ, before whom "every knee shall bow, whether in heaven or on earth or beneath the earth" (Phil. 2.9), and every tongue shall confess that He alone is Lifegiver and Lord. He is the one who lives and reigns forever. He is the one who, by His ever favorable will, distributes His Kingdom, His glory, and His inheritance from His Father to all who share in His Cross, His death, and His Resurrection, as "He is the firstborn to many of us" (Rom. 8.29).

Him do we beseech, from our Patriarchal and Ecumenical See, which has been touched by the blood and grace of martyrs, that He may grace the world with peace, that He may illumine people's souls with truth and righteousness, that He may bestow patience and encouragement on those who face adversity, and that He may grant the taste of salvation and life eternal to all believers. To Him, as conqueror of death and Prince of Life, be all glory, dominion, honor and worship, together with Father and the Holy Spirit, unto the ages.

Holy Pascha 2009

CHRIST IS RISEN AND GOD LIVES

In sullenness, one day in the nineteenth century, humankind heard from the lips of the tragic philosopher: "God is dead! We killed him! All of us are his murderers. . . . God will remain dead! What else are the churches but tombs and graves of God?"[12] And only a few decades later, we heard from the lips of his younger colleague: "Gentlemen, I declare to you the death of God!"[13]

These declarations of atheist philosophers shook the conscience of people. Much confusion ensued in the field of the spirit and of literature, of art and sometimes even of theology, where, especially in the West, there was debate even about a "theology of the death of God."

Of course, the Church never had the slightest doubt that God had died. This occurred in A.D. 33, on the hill of Golgotha in Jerusalem, in

---

12. The German philosopher Friedrich Nietzsche (1844–1900).

13. The French existentialist philosopher Jean-Paul Sartre (1905–80).

the reign of Pontius Pilate, the Roman governor of Judea. After suffering an unspeakable passion, He was crucified as a criminal and, at about the ninth hour of the preparation of the Passover, he said, "It is accomplished!" and surrendered His spirit. This is an unquestionable historical reality. The Only-begotten Son and Word of God, Jesus Christ, the true God, indeed died for our sake (see 2 Cor. 5.14). After assuming everything that we have (body, soul, will, energy, toil, agony, pain, sorrow, joy—indeed, all things except sin), He finally assumed our greatest concern, death, even in its most cruel and humiliating expression—namely, death on the Cross. On this point, we are in agreement with the philosophers. We would even accept that churches and temples are "the tombs and graves of God." Nevertheless, this God—who has died—we recognize, experience, and worship as "a most life-giving death." Only moments after that awful Passover, in the morning watch on that "first day of the Sabbath," on the day of the Lord, what occurred was the reason for which the divine economy of the flesh—the Passion, the Cross, and the descent into Hades—all took place. The Resurrection! And this Resurrection is an equally unquestionable historical reality!

This reality has immediate and salvific consequences for all of us. The Son of God, who is at the same time the Son of Man, was risen. God was resurrected together with all humanity, which He assumed—in the body that He received from the pure blood of the Most Holy Theotokos as well as in His sacred soul. He was risen from the dead, "resurrecting the whole of Adam in His loving-kindness." Christ's grave, the "empty tomb" of Joseph, is forever empty. Instead of being a grave for the dead, it is a memorial of victory over death; it is a fountain of life! The spiritual Sun of Righteousness has dawned "beautiful, as from a grave," granting the unwaning light, peace, joy, gladness, and eternal life. It is true that the temples were the "tombs" of God, but they were empty tombs, filled with light and replete with "the fragrance of life" (2 Cor. 2.16) as well as the smell of Paschal spring—brilliant, splendid, adorned in glory and with life-giving flowers of tangible hope. The death of God overturned the power of Hades; death itself was reduced to nothing more than a mere incident introducing humanity from death to life. The churches, those "tombs of God," are the wide-open gates of divine love, the opened entrance to the bridal chamber of God's Son, who "came out of the tomb as a Bridegroom," while we faithful enter therein and "celebrate the death of death, the annihilation of Hades, the beginning of a new, eternal way of life; and, thus rejoicing, we offer hymns to the cause—namely, the only blessed and glorious God of our fathers."[14]

It is fortunate, then, that God died because His death became the source of our life and resurrection. It is fortunate that there are so many of His "tombs" throughout the world, so many sacred temples, where each of us, when we are in pain, tired, and in need of consolation, can freely enter so as to lay before God the burden of our suffering, agony, fear, and insecurity—that is to say, in order to become rid of our death. It is fortunate that we have churches of the crucified, dead, risen, and living Christ, where—before the hopelessness of our time, the betrayal of all idols, of the "lowly gods" that have stolen our hearts, such as the economy, the ideology, the philosophy, the metaphysics, and all those "empty deceits" (Col. 2.28) of our "age of deception"[15]—we can find refuge, comfort, and salvation.

From the Ecumenical Patriarchate, the Mother Church, which experiences to the utmost the Passion, pain, Cross, and death as well as the Resurrection of Christ, we extend to all the faithful of the Church our wholehearted Paschal greeting and blessing, together with the embrace of our Lord Jesus Christ, who has risen from the dead and lives eternally, granting life to all people. To Him be glory, might, honor, and worship, with the Father and Holy Spirit for all the ages.

Holy Pascha 2010

PARTICIPANTS OF ABUNDANT LIFE

Once again, the sacred day of Pascha has dawned in full delight and splendor, dispensing joy, comfort, gladness, and assurance of life to all faithful, despite the heavy atmosphere that prevails in our world because of the widespread crisis with all its familiar painful consequences for our daily life.

Christ has risen from the tomb as divinely human; and humanity has risen with Him! The tyranny of death belongs to the past. The hopelessness of Hades' captivity has irrevocably gone. The only powerful giver of

---

14. Troparion of the Seventh Ode, Canon of Pascha.

15. From the Akathist Hymn, a sixth-century anonymous hymn dedicated to the Mother of God.

life, having through His Incarnation voluntarily assumed all of the misfortune of our nature and all that it entails (namely death) has already "brought death to Hades by the lightning of divinity,"[16] granting us life—and "life in abundance" (John 10.10).

This abundance of life, which was granted to us by the risen Lord, is ceaselessly slandered and assaulted by the devil—indeed, these actions are the source of his very name—although he is now weakened, completely powerless, and entirely ridiculous. The devil slanders life by means of the hubris that still prevails in the world against God, humanity, and the creation. The devil assaults life by means of the sinful tendency that exists within us like "old rust," using this to entrap us either into tangible sin or delusional belief. Hubris is the offspring of that "rust," while together they constitute the sinister couple responsible for disrupting relationships within ourselves and with others as well as with God and the whole creation. Accordingly, it is imperative that we purify ourselves of this rust with great attentiveness and carefulness so that the profuse life-giving light of the Risen Christ may shine in our mind, soul, and body, so that it may in turn dispel the darkness of hubris and pour the "abundance" of life to all the world.

This cannot be achieved by philosophy, science, technology, art, or any ideology; it can be achieved only through faith in what God has condescended for us human beings through His Passion, Crucifixion, and burial, descending to the depths of Hades and rising from the dead as the divine-human Jesus Christ. It is also expressed in the sacramental life of the Church as well as through laborious and systematic spiritual struggle. The Church, as the body of Christ, unceasingly and to the ages experiences the miracle of the Resurrection; through its sacred mysteries, its theology, and its practical teachings, it offers us the possibility of participating in that miracle, of sharing in the victory over death, of becoming children shaped by the light of the Resurrection and truly "partakers of divine nature" (2 Peter 1.4), just as in the life of every saint in the past and present.

The thorny weeds of passions growing within the depths of our heart, polluted by the rust of "the old self" (Eph. 4.22), must definitely be transformed as soon as possible in Christ, through Christ, and for the

---

16. Dismissal Hymn of the Resurrection, first tone.

sake of Christ and His living images that surround us—namely, our fellow human beings—into a bouquet of virtues, holiness, and righteousness. And so the sacred hymnist chants in timely manner: "Let us put on the robe of righteousness, which is whiter than snow, and let us rejoice today in the day of Pascha; for Christ, the sun of righteousness that rises from the dead, has showered on us the light of incorruption."[17] The white garment of righteousness was given to us symbolically on the day of our baptism; and we are invited to cleanse it continually through constant repentance, self-control, patience in pain, and relentless effort to fulfill the commandments of God, especially the supreme commandment of love. In this way, we are able to participate in the cross-bearing self-emptying of Christ in order that the Paschal gladness, radiant light, and joyful salvation may enter our life and world.

We address this from the Phanar, where we constantly experience the suffering of Holy Friday and the light of the Resurrection, as we express to you the affection of the Mother Church, wholeheartedly wishing on all the saving gift and the Paschal blessing of the Lord of Life, who rose from the dead.

CHRISTMAS ENCYCLICALS

BARTHOLOMEW
By the Grace of God,
Archbishop of Constantinople, New Rome, and Ecumenical
    Patriarch,
To all the Faithful of the Church:
Grace, mercy, and peace from Christ the Savior Born in Bethlehem

> The customary address and introduction of
> encyclical letters on the occasion of Christmas

Christmas 1992

THE CHURCH AS THE BODY OF CHRIST

"The Son, God and Lord, begotten of the One without beginning, incarnate of the Virgin, has appeared" once again, in order to enlighten

---

17. From Vespers on the Sunday of Thomas.

those in darkness, to gather those dispersed, to unite the created with the uncreated, to deify humankind. He is the King of kings and Lord of lords, who is born of the Virgin and before whom "every knee in heaven, on earth and beyond the depths of the earth, bends." Everything is united, reconciled and recapitulated in Christ, because He came to bring unity and peace, "that we might have life, and have it abundantly" (John 10.10). By His incarnation, Christ comes as man in full communion with God and as God in full communion with man. Thus, He becomes the real mediator of our own communion with God.

For this reason, persecuted until yesterday in the atheistic East and equally ignored by the materialistic West, He is revealed once again as the unique hope of humanity and as the only stable point of orientation. Now that this truth has been perceived anew, indeed "all of creation rejoices." Dwelling among us (John 1.14), He becomes as one of us "yet without sin" (Heb. 4.15). "Nature becomes new and God becomes human; whatever was has remained, and whatever was not has been acquired; He bore neither confusion nor division." "And do not ask how, for wherever God wills, the order of nature is changed. He willed, to Him it was possible, He descended, He saved; He reconciled all things to God."

His Church, as His extension to the ages, continues this work of salvation through His love and peace, which surpass all understanding (Phil. 4.7). Love and peace are His precious gifts to all those who struggle to vanquish their egos and overcome the isolation of apostasy. His Church, especially with its pastoral theology, gives us the means to face the various problems that plague humanity today in an historic and critical time. Through the Church, where we meet Christ, its head, He feeds the hungry, those who seek will find, those who knock will have the door opened to them, those who love will be loved, those in despair will welcome Him as bridegroom. *Emmanuel* means "God is with us." *Jesus* means "God is victorious." He is victorious over us, confronting evil, sin, and death; and we discover this truth and reality as unending bliss, as personal victory, as the kingdom of eternal love and blessedness.

Christ entered history; He assumed its entire weight, pain, and hideousness, emerging victorious and triumphant. This is why we ought to turn to Him—and to Him alone. He is the way, the truth, and the life. We celebrate Christmas and soon we shall close this year, glorifying God for all that He granted us. At the Ecumenical Patriarchate, we thank him for many gifts, and particularly for our blessed pilgrimage to the Garden of the Holy Theotokos, the Holy Mountain,[18] and for allowing us to visit the renowned island of Crete, whose pious and brave people seized the opportunity to manifest and enthusiastically declare their unshaken devotion and great respect for the Mother Church. On these trips we tasted the spiritual joy of the shepherd who observes his spiritual offspring bearing good fruit and thereby glorifies our Father in heaven.

May the builder of the Church strengthen its work and bless its children everywhere, invigorating them to fulfill His divine will. And let us all, with one mouth and one heart, "cry aloud to Him, offering up to Him hymns, singing together with the angels: 'Holy is Christ our God, who was incarnated for us; glory be to Him.'"

Christmas 1993

THE MYSTERY OF LOVE INCARNATE

> You have dawned, O Christ, from the Virgin,
> O perceivable Sun of Righteousness.

The gifts of God come noiselessly from within, as does the light of the dawning sun. And into the pure Virgin, who was humble (unlike the powerful of the earth), there came noiselessly and undetected the radiance of the divine light, the very Son and Logos of God, with the objective not simply of sanctifying her, but of becoming incarnate by her through the Holy Spirit and of distinguishing her as His true mother, the Theotokos.

And the Virgin experiences this divine visitation. She lives the mystery that surpasses every mind and all comprehension: "The pregnant Maiden has come to give birth to the Lord." She is astonished by the miracle: How is it possible for the child inside her to be simultaneously both her

---

18. This was the first occasion that Ecumenical Patriarch Bartholomew formally visited Mount Athos after his election and enthronement in 1991. The Holy Mountain lies within the ecclesiastical and spiritual jurisdiction of the Ecumenical Patriarchate. The Ecumenical Patriarch chose to open his Patriarchal ministry with a spiritual pilgrimage and personal retreat to this historical monastic institution.

Savior and her God? "Where God wills, the order of nature is vanquished." The humility of the Virgin brought God to earth. The personal, private fact of the conception by the All-Virgin and of her giving birth assumes cosmic dimensions, becoming cause for universal salvation.

"Today the heavens are filled with joy; Christ is born of the Virgin." All of human life and nature are blessed. Every pregnancy, as a result of this immaculate offspring, partakes of the divine. And by this divine conception all virginity is revealed to be prodigiously fertile. Without this virginal conception, everything human remains barren and in darkness. Through it, however, everything is illuminated by divine radiation. This is the expectation of nations, humanity's unexpressed desire and plea, which cannot be silenced.

"Human history awaits with patience the hour when the neglected person will be glorified," a renowned poet, indeed a non-Christian, once wrote. But the hour has come; the miracle has occurred. Christ, the perceptible Sun of Righteousness, has dawned from the Virgin and glorified humankind. He has illuminated the universe, overthrown the original curse of Eve, and annihilated the powers of Hades. "All things are stirred to ponder the annihilation of death." Death is annihilated. Humanity is now able to live.

This is why heaven and earth celebrate a feast divine yet human, personal yet universal. We celebrate the birth of the God-Man as well as the birth of the human being. God is born in flesh, and humankind is reborn in spirit. We have the true manifestation of God and the actual manifestation of humanity, the revelation of God's ineffable love and of the benevolence of human nature, with all of its hidden potential.

Truth has been revealed, not as a fleshless idea but as incarnate love, as the theanthropic Lord and the descent of divinity to earth, where it assumes and elevates human nature. It is not that someone has come to save by force what is mortal. It is not that someone has come to impose his view as some new order. "Our Savior," as an infant lying in a manger, "has visited us from on high." When the Almighty elevates us by humbling Himself, enriches us through His voluntary poverty and respects us who are lowly before God, then, to be sure, "the old kingdom passes into corruption through God's appearance in human nature, His appearance unto the newness of perpetual life." A new kingdom of grace is inaugurated; a new life is lived, granting to all "who are humble what comes from on high, and to the poor, spiritual wealth."

However, turmoil interrupts this sacred and unutterable joy. "Herod was troubled, because God appeared in flesh as savior of our souls." Neither Herod's nor Hades' authority and logic could bear the idea that the Virgin gave birth to God, that the humble was held in esteem, that the weak was raised, and that humankind was saved. So, he massacres the infants. To the angelic hymns and joy of the world is added "lamentation, weeping, and great mourning," so as to overshadow the joy, annihilate the God-Man, and dispel the love voluntarily sacrificed for the life and salvation of the world.

Thus, the theanthropic Lord confronts Herod's turmoil, and the violence of every period, with serenity and self-sacrifice. He spills His own blood, "forever slaughtered while sanctifying those who share in Him," so that the infants may live, all of creation may be transfigured, and we may enter the paradise of authentic freedom and divinization.

These two forces and kingdoms, the theanthropic and the "herodian," sacrificial love and tyrannical domination, will be contrasted to the end. The victory, however, belongs to love. That is because, although many ideas and powers that are patterned after Herod's example are in force today, the turmoil brought on by hostility and war threatens humankind and degrades life; selfishness condemns many to starvation; and consuming greed, void of the meaning of Christmas, often commends the prosperous to desolation and spiritual poverty. While all this happens, there is always, in the dead of winter and despite the darkness, a bright star guiding us fixedly to the place where Christ is born, the only place where one can, by grace, give birth to Christ.

"The divine Logos, incarnate once for all, is forever born, inviting those who so desire to be spiritually His, becoming a child and shaping Himself in them through virtues." This blessing, namely that Christ may be molded in the soul of each one of us through obedience, so that we may live "the joy that comes to all people," we pray will wholeheartedly come on all of you.

Christmas 1994

BEHOLD, THE NEW HAS COME

"This is the cause of our festival; this is what we celebrate today: God's advent to the world." We celebrate the ineffable mystery of divine favor, of the descent of love and peace, of joy and hope to creation. We rejoice in the wonder of converse between divine and human life, in the union of the uncreated and the created. We keep glad festival because the Son of God accomplishes His compassionate intervention, assuming the poverty of our life so as to enrich it with the gifts of His divine life. In the poetic language of our predecessor, St. Gregory the Theologian:

> He who is
>> comes into being,
>> the uncreated is created,
>> and the infinite is confined.
>
> He who enriches become poor,
>> for He impoverishes my flesh
>> that I may grow rich in His divinity.
>
> He who is fullness empties Himself,
>> for He is emptied of glory for a time,
>> that I may partake of His fullness.

To be sure, the "strange" and "wondrous" mystery of the Incarnation of God's Son lies outside the limits of human comprehension. It is a mystery not to be understood, "exceeding the mind's grasp and reach." Yet, though "the mystery will not bear inquiry," our Church lives the reality of the divine birth and ceaselessly declares, "We confess your grace, we proclaim your mercy, we do not conceal the great kindness."[19] Precisely herein lies the majesty of our Orthodox faith and life, able to vitalize any historical moment and elevate it to an occasion for participation in the divine.

And so the historical fact of God's Son becoming human is not an event of the past disconnected from and unrealized in the present; it is a contemporary reality with the potential for life and communion, accessible throughout the course of history. In celebrating the birth of Christ "in the days of Herod the king" (Matt. 2.1), the Church calls all faithful to become today's eyewitnesses and participants, in their own lives, of the mystery of the divine dispensation. "Come, faithful, let us see where Christ is born; let us follow where the star travels." Truly, for those who

---

19. Prayer from the Great Blessing of the Waters on the Feast of Epiphany (celebrating Christ's baptism, January 6) and from the sacrament of baptism.

believe, "there is born today of the Virgin He who holds all creation in His grasp." The event of Christ's birth does not vanish into the remote and unrepeatable past but is preserved within the Church as an ever present grace, relived in the heart of the believer, a living event that seals and shapes our entire life.

In this theological context, we are able to comprehend not only the meaning of Christ's birth but also the value of humanity, to whom God promises the possibility of becoming a God-bearer, of experiencing divine "infant leaps for joy" within the heart. The supreme honor and surpassing grace given to humanity is precisely the prerogative to recreate within the heart the wondrous mystery of the divine Incarnation, to offer one's own corruptible nature as manger, as room to contain the uncontainable.

And yet, though scriptural truth raises humankind to such a lofty state, the style and pace of modern life invariably cripples our spiritual powers. The conventions and distractions of the world leave us little latitude to know ourselves. Contemporary life largely ignores God, thereby also ignoring man. Ultimately, estranged from Christ, and despite progress and various successes, humanity is impoverished of any true riches and resources, unwise in wisdom and understanding, powerless in capacity and competence, insignificant in glory and grandeur.

Self-proclaimed saviors, "ignorant and unstable" (2 Pet. 3.16), wishing to exploit contemporary human powerlessness, but also our inmost desire to give meaning to life, push their own humanisms, promising a new era, a new paradise without Christ. In essence, these newfangled humanisms create a wretched picture of existential confusion, of the absence of God, of death—a vicious cycle within which human consciousness and conscience disintegrate. The world of drugs, all manner of quasi-religious pagan movements, anarchy, violence and terrorism, demon worship and body worship, but also religious insolence under the mantle of piety, expressed as disavowal of the Church's divine precepts—all these are phenomena of our age. In one way or another, they influence modern life and generate in human beings a fear and angst, a state of living that must be defined as pain, grief, loss of hope.

It is not as a spectator that our Church observes this contemporary scene; nor does it spurn humanity, so pitiable at the end of the second millennium. Its vigilant concern is to offer humanity hope for life, the enduring optimism of the gospel, the all-enabling conviction of divine love and presence. Its care is unceasing to present to people "who labor and are heavy-laden" the God-Man Christ, "the light of knowledge," "the Sun of Righteousness." Beloved shepherds and fellow pastors, beloved children in the Lord, it is apparent in our time, perhaps more than in any other period in history, that humanity stands in need of God's presence. Human beings can be freed of the terrors that beset them, that grind down their very being, only if they are prepared to center their fragmented existence in the divine Lord of life.

God incarnate has left us a treasure that the ages can never exhaust: His word and law, divinely revealed in both the Old and New Testaments. The culmination of this revelation is, as is well known, the Book of Revelation of the Apostle and Evangelist John, written on the island of Patmos exactly 1900 years ago. Therefore, in proclaiming the impending New Year 1995 as the "Year of Revelation," we call on all who honor God, His revealed truths, and the "chosen vessels" through whom He spoke to us "in many and various ways" (Heb. 1.1), that together we may celebrate this great and solemn anniversary of the whole Christian Church.

Communion with the compassionate Lord manifested in the flesh, true God and true Man, can overthrow the lawless autonomy of contemporary man, liberate him from the powers of darkness, and give him a new perspective and a new purpose in life. We who believe in God made flesh do not await some "new age," nor are we disquieted over the vaunted "new order of things." For we know well that the only birth-giver of a new humanity is Christ, who in His infinite love assumed flesh. "If anyone is in Christ, he is a new creation; the old has passed away, behold, the new has come. All this is from God, who through Christ reconciled us to Himself" (2 Cor. 5.17–18).

And so for us who have been found worthy of the Orthodox faith, there remains nothing but to approach the "strange wonder" of Christ's birth, the "miracle above all miracles," and to do so with penitence, devotion, and contrition of heart, in order to celebrate in godly manner the festival of Christ's nativity. "Acknowledge the birth and leap for joy . . . and respect the enrollment by which you are enrolled in heaven; be in awe of the birth by which you are freed of the bonds of birth-giving; honor little Bethlehem, which has led you back to Paradise; and venerate the manger where, though lacking reason, you were nourished by the Word" (St. Gregory the Theologian).

In offering doxology, then, let us cry to our Lord made manifest in the flesh: "Glory to God in the highest, and on earth peace, with which your advent has rewarded us, our Lord: glory to You." To Christ our Lord, born in Bethlehem, be glory and power to the endless ages.

Christmas 1996

THE SILENCE OF GOD

> You have dawned, O Christ, from the Virgin,
> You are the spiritual Sun of Righteousness.

From the humble Phanar, which, as the First Throne of the Orthodox Church, is charged with the burden of responsibility for shepherding the oikoumene, we address this joyful salutation to all humankind on the occasion of the Nativity of Christ. Here, we live the miracle of the birth of the God-Man in the cave, by sharing in the same experience; for there is an intimate affinity between the poverty of the Phanar, a meek and humble Church, and the manger of our Lord. Indeed, there is an inward relationship between the hushed words of blessing issued from the Phanar to the oikoumene, through the sacred service of our liturgical theology, and the light that shone forth in the cave illuminating all creation, when the Christ was born of the Virgin.

We perceive this First Throne as both a cross and a commission; we understand the ecumenicity of our patriarchate as a ministry to the truth of the Church and to the liberty, in Christ, of all people. Through its very existence and polity, the Ecumenical Patriarchate ever reverberates with the melodist's words on the Nativity of Christ: "Hearing this, let the oikoumene dance for joy." Dance and be glad! Not just a segment of humanity, but the whole oikoumene! Not just a portion of creation, but every part of creature! "Today all things are filled with joy; Christ is born of the Virgin." "You have dawned, O Christ, from the Virgin; You are the spiritual Sun of Righteousness."

The sun rises as a gift of blessing on the just and unjust; it does not distinguish one from the other. It does not exclude anyone from the benefit of its brilliant rays. It nourishes the good seed and the tares, leaving the sorting and winnowing to take place naturally at the time of harvest. Likewise, the spiritual Sun of Righteousness dawns on the whole of humanity with a divine love and a blessing imperceptible in its serenity and compassion. It is the mystery of a cry that takes place in the silence of God. It is not simply a manifestation of divine power but rather the revelation of God's ineffable love for humankind. He did not come, as He once did on Mount Sinai, mighty in power and dazzling with thunder and lightning, but God the Word was made manifest as an infant child lying in a manger.

Whoever truly loves, honors, and respects one's beloved would surely cringe to see that same loved one powerless and humbled rather than mighty and honored. But the Lord, "rich in divinity," made Himself poor for our salvation. The Word is "a wonder astonishing every conception," a mystery of divine condescension[20] and *kenosis*, the self-emptying of God. This is why at first it was not human beings but angels who sang "glory in the highest"; and it was the irrational beasts in the cave that cooed and caressed with their loving breath God the Word made flesh, who was to set free the human race from its own irrationality.

"The truth has come, the shadows have passed; God has appeared from the Virgin and among men, in a form like our own, deifying the human nature He took upon Himself." He deified what He assumed and bestowed freedom on humankind, granting us the potential to realize the meaning of life. He freed woman; she is no longer subservient to man. He freed all of humankind; it is no longer subservient to creation. He even freed creation; it is no longer subservient to whim and greed. The incarnate Lord desires to see all people free, to see us press forward, to see us attain full stature—to find life by voluntarily losing our life. The Lord modeled this love for us: He emptied Himself, He was humbled, He was hidden; and, having become invisible, He was made manifest after the Resurrection.

What was desired and expected from the ages is realized; opposites are united; fragments are brought together; breaches are bridged. Human nature is joined with the Holy Spirit! The Virgin Mother is honored! The God-Man is born! Indeed, what is born is the potential for humanity to live truly, to be free and by grace to attain divine-human life, through a

---

20. The Greek term *synkatavasis* signifies the ultimate divine benevolence and loving condescension, which was revealed in the incarnation of God's Son and Word, Jesus Christ. It implies that God "came down" to meet the world's needs.

nuptial relationship with incorruptible virginity, which itself gives birth to joy for all people, eternally and without change in a most exalted place.

And the lofty place, where these dread and awesome mysteries are consummated, is defined by the manger. It is humility, love, oblation, sacrifice for one another, following the example of the Lord. For we are no longer alone, whether we are aware of it or not: "Our Savior has visited us from on high." And we are no longer divided: "There is neither Jew nor Greek, there is neither slave nor free, there is neither male nor female: for we are all one in Christ Jesus" (Gal. 3.28).

Our heartfelt prayer is that we may all enjoy this true freedom and unity, which are the gifts of the incarnate Word of God, as we bless the Most Holy Virgin Theotokos, who gave birth to Christ, the Life-giver and Savior of our souls. For His is the dominion and unto Him be all glory and honor and worship unto the ages of ages.

Christmas 1997

DIVINE ASSURANCE

For unto us a Child is born; unto us a Son is given.

We have returned to the Ecumenical Patriarchate from a lengthy journey and pastoral visit to the flock of the holy and Great Church of Christ throughout the oikoumene. Over the past few years, as we have traveled through Europe and Asia, to Australia and most recently America, we have experienced the unforgettable blessing and joy of meeting so many beloved people.[21] We have seen faces shining with the light of hope, but also faces darkened by clouds filled with tears and despair.

The countenances of young and old alike remain deeply engraved in our heart. We have seen adults heavy-laden with life's responsibilities and young people full of high hopes for a good career. We have seen the sick and infirm on their bed of suffering and the aged at the twilight of their

---

21. Soon after his enthronement, the Ecumenical Patriarch visited the Orthodox communities of France and Great Britain (1995), Australia, New Zealand, and Hong Kong (1996), as well as the United States (1997). For a description of these pastoral visits, see Michael O'Carroll, *A Light from the East: The Ecumenical Patriarch Bartholomew I* (Santa Barbara, Calif: Queenship Publishing Company, 1998), 67–114.

life. We have heard the cries of young children, who are the hope for the renewal of our people. We have tangibly experienced just how small our world really is and just how fleeting life can be. We have seen how the light of hope and expectation shines in the eyes of people of all ages. And we have seen how much pain, suffering, and injustice exist in the world. We have seen how our weakness and sinfulness can demean the beauty of life, which by the love of God can become paradise even while all of us can be united to become one loving family.

Yet amid all of humankind's trials and tribulations, there comes the birth of a child, a divine gift to every family. Such a child is the harbinger of great joy and graces. Through him the family grows and is blessed with hope. Therefore, in this spirit of empathy and true understanding, we would like to address to all of you sincere words of gratitude and consolation. Having been graced by the joy of your love during our lengthy journey, we would like to give you something in return.

And what we wish to offer you, which was impossible for us to do fully before, now comes as a gift from heaven itself. From one end of the world to the other, the joyous message resounds: "For unto us a child is born; a son is given . . . and His name shall be called Angel of Great Counsel, Wonderful Counselor, Mighty God" (Is. 9.6). He is the expectation of the nations. He is the joy of all children. He is the gladness of mothers. He is the sanctification of human nature. He who is born is God and His mother is a virgin. What greater marvel has the world ever seen? Let all creation leap for joy and all inhabitants of the earth rejoice!

With the incarnation of God the Logos, and through His assumption and deification of our human nature, we have all become brothers and sisters. We can hope. We are encouraged. We draw strength. We feel tangible love. We marvel at the divine child behaving with humility. He is born in a cave. He reclines in a manger. He is wrapped in swaddling clothes. He enters into our poverty, our isolation, our desolation. He does not come as a mere visitor. He comes to grow up and become a man; He endures all the sufferings of the flesh, except sin. He suffers the icy cold of winter, the helplessness of poverty, the hatred of Herod, the bitterness of exile, the flight into Egypt, and the hardships endured by His all-holy mother and His foster father. He comes and saves us. Emmanuel is born! God is born and abides with us.

And so we experience the miracle, a miracle whereby God not only assumes human nature but the all-holy, pure Virgin also gives birth to God. Therefore, let heaven and earth be filled with the angelic hymn: "Glory to God in the highest, and on earth peace!" Glory and divine peace reign in heaven and on earth! Uncreated glory and lasting peace reign in the palace and sanctuary of peace, the liturgical world of the Church. This peace and glory in turn reign in the heart of every person of faith, who entrusts all of his or her life and places it in the hands of the incarnate Word of God. For without the Lord, the God-Man, without Emmanuel, we are alone. We are powerless, frail, and barren. But now we are children of God, brothers and sisters and coheirs with Christ.

At this time of the universal joy of Christmas, we do not send out letters written by human hand; instead, we announce to you the message of the God-Man: "You have dawned, O Christ, from the Virgin; You are the spiritual Sun of Righteousness." This Sun enlightens everything under the sun. He gives light to the ends of the earth and to the depths of the human soul. Whether we celebrate Christmas in the Northern or Southern hemisphere, during winter or summer, we all welcome the divine love and grace of the incarnate God.

We pray with all our heart that "the young child, the pre-eternal God" will abundantly bestow on all of you this love and grace, so that we may enter joyfully into the new year of His goodness. And so may we be counted worthy, eager, and ready to celebrate the millennial observance, two thousand years later, of that significant day in the history of the world, the day of our Lord's nativity. May His grace and infinite mercy be with you all.

Christmas 1998

HE EMBODIED ALL HUMAN EXPECTATIONS

Christ is born, glorify Him!

Christ the God-Man is born, and the melodist exhorts us all to glorify God. Indeed, we all spontaneously offer praise for the great joy and miracle of creation, which is the birth of every new life, of every newborn person, for it signifies the continuation of the natural existence of the human race. However, on this day we rejoice and offer praise not for just any natural birth. Today marks the birth of our Savior and the supernatural restoration of the human race. The pure Virgin is designated and revealed to be the Theotokos. It is through her Son that the human race is saved and that the miracle concealed from all ages becomes reality. The Logos, through whom all things were created, becomes incarnate; it is for Him that the universe was created and divinized.

Humankind was created in the image and likeness of the Creator, having as its final and ultimate purpose the ineffable joy of being divinized after having first given birth not to any simple human being but to God incarnate. It is this culmination that we celebrate today. Therefore, "Christ is born, glorify him!" The Theotokos gives birth to the God-Man; go out to meet Him! Through her purity and humility, the Theotokos, a mere human being and the immaculate temple of God, becomes worthy of embodying the expectations of all humankind, of giving birth not merely to an exceptional child or to an inspired prophet but to the God-Man and Savior Lord.

In the creed, we confess our belief "in one Lord Jesus Christ, the only begotten Son of God, begotten of the Father before all ages."[22] Today, then, we celebrate a joyous and surprising event. The pre-eternal Son and divine Logos is born in time of his all-holy mother, as the incarnate God. Today, humanity does not fashion by its own hands something similar to the divine, but the Virgin, through the Holy Spirit, bears God the Logos incarnate.

"Christ is born of the Virgin and Theotokos, give Him glory!" Through this wondrous birth, all can become partakers of divine glory; everyone can experience this joy, not as simple psychological euphoria or temporary delight, but as heavenly power, a power that triumphs over death. Each person who is inspired and guided by the life of the Virgin, who imitates her humility and extreme obedience to the will of God, is able to find inner peace from spiritual warfare and to arrive at a point of spiritual rest, being born from above and receiving eternal life in Christ. The entire tradition of the Church and the experience of our saints clearly assure us of this. The life of each of us is one of asceticism and struggle,

---

22. From the Symbol of Faith, formulated in Nicea (325) and Constantinople (381).

one of navigating the high seas of life; the end result and ultimate hope is to reach the serene and well-lit harbor of the love of God, which gives birth to our praise for Him.

"Christ is born, glorify him!" God is born as Theanthropos; His glory is made manifest before all humankind. His divine goodwill fills the entire person; and the incessant doxology to the all-good God for, His extreme graciousness in condescending to touch humanity, flows spontaneously from within. This eucharistic doxology is the source of purification. It enlightens our minds and reveals that God created and creates all things "very good." This multiplies our delight and converts our life into paradise. Everything in the life of a faithful person becomes cause for eternal joy and doxology.

St. John Chrysostom, whose sixteen hundredth anniversary since ascending the venerable Throne of Constantinople—sealed with the blood of martyrs—is observed this year, serves for us all as a bright example and model.[23] The end of his life was the emergence of unending doxology, which gushed forth from his heart. He journeyed into long and harsh exile. Somewhere along the way his venerable life ended with him offering his final and famous chrysostomian utterance: "Glory to God in all things." Beloved brother hierarchs and dear children in the Lord, "Christ is born, glorify him!" Give glory extensively and unceasingly, for Emmanuel has come to us and will remain with us. The glory of His divinity, the consolation of the Holy Spirit, and the warmth of divine love have come and will forever remain with us.

For this reason, we wholeheartedly pray that, through the intercessions of our all-holy Lady, the Theotokos and Ever-Virgin Mary, together with our father among the saints, John Chrysostom, our predecessor as archbishop of Constantinople, we will all receive strength from the inexhaustible grace of Christmas, so that we might live in a manner pleasing to God. May this fountainhead, this endless doxology to God, also be born in each of us, as a foretaste of the life to come and of the kingdom, which we pray that God the Logos, who was incarnate for us and for our salvation, will grant to all. May His grace and infinite mercy be with you all.

---

23. The Ecumenical Patriarch proclaimed 2007 "the year of St. John Chrysostom," marking the 1600th anniversary since his repose. See below, 80.

Christmas 1999

THE ULTIMATE MEANING OF HISTORY

Our holy Orthodox Church has passed down to us that we should celebrate the important events of God's saving work according to set periods and with set feasts, so that through their celebration we might appropriate divine grace and participate in those events spiritually and physically. Among the most important events of God's divine providence is the birth in the flesh of our Lord Jesus Christ, the celebration of which the Church has established from the earliest centuries of its existence.

Our connection to the crucial historical events of God's saving work must not be only sentimental in nature. The aim is not to remember joyful events simply to be happy or mournful events simply to grieve. Our connection to these events must include aspects of serious contemplation and deep appropriation of their grace. We meditate on past events in order to prepare for things to come, things for which we hope. In this manner, both individually and collectively, we seek to be essential participants in the actualization of the mystery of salvation. Past events of God's plan of salvation, as well as current events of the unfolding present, are comprehended by faith in Christ in the light of their *telos*—that is, their ultimate end, meaning, or fulfillment. The criterion of both the comprehension and the interpretation of past and present, as well as of all things as they unfold in time moving toward the future, is the reality of the "last things"—the journey toward the Kingdom of God.

"Truth is the reality of future things," says St. Maximus the Confessor.[24] Consequently, truth is also to be discovered in everything that contributes to our participation in that transcendent reality. It is not to be found in the changing or fleeting actualities of the world. It was for the restoration of humanity, that it might return it to its primordial beauty, and for the realization of the Kingdom of God, as the true life of full blessedness in the future eternal age, that Christ was born. God so loved the wayward world, which had distanced itself from Him by its own volition, that He "gave His only-begotten Son that whoever believes in

---

24. One of the greatest theologians and mystics of the early Church, St. Maximus (580–662) was an aide to the Emperor Heraclius and later became a monk. His title is an indication that he suffered persecution for his faith, although he did not die a martyr.

Him should not perish but have eternal life" (John 3.16). It was for our sake that "the Word became flesh and dwelt among us" (John 1.14).

The Orthodox Church continuously lives the revelation of the Incarnation of God's Word. It lives this event daily in the Divine Liturgy, where the whole mystery of the incarnate life of God's Word on earth is repeated. The Church lives all the great moments of Christ's saving ministry: His birth according to the flesh, His earthly dwelling among us, His teaching, Cross, Resurrection, and bodily Ascension. Finally, the Church lives the descent and indwelling of the Spirit as the Comforter. It lives our reconciliation with the Father through the Son. At the same time, the Church lives the future reality as "through a glass darkly" (1 Cor. 13.1), a future reality to which it aspires and that it earnestly seeks (Heb. 13.14).

The Orthodox Church knows that every believer's struggle to put on Christ takes place in the world, in time, and presupposes not only love for God but also love for one's neighbor expressed through readiness to bear the burdens of another as if our own (see Matt. 25.34 and 46, James 2.14 and 20). It is on this account that the Orthodox Church employs the most effective weapons—the proclaimed word and the grace of the sacraments as well as its icons, symbols, and feasts—and invites all faithful to a continuous struggle to imitate Christ so as to ascend to and assume the divine and ineffable beauty of the virtues of Christ. In a true spirit of pastoral care, the Orthodox Church takes this opportunity, on the completion of two millennia since the birth in the flesh of our Lord Jesus Christ, to call together her faithful members once again—just as she does each year, each Sunday, indeed each day, hour, and moment—to knowledge of Christ, to vigilance, repentance, prayer, ascetic struggle, and sobriety. The Church admonishes and exhorts everyone to spend the present life redeeming the time, "because the days are evil" (Eph. 5.16).

The Mother Church never ceases to pray and to do all in its power, both at all times and on each auspicious feast, for peace in the whole world, for the unity and stability of the holy churches, for reconciliation and friendly relations according to God, for respect for human life, freedom, and the natural environment, and, above all, for all human beings, in order that through repentance, love, and commitment to what is pleasing to the Lord, they may be saved by the grace of Christ, who was incarnate, crucified, and risen on behalf of all people. Only by His light is it possible for every inquiring soul to know who God is and what freedom, duty, love, and neighbor are as well as to distinguish between this knowledge and racial discrimination, ethno-phyletism,[25] religious fanaticism, and any form of religious zeal that is not enlightened.

And so we greet you paternally and bless all of you fervently. Above all, we exhort and beseech you: Open wide your hearts to love the Lord and Savior Jesus Christ, who became incarnate for us. Be assured that, beside Him, you will find eternal grace. We also bestow on all the faithful our Patriarchal blessing, wishing you a blessed Christmas and a joyous new year. May the dawn of the new millennium be without cause for grief. May it be peaceful, as well as in every way auspicious and blessed by the Lord. Brothers and children in the Lord, do not ever forget that Christ, who was born in a manger two thousand years ago, is our only hope, the hope of all, and the hope of the entire world. May His grace and great mercy be with all people.

Christmas 2000

CALLED TO LOOK UPWARD

"Christ is on earth, be exalted!" Beloved children in the Lord, this exhortation from St. Gregory the Theologian, proclaimed sixteen centuries ago, remains timely to this day. And it will always remain timely, so long as life continues on this planet. For this material life, which is unidimensional and exclusively worldly, is not fitting for our true nature as images of God.

Humanity typically looks downward and is attached to earthly and corruptible things, as if its entire existence is exhausted in them, and as if the world beyond this material creation is nonexistent. This is why the exhortation to "be exalted" is always timely. It serves as a strong reminder of the superiority of humanity in comparison to earthly, material things. However, this exhortation is not enough to move humanity, nor by itself can it justify "why" humanity must be raised above and transcend tangible earthly matters, rising to a spiritual search for some intangible source of satisfaction and joy.

---

25. The organization of the Church on the basis of ethnicity or race. Often, the word connotes discrimination based on nationalism.

The only reasonable and sufficient justification for this elevation of humanity above everything earthly and corruptible is that "Christ is on earth," as we read in the first part of the above exhortation. St. Gregory the Theologian is in fact crying out, "Be exalted, my fellow human beings, because Christ has descended on earth." Christ is not only human; He is not simply one of many human beings. He is perfectly human but at the same time also the incarnate Son and Word of God. He became flesh, assuming the form of a servant, to raise us mere human beings beside His heavenly Father, in order to deify us. Therefore, it is absolutely necessary, on the occasion of His human birth, for us to turn our attention upward, to lift up our mind and heart to the highest, in order to see whence He descended from and where He invites us to ascend.

He invites us to rise to the beautiful and incorruptible world of divine love that never fails. He invites us to rise to the beautiful and incorruptible world of peace that transcends all understanding, which God grants to those who love Him. He invites us to rise to the heavenly kingdom of the eternal and blessed life that is prepared for all those who love the Lord. It is only in this supreme spiritual space that all the deepest human desires are satisfied for genuine communion with the most desired and beloved person, our Lord Jesus Christ. He now sits at the right hand of the Father; the beauty of His person is ineffable; and the vision of Him fills our heart with joy, life, knowledge, perfection, and unsurpassed blessedness.

Christ, then, is on earth, beloved brothers and sisters, so that we may be exalted to the heavenly way of existence and life, which is none other than Christ's own existence and life. We shall not be alienated from this existence and life so long as we are in this present world and reality, which God in His love and wisdom has established as our dwelling. However, we shall be alienated from Christ's existence and life by captivity and submission to a materialistic and earthly life, which knows as its sole end only hopeless death.

Christ is on earth. Therefore, be exalted to the way of life that is Christ's. Out of love He healed the sick, fed the hungry, relieved the burdened, forgave the sinful, and overlooked nothing necessary to teach us the way of this new life, to render us "a new leaven," a new ferment, "new wineskins," full of new spiritual wine. From this, the new humanity in Christ is appointed, one that dwells on earth and lives in heaven. This new humanity in Christ rests its feet firmly on this earth, works good things in this world continually with its hands. Yet with its mind and heart, this new humanity is always raised upward, to the heavenly and the high, toward love for God and human beings, toward the practice of good deeds, of peace, reconciliation, hope, and life.

Bearing these things in mind, the holy Great Church of Christ, with its heart continually turned upward, does not fail to practice good deeds on earth through its faithful members and to invite them "to show leadership in good deeds for all necessary things." Evidence of this are three significant conferences that the Mother Church has organized and realized in Constantinople this year as the two thousandth anniversary of the birth of Christ in the flesh. These conferences included the Conference of Orthodox Youth, which met in June on the central theme "The Youth in the Church before the Third Millennium;" the International Scientific Conference, which convened a little later on the theme "The Creation of the World and the Creation of Humanity: Challenges and Problems in the Year 2000"; and the Clergy-Laity Conference, which met one month ago with representatives from the eparchies and parishes of the Ecumenical Patriarchate throughout the world in order to discuss the theme "The Parish as the Nucleus of Church Life: Experienced Reality, Contemporary Perspectives, and challenges."[26]

Through such activities as well as through our concern for the natural environment and for peace among peoples, nations, and the churches; our concern to curb social and political tensions; our concern to proclaim throughout the world the message of Christ's presence within this world, to proclaim the ministry of monastics and laity striving for holiness, and to proclaim the general invitation to a genuine experience of life in Christ, there is ample evidence that "Christ is on earth" for us to be raised to the heavens. And there is ample evidence that the One, Holy, Catholic and Apostolic Church embraces in its entirety this earthly life as a forestage and foretaste of the heavenly one, calling us to live on this earth in a way that raises us to the heavens. Furthermore, the presence today of our beloved brother Primates and representatives of the most holy local Orthodox Churches throughout the world in this venerable First Throne Church of Constantinople bears witness to the fact that all of these constitute the One, Holy, Catholic and Apostolic Orthodox Church, which

---

26. For the related occasional addresses by the Ecumenical Patriarch, see Chapter 2, "Patriarchal Exhortations."

is united in Christ and in the Holy Spirit, despite any administrative division.

"Christ is on earth." Therefore, beloved children in the Lord, exalt your life in a fitting manner for our Great Visitor. May His grace and infinite mercy be with you all.

Christmas 2001

SANCTIFICATION AND RE-CREATION

> She gave birth to her first-born son, wrapped him in swaddling clothes, and made him recline in a manger.
>
> Luke 2.7

The greatest event in the history of the universe, the Incarnation of the Son of God, was accomplished almost imperceptibly. As the sacred hymnist says in addressing the Lord: "Unnoticed, you were born in a cave." Truly, the incarnate Word of God was born of the Virgin maiden in a cave in Bethlehem on a silent night like all other nights, wrapped in swaddling clothes like all infants, and placed in a manger as a sign of extreme humility. At a certain moment, the angel of the Lord appeared and declared to the vigilant shepherds: "Today, a Savior was born to you, who is Christ the Lord" (Luke 2.11). Suddenly, a multitude of the heavenly host appeared, praising God, though soon all the angels departed and the silence of the night succeeded their short-lived doxology. In this way, the greatest event of all ages, God becoming human, was covered in silence. It was announced, revealed, and silenced. Out of millions of human beings alive at the time of the birth of Christ, only a few shepherds were informed of the miraculous event.

God, then, does not project His saving work. He does not impose His presence in human hearts or human lives. The great mystery of divine dispensation operates, by and large, internally and mystically. At the same time, our most essential work, the work of appropriating the grace of God, which sanctifies our hearts, is also mystically accomplished in our heart, as if in another cave. Undoubtedly all apparent good works are useful and praiseworthy. The Lord Himself exhorts: "Your light should shine before our fellow human beings, that they may see our good works and glorify our Father in heaven" (Matt. 5.16). The Apostle Paul also recommends that we learn "to lead in good works for meeting necessary needs, that we may not be fruitless" (Tit. 3.14).

Our most serious and important work, however, is sanctification, which is accomplished through the grace of God as well as through observance of the divine commandments and inconspicuous internal work, all aimed at purifying our inner life of every evil thought. Pursue peace with all, and acquire sanctification, without which no one can see the Lord, as the Apostle recommends. And he adds two fundamental elements for our sanctification: Take care, lest you find yourselves far from the grace of God, that you let exist within you no root of bitterness, which may cause trouble whereby many may be polluted (Heb. 12.14–15).

All of us, as faithful, desire that our heart will become the new cave where Christ is received, so that we may be reborn. What is required for this to be achieved, beyond apparent good works, is the invisible work of purifying our heart of every tumult and bitterness, of evil memories and vain imaginations, so that the grace of God may sanctify it and Christ may find it appropriate to dwell within us. There, in the purified cave of our heart, the great mystery will be accomplished, on account of which Christ was born in the cave of Bethlehem. Our existence will then be sanctified and deified, and we shall be reborn in the Holy Spirit. In this way, reborn and renewed, we shall partake of the whole life of Christ from His birth to His crucifixion and His subsequent resurrection and ascension into heaven.

Bearing these things in mind, let us celebrate, according to St. Gregory the Theologian, "not in festive but in godly manner, not in worldly but in transcendent manner, not for what is ours but for what is God's, not for the purpose of creation but for the purpose of re-creation."[27] May we all become worthy to see Christ being born and received in our hearts. Then, in godly manner we shall celebrate the joyous feast of the invisible birth of Christ, through our wholehearted participation in the warm welcome extended to Him by the world. May the grace and rich mercy of Him, who was born in Bethlehem and made to recline in a manger, Christ our Lord and God, be with you.

---

27. See PG 36.316AB.

Christmas 2002

GOD AS LIGHT

> Our Savior visited us from on High, and we who were in darkness and in shadow found the truth.

The desire for truth is ancient and universal among human beings. The human race has made and continues to make strenuous efforts to approach it. It is surely with good reason that truth is sought, because knowledge of truth emancipates us from deceit and its consequences. Unfortunately, however, in our search for truth, we do not always follow the right path. There have been and continue to be many erroneous doctrines that have demanded and continue to demand recognition as expressions of truth. Today, more than ever, the proponents of certain eastern or other antique philosophies endeavor to present these doctrines as new and as endowed with cosmic or supernatural power. They try to persuade us, on the basis of many claims of spiritual experiences, that they possess the full truth and greatest power.

However, beloved children in the Lord, we know very well from our experience that the birth of our Lord Jesus Christ, which we celebrate with great solemnity today, "dawned the light of knowledge on the world." The Holy Gospel informs us that, through the birth of our Lord Jesus Christ, "the people who sat in darkness saw a great light, and those in the land and in the shadow of death were met with a light that dawned upon them" (Matt. 4.16). This is what the sacred hymnist declared poetically when he wrote, "We who were in darkness and shadow have found the truth."

The truth we have found is not an intellectual proposition, a formulation about the world, God, and humanity. It is the Creator of the world Himself, the Son and Word of God, our Lord Jesus Christ, He who was born humbly in an insignificant cave for our salvation and revealed to us His infinite love for the world, for the righteous and sinners alike. He assured us that He is Himself the Way, the Truth, and the Life. If we find Him, we need no other truth, because He is the only truth and the fullness of truth. We do not need eastern or other dubious teachers of any origin and with any promise. On the contrary, we know that the wise men too, while in error about everything else, came from the East to venerate our Lord Jesus Christ as king. This Christ, who out of love emptied Himself of royal glory and became assimilated with lowly humankind, so that He may assimilate us to God, is the one whom we ought to love and follow with all our soul and all our mind.

Let us follow the example of the humble shepherds of Bethlehem, and also of those wise men to whom "a star showed the Word that existed before the sun, coming to put an end to sin." Let us refuse to listen to those contemporary wise men and shepherds who, instead of following Christ, point to other false saviors. Salvation lies nowhere but in Christ. It is only from Christ that we expect to benefit as individuals, as nations, and as humanity. If we stand aloof from Him, we shall find ourselves in darkness and in the shadow of lies, and we shall reap the bitter fruit of humanity in deception, traveling on the deadly paths of falsehood.

Grace and truth came through Jesus Christ (John 1.17). Joy, peace, salvation, and every good thing is found only in Him. "Glory to God in the highest," who was well pleased that His own Son and Word would become incarnate for us and transmit to us His full truth and saving grace. Glory, praise, and thanksgiving are also due to Jesus Christ, born in a humble manger, and to the Holy Spirit, who constitutes the Church and inspires the faithful.

In reminding you of these things, we wholeheartedly bestow on you our paternal wishes and patriarchal blessings, fervently praying that you may pass in peace and joy the holy feasts of the Twelve Days of Christmas as well as the new year of the Lord's favor that is at hand. May the grace and mercy of our Lord Jesus Christ, who was born in a manger in Bethlehem for our salvation through the Ever-Virgin Mary, the Theotokos, be with all of you.

Christmas 2003

GOD AS LIFE

By God's dispensation, we are once again celebrating the great and joyous feast of the birth of the incarnate divine Logos. Our most merciful God, who created man and endowed him with the gift of self-consciousness and the capacity to know and communicate with others, preordained him ultimately to partake in the joy of love. God did not abandon man when, on rejecting His love, he chose to become estranged from the

Creator. This choice, made by the first-created human beings, proved detrimental and fatal. It brought spiritual death to humankind, turned life materialistic, and gave rise to selfishness. This was a predicament from which humankind could never escape alone.

It was precisely for this reason that the Word of God graciously condescended to assume human flesh; in so doing, He healed human nature so that, reborn in Christ, humanity would love God anew in the person of Jesus Christ. This restoration of the loving relationship between humanity and God is the source of the greatest joy in the universe. It is a gift offered by God to the world and for which the angels sang on the night of Christ's birth in Bethlehem. It is this very restoration that we celebrate joyously and spiritually, sharing, to a certain degree, in all the material gifts given by God to alienated humanity—gifts that clearly indicate God's love for the world.

Most of our fellow human beings revel in opportunities for worldly joy. They are preoccupied with the enjoyment of the abundant riches and numerous entertainments and pleasures with which developed countries are replete, all the while forgetting the deeper meaning of the birth of Christ. At times, even devout and faithful Christians are misled by such secular temptations. They too sometimes overlook the true meaning of the nativity of Jesus Christ, neglecting the spiritual experience of this event that is of such tremendous importance for our lives.

The great importance of this birth rests on the fact that God assumed flesh and became human so as to deify human nature. He took on flesh in order to offer humankind the potential for fullness of growth and, ultimately, the potential to become one with God. All human joys and pleasures are trivial and minuscule compared with the joy of sharing in the life of Christ. Nevertheless, humankind is unconcerned with this potential. It is content with mortality and malice, while setting goals that are minimal and mundane. It tends to alter the feast of Christmas so that it becomes a universal celebration of a purely seasonal nature, totally anthropocentric and completely disconnected from the Church and its Christian content. To counter these tendencies, Christians should make every effort to realize consciously the deeper spiritual meaning of the incarnation and birth of God's Word. This is what concerns us directly; it affords us the opportunity to partake in the life of Christ, which is an ineffable mystery, an opportunity inevitably filling us with infinite and inalienable joy. Yet, to receive this joy and peace, we must accept this invitation and its implications. We must love Jesus Christ, who gave us this opportunity; we must seek divine grace and allow ourselves to change through God's grace.

Beloved faithful, our Lord, who was born in a cave and lay in a manger, expects that we open our hearts so that He may reside within us, as if inside another cave. From within our hearts, He will guide our thoughts and feelings toward everything that is good and beautiful. He will become our travel companion and illumine our hearts with love and happiness. Let us cleanse our hearts of malevolent addictions, evil habits, spiritual bondage, and sinful intentions; let us purify our hearts through confession, whereby our souls become purer than snow. Then, with sacred anticipation, we shall be ready to welcome Jesus Christ as an infant in the manger of the heart. Then, gradually, by following the commandments, Christ will be formed in us (Gal. 419) and we shall reach the fullness of the measure of His stature (Eph. 4.13).

We warmly embrace you on the occasion of this special day and wholeheartedly bestow on you our paternal wishes and patriarchal blessings. We pray that Christ, the Prince of Peace, may put an end to wars and bloodshed, bringing peace to our agitated world. We further pray that you may all celebrate these holy days with peace and joy under the protection of God, through the intercession of the most holy Theotokos and of all the saints. May the grace and abundant mercy of Jesus Christ, who was born in a cave and laid in a manger, be with you all.

Christmas 2004

GOD AS HUMILITY

It is with amazement and wonder that we approach face-to-face, particularly during these days, the incarnation of the Son and Word of God, who was born of a Virgin in a manger, something impossible for both humankind and the angelic orders to conceive. Yet, as the faithful celebrate this joyful event, when by divine graciousness a Savior was born to us, humankind is shattered by the social conflict of injustice as well as by the natural disaster of earthquakes, which bring turmoil and trouble to all those who love peace. In the drive for social experimentation, social structures are being destabilized; spiritual quests are derailed by self-destructing cults; and unprecedented natural disasters are occurring in different places of the planet. All around, one sees disorder and confusion, murder and devastation. The vision of peace seems unwelcome and suppressed. Uncertainty, anxiety, depression, lack of meaning, frequent indifference, and often even hate have found their foothold.

Millions of our fellow human beings find themselves struggling, both morally and physically, trapped beneath this natural, social, and spiritual wreckage. Many of them, unable to cope with this situation, are stricken with various psychological and physical injuries. Others seek out the guilty and engage in vindictive acts against those whom they believe responsible for their troubles. Still others, unable to determine who is responsible and unable to address them directly, express dissatisfaction through acts of terrorism directed against the innocent. Some even exploit this destabilization, attempting to profit at the expense of their neighbor. And yet others, having entrenched themselves in wealth or power, live in a secluded world, neither feeling the pain of others nor being willing to ease this pain. All of these people have not known the salvation received through the newborn Christ. In many cases, out of despair that there can be no redemption, they do not even seek out salvation. Instead, through their own efforts, they strive for solutions to their problems and many times resort to the power of evil, which only increases confusion and pain.

Beloved children in the Lord, we believe and know well that salvation is to be found nowhere else but in Christ and that there is no other name by which we may be saved than that of Jesus Christ. Our certainty is not shaken by our knowledge that the Word of God appeared as a humble human being, as a weak infant, as a lamb bearing the sin of the world, and as a savior accepting the Cross and death. We are not alarmed that most people do not accept the message of love and humility, which, as He taught, are necessary in order for them to be saved.

Bearing in mind the example of our Savior, we recognize the saving power of humility and love, which are voluntarily crucified—these two supernatural attributes of divinity, which fallen humanity imitates so reluctantly. With much love and humility, we repeat to all people the saving message of Christ, proclaimed not only through words but also through His sacrifice on the Cross, which conquered death through the Resurrection. For the sacrifice out of love is sealed by the death of Christ. His death, however, does not bring the transformation of the world to a conclusion. That is accomplished in the triumph over His death through Resurrection. This is the content of salvation about which we speak. Death will never have dominion over us because Jesus Christ, who is newly born, has trampled it and abrogated its power.

A Savior has been born to us this day! He did not come wielding earthly power but came with the power of humility; the almighty and incomparable power of love was sacrificed selflessly and unconditionally. We have no delusions or false hopes when we claim that the world in its entirety will soon accept these truths. We know, however, that, as long as the world does not accept and apply them, it will continue to live in the torment of mutual destruction, moral derailment, and meaninglessness.

And so we appeal first to the faithful: Let us invite Christ to be born in our hearts, not as an emotional, short-lived sensation of worldly euphoria but as a radical change of the soul, as our rebirth in Christ, so that the divine attributes of love and humility may constitute the fundamental elements of our existence. With ardent love and humility, we invite all our fellow human beings, whether they know Christ as God or not, to draw near to Jesus Christ in order to receive from Him peace in their hearts, knowledge of the purpose of life, negation of pain, and joy of life.

May Christ, through the intercession of the most holy Theotokos, who gave her own flesh to the Savior Christ, and of our holy predecessors among the saints, John Chrysostom and Gregory the Theologian, whose sacred relics have recently been returned to our Church,[28] and of all the saints, be born in the manger of all our hearts and reside there permanently so that we may live with Him the joy of His presence, indescribable love, and extraordinary humility.

Christmas 2005

GOD AS UNCONDITIONAL LOVE

> For God so loved the world that he gave his only Son, so that all who believe in him may not perish but have eternal life.
>
> John 3.16

---

28. The sacred relics of these saints were solemnly restored to the Ecumenical Patriarchate as a gift from Pope John Paul II in November, 2004. See Chapter 4, "Ecumenical Addresses," 284.

The human soul feels a deep need to be loved. The widespread sense that life has no meaning plagues our younger generation in particular and may be blamed precisely on the absence of love. Our fellow human beings are for the most part trapped in their individual pursuits, and, through the acquisition of material goods, carnal pleasures, and worldly fame, seek to fill the emptiness caused by this lack of love. Yet, the soul is satisfied only with personal love, which exists in the Lord and holds the world together, acknowledging all by name. It is offered to all generously. God created the universe through His Logos, out of love, so that all may participate in the joy whose source is found in this personal love.

However, from the first-created human being and throughout history, humanity has rejected the love that the Creator has offered, turning instead to a faceless world and unsuccessfully seeking recognition through the pursuit of superiority and satisfaction in self-absorption. A world of competition, hatred, and bloodshed has emerged. We continue to experience it as daily reality. By contrast, God's love never diminishes, regardless of our rejection; for God sent His only-begotten Son out of love, not to judge people for going astray but rather to save the world (John 3.17). He was born of the Virgin Mary, in a humble manger, to show that might, fame, and material riches, in which humankind seeks joy and salvation, are not the true sources of life and happiness. Christ came to Bethlehem to proclaim the message of God's unconditional love for humankind. God has continued to offer this immense love for the two thousand years since Christ's birth. His Son and Word came to the world as a weak and innocent infant, filled with love and yet threatened with death by Herod, who represents that part of humanity that loathes love even when it is offered through the innocent and peaceful eyes of a child.

Many people erroneously think of God as an unyielding judge rather than as an affectionate father who, with love and forgiveness, awaits the return of His prodigal son. So they have distanced themselves from the incarnate God, the glory of God the Father, and the consubstantial Holy Spirit; they have broken away from the life-giving and loving Holy Trinity and thereby rendered their world secular, deprived of hope in God and of genuine love. They have turned to substitutions for divine love, basing their hopes on the expansion of power in the secular world, on the accumulation of wealth, on the subjugation of nations, on the global expansion of trade, and even on the promulgation of ideas against God. They disregard, even deny, the reality of death, turning to anything and everything to alleviate the stresses arising from a life without love. Unable to find deliverance from their despair in such pursuits, some are driven to reject the greatest gift of God to humankind—life itself.

Nevertheless, beloved children, the love of God is an undeniable reality. Our Lord Jesus Christ waits to be born in the heart of each of us in order to bring to everyone the meaning of life. This means that He has chosen us to enjoy life in mutual love and to experience the fulfillment of our existence in our relationship with Him, the incarnate God, and with our fellow human beings and all creation. "Blessed be the God and Father of our Lord Jesus Christ, who has blessed us in Christ with every spiritual blessing in the heavenly places, just as He chose us in Christ before the foundation of the world to be holy and blameless before Him in love" (Eph. 1.3–4).

Love is the equivalent of the foundation and roof of a building, the beginning and end of life, the Alpha and Omega of creation. The mysteries of the manger and birth, the Cross and Resurrection, the Ascension and continuing presence of Christ on earth—all point to love. The hymn of the angels that is chanted during the Nativity service, "Glory to God in the highest, and on earth peace, good will among all" (Luke 2.14), is an expression of the admiration that the angels felt when they realized the inconceivable love of God. Christ tolerated crucifixion among outlaws not out of weakness, which is a quality unbefitting an omnipotent God; He tolerated it out of love. All of God's actions are filled with love for the world.

Let us, then, beloved children, abandon the course that leads to secularism. Let us return to our heavenly Father in repentance. Let us approach Jesus Christ, who was born as our brother, who came into the world out of love for us, as we had been deceived and had distanced ourselves from Him. His love for us is a fact. In His presence, there is no fear but only forgiveness, peace and joy. May the grace, blessing and abundant mercy of God be with you all during this Nativity season and throughout your lives, unto the ages of ages.

Christmas 2006

GOD AS COMMUNION

God on earth, man in heaven; all became mingled together.

St. John Chrysostom

The human mind finds it difficult to comprehend the immense change resulting from the birth of Christ. He who was born in the manger in Bethlehem was not an ordinary child like those born every day. He is the Creator of the universe, who descended to our level in order to raise His creation back up and restore humanity to the heights from which it had fallen. According to the plan of the Creator, who is full of love, humankind was created with the capacity to achieve divinity. But humanity strayed from the right path and became enslaved to decay and death. To restore within humanity the potential to become divine, God had to become incarnate, to assume flesh for the sake of fallen man who, as a creature of this world, could not transcend mortal human nature and become divine of his own accord.

The notion of God's incarnation was something that not even the most vivid human imagination could conceive; no one dared consider this unexpected possibility. Only the Prophets, inspired by the Holy Spirit, foretold such an occurrence as conceivable and possible through God. Indeed, on the night of Christmas, the unexpected became real. "God [is] on earth, man in heaven," exclaims St. John Chrysostom in admiration and awe. This world-altering event is not irrelevant to our life. Its significance is not exhausted in fleeting celebratory festivities. We ought to contemplate the new situation with great seriousness and soberness. The birth of Christ gives us the opportunity to transcend our mortality, ascend to heaven, live with Christ, be reconciled to God, enjoy His adoption, and experience the inexhaustible joy of divine love unto the ages.

Let us, therefore, celebrate spiritually, together with the angels and saints, the grace of God offered to the world. And let us begin a new life, a life worthy of the calling of the incarnate God. The stirring event of Christ's birth, though inconspicuous, has effected a profound change in the universe and particularly in each of us. We should take care not to undervalue its importance simply because the circumstances in which it took place were humble. Nor should we celebrate the event in the boisterous and superficial manner that would befit a seasonal celebration with no other significance except as an opportunity for secular festivity.

While the events surrounding the birth of our Lord Jesus Christ are not visible to mortal human eyes, there are some who, by the grace of God, have seen and described the deeper events and resulting mystical change. Here is how our saintly predecessor on the Patriarchal Throne of Constantinople, John Chrysostom, describes this sacred and dazzling event:

> Angels joined the choirs of men, men had fellowship with the angels and other celestial powers; and one might see . . . reconciliation made between God and our nature, the devil brought to shame, demons in flight, death destroyed, paradise open, the curse eradicated, sin obliterated, error driven off, truth returning, the word of piety everywhere sown and flourishing in its growth, the heavenly city planted on earth, angels continually brought to the earth, and abundant hope for things to come.[29]

Beloved brothers and sisters, may we see this very hope for things to come realized in our life through the prayers of St. John Chrysostom, who, together with all the saints, intercedes for us with the Lord in heaven. This coming year marks the sixteen hundredth anniversary since the repose of this saint. Therefore, the Ecumenical Patriarchate proclaims this as the year of St. John Chrysostom, and we urge the faithful to study his work and examine his life.

"Christ is born; glorify Him! Christ is come from heaven; go out and meet Him! Christ is on earth; be lifted up!" To this God, who so loves humankind that He was born for us in flesh, be all honor, thanksgiving, glory, and worship unto the ages of ages.

Christmas 2007

GOD AS PERSONAL LOVE

Christ is born; glorify Him!
Christ comes from heaven; go out and meet Him!

It is with great joy that our Church invites us to glorify God for the loving presence on earth of Christ in His divine-human hypostasis, being one of the three persons of the Holy Trinity. We must, therefore, examine carefully the true and life-giving significance of the incarnation of the Son and Word of God. For, first, it reveals to humanity that God is personal and is made manifest to us as personal, just as He has also created us as

---

29. PG 57.15–16.

persons; second, it reveals to us that God embraces us with His love. These two truths, the personhood of God and the reality of His love, express fundamental tenets of our faith, which of course we have heard about many times. Still, their impact on our lives is not as great as it should be, inasmuch as many of us neither experience Christ's boundless love for us in a personal way nor return the love to Him so that by grace we may also share in His other properties.

If others, who have not known this personal God and, as a result, drown in their search for an impersonal being that they perceive as divine, are somewhat justified in the frustrations of their quest, we Orthodox Christians are not at all justified in following ways that lead only to impasse. For, instead of seeking God as person and approaching Him in the one who loved us—namely, Jesus Christ—those who are so deceived desperately strive to become divine through their own powers, just as Adam did by obeying the evil one. However, the true and personal God, who is known only through Jesus Christ—the one born in a manger out of love for the world—promised us adoption and return to the bosom of the Father as well as deification by grace through Christ. It is only through Christ that one can fulfill the universal human desire to transcend corruption and the isolation of existence without love.

Let us, therefore, direct the gaze of our heart toward the newborn Jesus Christ in the manger, so that, by considering His love for us, we might love Him with all our heart, mind, and being. It is only through the love of Jesus Christ that we may by grace become participants also in His divine nature, just as through love He shared in our human nature. Other experiences and worldly ecstasies as well as purely anthropocentric ideas do not lead to an encounter with the truly personal God of love but only to a deep and cold darkness, to the gloom of eternal destruction, and to a complete abyss.

For this reason, beloved children, love Jesus Christ, who out of love for us and for our salvation became human; come to know the communion of His love, with the Father and the Holy Spirit. Indeed, there is nothing sweeter than the love of this personal God. The great herald of divine love is the one who identified God with love—namely, St. John the Evangelist and theologian, who twice pronounced the supreme utterance, that "God is love" (1 John 4.8, 16). After him, the great herald is St. Paul the Apostle, who loved God to the end and posed the fervent question, "Who

can separate us from the love of Christ?" Neither sorrow nor sword, neither death nor any other love can be more powerful than Christ's love for
us (Rom. 8.39). In remembrance of these loving words of St. Paul, and in
celebration of his birth two millennia ago, we declare the coming year
2008 as the Year of the Apostle Paul.[30]

We pray paternally and wholeheartedly that Jesus Christ, who was born
in a manger out of love and for our salvation, may render our hearts as
His manger, through the intercession of His Ever-Virgin mother, together
with that of our predecessor St. John Chrysostom, to whose blessed memory we had dedicated this past year, and of another Patriarchal predecessor, St. Nephon, restorer and second founder of the Holy Patriarchal and
Stavropegic Monastery of St. Dionysius on Mount Athos,[31] which next
year celebrates the five hundredth anniversary since his repose. We pray
through the intercession as well of Saints John and Paul, both Apostles
par excellence and heralds of God's love, and through the intercession of
all the saints, that He may reveal to everyone His profound and personal
love.

We invoke on all of you His grace and rich mercy. Merry Christmas!
May the Twelve Days of Christmas be blessed, and may the new year be
spiritually fruitful.

Christmas 2008

PARTAKERS OF DIVINE NATURE

The great and sacred day of Christmas, the mighty citadel and matri-
arch of all feasts, has dawned, inviting each of us to a spiritually uplifting
encounter with the Ancient of Days, who became an infant for us. St.
John of Damascus underscores this reality: "By the grace of God the
Father, the only-begotten Son and Word of God, who is in the bosom of
the Father, consubstantial with the Father and the Holy Spirit, the pre-
eternal and perfect God, who is without beginning, condescends to us as

---

30. For the related occasional address by the Ecumenical Patriarch, see Chapter 4,
"Academic Discourses," 371.

31. One of the twenty monasteries on Mount Athos, Dionysiou Monastery was
founded in the fourteenth century.

His servants, becoming fully human and achieves that which is newer than new, the only new thing under the sun."[32]

This incarnation of the Son of God is not merely symbolical, like the incarnations of the numerous gods in mythology; it is reality, a truly new reality, "the only new thing under the sun." It occurred at a specific historical moment during the reign of the Emperor Octavian Augustus some 746 years (according to new astronomical data) since the establishment of Rome. It occurred among a specific people, in the house and line of David (Luke 2.4); in a specific place, Bethlehem of Judea; and with a specific purpose: "He became human in order that we might become divine," in the succinct words of Athanasius the Great.[33]

The event of God's incarnation gives us the opportunity to reach the extreme limits of our nature, which are identified neither with the "good and beautiful" of the ancient Greeks and the "justice" of the philosophers nor with the tranquility of Buddhism and any transcendental "fate," or so-called karma. Nor again is it identified with any "harmony" of supposedly contradictory elements of some imaginary "living force." Rather, it is the ontological transcendence, through Christ, of corruption and death. It is our integration into His divine life and glory. It is our union, by grace and through Him, with the Father in the Holy Spirit. These are our ultimate limits: personal union with the Trinitarian God! And Christ's nativity does not promise any vague blessedness or abstract eternity; it places "in our hands" the potential of personal participation in God's sacred life and love in an endless progression. It grants us the possibility not only "of receiving adoption" (Gal. 4.5) but also of becoming "partakers of divine nature" (2 Peter 1.4).

Of course, amid the global confusion and crisis of our time, these truths have a strange echo. Most people's hope, resting on worldly "deities," is daily proven false. The dignity of the human person is humiliated and crushed by numbers, machines, computers, stock markets, and diverse flags of vain ideological opportunism. Nature is blasphemed; creation groans; young people despair and protest against the injustice of the

---

32. *On the Orthodox Faith* III, I in PG 94.981–84.

33. *On the Divine Incarnation*, chapter 54. St. Athanasius (293–373) was a deacon during the First Ecumenical Council of Nicea (325), later archbishop of Alexandria, and a leading theologian against Arianism.

present as well as against the uncertainty of the future. "Darkness, clouds, storms, and noise" (Deut. 4.11) prevail in our world, giving the impression that even the light of hope that dawns in Bethlehem is threatened with extinction, and the angelic hymn of universal joy—"Glory to God in the highest, and on earth peace, good will among all" (Luke 2.14)—is in danger of being overcome.

Nevertheless, the Church calls everyone to sober attention, a reevaluation of priorities, and the search for the divine in every person. Indeed, the Church will not cease to proclaim, with all the strength acquired through its two millennia of experience, that the child in the manger in Bethlehem is "the hope of all ends of the earth," the Word and purpose of life, the redemption sent by God to the whole world.

We share this good news with much love from the Throne of the Great Church of Christ in Constantinople, which has been decorated with the blood of martyrs, proclaiming it to all children of the Ecumenical Patriarchate and to every person who thirsts for Christ. We invoke on all of you the mercy, peace, and grace of God as well as the saving gift of the only-begotten Son of God, who came down from heaven—for us and for our salvation—and was incarnate of the Holy Spirit and the Virgin Mary, becoming human. To Him, together with the Father and the Holy Spirit, belong all glory, power, honor, and worship unto to the ages.

Christmas 2009

THE WHOLE WORLD REJOICES

> Heaven and earth have united
>   through the birth of Christ.
> Today, God has appeared on earth,
>   and humanity has ascended to heaven.
>
> Christmas hymn

The distance between God and humanity resulted from sin but has been abolished through the assumption of human nature by the only-begotten Son and pre-eternal Word of God. It was God's good will, His initiative and desire, that the incarnation of His Son should eliminate that distance and unite heaven with earth, creation with its Creator. During the Feast of the Entrance of the Theotokos,[34] the Church chanted, "Today is the beginning of God's good will and the proclamation of human salvation." During that feast, through the dedication of the blessed Mary to the temple and through her preparation as the bearer of the boundless God, the road was paved for God's dispensation to humanity through the incarnation, foretelling our salvation.

During the Feast of the Annunciation,[35] when the divine Inconceivable was conceived, through the Holy Spirit, in the womb of the Theotokos, divine nature began to coexist with human nature so that, in the words of St. Athanasius the Great, "we might become deified," and the Church again chanted, "Today is the beginning of our salvation and the revelation of the pre-eternal mystery; the Son of God becomes the son of the Virgin." And so the "divine good will" welcomed at the Entrance, as well as the salvation that was initiated at the Annunciation, are today rendered a tangible reality as we celebrate the great holy day of Christmas. Today, "the Word assumes flesh and dwells among us" (John 1.14), while the angels celebrate, chanting, "Glory to God in the highest, and on earth peace, good will among all" (Luke 2.14).

With the Incarnation of the Divine Word, the salvation of the human race has already potentially occurred. Those who believe in Jesus and live in accordance with the faith, fulfilling His commandments and practicing His teaching, are thereby elevated to the status of friends of God and become participants with Him in His sacred work! They become "partakers of divine nature" (2 Peter 1.14), gods by grace! This takes place exclusively within the Church, where we are reborn in Christ and adopted by the Father through holy baptism and through the holy sacraments as well as through the cultivation of virtue, so as to be filled with divine grace and the Holy Spirit while growing "to maturity, to the measure of the full stature of Christ" (Eph. 4.13) until we can say, like St. Paul, "It is no longer I who live, but it is Christ who lives in me" (Gal. 2.20). Those who acquire such perfection are regarded by Christ not simply as His friends or brothers and sisters but as members of His very body. This is why, from the height of the Cross, He would say to His most holy mother of the Evangelist John, "Woman, here is your son," and to John, "Here

---

34. November 21.
35. March 25.

is your mother" (John 19.26–27). Christmas, therefore, opens wide the door of human "christification" and deification by grace. And for this reason "the entire creation rejoices in celebration and the heavens delight with us" on this day of salvation and special significance.[36]

With these joyful and hopeful realities before us, from the sacred See of the Ecumenical Patriarchate at the Phanar, we extend to you our fervent, festive congratulations and wholehearted Patriarchal wishes on this central occasion of the Christian calendar. We greet all of our beloved faithful throughout the world, the beloved children of the holy Mother Church—clergy of all ranks, monastics and laity, pastors and parishioners, and especially those suffering or experiencing sorrow, need, or trial. May the pre-eternal Son of God, who was born in a cave and lay in a manger— who for our sake became Son of Man—render all of us worthy of His self-emptying love and His sacred, venerable incarnate dispensation.

LENTEN ENCYCLICALS

Catechetical Address
On the occasion of the commencement of Great Lent
BARTHOLOMEW
By the Grace of God,
Archbishop of Constantinople, New Rome, and Ecumenical
    Patriarch,
To all the Faithful of the Church:
Grace, mercy, and peace from Christ the Savior Christ
Together with our own prayer, blessing, and forgiveness

> The customary address and introduction of
> encyclical letters on the occasion of Great Lent

Great Lent 2000

PREPARING FOR LENT

Our holy Orthodox Church, through the Holy Fathers, has designated the period of Great Lent as an annual occasion of repentance. Of course, repentance is necessary each day and every hour. However, during Great

---

36. From a hymn after Christmas, chanted on December 28.

Lent, our Church invites us to deeper experience of that repentance. What is the deeper significance of this repentance that our Church so highly recommends? Many say: "I do not feel that I have committed any sin, and so I have no need of repentance." Yet the Holy Fathers emphasize that repentance is required not only of sinners but even of those who have attained perfection. A Christian, then, may wonder: "For what mistakes must the perfect repent?"

During the period of the Triodion,[37] the preparatory stage for Great Lent, which itself is a period of preparation and prayer, our holy Church presents us with three examples of persons who, while in fact needing repentance, did not realize its importance and consequently failed to repent. The Church presents us as well with another person who did in fact repent sincerely. Naturally, all of us are familiar with the sinful Publican. Conscious of his many sins, he did not dare raise his eyes to heaven but instead beat his breast, saying, "God, be merciful to me, a sinner." Nevertheless, not all of us are aware of his sinfulness, and so we are at a loss as to why and of what sins we must repent. The answer is provided by three repugnant personalities, which the holy gospel gives us as examples to avoid.

The first is the Pharisee, who is well known to all of us. This man kept certain precepts of God's law, particularly those that were external and visible to others. He conveyed to others and himself had the impression that he was a good man, while at the same time inwardly condemning his neighbor of various sins. The impression that we are good, particularly when accompanied by condemnation of others for their failings, indicates a state of spiritual illness. It reveals a soul unaware of reality and in need of a change of attitude in order to know the truth about itself and others and to be liberated from delusion. In order to be saved, the soul must, in all humility and repentance for its arrogance, approach Christ, who is meek and humble of heart.

The second repugnant personality presented by the holy gospel is the supposed "good" son in the parable of the Prodigal Son; this was the

---

37. A period in the liturgical cycle of the Orthodox Church calendar, which includes a pre-Lenten season, the forty days of Great Lent itself, and Holy Week, concluding with the midnight office of Holy and Great Saturday. See Kallistos Ware, ed., *The Lenten Triodion* (South Canaan, Pa.: St. Tikhon's Seminary Press, 2002).

elder son, who was not profligate. He neither wasted his Father's property nor committed the same sins as his prodigal brother, and so he felt no need to repent. However, all of us understand that he was hardhearted and self-centered, that he could not endure the warm reception that his father prepared for the repentant, prodigal brother on his return. So the elder son, too, needed a change of attitude. He needed to repent in order to recognize the delusion of his ways and be saved by his father, who—like God—desires that all may be saved and come to the knowledge of truth.

The third type that the holy gospel presents and admonishes to avoid during the period of the Triodion is represented by the myriad of people who are hardened and indifferent before the pain of their neighbor: those who offer no food to the hungry when they themselves are filled; those who offer no drink to the thirsty when they themselves are quenched; those who do not clothe the naked when they themselves are adequately clothed; those who show no concern for those in prison when they themselves enjoy freedom; those who in general are interested in their own well-being and remain indifferent to the needs of others.

No matter how much we wish to conceal the spiritual condition of our soul so as to make it appear beautiful, it is impossible not to discover within its depth certain elements represented these three repugnant persons, who considered themselves to have no sin and to be in no need of repentance but instead to be deserving of God's justification. All of us must repent, in order to plant in our heart the seed of the love for other people, for compassion, and for mercy as well as for our acceptance of every brother and sister who returns and repents, recognizing that our virtues are as naught before God and that all of us are debtors—embracing all of this in love and humility, in self-awareness and the struggle to purify our minds of intellectual pollution and of misdirected, self-centered ideas and thoughts.

Beloved children in the Lord, we Orthodox Christians have a special obligation to experience the spiritual life of our Church, so that our non-Orthodox brothers and sisters may also discern the grace of God that is in us and praise God for the Orthodox faith. However, to experience the Orthodox spiritual life, we need repentance, a profound change of attitude, and avoidance of the examples of spiritual error presented above. We also need humility and self-knowledge so that God's grace, which is granted to the humble and not the prideful, may also come upon us. For God is able to raise up children of Abraham from among the stones—that is to say, to create faithful out of those who love Him and who love other people. If we are not found to be worthy laborers of His vineyard, God will give it to others who will prove more capable of producing good fruit.

Therefore, let us devote ourselves to the struggle of repentance, so that we may be continually transfigured in newness of mind, living and practicing the spirit of the law—namely, discernment and mercy, love and humility, acceptance of others, desire for the salvation of all, and sincere concern for the whole world. Let us remove ourselves from any self-serving complacency and embrace the heritage of our Fathers. For only then will we become like our Father in heaven—when we receive our prodigal brothers and sisters with the same open embrace with which the father in the parable welcomed the Prodigal Son, when we reject the attitude of the elder brother. This change of heart, this repentance, is what we seek and what, according to the Church Fathers, supersedes other ascetic feats, which are useful only when they relate and lead to this change, not when they increase a false sense of virtue.

May the Almighty Lord enlighten our hearts so that we might understand how much each of us requires a revision of our ways, so that we might destroy the old structure of our established ways of thinking and replace them with a new system of convictions proposed by the only restorer of the world and redeemer of humanity, our Lord Jesus Christ. To Him is due is all honor and worship, unto to the ages of ages.

Great Lent 2001

THE ASCETIC WAY

Our holy Orthodox Church always reminds us that we must be disciplined in virtue because our all-good Creator offered to the first-created the way of ascesis—namely, the deliberate control of desires so as to approach divine likeness. Ascesis did not concern only the first-created. It is also crucial for all Christians, who struggle continually throughout their lives. Our holy Church, knowing the human tendency to slacken and even relinquish the effort to exercise an ascetic discipline and maintain an ascetic disposition, has instituted particular periods of ascetic struggle that are more intense. These periods precede the great feasts and normally comprise great fasts, because God's commandment to the first-created included a commandment to abstain from food.

We have begun our entrance into the period of holy and Great Lent, which is the principal ascetical period of the ecclesiastical year, constituting our preparation to welcome the great feast of Pascha, the Resurrection of Christ and His victory over death, the darkest enemy of humanity. "The arena, then, of the virtues has been opened," as our Church chants.[38] And we are all invited to enter, "those of us who wish to struggle for the prize, girding ourselves for the noble contest of the fast." Of course, fasting is not the only contest that we are called to undertake during this season. Nor is the purpose of ascesis to measure our achievements. It is to render our soul pure and good, replenishing it with demonstrated love toward God and our neighbor by means of trust in divine providence and peace, faith and prayer—that is, through spiritual communion with God.

This communion with God is hindered by solipsism, a spirit of self-sufficiency, egocentrism, and arrogance as well as by the pharisaic mask of self-justification and self-satisfaction. By the same token, this communion with God is enhanced by opening our heart toward our neighbor—by love, charity, compassion, sympathy, humility—and, in general, through a sense that we need the presence of other persons in our life. This is why Orthodox Christian ascesis is based not on amassing achievements for the increase of human vainglory but on increasing love and humility. An Orthodox Christian practicing ascesis knows that nothing can be achieved without God's grace and consequently seeks only to reach a spiritual condition conducive to divine grace—to reach, that is, the state of selfless, peaceful, and humble love. An Orthodox Christian, aware that even this condition is a divine gift, will always remain humble and rejoice in God. Such a person knows well that, if one is filled with pride like the Pharisee, if there is no continual struggle for humility and self-knowledge, then the protection of divine grace will be lost and one will be reduced to a state of spiritual aridity and barrenness. Consequently, the more we receive grace, the more we perceive our own unworthiness for this divine gift and for its grandeur.

---

38. The opening hymn of the season of Great Lent.

Behold, then, the straight path indicated to us by the Church, a path traveled successfully by thousands of faithful before us and traveled today by thousands of our brothers and sisters. Let us enter on this path. Let us fight the good fight—of fasting and prayer, of selfless love and humility—that raises us high, in order that we may receive in purity the life-giving Resurrection of our Lord Jesus Christ.

Great Lent 2003

FORGIVENESS AND GRATITUDE

Tomorrow marks, once again, the beginning of the period of holy and Great Lent. It is well known that this is a season of spiritual exercise, a time when we are assisted by prayer and fasting. Our Church, however, places great importance on sincere repentance, as we learn, from the outset of the Triodion, with the parable of the sinful Publican, who repented and was saved, and with the example of the haughty and unrepentant Pharisee, who was condemned despite observing the commandments of the law.

Today, the sacred gospel stresses that our repentance is acceptable only if we forgive all those who wronged us. Indeed, in the Lord's Prayer, we daily ask of our heavenly Father to "forgive us our trespasses even as we forgive those who trespass against us." The question, however, arises whether, in repeating these words, we truly forgive those who wrong us. Or do we repeat the words of this prayer out of habit, without being fully conscious of their significance and consequence?

My beloved spiritual children in the Lord, there are two characteristics of the noble and sensitive Christian soul. The first is the disposition—after the example of our Lord, who forgave and prayed for those that crucified Him—to forgive those who harm us; and the second is the disposition to give thanks to our great benefactor, our Lord Jesus Christ, and to every fellow human being who supports us. Our entire Church is full of gratitude to God, and the sacrament of the Eucharist constitutes an expression of this gratitude. Its very name, Divine Eucharist, implies and enforces this; moreover, the constant repetition of "glory to the Father and the Son and the Holy Spirit, now and always and unto the ages of ages" is an overflow from our hearts, which are filled with thanksgiving.[39]

The heart that forgives and gives thanks is full of joy and happiness. On the contrary, the heart that is full of ingratitude and acrimony lives in the terrible antechamber of voluntary hell. The ungrateful person is never satisfied; the dissatisfied person is thoroughly miserable. At the same time, the resentful person, who constantly brings to mind the evil suffered at the hands of another, cannot find peace. For the very memory of that evil becomes a new appropriation of evil, a continuous resuscitation of evil, which is no longer the fault of the person who committed it once but of the person who suffered it and yet does not wish, or is unable, to forgive. Nevertheless, the presupposition of our forgiveness by God is that "we forgive those who trespass against us."

Great Lent will be of benefit to us only if we enter the spiritual battle with the powerful weapons of forgiveness for those who have harmed us and only if we express gratitude to those who are our benefactors—principally, of course, to our Lord Jesus Christ, who forgives our sins and prepares for us a place of peace and blessedness. No one whose heart is resentful or ungrateful is accepted into this place of peace and blessedness.

It is our wish to all of you, beloved children, that we shall journey through this period of the holy and Great Lent with spiritual and bodily health as well as with repentance, so that we may arrive at the end, purified from every stain of ingratitude and resentment and filled with a spirit of forgiveness and thanksgiving, having our own sins forgiven and our hearts fulfilled in peace and ineffable joy.

Great Lent 2004

THE WAY OF REPENTANCE

At the beginning of the Triodion, a heart-searching hymn is chanted: "Life-giver, open for me the doors of repentance."[40] It is immediately evident that our holy Orthodox Church has devoted a great deal of this

---

39. One of the shortest liturgical phrases and most popular prayers in the Orthodox Church.

40. From the Matins service of the first Sunday of the Triodion, which commemorates the Publican and the Pharisee.

season and of the entire year to repentance. Moreover, at every hour and every day, it reminds us of the need to repent. The Church is fully aware that repentance is the starting point of spiritual life and of salvation for every human being. The fact that both St. John the Forerunner and our Lord Jesus Christ Himself inaugurated their preaching with a call to repentance attests to this truth.

As revealed in the meaning of the Greek word itself, *metanoia*, repentance consists of a "changing of minds," a transformed spiritual attitude toward the world and God. It entails the renunciation of sin and the decision to live henceforth according to God's commandments. And so repentance is primarily the renewal and change of our way of thinking, of how we evaluate elements of the material and spiritual world. It is also a reordering of our hierarchy of values, the values by which we regulate our lives.

If we have given priority to the accumulation of wealth, we should now strive to use financial goods to enhance the public welfare. If we have primarily sought to satisfy our individual needs, we should now attend to the needs of others, starting with those close to us and advancing to the broader family of society and even the entire human race. If our concern has been to attain success, then we should extend this concern to make it one that we apply to the next life. If our studies and research have been limited, covering only areas of the human sciences and the arts, we should delve into the sacred science and the art of spiritual life. If we have been anxious to secure relationships with the powerful, we should make every effort to form friendly relationships with the spiritual, especially our Lord Jesus Christ, the Theotokos, and the saints. If we have believed that our judgment and understanding are superior, then we should learn the way of humility. In general, we will be able truly to repent if we reevaluate our beliefs and reassess our practices in order to align ourselves with the Church. These are fundamental principles of the sacred gospel and, ultimately, the saving teachings of our Lord.

Furthermore, repentance must be accompanied by confession of sins to a suitable confessor. This should be done in total honesty and utter humility. God has bestowed His authority on spiritual confessors to bind and to loose sins. Repentance without confession of sins is inconceivable and even impossible. In the sacrament of confession, through the grace of the Holy Spirit, the disciple of Christ is cleansed of all impurity. The wounds caused by passions are healed, and the Christian is spiritually renewed, receiving strength to continue the good fight. Continuous repentance is mandatory, as the Church Fathers teach, even for the pious and perfect, if there are any such, because spiritual perfection is infinite.

Beloved brothers and sisters in Christ, let us refrain from saying that we have no sins or that we need not repent, for we run the risk of assuming the blameworthy arrogance of the Pharisee. We all need to repent, since we all constantly need to learn God's will for us to love and forgive. We need to acquire greater passion for the spiritual life, despite any success we might have achieved in that regard.

May our loving God, through the intercession of the most holy Theotokos and of all His saints, bless us that we may traverse this holy period of Lent in health and repentance, so that, cleansed and restored, we may approach the holy Pascha and partake in the joy of the Resurrection.

Great Lent 2005

THE PERIOD OF FASTING

> The time has come for the beginning of spiritual toil, the victory against demons, the fully armored self-restraint, the grace of angels, our bold confession to God.
>
> Lenten Triodion

The period of holy and Great Lent interrupts the dullness of our routine; it is the ultimate time of spiritual struggle. One more arena of toil opens up before us, an arena where not only the body strains but also the spirit—a great arena, in which all of us can and must participate. This "arena of virtues" does not have stands; it has no room for spectators; it only provides a track for contenders; from heaven above are watching the judge and spectators—that is, the Lord, who establishes every good struggle of faith, and the saints, who have already participated and excelled in these struggles, having received their wreaths and trophies. They watch and encourage our efforts, admiring our accomplishments.

We entered this arena of spiritual struggle essentially from the moment we were baptized. It was then that we renounced Satan and his works, clothing ourselves with our Lord Jesus Christ, as with a robe whiter than snow, and promising to follow Him throughout our life. Selfishness and vainglory, in conjunction with the unceasing "war" waged against us by the devil, render us lethargic, and so we abandon our exercise in Christ, sinking into forgetfulness and indifference. Following that path, we stray from the source of life, from Christ, until we are completely separated from Him. For, even as Christ is life, estrangement from Him implies deprivation of life, of joy, and of light. And so the Church, in its care and wisdom, established this period of fasting and prayer so that we may all remember the duties ensuing from our holy baptism and understand that we are, by definition, athletes participating honorably in various sacred exercises, including charity, forgiveness of one another, patience in hardship, perseverance in pain, and the expression of love.

Fasting relieves the body from unnecessary weight; it empowers prayer, humbles the sense of one's worth, and "opens up the gate of repentance." Physical "repentance" strains and exercises the body, but it also constitutes a clear demonstration of our self-knowledge that we are all sinful and fallen people and that, in repentance, we humbly ask God to bring us back to life. It is a spiritual confession and prayer that the body partakes of as well. Charity sanctifies such fasting and makes our prayer more agreeable to our merciful God. Our patience in illness, pain, and sorrow follows the footprints of the martyrs and secures for us tremendous reward. Forgiving those who harm us and loving our neighbor—these seal our authenticity as Christians and render us imitators of Christ. Moreover, the frequent study of sacred Scripture, the Church Fathers, and the saints' lives gives our spirit the nourishment required to fight well and to fight to the end.

The appropriate hymn of piety that we repeat with prostrations during Great Lent is the prayer of St. Ephraim the Syrian: "Lord and Master of my life, do not give me a spirit of idleness, curiosity, lust for power, and preoccupation with trivialities. Rather, give me, your servant, a spirit of prudence, humility, patience, and love. Yes, Lord, make me able to see my own faults and not judge my brother, for you are blessed unto the ages of ages."[41] In this prayer, we invoke the Lord and Master of Life, asking to be delivered from the four main evil spirits, the four most hideous passions. We also ask to be endowed with the four principal good

---

41. An Assyrian deacon, St. Ephraim (306–73) is a beloved poet and hymnographer of the Orthodox Church.

spirits, the four most beautiful virtues. At the same time, we ask that we be given the virtue of self-knowledge, so that we may be concerned with our own sin and not with that of others. This prayer may very well be the most wholesome and remarkable prayer of repentance!

So let us enter the holy arena. Let us begin the good struggle of repentance and purification through fasting, self-restraint, forgiveness of one another, patience, acts of charity, prayer, and love. Let us struggle with grace and honor, like all the saints—with yearning for Christ and with spiritual nobility, with humility but also with fervor. The Mother Church, from the See of the humble but perpetually bright Phanar, which has known a multitude of martyrs, conveys its blessings on all and lovingly urges that no one remain inactive or indifferent to the trumpet calling us to spiritual exercise. "The time has come," beloved brothers and sisters in the Lord. The word "time" here does not imply merely earthly time; it also, and most especially, signifies the "opportunity" to be seized.

Blessed be God, who presents us with yet another Lenten period, yet another opportunity to struggle spiritually and to triumph over the devil, sin, and death—with yet another season for repentance and salvation. To Him, our Savior God, belong the glory and power unto the ages.

Great Lent 2006

THE RETURN OF THE PRODIGAL

> Let us listen to the Scriptures on the Prodigal Son who regained wisdom, and let us follow the good example of his repentance.
>
> Sunday of the Prodigal Son, from the *Oikos*

By the grace of God, once more we are entering the period of the Triodion, during which the holy Orthodox Church invites everyone to repentance. Although, according to the Church Fathers, authentic repentance is necessary even for those who are faultless in faith and virtue, many Christians do not understand that they are in need of repentance at all. Other Christians refuse to repent, convinced that they have not done anything to trouble their conscience or require repentance.

However, repentance is a process much deeper than mere acknowledgment of our sins or recognition of our errors. Sincere repentance should primarily address the thoughts and reflections, the beliefs and motivations, from which our deeds arise. Our Lord Jesus Christ taught us that evil thoughts pollute us in the same way as evil deeds—that, in the eyes of God, harboring evil thoughts is tantamount to committing evil. Remaining indifferent toward our fellow human beings, being shut up in our selves and our desires, feeling bitterness toward others, lacking love and feeling hatred, harboring feelings of superiority, self-affectation, ambition, sensuousness, or avarice—all of these make for a person remote from the ideal of the healthy human being. The ideal, healthy human being is characterized by love, humility, meekness, peace, and forgiveness. Therefore, we all need repentance; we all need to change our mentality and perceptions with respect to good and evil, for we are all of us very far from being ideal.

We all observe the actions of others. Indeed, we often criticize others for cruelty, ignorance, and self-assurance in their stubbornness. We criticize other people for insisting that, despite their inadequacies, their deeds, thoughts, and judgments are beyond criticism. However, we need to reflect on whether other people see us in the same light. We need to consider which of our notions require change, which feelings need improvement, what information requires discernment. In examining ourselves in this manner, we will realize that we too lack much; we may realize our own shortcomings. The Church Fathers consider the vices of ignorance, negligence, carelessness, and indolence as sinful—conditions that most of us hardly consider abnormal but that nonetheless require radical repentance.

Besides these sins, there is the inadequacy of our love for our fellow human beings and for God. There is always room for much improvement. We need repentance for our deficiency of love; we need to demonstrate greater love for others; we need to remove from our hearts any condemnation of others; we need to dispel feelings of arrogance, bitterness, and resentment toward others; for negative feelings, we need to substitute forgiveness and prayer; we should be benevolent to all our fellow human beings—even, and perhaps especially, to those who hate, persecute, and harm us.

Christ is ready to accept such repentance. All of heaven rejoices when sinners truly repent; indeed, great joy as well as a sense of freedom and relief also overwhelm every Christian who offers genuine repentance. A person who clings to feelings of hatred ultimately inflicts more pain on himself than on others, for the people he traumatizes and hurts may take comfort and transform their pain into prayer and peace. By contrast, the person who envies and hates lives an endless internal suffering.

Therefore, the repentance of every person is inevitable. The time will surely come for each of us when we shall find ourselves face-to-face before the truth; then we will realize how far from true love we were during our life. Blessed is the one who repents like the Prodigal Son; such a person is welcomed by our heavenly Father. Miserable will be the one who refuses to change or repent; for such a person is left without hope. Let us, therefore, listen carefully to the story of the Prodigal Son, beloved children, and let us repent a good repentance.

Great Lent 2007

STRIVING FOR THE GIVER, NOT THE GIFTS

The time has come; this is the beginning of spiritual struggles.

From the *Ainoi* hymns, for Cheese Fare Sunday,
or Forgiveness Sunday, the eve of Great Lent

With these words, the sacred hymnist reminds us of our obligation to intensify our spiritual struggles for the benefit of our spiritual training and progress during this period of holy and Great Lent. Humanity long ago realized that good things can be acquired only through hard work. The Church Fathers realized that, in order for us to savor divine love— "the contempt of repose is necessary," according to a characteristic saying of Abba Isaac the Syrian.[42] Material goods are what we pursue and acquire; but we understand that we must be prepared to forgo these for the sake of God and others. By contrast, spiritual goods are offered to us by God; they are granted on the condition that we love the giver and not the gifts—a much harder truth to grasp. The Lord Himself made it clear to us when He exhorted us to "seek first the kingdom of God and its righteousness," adding that "all these things shall be added to you" (Matt.

---

42. Also known as St. Isaac of Nineveh (d. 700), Abba Isaac is among the most popular and influential mystics of the Orthodox Church.

6.33). Moreover, the Lord assured us that whoever surrenders his or her life for the love of God will be the one who ultimately saves it.

Beloved children in the Lord, when we return to Him, our Father who is in heaven, who loves us and desires only our blessedness—the giver and source of everything good—will give us everything we need, just as the father gave to the prodigal son on his return. The best robe, the fattened calf, the ring on our finger, the festive gathering, and, most important, His paternal embrace—these He will surely give us. In order for us to return to this paternal embrace, however, we must turn away from sin and selfishness, which are represented by the carobs eaten by the pigs; we must prove, through voluntary spiritual struggle, our honest desire for and dependence on God's love. The true nature of this spiritual struggle consists in aiming for God's love as the object of our quest and in abandoning inferior desires, such as for food and material goods. Therefore fasting, one of the most important ascetic practices of Great Lent, is not a rejection of food itself but rather a voluntary deprivation of self-sufficiency that food enables our body to maintain. The goal is twofold—for the soul to disengage from exclusive interest in the ego and for the body to become obedient and well-trained in order to serve but not rule the human person.

Furthermore, the goal of spiritual struggle is not the acquisition of virtues or of any such extraordinary abilities. On the contrary, it is the expression of passionate desire to encounter our Lord Jesus Christ, in whom everything is recapitulated and from whom everything derives. The divine Word clearly proclaims that, without Him, we can do nothing; and the sacred Psalmist reminds us that, unless the house of the soul is built by the Lord, we struggle in vain. Therefore, we Christians devote ourselves to the love of Christ, voluntarily surrendering all other less important forms of love and devotion so that we may become worthy of welcoming His presence in the house of our souls. When we have achieved this, through the grace and blessing of God, then peace, joy, and perfect love will be established permanently in our existence.

This is why the spiritual struggle of Great Lent is practiced neither with depression nor with ostentation but with as much joy and secrecy as possible. If there is any desire to show off, then the goal of divine love is replaced by self-satisfaction; if there is depression and sorrow, joy and the voluntary nature of the effort depart, while the person fasting experiences a state of oppression and constraint, which is not pleasing in God's eyes. The spiritual struggle should be practiced with joy; its main goal should be to introduce our heart to the love of God, though which every sorrow and vindictiveness, as well as all complaints and grievances against our neighbor, are thoroughly expelled. Then the unshakable and incomparable peace of God will radiate within us and around us.

May we all journey through the arena of Great Lent with spiritual discipline so that we may enjoy, in all its fullness, the joy of the Resurrection of our Lord Jesus Christ, whose grace and rich mercy be with all of you.

Great Lent 2008

CHANGING OUR WAY AND OUR WORLDVIEW

During this period of holy and Great Lent, the Church calls us to repentance. Doubtless, as contemporary people hearing this ancient invitation to repentance, we feel uncomfortable because we are accustomed to a certain way of life and do not wish to question it. That leads to a feeling of insecurity, because then the ideological structure within which we take refuge is clearly at risk. However, deeper examination compels us to accept that such fears do not conform to reality. Rather, they lead us to justify ourselves and excuse our sinfulness (Psalm 140.4). When a person justifies his or her actions and self-vindicates on the basis of erroneous values, significant harm occurs; inevitably, the moment will come when the truth emerges and we find ourselves without excuse. Then, however, it may be too late to adjust our convictions—that is, to repent of our errors and sinful behavior, which we formerly justified.

Now, as Christians, we may be used to hearing about and practicing repentance, and we do not feel disagree with our Church's call to it. However, there is a need for us to make a deliberate and conscious effort to recognize that authentic repentance has two objectives. The first objective is threefold: renouncing sin, refraining from sinful acts, and making amends for the consequences of our sins. For example, the publican Zaccheus, who sincerely repented during his encounter with Christ, demonstrated his repentance in a practical way by repaying fourfold the very people from whom he had unjustly seized wealth.

The second objective of repentance is that we change our mentality. We should replace our usual frame of mind with a loftier one; or, in the words of the Psalmist, we must ascend in our hearts (See Psalm 83.6). This objective must be pursued especially by those who are unconvinced by their consciousness of specific sins. For example, in practice, our love surely falls short of what we understand perfect love to be; likewise our understanding of humility. For when we compare our own spiritual state to the perfection of God, which we are called to imitate, surely we shall see our shortcomings and realize the endless road we must traverse in order to find ourselves in the path of those who are like God.

As we examine the quality of our inner peace, we will ascertain that we fall short of the peace of Christ, which surpasses all understanding. (Phil. 4.7). Pondering the degree to which we entrust our lives to God's providence, we sadly realize that we are often seized by anxiety and uncertainty about the future, as if we were of little faith or even entirely deprived of it. In general, on examination of the purity of our conscience, we will realize that we fall short of understanding correctly the many feelings we harbor within ourselves, feelings that are detrimental to our purity, feelings we often mistake as being natural and healthy. And so we need a new, more complete enlightenment of our conscience, so that we may be in a better position to think critically about our shortcomings. No one can claim to judge oneself perfectly. By the same token no one can claim to have no need of a renewed mind, an enlightened mind, a transformed mind—ultimately, a mind of repentance.

The call of our Church to repentance is not merely a call to self-reproach. The latter can be useful, like deep contrition and tears of repentance; but of themselves these qualities are all insufficient. We need to experience the joy emanating from forgiveness granted by God. We need to experience both a sense of deliverance from the burden and bondage of sin as well as a sense of God's love for us. Repentance means cleansing and enlightenment of mind, greater love for Christ and His creation, and the freedom and joy that come from the newness of life into which we continually grow and mature.

Therefore, beloved children in the Lord, let us accept the invitation of our Church to repentance. Let us who have fallen short through sin cleanse ourselves through confession. Let us constantly examine our own presuppositions so that our judgments and thoughts may be godly, pure, and true. Finally, we paternally pray that all of you may enjoy every assistance and grace of the Lord on the road to repentance and throughout your renewed life in Christ.

Great Lent 2009

THE CHURCH AS OUR HOME

> Come, all peoples, let us today welcome the gift of fasting, the period of repentance granted to us by God.
>
> Monday, First Week of Great Lent

The fast recommended by our holy Church is not about deprivation but about charisma. And the repentance to which it calls us is not about punishment but about blessing. When the Church urges us, through the words of Scripture, not to store up for ourselves treasures on earth, "where moth and rust consume" (Matt. 6.19), but instead to store up treasures in heaven, "where there is no corruption" (Matt. 6.20), it is telling us the truth. For the Church is not of this world, even though it lives in and understands this world. It understands humanity and its needs. It understands our age and our fears. This is why, with calmness and steadfastness, the Church invites all to repentance. This is why it discourages its children from taking the wrong path, from treasuring their own labors and basing their hopes on unstable foundations. Instead, it encourages them to store up treasure in heaven; for where our treasure lies, there also is our heart.

The treasure that cannot be corrupted and the hope that does not shame is precisely God's love, the divine force that binds all things; it is the incarnate Word of God, who stays with us forever. He is the sanctification of our souls and bodies—for He did not come to judge but to save all people. He did not come to criticize but to heal the world. "He wounds with compassion and demonstrates compassion with fervor." He abolished the one who held the power of death—namely, the devil. He annihilated the sorrow of death—namely, the joyless form and dark presence of death, which darkens and defiles all of our life and joy. This is why, when our heart is directed toward the divine-human Lord, who has authority over the living and the dead, everything is illumined and transformed.

Indeed, when the Apostle exhorts us "not to set our hopes on the uncertainty of riches, but rather on God who richly provides us with everything for our enjoyment" (1 Tim. 6.17), he is assuring us that the true enjoyment of life is exactly what God offers us, while we are simply to receive it with gratitude and thanksgiving. Then the little becomes abundant, because it is blessed; and the fleeting and momentary shine with the light of eternity. Then not only do the joys of life contain something eternal, but the trials and tribulations of life become occasions of divine comfort. The divine economy of salvation is assured, for God is "the one who provides everything with depth of wisdom and loving-kindness." And the deposit of our labors is secured, for "we surrender all of our life and hope" to the incarnate Word. So when the gospel tells us to aspire to heaven, it is speaking literally, for it brings us down to the reality of earth, which has become heaven.

This is the certainty experienced and professed by the Church: "Through your Cross, O Christ, there is one flock and one church of angels and human beings. Heaven and earth rejoice together. Lord, glory to you." The Church grants us the opportunity to experience this miracle of earth-become-heaven. Our roots lie in heaven. Without the Church, we are uprooted and homeless. For the Church is our home. When we return to the Church, we return home; we come to ourselves, like the Prodigal Son. When we are estranged from the Church, we are lost and meaningless. When we approach the Church, we perceive the authenticity of what is true. We behold the heavenly Father awaiting and welcoming us outside our home. We are convinced by the sense of goodness and beauty; we sense the presence of God's powerful love, which overcomes death; and we no longer sense corruption or the doubt that mocks. Therefore, beloved, let us heed the divine invitation to enter the ocean of fasting in order to reach the harbor of light and enjoy resurrection with all the saints.

Great Lent 2010

THE CIRCLE OF FORGIVENESS AND JOY

Tomorrow, we enter the period of holy and Great Lent. In the Lenten Vespers of Forgiveness chanted this evening,[43] we will hear the sacred

---

43. On the eve of and in preparation for Great Lent, the Orthodox Church celebrates the solemn Vespers of Forgiveness. At the conclusion of the service, the congregation practices the ancient rite of forgiveness by forming a circle around the interior of the

hymnist urging us to "begin the time of fasting with joy, submitting ourselves to spiritual struggle," as we prepare to welcome the great Passion and joyful Resurrection of our divine-human Lord.

Therefore, what is demanded is a joyful disposition, in order that, in purification and prayerfulness, we might fervently embrace the spiritual struggle of this period of contrition. Fasting, abstinence, frugality, controlled personal desires, intense prayer, confession, and other similar ascetic practices are essential to the period of Great Lent and should not be considered burdensome obligations or unbearable duties that lead to despondency or dejection. When doctors recommend diet or exercise as necessary prerequisites for health and vigor of body and mind, the first advice they offer is to maintain a pleasant mental disposition, which includes smiling and positive thinking. The same applies to the spiritual period of fasting that lies before us. Great Lent should be regarded as an invaluable divine gift. It is a sacred time of divine grace, which seeks to detach us from things material, lowly, and corrupt in order to attract us to things superior, wholesome, and spiritual. It is a unique opportunity to remove from the soul every passion, to rid the body of everything superfluous, harmful, and mortal. And so it is a time of immense rejoicing and gladness. A genuine feast and exhilaration!

Nevertheless, beloved children, the fasting expected of us by the Church, as well as the abstinence, frugality, restriction of personal desires and unnecessary pleasures or expenses—all of these constitute literally a prescription for salvation. It is especially true this year, when our world has experienced a global economic crisis, marked by imminent danger of bankruptcy not only for individuals and companies but also for entire nations. The threat looms of destructive consequences in the form of skyrocketing unemployment, resulting in widespread poverty, rampant depression, social turmoil, increased crime, and other such calamities. Great Lent instructs us to journey daily with a little less, without the arrogance of extravagance, waste, or display. It encourages us to surrender all forms of greed and ignore the challenges of commercial advertising, which constantly promotes new and false needs. It encourages us to limit ourselves, in an attitude of dignified, deliberate simplicity, to what is absolutely essential and necessary. We are not to be reduced to a consuming

church, with each person asking, receiving, and giving forgiveness to every other person in attendance.

or compulsive herd of mindless and heartless individuals but rather to become a society of sensitive and caring persons, sharing with and supporting our neighbor who is in poverty or suffers the effects of economic recession.

Finally, Great Lent informs and instructs us about patience and tolerance in moments of smaller or larger deprivation, while simultaneously emphasizing the need to seek God's assistance and mercy, to place our complete trust in His affectionate providence. That is how Christ envisions Great Lent. That is how the saints lived Great Lent. That is how the Church Fathers undertook the struggle of Great Lent. That is how our faith has traditionally perceived Great Lent. That is how the Church of Constantinople, in its spiritual ministry and unceasing vigilance, has always projected Great Lent and how it continues to proclaim Great Lent, particularly in the current global circumstances. In sharing these pastoral thoughts and words from the historical and holy Phanar, we extend to all of you our paternal prayer and spiritual blessing for a fruitful journey through the period of Great Lent.

2

Patriarchal Exhortations

Addresses to Orthodox Hierarchs and Faithful, Clergy and Laity

KEYNOTE ADDRESSES AND INTRODUCTORY
EXHORTATIONS AT THE MEETINGS
OF ORTHODOX PRIMATES

*First Synaxis of the Heads of Orthodox Churches,
Ecumenical Patriarchate, March 13, 1992*

SOMETHING IS STIRRING IN OUR CHURCH

With gratitude we offer glory above all to the holy God of our Fathers for having deemed us worthy of manifesting, through this fraternal synaxis,[1] "the unity of the Spirit in the bond of peace" (Eph. 4.3) and of witnessing to our world the unity, peace, and love by which we are bonded to each other in Christ. We express our sincere thanks to each one of you, beloved brothers, for the effort you have made to come to this city, rich in history and significance, so that the Primates of the local holy Orthodox autocephalous and autonomous churches may be gathered together.[2] Many of you have in the past suggested and proposed such a

---

1. Greek for "gathering" or "assembly."

2. These Churches include the four ancient Patriarchates: the Ecumenical Patriarchate (Church of Constantinople), the patriarchate of Alexandria, the patriarchate of Antioch, and the patriarchate of Jerusalem. They also include modern churches and patriarchates, including the patriarchate of Moscow, the patriarchate of Serbia, the patriarchate of Romania, the patriarchate of Bulgaria, the patriarchate of Georgia, the Church of Cyprus,

synaxis both to my predecessor, the late Ecumenical Patriarch Dimitrios, and recently to our Modesty.[3]

These suggestions, together with the invitation on our part, as well as the response by all the brethren who were able to accept it, are manifestations of our conviction that something extraordinary is happening today in the world and in our Church, which lives and moves in the world without belonging to this world (John 17.16). All of this increases our responsibility as shepherds of the people of God and as, by God's grace, Primates of our local churches.[4] It imposes the need for even greater vigilance, action, and coordination of our resources, requiring a manifestation, at all costs, of unity, concord, and unanimity to the outside world during this critical and historic moment, despite any internal differences of opinion, which are so typical of any family.

THE POWER OF TRADITION

At this moment, the world expects the salvific word of Orthodoxy. The hour of Orthodoxy, out of a sense of duty and as a result of its capabilities, has arrived in the contemporary world and age. Guided by the holy Scriptures and by sacred tradition, we are blessed in the Orthodox Church to treasure the authentic teaching, not only about the Triune God but also about humanity created in the image of God and about all of creation, even those parts not endowed with reason.

Together with the Apostles, the martyrs, the Fathers, and the saints from every region and from each era, we confess the apostolic faith, which we celebrate in a special way when we stand around the holy altar, offering the divine Eucharist, as we shall do together, with God's help, during the forthcoming great feast of the Sunday of Orthodoxy. All of us together, as a single body nourished by the Holy Spirit, glorify God, the Father of

---

the Church of Greece, the Church of Poland, the Church of Albania, and the Church of the Czech Lands and Slovakia. This meeting included the primate of the Autonomous Church of Finland. As of 1999, the other autonomous church is the Church of Estonia.

3. Ecumenical Patriarch Bartholomew was the first to convoke such assemblies of heads of autocephalous churches: in Istanbul (1992, very soon after his enthronement), on the island of Patmos (1995), in Jerusalem/Bethlehem and Istanbul on the occasion of the new millennium (2000), and more recently in Istanbul (2008).

4. For a list of participating hierarchs, see Chapter 5, "Messages and Declarations,"

our Lord Jesus Christ, in various tongues and in different places "from the rising to the setting of the sun" (Ps. 113.3).

We honor our brothers in the faith who remained loyal to our Lord and Savior during periods of difficulty or even persecution, particularly in recent times. We have been encouraged by their witness. We have been strengthened by their prayers. In troublesome times, God "has not been left without a witness" (Acts 14.17). May their memory be eternal! Now, when the clouds and storms have passed, we are called as Primates and as Orthodox churches to offer our irenic witness to those near and far. Again, our witness will not be easy. Many forces are today working against us to reject the reality of God and diminish the dignity of the human person. But we place our complete trust in the Lord God. We know that His yoke is easy and His burden is light (Matt. 11.30).

Beloved brothers, this present holy synaxis of ours invites us, at the commencement of Holy and Great Lent, with fear of God, to recall our responsibilities as shepherds of Orthodoxy before peoples and nations for which Orthodoxy constitutes the only hope. Once again, we commend ourselves and each other, our whole life and ministry, and our fellow Christians and churches, to Christ our God. He calls each of us to be the "light of the world" (Matt. 5.14) and the "salt of the earth" (Matt. 5.13). And He exhorts us: "Let your light shine before others, that they may see your good works and give glory to your Father in heaven" (Matt. 5.16).

A CRITICAL PRESENCE

If this is true in heaven, and if it is true from the time that the Church began, it is more valid today, as the Lord gave many of us new opportunities to fulfill His commandment to preach the gospel to all of creation. In many parts of the world, at this very moment, great social and political changes are taking place. And we recognize the deep yearning in the hearts of many people for Christ and His Church. In these times, we believe that the Lord is calling us not only to be vigilant, so as to maintain our faith, but also to have the courage to declare this faith everywhere, that the world may in the end believe (John 17.21) and be saved. Our times demand prophecy.

Holy brothers in Christ, our deliberations here have been carefully and meticulously prepared by our plenipotentiary representatives who gathered at our Patriarchal Metochion[5] in Ormylia, Chalkidiki.[6] To them, therefore, we express our thanks. One of the topics we will discuss here is that of our relations with Christians outside of Orthodoxy. This discussion occurs against the background of events in countries of the former "iron curtain." There also appears to be great interest in this topic among the non-Orthodox. Certainly, our communication and our dialogue with brothers and sisters outside the Orthodox Church imply neither the acceptance of their doctrinal positions nor the depreciation of the historical teachings of our Orthodox faith. We humbly consider that these dialogues are beneficial in our search for ways to overcome differences and in our effort to enlighten others of our positions, albeit without sacrificing anything essential to our faith. Our Orthodox Church, containing the fullness of truth, also has a corresponding responsibility to contribute to the healing of divisions among Christians.

Of course, we recognize the responsibility of our Church, which, according to the Apostle, "has no spot or wrinkle, or any such thing" through deviation from the ancient forms, never having accepted or added or subtracted any kind of doctrinal innovation. Still, influenced by assaults against the Church, we sometimes falter in our responsibility to offer unceasing witness to our faith.

ARTICULATING THE FAITH

What can we say about environmental issues, missionary activity, schisms in the body of the Church, the position of Orthodoxy within a united Europe, or the other topics that have been included in the various memoranda that you, brother Primates, have coauthored and signed? All these are such current and timely, burning issues, which rightly attract our attention and assume priority, precluding, for the moment, the inclusion of other important issues on the agenda of our sessions here.

---

5. Greek for "dependency," referring to a monastery, parish, or property that receives clergy from another community.

6. A peninsula in northern Greece.

On those subjects that have been selected, a lengthy and comprehensive discussion took place in the Inter-Orthodox Preparatory Committee of our synaxis, which has also prepared, on behalf of all of us, the text before us. We believe that this text adequately expresses our common positions on the topics to which we have referred, so it may become the basis for a text of our message[7] to our faithful and to the world, which will be proclaimed in the context of our fraternal liturgical concelebration.[8] Therefore, let us love one another, so that with one mind we may confess the faith of the Apostles, the faith of the Fathers, the faith of the Orthodox, the faith that sustained the universe.

Fifth Synaxis of the Heads of Orthodox Churches,
Ecumenical Patriarchate, October 10, 2008

A SACRED OBLIGATION AND CONVOCATION

1. To the Trinitarian God, we offer praise and glory that we have been counted worthy once again to gather in the same place, here at this sacred center, as persons entrusted by His mercy with the ministry of leadership in the local most holy autocephalous and autonomous Orthodox churches, in order to affirm our sacrosanct unity in Christ and deliberate on matters that concern the Church in the fulfillment of its mission in the contemporary world.

It is with much gladness and ineffable joy that our most holy Church of Constantinople and we personally welcome you all, the most venerable and reverend heads of the local most holy Orthodox churches, as well as the representatives of those unable to attend in person, together with your honorable entourages.[9] We greet each one of you warmly with a sacred embrace, exclaiming with the Psalmist, "How wonderful and sweet it is for brethren to dwell in the same place." We express our gratitude to all of you for responding with eagerness and fraternal love to the invitation of our Modesty that we assemble here; for you have undergone much

---

7. See Chapter 5, "Messages and Declarations," 382

8. The concelebration of the Divine Liturgy at such gatherings is always the supreme expression of unity among Orthodox churches in full doctrinal and liturgical communion with one another.

9. For a list of participating hierarchs, see Chapter 5, "Messages and Declarations," 411.

sacrifice and toil in order to travel to our city. Therefore, we deeply appreciate this response on your part as evidence of brotherly love but also of your concern for the support and reaffirmation of unity within the most holy Orthodox Church, of whose unity we have been assigned guardians, keepers, and guarantors by divine grace.

2. From the moment that, by God's mercy, we assumed the reins of this First Throne among Churches, we have regarded it as our sacred obligation and duty to strengthen the bonds of love and unity of all those entrusted with the leadership of the local Orthodox churches. And so, in response also to the desire of other brothers serving as heads, we assumed the initiative of convoking several occasions for synaxis: first, in this city on the Sunday of Orthodoxy in 1992; then, on the sacred island of Patmos in 1995; and thereafter, we had the blessing of experiencing similar encounters and concelebrations in Jerusalem/Bethlehem and the Phanar on the occasion of the beginning and end of the year 2000 as we entered this third millennium of the Lord's era.[10]

Of course, these occasions for synaxis do not constitute an "institution" by canonical standards. As is well known, the sacred canons of our Church assign the supreme responsibility and authority for decisions on ecclesiastical matters to the synodal system, wherein all hierarchs in active ministry participate either in rotation or in plenary. This canonical establishment is by no means superseded by this synaxis of the heads of churches. Nevertheless, from time to time such a synaxis is deemed necessary and beneficial, especially in times like ours, when personal encounter and conversation among responsible leaders in all public domains of human life is not only increasingly possible but also increasingly essential. Therefore, the benefit gained from a personal encounter of the Heads of the Orthodox churches can, with God's grace, only prove immense.

THE YEAR OF ST. PAUL

3. This synaxis, beloved brothers in the Lord, occurs within the context of a great anniversary for the Orthodox Church and, indeed, for the entire Christian world. For while the precise date of the birth of St. Paul,

---

10. For the official statements issued at these meetings, see Chapter 5, "Messages and Declarations," 411

the Apostle to the Gentiles, is not known, it is conventionally estimated around the year A.D. 8, or two thousand years ago. This has led other Christian churches, such as the Roman Catholic Church, to dedicate the present calendar year as the "Year of St. Paul"; it was clear that the Orthodox Church, which owes so much to this supreme Apostle, could not do otherwise.[11]

The first and greatest obligation to St. Paul is the preaching and entire Apostolic ministry of this "chosen vessel of Christ" in founding the churches that today lie within the jurisdiction of the Orthodox patriarchates and autocephalous churches—for example in Asia Minor, Antioch, Cyprus, and Greece. Bearing this obligation in mind, the Ecumenical Patriarchate decided to organize a journey of pilgrimage in certain regions within its canonical confines where St. Paul preached,[12] and fraternally to invite thereto the other heads of the most holy Orthodox churches, that together we might honor this great Apostle as well as all that was endured and realized by him "with far greater labors, far more imprisonments, with countless floggings, and often near death . . . on frequent journeys, in danger from rivers, danger from bandits, danger from [his] own people, danger from Gentiles, danger in the city, danger in the wilderness, danger at sea, danger from false brothers; in toil and hardship, through many sleepless nights, hungry and thirsty, often without food, cold and naked" (2 Cor. 11.23–27). And all this in order to found and establish the churches, whose pastoral care and direction the Lord's mercy has also assigned to us.

Another obligation entailed by St. Paul's "labor of love" relates to his teaching, articulated in his epistles and the Acts of the Apostles, written by St. Luke the Evangelist, his coworker in the gospel. This teaching

---

11. The Ecumenical Patriarch had announced the dedication of 2008 as the Year of St. Paul during his Christmas encyclical in December 2007. See Chapter 1, "Patriarchal Proclamations," 80

12. This event was held immediately following the synaxis (October 10–12, 2008), from November 12–16, 2008. Specifically organized within the context of the Year of St. Paul and within the ecclesiastical framework of, and as a scholarly offering to, the synaxis, the symposium drew recognized scholars from diverse Christian communions and numerous countries for a symposium, officially opening in Istanbul and proceeding through the cities of Smyrna, Ephesus, Perge and Antalya (in Asia Minor) as well as through Lindos (Rhodes) and Kaloi Limenes (Crete), where it officially concluded.

expresses "the exceptional character of the revelations" (2 Cor. 12.7) of which St. Paul was counted worthy by the grace of the Lord, and throughout the centuries it has remained a guide and compass for the Church of Christ, the foundation of the doctrines of our faith, and an inviolable rule of faith and life for all us Orthodox Christians. The theology of the Church has always drawn and will continue to draw from the depth and breadth of concepts in St. Paul's teaching.

4. This is why we deemed it appropriate, in the context of these Pauline celebrations, to organize an international and inter-Christian scholarly symposium,[13] where select participants from the Orthodox Church as well as from other Christian churches and confessions may address and analyze topics related to various dimensions of St. Paul's life and teaching as we journey in pilgrimage and visit the sacred places where the Apostle to the Gentiles preached and ministered.[14] The texts of their presentations will be published in a special volume, which, as we hope, will contribute to Pauline studies.[15]

As will undoubtedly become clear from the proceedings of this symposium, the teaching of St. Paul does not simply concern the past; it has, today as ever, immediate relevance in our time. For our own synaxis in particular, this teaching is extremely significant, chiefly with respect to one of its fundamental aspects—namely, its emphasis on the crucial and always topical subject of the unity of the Church, which, as we mentioned

---

13. For the addresses by Ecumenical Patriarch Bartholomew at the opening and closing sessions of this event, see Chapter 4, "Academic Addresses," 371

14. His Eminence Archbishop Demetrios of America was chairman of the academic committee and presided over the sessions (with Rev. Dr. John Chryssavgis serving as secretary), while His Eminence Metropolitan Gennadios of Sassima chaired the organizing committee. The Ecumenical Patriarch led the symposium, accompanied by the patriarch of Alexandria, the archbishop of Cyprus, the archbishop of Athens, the archbishop of Albania, and the archbishop of Prague as well as by representatives from every autocephalous and autonomous church, including the patriarchates of Antioch, Jerusalem, Moscow, Serbia, Romania, Bulgaria, and Georgia as well as the churches of Poland, Finland, and Estonia. The Roman Catholic Church was represented by personal delegates of Pope Benedict XVI. Speakers included His Eminence Archbishop Demetrios, Bishop Tom (N.T.) Wright of Durham, Prof. Helmut Koester, Prof. Karl Donfried, Prof. Brian Daley, Prof. Ioannis Karavidopoulos, and Prof. Turid Karlsen Seim.

15. See Demetrios Trakatellis and John Chryssavgis (eds), *In the Footsteps of St. Paul: An Academic Symposium* (Brookline, Mass.: Holy Cross Seminary Press, 2010).

earlier, constitutes a great responsibility and concern for all bishops in the Church and especially for the heads of churches.

LEARNING FROM ST. PAUL AS THEOLOGIAN OF UNITY

5. St. Paul is perhaps the first theologian of church unity. Since its foundation, the Church has experienced unity as a fundamental feature of its life. After all, this was an explicit desire of the Church's founder, expressed with particular emphasis in the prayer to His Father just prior to His passion: "I ask not only on behalf of these, but also on behalf of those who will believe in me through their word, that they may all be one. As you, Father, are in me and I am in you, may they also be one in us, so that the world may believe that you have sent me. The glory that you have given me I have given them, so that they may be one, as we are one: I in them and you in me, that they may become completely one" (John 17.20–23). However, St. Paul is the first to develop and explore this unity in detail; and he toiled for this unity like no other among the Apostles.

Indeed, just as St. Paul preached the gospel enthusiastically, so also did he labor for church unity passionately. His "anxiety for all the churches" (2 Cor. 11.28) and their unity in Christ consumed his entire existence. As St. John Chrysostom observes: "He bore responsibility not only for a home but for cities, provinces, nations and the whole oikoumene; indeed, he was anxious about so many and so diverse important matters, for which he suffered alone and cared even more than a father for his children."[16]

Nothing else brought such sorrow to the Apostle's heart than the lack of unity and love among members of the Church: "If you bite and devour one another, take care that you are not consumed by one another," he writes with great pain to the Galatians (Gal. 5.15). Moreover, in addressing the Corinthians, he appeals to them "by the name of our Lord Jesus Christ, that all of you be in agreement and that there be no division among you, but that you be united in the same mind and the same purpose" (1 Cor. 1.10). When he ascertains that the faithful in Corinth are divided into parties, he cries out in sadness: "Has Christ been divided?" (1 Cor. 1.13).

---

16. PG 61.571B.

Truly, then, for St. Paul, schism in the Church is as frightening and horrible as the division of Christ Himself. For, according to the great Apostle, the Church is "the body of Christ," constituting Christ Himself. "Now you are the body of Christ and individually members of it," he writes to the Corinthians (1 Cor. 12.27). We all know how St. Paul insists on characterizing the Church as "the body of Christ," an image he articulates extensively in the twelfth chapter of the First Letter to the Corinthians. This concept is not metaphorical but ontological. Division in the Church renders the very body of Christ divided. In fact, division is so repulsive and horrible for St. John Chrysostom, according to his interpretation of St. Paul's letters, that he claims that not even martyrdom can erase the sin of someone who causes division.

Consequently, we could ask what St. Paul might say today if he were to encounter the indifference of so many of our contemporaries for the restoration of unity in the Church. Surely he would rebuke them harshly, as perhaps he might do with each of us in our tolerance or neglect before the numerous schisms and divisions invoking the name of Christ or even the name of Orthodoxy. One cannot properly honor St. Paul if one does not simultaneously labor for the unity of the Church.

6. It is this kind of struggle for the unity of the Church that St. Paul undertook with a view to bridging the gap between Gentile Christians and Jewish Christians who tended toward judaizing. It is well known that, in the churches St. Paul founded among the Gentiles as well as in the church of Jerusalem, there existed differences seriously threatening the fabric of the early Church. These differences had to do with whether or not one should keep the precepts of the Mosaic Law and were particularly pronounced when they touched on the question of whether Gentile Christians should practice circumcision. Paul's attitude on this matter was particularly instructive. There we may discern the first seeds of Church practice that later became known in the canon law of our Orthodox Church as "economy" (or dispensation, *oikonomia*). Like the Law of Moses, the sacred canons must be respected; nevertheless, they cannot also fail to take into consideration the human person, for whom, after all, the Sabbath (namely, the Law) was made, in accordance with the familiar phrase of the Lord (see Mark 2.27). Echoing the spirit of our Lord, St. Paul insisted on his position, pointing to the way of *oikonomia* in his

concern that Church unity not be disrupted by the imposition of unbearable burdens on the shoulders of the weak.

Even the manner in which St. Paul chose to preserve Church unity at that very critical moment was enlightening. At his initiative, a solution was reached through the convocation of a council in Jerusalem, which by the grace of the Holy Spirit ultimately safeguarded the unity of the Church (see Acts 15). And so, while St. Paul was convinced of the correctness of his opinion, he was not satisfied merely to insist on what he believed to be true. His passion for the unity of the Church led him to the only possible and valid defense of his position, which lies in the conciliar decision itself. The Church upheld this way through the ages, defining through synods exclusively what is truthful and what is heretical. It is only in our time that we observe among Orthodox the phenomenon of individuals or groups pressing their opinions, sometimes persistently opposing conciliar decisions of the various churches. Yet, according to the example of St. Paul as well as of the Church through the centuries, both truth and Church unity are preserved only through synods.

UNITY AS ECUMENICAL

7. At the same time, Church unity for St. Paul is not merely an internal matter of the Church. If he insists so strongly on maintaining unity, it is because Church unity is inextricably linked with the unity of all humanity. The Church does not exist for itself but for all humankind and, still more broadly, for the whole of creation.

St. Paul describes Christ as the "second" or "final" Adam—as humanity in its entirety (see 1 Cor. 15.14 and Rom. 5.14). And "just as all die in Adam, so all will be made alive in Christ" (1 Cor. 15.22; see Rom. 5.19). Just as the human race is united in Adam, so also "all things are gathered up in [Christ], both things in heaven and things on earth" (Eph. 1.10). As St. John Chrysostom remarks, this "gathering up" (or recapitulation, *anakephalaiosis*) signifies that "one head had been established for all, namely the incarnate Christ, for both humans and angels, the human and divine Word. And they were gathered under one head so that there may be complete union and contiguity."[17]

---

17. PG 62.16.

Nevertheless, this "recapitulation" of the entire world in Christ is not conceived by St. Paul outside the Church. As he explains in his letter to the Colossians (1.16–18), in Christ "all things in heaven and on earth were created and . . . in him all things hold together" precisely because "he is the head of the body, the Church." "[God] has made him the head over all things for the Church, which is his body, the fullness of him who fills all in all" (Eph. 1.22–23). For St. Paul, then, Christ is the head of all—of all people and all creation—because He is at the same time head of the Church. The Church as the body of Christ is not fulfilled unless it assumes in itself the whole world.

There are many useful conclusions that we may gain from this ecclesiology of St. Paul. We confine ourselves to pointing out, first, the importance—for the life of the Church in general and for the ministry of us all in particular—of the duty of mission. The evangelization of God's people, as well as of those who do not believe in Christ, is the Church's supreme obligation. This obligation—at least when it is not realized aggressively (as it was in the past, primarily in Western Christianity) or deceptively (as is the case with various forms of proselytism) but with love, humility, and respect for the cultural particularity of each person and race—is a response to the Lord's desire that, through the unity of the Church, "the world may believe" in Him (John 17.21). So we must in every way encourage and support the external mission of the Church wherever it is practiced, particularly in the jurisdiction of the Patriarchate of Alexandria within the vast continent of Africa.

However, even within our churches, the need or, indeed, the obligation to evangelize is today rendered imperative. We must become conscious that in contemporary societies, especially in the context of Western civilization, faith in Christ can by no means be taken for granted. Orthodox theology cannot today be developed or expounded without dialogue with modern currents of philosophical thought and social dynamics as well as with various forms of art and culture in our time. In this regard, the message and overall word of Orthodoxy cannot be aggressive, as, unfortunately, it often is, rendering it of no benefit at all. Rather, it must be dialectical, dialogical, and reconciliatory. We must first understand other people and discern their deeper concerns; for, even behind disbelief, there lies concealed a search for the true God.

Finally, the connection between the unity of the Church and the unity of the world, on which the Apostle to the Gentiles insists, imposes on us the need to assume the role of peacemakers within a world torn by conflict. The Church cannot—indeed, it must not—in any way nurture religious fanaticism, whether consciously or subconsciously. When zeal becomes fanaticism, it deviates from the nature of the Church, particularly the Orthodox Church. By contrast, we must develop initiatives of reconciliation wherever conflicts among people either loom or erupt. Inter-Christian and interreligious dialogue is the very least of our obligations; and it is one that we must surely fulfill.

However, the modern world is unfortunately plagued by a crisis that cannot be reduced to interpersonal relations but extends to the relationship between humanity and the natural environment. According to St. Paul, as we have already observed, Christ constitutes the head of all, of things visible and invisible—that is, of all creation, while the Church as His body unites not only humanity but the whole creation. Therefore, it is abundantly clear that the Church cannot remain idle before the crisis that affects humanity in relation to the natural environment. It is our obligation to assume every possible initiative: first, so that our own flock may become aware of the demand for respect toward creation and avoid any abuse or irrational use of natural resources; second, so that we may support every effort that aspires to the protection of God's creation. For, as everyone today acknowledges, the cause of the environmental crisis is profoundly spiritual, the result primarily of human greed and indulgence, which characterize modern man. With its long ascetic tradition and liturgical ethos, the Orthodox Church can contribute greatly to a confrontation of the crisis that now threatens our planet. In full recognition of this, the Ecumenical Patriarchate has—already since 1989, as the first church to do so in the Christian world—issued an encyclical signed by our venerable predecessor Patriarch Dimitrios, establishing September 1 of each year as a day of prayer for the protection of the natural environment. It has also, since that time, promoted a series of activities, such as the organization of international symposia involving scholars and religious leaders who are invited to ascertain various ways of protecting God's creation from imminent destruction. We invite and appeal to all our sister Orthodox churches to support this endeavor of the Ecumenical Patriarchate;

after all, our obligation and responsibility before God and history is something we all bear in common.

8. And now, beloved brothers in the Lord, let us turn our thought to the internal affairs of our Orthodox Church, whose leadership the Lord's mercy has entrusted to us. We have been deigned by our Lord to belong to the one, holy, catholic and apostolic Church, whose faithful continuation and expression in History is our holy Orthodox Church. We have received and preserve the true faith, as the holy Fathers have transmitted it to us through the ecumenical councils of the one undivided Church. We commune of the same body and blood of our Lord in the Divine Eucharist, and we participate in the same sacred mysteries. We keep basically the same liturgical *typikon* and are governed by the same sacred canons. All these safeguard our unity, granting us fundamental presuppositions for witness in the modern world.

Even so, we must admit in all honesty that sometimes we present an image of incomplete unity, as if we were not one Church but rather a federation of churches. This is largely a result of the institution of autocephaly, which characterizes the structure of the Orthodox Church. As is known, this institution dates back to the early Church, when the so-called "pentarchy" of the ancient apostolic sees and churches—namely, of Rome, Constantinople, Alexandria, Antioch, and Jerusalem—was still valid. The communion or "symphony" of these sees expressed the unity of the universal Church in the oikoumene. This pentarchy was severed originally after the tragic schism of 1054 between Rome and Constantinople and afterward between Rome and the other patriarchates. To the four Orthodox Patriarchates that remained after the Schism, from the middle of the second millennium to this day, other autocephalous Churches were added until we arrived at the present organization of the Orthodox Church throughout the world today.

Yet, while the original system of pentarchy emanated from respect for the apostolicity and particularity of the traditions of these ancient patriarchates,[18] the autocephaly of later churches grew out of respect for the

---

18. For more on the notion of apostolicity, see Francis Dvornik, *The Photian Schism: History and Legend* (Cambridge: Cambridge University Press, 1948).

cultural identity of nations. Moreover, the overall system of autocephaly was encroached in recent years, through secular influences, by the spirit of ethno-phyletism or, still worse, of state nationalism, to the degree that the basis for autocephaly now became the local secular nation, whose boundaries, as we all know, do not remain stable but depend on historical circumstance. So we have reached the perception that Orthodoxy comprises a federation of national Churches, frequently attributing priority to national interests in their relationship with one another. In light of this situation, which recalls somewhat the situation in Corinth when the First Letter to the Corinthians was written, the Apostle Paul might well ask: "Has Orthodoxy been divided?" This question is posed also by many observers of Orthodox affairs in our time.

Of course, the response commonly proffered to this question is that, despite administrational division, Orthodoxy remains united in faith, in the sacraments, etc. But is this sufficient? When before non-Orthodox we sometimes appear divided in theological dialogues, for example; when we are unable to proceed to the realization of the long-heralded Holy and Great Council of the Orthodox Church; when we lack a unified voice on contemporary issues and, instead, convoke bilateral dialogues with non-Orthodox on these issues; when we fail to constitute a single Orthodox Church in the so-called Diaspora[19] in accordance with the ecclesiological and canonical principles of our Church—how, then, can we avoid the perception of division in Orthodoxy, especially of division on the basis of non-theological, secular criteria?

We need, then, greater unity in order to appear to those outside not as a federation of churches but as one unified Church. Through the centuries, and especially after the Schism, when the Church of Rome ceased to be in communion with the Orthodox, this Throne was called—according to canonical order—to serve the unity of the Orthodox Church as its First Throne. And it fulfilled this responsibility through the ages by convoking an entire series of pan-Orthodox councils on crucial ecclesiastical matters, always prepared, whenever duly approached, to render its assistance and support to troubled Orthodox churches. In this way, a canonical order was created and, accordingly, the coordinating role of this

---

19. Referring to the "dispersion" of Orthodox faithful throughout the world as immigrants to various countries.

Patriarchate guaranteed the unity of the Orthodox Church, without in the least damaging or diminishing the independence of the local auto-cephalous churches and without interfering in their internal affairs. This, in any case, is the healthy significance of the institution of autocephaly: while it assures the self-governance of each Church with regard to its internal life and organization, on matters affecting the entire Orthodox Church and its relations with those outside, each autocephalous Church does not act alone but in coordination with the rest of the Orthodox churches. If this coordination either disappears or diminishes, then auto-cephaly becomes "autocephalism" (or radical independence)—that is, a factor of division rather than of unity for the Orthodox Church.

Therefore, dearly beloved brothers in the Lord, we are called to con-tribute in every possible way to the unity of the Orthodox Church, tran-scending every temptation of regionalism or nationalism so that we may act as a unified Church, as one canonically structured body. We do not, as during Byzantine times, have at our disposal a state factor that guaran-teed—and sometimes even imposed—such unity. Nor does our ecclesiol-ogy permit any centralized authority that is able to impose unity from above. Our unity depends on our conscience. The sense of need and duty that we constitute a single canonical structure and body, one Church, is sufficient to guarantee our unity, without any external intervention.

VISION AND ACTION FOR THE FUTURE

In consideration of all these things, and with a sense of our Church's obligation before God and history in an age when the unified witness of Orthodoxy is judged crucial and is universally expected, we invite and call on you fraternally that, with the approval also of our respective holy syn-ods, we may proceed to the following necessary actions:

> To advance the preparations for the Holy and Great Council of the Orthodox Church, already commenced through pan-Orthodox preconciliar consultations.
>
> To activate the 1993 agreement of the Inter-Orthodox Consultation of the Holy and Great Council in order to resolve the pending matter of the Orthodox Diaspora. Regarding these concerns, the Ecumenical Patriarch-ate, in its status and responsibility as the coordinator of pan-Orthodox matters, intends to call, in the upcoming year of 2009, a pan-Orthodox

meeting, to which, like the pan-Orthodox meetings in Rhodes, all of the autocephalous churches will be invited.[20]

To strengthen, by means of further theological support, the decisions taken on a pan-Orthodox level regarding participation of the Orthodox Church in theological dialogues with non-Orthodox.

To proclaim once again the vivid interest of the entire Orthodox Church in the crucial and urgent matter of protecting the natural environment, supporting on a pan-Orthodox level the relative initiative of the Ecumenical Patriarchate.

To establish an Inter-Orthodox Committee for the study of matters arising today in the field of bioethics, on which the world justifiably also awaits the Orthodox position.[21] At this point, we remind this venerable assembly that some years ago the Ecumenical Patriarchate, through official letters, had recommended to our sister Orthodox churches that each designate an expert as their representative in order to form an inter-Orthodox committee on bioethics; however, only a few responded. We shall return to this issue in the near future, and we ask that hereafter you do not delay in responding, so that this inter-Orthodox committee may be formed and assume its work.

We deemed it proper to offer these proposals for your consideration, in our wish that this synaxis, after making possible the exchange of more-general thoughts, may also conclude with several specific decisions whereby the unity of our Church will be expressed in deed. After all, this is what public opinion expects of us, both among our own flocks but also in the world around us. You are certainly able to add other proposals to these, should this be deemed necessary, Your Beatitudes and most eminent brothers.

In closing our address, we express once again glory to our all-good God for vouchsafing that we convene in the same place, within the context of

20. At the invitation of His All Holiness Ecumenical Patriarch Bartholomew, following the consensus of the heads of Orthodox churches, as expressed during their meeting at the Phanar (October 10–12, 2008), the Fourth Preconciliar Pan-Orthodox Conference met at the Orthodox Center of the Ecumenical Patriarchate in Chambésy, Geneva (June 6–12, 2009).

21. In 2001, His All Holiness invited the Heads of Orthodox churches to designate representatives for such a committee. While many churches were eager to participate in such an initiative, others were hesitant.

the Pauline celebrations, and we pray that our brotherly fellowship in the Lord during these days will unite us still more in the bond of love.

"Now to Him who by the power at work within us is able to accomplish abundantly far more than all we can ask or imagine, to Him be glory in the Church and in Christ Jesus" (Eph. 3.20–21).

ADDRESSES TO ORTHODOX PATRIARCHS

Funeral Oration for Patriarch Alexei II, Moscow, December 9, 2008

AN INSPIRED AND DISTINGUISHED TENURE

> As for me, I am already being poured out as a libation, and the time of my departure has come. I have fought the good fight, I have finished the race.
>
> 2 Tim. 4.6–7

Like a sharp arrow, the heart of the Orthodox Church militant was pierced in recent days by the announcement of the unexpected repose of the venerable Primate of our sister autocephalous Church in Russia, our beloved brother and concelebrant Alexei.[22] Therefore, we open our occasional farewell address with the timely words of the heavenly Apostle Paul to Timothy, inasmuch as we are absolutely convinced of the unbroken continuity in martyrdom and in confession, perpetual expression and dynamic faith, that are manifest from time to time in virtuous individuals who follow St. Paul's example in their life. Of course, there is never an absolute identification between St. Paul and these individuals. Nevertheless, we are able to draw this intimation because, in all places, indomitable fighters boldly bear the cross of the same "good fight," continuing in this way the same ministry and mission through the centuries.

And as a fighter, our late brother is a deserving recipient of these words as well as of the crown that awaits him. For he journeyed with dignity and humility along the difficult path of his supreme yoke and highly responsible ministry as Primate. Yet, in full recognition of his pioneering

---

22. Patriarch Alexei died on December 5, 2008. He had recently attended the synaxis of heads of Orthodox churches that was organized by the Ecumenical Patriarchate in Istanbul (October 10–12, 2008). See above, 110

contribution to the revival and establishment of his flock, replete with wounds—a flock under the providential care of our Lord as Shepherd of shepherds, who is appointed to be its inspired leader—we are able to apply to him St. Paul's words as an expression of gratitude to God for offering in the person of this worthy hierarch an imitable example for His struggling people.

The late Patriarch Alexei skillfully administered his Church and was able to lead the Orthodox Church of Russia out of the limited boundaries of its internal turns and turmoils. As a simple hierarch, before being elevated to the position of leading bastion of the Patriarchal See, he encountered the stubborn and fanatical opposition of inimical authority. This consolidated in his heart both the conviction with regard to the endless, unyielding struggle and the expectation of the evidence of resurrection that derives from the power of the Cross. Indeed, the blessed hope of this expectation and anticipation of martyrdom was achieved in the days of his inspired tenure as patriarch, when that deplorable spectacle tolerated over numerous years by his humble predecessors at last disappeared, so that—to quote our own great predecessor, St. Gregory the Theologian—"Jerusalem was erased and the honorable and golden sons of Zion were led in captivity, while thousands fell and the earth was covered with their blood and corpses."

Today, as we gather around the venerable body of the Patriarch, in the midst of a mourning Church, we profess and proclaim: "How awesome are the works of the Lord!" In the abundance of His strength, His enemies were revealed to be liars; we have seen His works, and we know that He is far more powerful that the sons of men; for His eyes have looked on this blood-stained flock, and those who harassed the Lord's people were unable to realize their complete destruction; instead, the Lord of all power granted life to the souls of His people and led them to a place of refreshment; the ineffably loving Lord protected them from the wiles of the evil ones; God showed mercy on His people and gave them a Patriarch who was great in achievements and bold in crises, so that, through the inexhaustible strength of the Patriarch's boundless love and longsuffering tolerance, God might preserve the integrity of this bruised vineyard and grant support to the shaken conscience of the Church.

He was truly distinguished as a reviver and a brilliant illuminator of the faith in word and deed, working toward excellent cooperation with our sister Orthodox churches throughout the world.

He looked toward the First among the Thrones, the Church of Constantinople, as a womb of regeneration for the superb people whom he selflessly shepherded. Whenever the slightest cloud overshadowed the general comity, it was swept away by a heavenly breath of love and the hierarchical order based on the sacred canons.

He was extremely appreciative of the missionary witness that the Mother Church of Constantinople provided on occasion to this sacred and glorious land of Russia, recognizing it as a principal cause and fundamental contributor to the revival achieved here.

It is in the same spirit that the Mother Church, too, always communicated with him. We often followed and studied how the life of this large church developed during his inspired tenure. We were filled with surprise after surprise; the organization of the Church was perfect, disciplined, and fruitful; there were extraordinarily beautiful churches and splendid monasteries with thousands of monks and nuns; there were theological academies, holy seminaries and, in general, everything in which any well-cultivated Orthodox church must take pride; we have seen them all and duly admired them. The existing spiritual bond between this deeply fertile church and us grew ever stronger, adding the refreshing heavenly taste of authentic experience to the vibrant global community in our time.

This sacred bond was strengthened as well by the ardent and active late Patriarch when recently we had the inexpressible joy of celebrating in common both in Kiev of the Ukraine[23] and in the Royal City.[24] Nothing troubling could possibly forewarn us of his repose, sudden and painful for the entire Church. However, the ways of the Lord are different; the tireless Patriarch Alexei reached the end of his human life, as the Lord determines this for us all. He concluded his brilliant ecclesiastical journey, "having fought the good fight" as a soldier of Christ in the position he was appointed.

As those of us who are left behind consider the results of his fellowship with us as well as his unhindered leadership of this eminent Church of Russia, let us ask ourselves if it is proper for sorrow to prevail overwhelmingly in the present gathering. When the earthly Church sees off one of its distinguished members—indeed, one who is also an exceptionally fruitful

---

23. July 27, 2008.
24. Constantinople, October 12, 2008.

Primate, who admittedly retained spiritual vigilance over his people to his last breath—then pain is transformed into joyful mourning, and sadness over loss becomes joyful sorrow, filled with peace.

The Lord's word, on which the late Patriarch based his whole life and manifold ministry, offers an entirely different dimension to today's event: "Those who believe in me, even though they die, will live. And everyone who lives and believes in me will never die" (John 11.25–26).

The Hundred-Twentieth Anniversary of the Recognition of Autocephaly and Eightieth Anniversary of the Elevation of the Romanian Orthodox Church to the Rank of Patriarchate, Bucharest, March 5, 2005

Address before the special session of the Holy Synod and the National Church Assembly of the Church in Romania

A MILESTONE OF UNITY

For us who are gathered here today in the name of our Lord Jesus Christ, who, according to His promise, is also here with us and among us, these moments are indeed touching and joyful to the utmost. We have gathered together to celebrate a multitude of happy anniversaries: the eightieth of the elevation of the most holy autocephalous Church of Romania to patriarchal rank; the hundred-twentieth of the recognition of her autocephaly by the Ecumenical Patriarchate; the ninetieth of the birthday of her Primate, our beloved brother and concelebrant, His Beatitude, Patriarch Teoktist; and the fifty-fifth of his consecration as prelate.[25]

It is love that causes the joy of this encounter and vouchsafes this wondrous reality, in which no linguistic, or ethnic, or any other kind of difference, can do anything to prevent our sense of unity and spiritual communion with all. Such an experience of unity is the paramount achievement of human existence, which is why it is also the sign of our spiritual struggle that is the most attacked by the barbs of the evil one. There are those who seem incapable of comprehending the spiritual unity

---

25. Patriarch Teoktist (1915–2007) became Patriarch of the Romanian Orthodox Church in 1986.

that we experience within the Orthodox Church, those who hold that declaration of autocephaly of a church implies that the unity of the Orthodox Church is fragmented.

Yet, it is not at all so. The unity of the Orthodox Church is neither administrative nor external: it is spiritual. We, Orthodox Christians, experience our unity with one another and—in a different fashion, of course—with all our fellow humans: yes, even with our departed brothers and sisters throughout the centuries. We experience the grand unity of God's creation and imbibe every aspect of this unity as it emerges from the material and the spiritual world. We sense that, despite its variety of forms, the universe, and humanity as a part of it, is imbued by one unifying principle and purpose: that there is one purpose and one temporal end, and, furthermore, one center from which the world emerged and to which it tends with yearning. For all those who believe in unity, the one, sole model thereof, to which we must all tend, with a view to achieving our "likeness" with our archetypal image, is the unity between the three persons of the Holy Trinity, the perfect unity of will and action. That perfect unity of the faithful, "according to the likeness" of the Trinitarian unity, constitutes the main request of our Lord's intercessory prayer, which we all know and which we must always keep within our sight. For our Lord ascribed such great importance to this unity that He caused the persuasiveness of any preaching of our gospel to depend on whether we have unity among ourselves. His utterance "that they all may be one; as you, Father, are in me, and I in you, that they also may be one in us: that the world may believe that you have sent me" (John 17.21)—this bears witness that if we, as preachers of the gospel, lack unity among ourselves, we will not manage to convince our neighbor that our Lord Jesus Christ was sent by God to save the world.

History has confirmed the truth of this utterance by the Lord, because, from the moment that Christians, and especially those who preached the gospel, were split, divided, and sundered from one another, so that Christian groups that disagreed with and confronted one another were established, people began to distance themselves from such preachers, and from Christ. The secularization, particularly of non-Orthodox churches, is both evident and marked, both typical and widespread, and—like a virulent disease—it is also spreading over some of the Orthodox.

Perhaps it is not readily understood that the failure of our preaching is due to our lack of unity as preachers. Quite possibly, the evil one seeks to persuade our preachers that there are reasons other than lack of unity that render their preaching less than persuasive. Then, perhaps there are some who remain content with the externalities of an organizational, racial, or similar type of unity, who do not realize that the unity of the faithful, as demanded by our Lord, is utterly profound and spiritual, hearkening to the model of unity offered by the Holy Trinity: "even as we are one," in the Lord's words. Such spiritual unity does not do away with the particular personality of any person. It does not cause any person, with his or her peculiar features, to disappear. It constitutes an outpouring and expression of love and freedom; and, for that reason, it occasions gladness. For it is well known that love and all superior sensibility can grow only in freedom. It cannot be achieved by coercion, as a result of pressure from without or from within. The movement toward unity with the other is the outpouring of love alone—of this attribute of God that is unifying, causing the world and those who approach Him to cohere.

This is why unity among the faithful constitutes proof of their unity with Christ. If unity does not exist among human beings, it can be adduced that their unity with God is also wanting. This means that all actions that strike against the unity of humanity constitute a departure from God and do not stem from Him. Of course, there are those among our neighbors who, in their error, preach hatred and the extermination of others, as if that were God's commandment, and so they seek to justify their terrorist acts—acts of satanic provenance—as acts pleasing to God. But they are in error; for God, being love, is filled with mercy and pity, seeking no one's perdition.

This is the faith and the living experience of us Orthodox Christians. It is the actual living experience, whose truth the saints have known, as have many ordinary people among the faithful, and therefore they speak of it from their experience. Gladness and peace stem from love and from a sense of unity. Distress and sadness, disorderliness and war, come from souls that are deficient in love and are dominated by feelings of hatred, loathing, bitterness, and division. Of course we realize that, for us humans, the perfection of our unity as sought by Christ, and as may be achieved within Him, is no easy task. The advice of the Holy Fathers is to regard our fellow humans as being at one with us and to feel their pain as if it were our own—and also to feel their gladness as if it were our own. This, however, is an ideal that few attain, though it is an ideal to whose summit all of us Orthodox Christians should aspire.

There is, however, one serious obstacle. This is each person's will, which is usually given priority and seeks that the will of all others conform to it. Our own will is, of course, the unavoidable consequence of the independence of each one's individual personality. That is why it is not possible, or, to say the least, it is not easy to coordinate human will into one single point that would be acceptable to all. The only way to harmonize the will of every human being is to harmonize people's will with one paramount will that is revered by all. This sublime will cannot but be God's will. If in its place we posit any human will whatsoever, conflict is most certainly bound to arise. Therefore, perfect unity for humanity can be achieved only within Jesus Christ, in whom all is recapitulated.

Until this is achieved, it is necessary to look toward such unity as toward a desirable goal and to ascend the ladder leading to it, step by step. In all areas of ecclesiastical life, as well as of political, international, social, and family life, we are lagging with respect to the achievement of this objective. The germ of division is widespread and continually causes rifts and conflicts. Tolerance, a conciliatory spirit, and forgiveness are not held in sufficiently high regard. Therefore, there lies before us an extremely broad field where we might work to inculcate the notion of unity as a necessary prerequisite for peace and prosperity as well as for our profound and inalienable joy.

It is such a joy that we experience today as, in a spirit of unity with you, we jointly celebrate the anniversaries we have mentioned. And this joy is such that no one can deprive us of it, for we know that the autocephaly and emancipation granted by the Mother Church to her daughter-come-of-age, the Most Holy Church of Romania, has rather consolidated, and most assuredly has in no way detracted from, the bonds of love and cooperation. With such feelings of love and unity, we congratulate you on these anniversaries, wishing that all the blessings of the Lord may be showered on you and praying for your progress in all good works, and especially such as lie within Christ's spirit of unity—which is the foundation of all spiritual ascent and of all inalienable joy—that they may be vouchsafed to all your Church, and nation, and people as well as to each member thereof.

First Official Visit by Patriarch Kirill of Moscow and All-Russia to the Phanar, Ecumenical Patriarchate, July 5, 2009

Homily during the concelebration of the Divine Liturgy in the Patriarchal Church of St. George

VISION OF UNITY

It is with great joy, deep love, and much honor that we welcome you today to the court of that church from which the unwaning light of the holy and blameless Orthodox faith was conveyed to the noble and blessed Russian people, whom we behold at this moment in the precious person of Your Beatitude. We greet and embrace you wholeheartedly, praying that the Lord may bless your people with His grace, establishing them in "the faith once delivered to the saints" (Jude 3) and increasing the seed of the gospel that they received from here.

This first and formal visit of Your Beatitude in your capacity as Patriarch to the See of the Ecumenical Throne[26] is replete with sacred symbolism and ecclesiological significance. For it demonstrates clearly the indissoluble bond between our two churches as well as the prevailing sacred and inviolable order of unity within our holy Orthodox Church. Therefore, the Ecumenical Patriarchate justifiably records your visit here in the pages of history, as it is an event of special importance, and offers glory to the Founder of the Church for granting us this gift and blessing.

The common celebration of the Divine Eucharist today, Your Beatitude, constitutes the supreme expression of our unity. For, as we know— and as the Church Fathers teach, from the Hieromartyr Ignatius, bishop of Antioch,[27] to St. Symeon, archbishop of Thessalonika,[28] and Nicholas Cabasilas[29]—the Church is realized and revealed as the body of Christ particularly and primarily in the Divine Eucharist. As St. Nicholas Cabasilas wonderfully observes, between the Church and the Divine Eucharist

---

26. July 4–6, 2009. The visit to the Ecumenical Patriarchate also marked the beginning of Patriarch Kirill's "irenic visits" to sister Orthodox churches.

27. Ignatius of Antioch (d. during the period 98–117) was one of the early Apostolic Fathers.

28. Symeon was Archbishop of Thessalonika from 1416 until his death in 1429.

29. A Byzantine liturgical commentator, Nicholas Cabasilas (c.1319–91) is the author of the study *On the Divine Liturgy* and the treatise *On The Life in Christ*.

there is not an "analogy of likeness" but an "identity of reality." It follows, therefore, that "if one could see the Church of Christ . . . then one would see nothing else but the Body of the Lord."

Therefore, having just celebrated together the Divine Liturgy, we manifested in time and place the very Church of Christ; by participating in the one bread and the same cup, we have been united in the communion of the one Spirit. This unity, which is achieved in the common cup, cannot be taken from us by anyone. "Neither sorrow nor sadness nor persecution nor hunger nor nakedness nor danger nor the sword," to quote the Apostle (Rom. 8.35), nor again any other power or scheme by the enemy, count as anything before the unity that we share in the body of Christ. Certain shadows and small clouds may from time to time conceal the warm relations among our sister churches,[30] but these are only temporary. With the love of Christ, "they pass quickly," according to the words of our saintly predecessor John Chrysostom. After all, the obligation remains with us, who are entrusted with the responsibility and ministry of leadership in our churches; and we must discover the solutions to whatever problems may arise, doing so in a spirit of peace and love and with the explicit purpose of securing the unity of our holy Orthodox Church.

Still fresh in our memory as an example of this strong will among our Churches, and ratifying the importance of securing at any cost the unity of our holy Orthodox Church, is the wonderful unanimity realized during the recent Fourth Pre-Conciliar Pan-Orthodox Conference, which took place at our Patriarchal Center in Chambésy-Geneva,[31] where important measures were taken to resolve the question of the Orthodox Diaspora—a

---

30. Relations between the patriarchates of Constantinople and Moscow were strained because churches in certain former Soviet states, such as Estonia, had sought independence from the Russian Orthodox Church by appealing—in accordance with ancient custom and traditional practice—to the Ecumenical Patriarch. The Russian Church does not recognize the Estonian Apostolic Orthodox Church as an autonomous canonical structure, claiming that it was created in 1996 by the Ecumenical Patriarchate on territory already controlled by Moscow. Under Estonian law, however, the Church of Estonia is legal successor to the pre–World War II Estonian Orthodox Church, which was proclaimed independent by the Church of Russia. More recently, the Ukrainian church had sought the Ecumenical Patriarchate's support for independence from the Moscow Patriarchate after centuries of Russian influence.

31. June 6–12, 2009.

development removing one of the more serious hurdles in the journey of our Orthodox Church toward the realization of the Holy and Great Council, which was decided with pan-Orthodox consent. We would like to take this opportunity, at this sacred moment, to express our satisfaction and gratitude for the constructive cooperation manifested during the same conference by your church's delegation, which, together with the other delegations of the sister Orthodox churches, contributed to the success of that conference. Let us hope that a similar spirit of splendid cooperation will also mark the inter-Orthodox preparatory commission that will convene next December for the purpose of finalizing preparations for the Holy and Great Council, which the world, both within and outside Orthodoxy, awaits with eagerness.[32]

THE PRIMACY OF UNITY

Indeed, Your Beatitude and Holy Brother, everyone has their eyes focused on us, expecting us to lead them by word, but especially by our example, in the way of reconciliation and love, which is so imperative today. This is why it is crucial that we demonstrate an unswerving readiness above all to promote in every way our pan-Orthodox unity. We already share the same faith, articulated and proclaimed by the holy synods. We enjoy the same worship, as this was formulated in this city and then transplanted to the other Orthodox churches. We have the same canonical order, unalterably defined by the order and regulations of the holy ecumenical councils. Our unity is based on these foundations. The structure of our Church into patriarchates and autocephalous Churches in no way implies that we constitute churches and not a Church.

Of course, the Orthodox Church does not have at its disposal a primacy of authority; however, it also does not lack a coordinating body, which, instead of imposing, rather expresses the unanimity of our local churches. This ministry is realized humbly—out of a long and sacred tradition—by this sacrificial throne in absolute faithfulness to the prescriptions of Orthodox ecclesiology.

---

32. The inter-Orthodox preparatory commission met in Chambésy-Geneva (December 10–17, 2009) to discuss the manner of declaring autocephaly and autonomy as well as the question of the diptychs (that is, the order and rank of the Orthodox churches).

Nevertheless, the unity of our holy Orthodox Church is not an end in itself. In accordance with the words of the Lord shortly before His Passion, the goal of the unity of His disciples, according to the model of the Holy Trinity, is "that the world may believe that You have sent me" (John 17.21). As "catholic," the Church extends by conveying God's love to all people and to the material creation itself. We exist as Church not for ourselves but for humanity and creation. We offer the Divine Eucharist "for the oikoumene" and for all creation. Consequently, we cannot remain indifferent in a spirit of self-sufficiency and self-love, complacent and proud that we "have found the truth," indifferent to or even disdainful of those who are outside the walls of the Orthodox Church.

For this reason, dearly beloved Brother in the Lord, we rejoice that the Most Holy Church of Russia, despite certain reservations or objections from within some of its circles, fully participates in the theological dialogues that are approved on a pan-Orthodox level with non-Orthodox Christians, contributing for a long time now to the promotion of Christian unity. There are of course difficulties that we encounter; more than often, there are even disappointments. Your Beatitude has great experience in this area, knowing well how difficult and rough this journey is. Yet, it is a journey that we are obliged to undertake according to the commandment of the Lord, albeit through spiritual toil and turmoil, always remaining faithful to the truth we have received "until all of us reach the unity of faith" (Eph. 4.13).

Beyond this, the burning and urgent problems of contemporary humankind rise before us, problems accentuated by our tendency toward self-love and hedonism, which are unfortunately presented, cultivated, and promoted by the modern world. These problems increase daily in contemporary societies; indeed, as a result of the existing trends of so-called globalization, they tend to assume ecumenical character. The worship of mammon, which led to the present financial crisis; the unjust distribution of wealth, which widens the gap and heightens the contrasts between social groups; wars and conflicts, which are followed by the oppression of the weak by the powerful, leading masses of people to embark on a search for a better life, far from their homeland; the rise of crime and every form of moral deviation and decline—all these have profound spiritual roots and oblige the Church of Christ to articulate and contribute an answer to this condition, by means of all spiritual resources available, and to cultivate a moral sensitivity within contemporary society.

Your Beatitude has shown particular sensitivity in these issues, proving your intense interest and concern.

However, our Church, too, the Ecumenical Patriarchate, demonstrates similar sensitivity in confronting such problems of the contemporary world, such as the environmental crisis that plagues the planet and humankind, even as we strive to reveal the deeper, spiritual, and moral causes of this crisis and raise awareness among people—and especially the faithful—about the seriousness of the crisis and the urgent need to take measures to resolve it. Moreover, conscious of the seriousness of these problems and aware of the Church's obligation, the Ecumenical Patriarchate has already taken the initiative to organize an inter-Orthodox bioethics committee, in which the Most Holy Church of Russia kindly participates through its appointed delegation.

Your Beatitude and beloved Brother, as all of us know, the Orthodox Church is fundamentally traditional. It respects and preserves the past as an invaluable deposit inherited from all preceding generations. Examples of this include the unbroken succession of saints, great hierarchs, fathers and mothers, teachers and missionaries, apostles and prophets, martyrs and ascetics, whose head and leader is our Lord Jesus Christ, who remains "the same yesterday and today, and to the ages" (Heb. 13.8). The saints of the Church constitute our common treasure, irrespective of where they lived. These saints have also been granted to our Church by the saint-bearing land of Russia, which continues to offer such saints to this day. This cloud of witnesses covers and protects all of us even at this historical concelebration, calling us to imitate their God-pleasing life in order that we may recall that we belong to the one, holy, catholic, and apostolic Church, as we confess in the symbol of our Faith.

However, this commitment to tradition by no means constitutes a brake to our life in the present or to our witness within the contemporary world. The Orthodox Church pays close attention to the quests, needs, and concerns of modern man. It is always present and prepared to stand by human suffering, just as the Good Samaritan did in the parable. So let us join hands as two churches, together with the other Orthodox churches, "with one mouth and one heart,"[33] as one united Church of

---

33. From the Divine Liturgy of St. John Chrysostom, immediately preceding the recitation of the Symbol of Faith.

Christ, to celebrate "the liturgy after the Liturgy,"[34] bearing the bread of life to those hungry and thirsty for righteousness and love. Our unity transcends the narrow limits of any nationalism or racism; may it also offer to those near and far a sense of hope that the world cannot provide—hope for a world of peace and love. May the Divine Liturgy that we have just celebrated be continued as our common journey in the world toward the Kingdom of God.

With this prayer, then, we embrace you, dearly beloved Brother, expressing our gratitude for your blessed visit here and entreating our Lord God to protect, preserve, and strengthen you in your supreme ministry for the benefit of His entire holy Church.

EXHORTATIONS TO CLERGY AND FAITHFUL OF THE ECUMENICAL THRONE

Synaxis of Bishops, Ecumenical Patriarchate, August 29, 1998

> Address to the synaxis of bishops within the immediate jurisdiction of the Ecumenical Patriarchate throughout the world

AWARENESS OF OUR FAITH

Most holy Brothers and concelebrants in the Lord, by the grace of God we are gathered again in this place of martyrdom and sacrifice, to evaluate the things that have occurred over these past two years and to offer one another our support. As we gather, we remember those of us departed from this life and also those who for whatever reason cannot be with us. We pray for the repose of the departed ones, and we affirm to the others that we consider them spiritually present with us.

During the past two years, Orthodoxy has been sought by many. We answered to those who inquired of us. Probably our words were not always well received, especially when people compared them with our actions. This is what influenced our choice of theme for this gathering: "Orthodox in Full Awareness." As Orthodox, we have only one reason to exist: namely, to proclaim to the world the unadulterated truth and to

---

34. An expression describing the deeper impact and wider influence of the liturgy in and for the life of the world.

share the pure light of Christ, which is Orthodoxy. We can offer this pure light only if we ourselves are purified, according to the saying of our predecessor St. Gregory the Theologian: "We should be enlightened ourselves before we illuminate others." Certainly, we live in the light of Christ, but the degree of light differs, not only between us but also within each of us, from one moment to another. The reason for this is that we are in a state of constant development in the matter of being illuminated by the divine light. The purpose of this synaxis is precisely to expound on and expedite this process.

The following brothers have graciously accepted the invitation to study various aspects of the general theme: Metropolitans Irenaeus of Kydonias and Apocoronou, Anthony of Hierapolis, Augustine of Germany, and Maximos of Ainou. The sub topics are: "Secularization as a Reality and as a Threat to Contemporary Orthodoxy," "Unacceptable Foreign and Heterodox Incursions of Practices and Ideas in the Orthodox Domain," "The Ecumenicity of Orthodoxy as a Contemporary Way of Life," and "The Challenge of Metaphysical Experiences Outside Orthodoxy, and the Orthodox Response to These."

THE CHALLENGE OF THE WEST

This year's theme continues the previous one, "The Stand of Orthodoxy in the Presence of the Challenges of Western Civilization."[35] Two years ago, the emphasis was on our response to the West; this time the emphasis is on our self-awareness as Orthodox and on the influence that the message of the Western world has on us. We are in a give-and-take relationship. We impact on one another. So there is always the danger that our message will reflect not the unadulterated truth but rather elements of non-Orthodox teachings. The *neptic* Fathers[36] correctly instructed us to watch our minds and guard them against thoughts that try to enter and produce fruits that are the result of alien seed and sowing.

---

35. Ecumenical Patriarch Bartholomew was the first ever to convene assemblies of hierarchs of the Ecumenical Throne throughout the world. These gatherings have normally taken place biennially in Istanbul since 1994. For a brief history, see the address entitled *Synaxis of Bishops*, 2002 (below), 143.

36. From the Greek word *nepsis*, meaning "soberness" or "vigilance." The term refers to the ascetic writers normally associated with the *Philokalia*.

In recent centuries, the lack of a comprehensive educational system in Orthodoxy has led our people to pursue graduate studies at heterodox educational institutions. These people brought to the Orthodox domain ideas that are not purely Orthodox. In addition, immigrants to non-Orthodox lands sometimes returned, bringing back with them practices that were copied from the heterodox. St. Paul's words should be our guide: "Test everything; hold fast to what is good" (1 Thess. 5.21). This is the purpose of our present conversation: namely, to point out which of these ideas are acceptable and which are to be rejected. We are motivated not by intolerance but by the wish to safeguard the life-giving truth of the Orthodox faith against their latent falsification.

Orthodox theological schools will contribute to our effort. Let more Orthodox schools and chairs be established. Let Halki reopen.[37] But Orthodoxy is not only a matter of intellectual understanding, of true faith and mind. It is first of all a matter of proper living, of correct participation in the glory of the Lord (2 Cor. 3.18). Theological schools and proper Orthodox scientific training are not enough. An Orthodox way of life is needed, one that will permeate our entire existence and impact the actions of our everyday life.

From a phenomenological perspective, Orthodox people are very much like others. Their relationship to God, their fellow human beings, and the world is, however, such that their heart is always filled with peace, love, hope, faith, and constant confidence in God's providence, no matter what the circumstances in which they live. This trust in God and in His intervention in history, as expressed by the Psalmist (Ps. 15.8), constitutes the immanent experience of the transcendent in the life of the Orthodox Christian. God is always present and active; the Orthodox Christian does

---

37. The theological school of Halki was established in 1844 and forcibly closed by Turkish authorities in 1971. It served as the principal training seminary of the Ecumenical Patriarchate for numerous years. Ecumenical Patriarch Bartholomew has long campaigned for and pledged its reopening. In a speech before the Turkish Parliament on April 6, 2009, U.S. President Barack Obama reaffirmed the need for Turkey to allow the reopening of Halki Seminary: "Freedom of religion and expression lead to a strong and vibrant civil society that only strengthens the state, which is why steps like reopening the Halki Seminary will send such an important signal inside Turkey and beyond. An enduring commitment to the rule of law is the only way to achieve the security that comes from justice for all people." See http://www.archons.org/news/detail.asp?id = 303.

not need or desire to build an immanent Kingdom of God, so to speak, without God, as do many contemporary people who act as if God were inactive and as if man were the only agent in history.

At this point, we are touching on the first subtopic of our synaxis, secularization as a threat for Orthodoxy today. Secularization may be defined as the removal of what is sacred, supernatural, and sacramental from our lives. This reduces our church life to mere ritual, to a show that satisfies our artistic desires, aesthetic demands, and the need for variation in our daily boredom; yet, our inner being does not participate, because in it there is no encounter with a "Thou," whom our inner being loves and desires to meet. Our personal spiritual life is thus reduced to mere external good manners, conformity to ethical rules, and external correctness. Our experience, however, is not governed by the Spirit of God; it does not receive and reflect the uncreated energies of the divine grace. And so the simple man, who is without grace, offers himself to his fellow human beings, but he is not at rest; for man seeks the Lord Jesus, even when he is not conscious of this desire.

THE IMPACT OF SECULARIZATION

Secularization changes the Church into a mundane institution; it changes the faithful into a non-deified person. Both are deprived of Christ, even if His name still happens to be mentioned. Secularization has already affected many members of the Orthodox Church, especially in places where Orthodoxy is surrounded by highly secularized Western societies.

Secularized Orthodox communities count their progress in terms of money, number of members, social activities (included in this list at times are even Divine Liturgies!), the number of state institutions under their supervision, and the like. The Orthodox Church cares about this life, just as for the life hereafter. Its members should know how to preside over good works. They cannot, however, afford to forget Christ; they cannot just practice His commandments without having a personal relationship with Him.

Secularization is a dangerous illness; it does not drive people from the church but rather transforms the church into something mundane, depriving it of its metaphysical worldview. Western theology has in many ways contributed to this secularization. It is important for Orthodoxy to pinpoint departures of even well-known and respected theologians from the pure Orthodox faith. Constant use of our Patristic sources and the teaching of their correct doctrine is mandatory.

The issue of secularization is always contemporary. The attack on the Orthodox mind and life in the Holy Spirit is constant, merciless, and not always immediately perceived. It has an impact on us without our knowing it. This is why it should be extensively studied. The influence of secularization on the Orthodox *phronema* (mind) belongs to the category of foreign practices and ideas that are unacceptable, which is the object of study in our second subtopic. Other foreign and heterodox practices will be identified, studied, and refuted by the Orthodox. These practices should be rejected with prudence, because some of them are by now old habits. One should be careful about how to proceed, lest we do damage to the healthy part of the body as we work to reject the elements that are foreign.

THE EXPERIENCE OF THE FATHERS

We now come to the third subtopic, on metaphysical experiences. Western scholasticism reduced the divine truths and, indeed, God Himself to mere concepts. Communion with God is a conceptual enterprise. And so the genuine experience of God, beyond concepts and ideas, the participation in the uncreated light and, generally, the uncreated energies—all of this becomes an impossibility for the West. All metaphysical experiences of religions can become a deception, illusion, trance, and the like. On this subject the opinions of Barlaam and Akyndinos, refuted by St. Gregory Palamas,[38] are well known.

Unfortunately, some Orthodox theologians even today are influenced by the doctrines of the adversaries of St. Gregory Palamas. They doubt the authenticity of well-attested metaphysical experiences, such as those, for example, of St. Symeon the New Theologian, even when these are indisputably accepted by the Church.[39] The result is that the experience of the

---

38. Among the foremost mystics of the Orthodox Church, Gregory Palamas (1296–1359) was archbishop of Thessalonika and a prominent spokesman for Hesychasm.

39. Perhaps the most popular mystic of the Orthodox Church, Symeon the New Theologian (949–1022) is one of only three saints to receive the title "theologian" (the others being St. John the Evangelist and St. Gregory the Theologian) and profoundly embodied the tradition of Hesychasm.

divine was prohibited to the Christian in the West as well as in the "westernized" East. Consequently, experiential contact with the non-earthly world was left to those influenced by various evil spirits—namely, to those who are non-Christians and to the Christians who are deceived by them. Various likeminded movements have proliferated, some of them leading their followers to suicide or even to criminal acts against innocent people. And so our pastoral problem is to confront, for the further protection of the Orthodox flock, the flood of foreign messages addressed to our faithful.

Orthodox Christians, on the one hand, believe that there is a reality different from the earthly one. It consists of the All-holy Trinity, whose life is made accessible to us through Christ in the Holy Spirit and in the uncreated energies of the divine grace; it consists of the saints of our Orthodox faith, of which the leader is the true Holy Theotokos. On the other hand, when influenced by a westernized spirit, these Orthodox behave as if this reality does not exist at all.

However, tens of thousands of their fellows, from all religious traditions, reassure them about genuine and tangible spiritual (or metaphysical) experiences. The dilemma is an existential one. The right path is that of the unadulterated Orthodox tradition, which neither accepts nor rejects these experiences but rather struggles to "discern" the spirits, in light of St. John's words: "Brothers, do not believe in any spirit; but test the spirits, to see if they come from God" (1 John 4.1). We certainly know that most of these experiences are the product of deception (*prelest*),[40] more spiritually deceptive than any deception of the senses. They are existential experiences caused by evil spirits of deception, which are temporarily vested with a garment of truth.

The Orthodox Church has a responsibility to give the right answer both to its own children and to anyone else, especially when (as in, for example, in the case of the charismatic movement) these experiences are considered as coming from the Holy Spirit and occur within the Church.

The best answer is, first, that of the saint, who has the experience of the supernatural world and the gift of discerning the spirits. Second, in the saint's absence, those who have had experiences outside the church, led by a deceitful spirit, can, when they turn from their deception (*prelest*), be of

---

40. From a Russian term, signifying "spiritual delusion."

great influence. Third, people who may not themselves have these experiences but are well versed in the teachings of *Philokalia*[41] and the *neptic* Fathers can also be of help. The *neptic* Fathers have prudently and clearly described both the characteristics of genuine supernatural experiences coming from the Holy Spirit and the signs through which these experiences are distinguished from the deceitful experiences involving evil spirits.

CHALLENGES OF THE PRESENT

Unfortunately, spiritism, the occult, black magic, magic celebrations, and the like have flooded our world. They are projected by the mass media, provoking curiosity and encouraging involvement. Only to assume a negative position is not sufficient. Responsible study and response are very much needed.

Regarding the ecumenical dimension of Orthodoxy as an ideal and as a commandment, it is not necessary to say too much here. All of us are in agreement about this. But much improvement is needed. First, Christian churches continue to turn within themselves. Second, quarrels among Orthodox jurisdictions continue to exist. Third, quarrels exist within individual churches as well. Our task is great, difficult, and critical. Our responsibility is to continue to proclaim the good news of unity and reconciliation.

As we conclude the second millennium of our Christian era, we see the Church of Christ adorned with the sacred blood of its children. Unfortunately, some of the wounds are not inflicted by its enemies. The task of healing the wounds will be our responsibility, so that the Orthodox may enter the third millennium as a loving and united family.

The unity for which Christ prayed and genuine Orthodox witness—these should be our main concerns. Secular people are ahead of us in this respect. They sever associations imposed from without, but they create new alliances. For they know that cooperation contributes much more to growth and progress than does isolation.

And now, let us consider certain events that have occurred during these past two years. The Albanian Church has established a synod. The Estonian

---

41. An anthology of texts on prayer written between the fourth and fifteenth centuries, originally compiled in the eighteenth century by St. Nikodemus of the Holy Mountain (1749–1809) and St. Makarios of Corinth (1731–1805).

Church is still under a *locum tenens*. The Church of the Czech Republic and Slovakia is now canonically proclaimed as autocephalous by the Mother Church. Part of the former Old Calendarists of Astoria (New York) are now reunited with the Ecumenical Throne. The creation of an office for the Ecumenical Patriarchate in Athens is under way, as is an office for the Ecumenical Patriarchate in the Church of Greece in Brussels.

In Thessalonika, the intra-Orthodox meeting drew up regulations both for the revision of our relations with the World Council of Churches and for our participation in its deliberations and worship.

The Mother Church keeps an eye on the development of all Orthodox churches throughout the world. We are grieved at the problems of the Churches of Bulgaria, Ukraine, and Estonia.

We visited the metropolitanates of the Ecumenical Throne as well as other Orthodox and non-Orthodox churches. These visits have produced much good will and will continue in the future.

There is not enough time to tell you everything about the following: intra-Christian and interreligious dialogues, initiatives dedicated to the protection of our environment, the celebration of the first millennium of Xenophontos Monastery on Mount Athos, the restoration of the Megali tou Genous Scholi (Great School of the Nation),[42] the reopening of the Theological School of Halki, the preparation of the Great and Holy Synod, and so on. With regard to the latter, please read about the process leading to the Great Synod in the journals *Episkepsis*,[43] *Klironomia*,[44] and *Orthodoxia*.[45]

In closing, we turn over the meeting to the other speakers. It is our hope that the Lord will help us to help one another, by sending down on

---

42. The continuation of the Great Patriarchal School of Byzantium, in its current structure, the school has functioned as an institution of learning for some 550 years, since being established by the Ecumenical Patriarch in 1456, immediately following the fall of Constantinople in 1453.

43. The formal weekly newsletter of the Orthodox Center of the Ecumenical Patriarchate in Chambésy, Geneva. The journal first appeared in 1970, edited by Metropolitan Damaskinos of Switzerland (now retired and currently metropolitan of Adrianoupolis).

44. The formal quarterly publication of the Patriarchal School of Patristic Studies, located at Vlatadon Monastery in Thessalonika and founded in 1969. Among the founders and original editors of the journal was Archbishop Stylianos of Australia.

45. *Orthodoxia* first appeared in 1926, and publication was interrupted in 1963, when the printing press of the Ecumenical Patriarchate was closed by the Turkish government. It resumed publication under Ecumenical Patriarch Bartholomew in 1994.

us the abundant grace of His Holy Spirit. For, without this, we will not be able to understand or do anything.

Synaxis of Bishops, Ecumenical Patriarchate, September 1, 2002

> Address to the synaxis of bishops within the immediate jurisdiction of the Ecumenical Patriarchate throughout the world

THE HISTORY OF OUR ASSEMBLIES

According to our established custom,[46] we have gathered again this year for a brotherly synaxis in order to discuss in a fraternal manner the most important spiritual issues that we face in the pastoral care of the sacred metropolises that have been entrusted to us. We address to all, those who were able to come and those who were not, a salutation of love and honor, and we welcome those present to the courts of the Mother Church, the Great Church of Christ. We wish you a pleasant stay, a good outcome to the discussions, illumination from God, and the presence in our midst of the Holy Spirit and of Christ Himself, in whose name we have gathered.

As is known to all of you, the issues that concerned us at the first synaxis of the hierarchy of the Ecumenical Throne in 1994 were mainly pastoral and included the issue of mixed marriages and the problems related to it, the present state of the liturgy and the measures that need to be taken, clerical vocations and education of our clergy, and theological dialogues.

At the second synaxis of 1996 we studied the alien environment within which the majority of the Orthodox *omogeneia*[47] finds itself. We concentrated especially on various aspects of Western civilization, the mass media, and contemporary society.

In 1998, our third synaxis focused its attention on the self-consciousness of the Orthodox Church and studied the basic theme "Being Conscientiously Orthodox" and the subthemes of metaphysical experiences

---

46. From the outset of his tenure, Ecumenical Patriarch Bartholomew organized regular assemblies for presiding heads of autocephalous Orthodox churches (since 1992) as well as biennial assemblies of hierarchs within the jurisdiction of the Ecumenical Patriarchate throughout the world (since 1994).

47. I.e., community based on common roots, religious or cultural.

outside Orthodoxy as well as of secularization and heterodox influences on the Orthodox ethos and mind.

The year 2000 was dedicated to the anniversary event and celebration of the second millennium since the birth of Christ.

As it appears from the list of themes discussed in our preceding synaxis meetings, our concern has been, on the one hand, about our self-consciousness as Orthodox (especially in 1998) and, on the other hand, about the challenges posed by the different religions and the foreign world that surrounds us. The proper personal and pastoral response to these challenges requires full knowledge of the specific qualitative difference between our faith and other worldviews. It requires as well a clear demarcation between right and wrong ideas or convictions that circulate both among Orthodox and among non-Orthodox in the societies in which we live. In this way, we are able to prevent the general membership of the Orthodox Church from unrestrainedly adopting the wrong ideas and convictions that seem often to prevail in society at large—ideas and convictions that in a certain way turn to naught the specific qualitative difference between the Orthodox faith and other faiths or that have the effect of associating this faith with what are in fact secondary issues, such as the calendar issue, the ethnic origin of the Orthodox, and so forth.

SPIRITUALITY, DOCTRINE, AND MISSION

In light of this it was deemed helpful in this year's synaxis to continue to delve into the self-consciousness of the Orthodox Church and to study the foremost theme of the purpose of the Church and of our Christian life as well as the practical consequences of that purpose for contemporary humanity in general. We will consider this theme under the following four subthemes: virtue and holiness, the dogma and life of the Orthodox Christian, dogmatic sensitivity and excesses or deficits, and the decision between Orthodox isolationism and sacred missionary outreach to the heterodox.

Surely all of us know in theory the purpose of the Church and of the Christian life, which is our personal incorporation and the incorporation of our flocks into Christ. The purpose is not simply that we "put aside" evil or aim for an anthropocentric acquisition of the virtues but that we "put on" Christ, "so that what is mortal might be swallowed up by life," in the graphic expression of the Apostle Paul (2 Cor. 5.4). We all know that the Orthodox Church is not a secular institution whose mission is spent in the conservation of certain traditions, either ethnocentric or religious, and in the execution of impressive Byzantine rituals. Neither is it merely a philanthropic organization that labors for the establishment of social welfare. Nor again is it merely an administrative register of certain generations or races, entrusted with the protection and safekeeping of these and the memory of their ancestors. Although the Orthodox Church adopts and fulfils with great interest and zeal all these duties and embraces all the problems of contemporary human society, it is nevertheless something much more important than all these. More specifically, it is the presence of the living Christ among human beings—Christ extended unto the ages of ages.

And so, by returning to the theme of the purpose of the Church and of the life of the believer, we do not seek to find a theoretical response to an academic question. We seek rather to stimulate a self-examination and self-awareness concerning the question of how far in our daily pastoral care this purpose or, rather, this supreme objective of coming to be in Christ and thereby being sanctified, both in the case of ourselves and our flocks, retains the priority it deserves, or whether it is obscured by our preoccupation with the cares of this life and the variety of our other duties or is even entirely overlooked.

This is because, as is known, we were given the apostolic command "to apply ourselves to good deeds so as to help cases of urgent need" (Titus 3.14). We are obliged, therefore, to make provisions for practical philanthropy, instruction, liturgical order, and the preservation, renovation, and complete reconstruction of necessary buildings as well as for catechism, the publication of books and periodicals, and the organizing of activities—all of which contribute to the solidarity of the faithful in the Church, to inter-Christian relations, and so much more. All these, however, must take place in relation to and always in light of the main and fundamental purpose of the Orthodox Church and the Christian life, and not in ignorance of it. We must not turn the Orthodox Church into an anthropocentric organization that serves only these temporal goals and maintains a Byzantine ritual tradition only externally. Such a process leads to secularization, is oblivious to the true presence of divine grace and of the Holy Spirit as the comforter in the life of the Church and of the believer, and debases the Orthodox Church to the level of a humanistic confession, or like a man-centered religion, well organized and active but ontologically deprived of the transforming experience of the presence of Christ and of the Holy Spirit in its daily life.

Contemporary man seeks, in a way similar to that of any man of any other epoch, the transcendence of corruption and death, of captivity and slavery, which he experiences as a suffocating grip and strangulation of his existence. He shakes off his existential anguish by engaging in a variety of activities, through which he tries to fill his existential emptiness and to give meaning to his meaningless life. However, in moments of quietness he is confronted with the agonizing question: What is the purpose of life? What is the purpose of any endeavor and success sealed by the gravestone? This is why he listens with great interest to the deceiving sirens of various religions that promise metaphysical paradise and lead to well-known mass suicides, to acts of escape from this difficult world and its anguished reality, and to supposed entry into a paradise of the afterlife, or to psychedelic or ecstatic experiences, into which some enter through the influence of harmful substances that cause sensualist or mental disturbances, false sensations, and even death.

ONE THING ALONE IS NECESSARY

The Apostle Paul graphically describes the captivity of the man who practices not the good that he desires but rather the evil that he does not want and who cries out in agony, "Wretched man that I am! Who will deliver me from this body of death?" (Rom. 7.24). He also gives the answer, from direct experience: "Thanks be to God through Jesus Christ our Lord" (Rom. 7.25). Are we in a position to declare to contemporary man that we have the experience of obtaining in and through Christ this freedom from the body of death, that we obtain it because we have passed with Christ from death to life, experience the miracle of the Resurrection as a vivid reality, and possess the grace that can make him, contemporary man, alive too? Can we offer immortality in Christ as something that we possess, or can we hand it over as something that we received in our very being from our Church Fathers and from Christ and the Holy Spirit?

If yes, then we serve the main purpose of the Orthodox Church, which is the concrete gospel of the trampling down of death and slavery by

Christ and by those who believe in Him; this is also the dawn of freedom and immortality that is in Christ for every believer; the unburdening of all "those who labor and are heavy laden" (Matt. 11.28) from the weight of their guilt, insecurity, and threat of destruction so that they may enter instead into the land of inner peace, joy, and knowledge of the person in Christ, meek and humble in heart—a knowledge that is equal to eternal life.

Daily works, administration, the meeting of social and pastoral needs, serving at table, education, catechism—these will never cease or be laid aside. But neither should "the one thing that alone is needful" (Luke 10.42) be neglected. The feeling of eternal life in Christ and in the Holy Spirit is clearly distinguished from all the abovementioned concerns. Yet, this feeling is not an intellectual or emotional conception of ideas, a conception that constitutes a depiction of a reality that we have not beheld and touched. Rather, it is a personal experience of grace, a personal and true experience of the dazzling presence of Christ and of the Holy Spirit, a sincere and affirmative response to the question that the Apostle put to those who had been baptized in the baptism of John, asking "whether they received the Holy Spirit" (Acts 19.2).

This presence of the Holy Spirit in our life and in the life of our Church is the main purpose of the Church's existence and of our life, resulting in our Church's ecumenicity and catholicity being sown within our heart, just as in the vision of Peter before visiting Cornelius. It is this sense that also gives wing to our sacrificial love and makes rivers of living water gush forth from our lips and our entire existence, refreshing thirsty souls. It is this sense again that raises up through our humility the burdens of human beings and soothes their wounds and pains; and this again, that, in a word, constitutes the specific qualitative difference of the Orthodox Church vis-à-vis any other confession or religion.

DOCTRINE AND LIFE: BELIEVING AND DOING

The clarification of certain related issues is intended to occur through the development of the specified subthemes. In the subtheme of virtue and sanctity, the intention is to stress that virtue alone, as characterizing a life congruent with the dictates of ethics, does not suffice for the Orthodox Christian. Surely the Christian has to be virtuous as a matter of duty.

The Apostle Paul presumably means this when he writes that "if there is any virtue or any praise, think about these things" (Phil. 4.8). Yet, the Christian ought to proceed beyond the virtuous life and move forward to self-sanctification—in other words, to union with Christ through love, prayer, the sacraments, and adherence to His will. And so, through self-purification, the Christian becomes the dwelling place of Christ and of the Holy Spirit, as Christ lives in him, and he has the mind of Christ and the heart of Christ and all his virtue being related to Christ. This is because the Orthodox Christian is not simply socially and individually conformed to the dictates of humanist-centered and social-centered ethics. He who lives in communion with Christ becomes, as a result, virtuous according to measure of the commandments of Christ.

This is also related to the theme of dogma and life. It is held by many, and especially by Protestants, but also (through the influence of Protestants) by many Orthodox, that virtuous life is sufficient and that to be concerned with the doctrines of the faith is superfluous. The truth, however, that dogma specifies is not only life in the spiritual condition of man vis-à-vis God and his fellow human beings but also the various pressing, temporal questions relating to life on earth.

Between him who feels that God is a judge that punishes and him who feels that God is a father that is merciful and forgiving, the difference in the attitude to life is huge. Consider a spiritual father who sees himself as a judge appointed to pronounce penalties relative to the weight of transgressions, and compare him to a spiritual father who sees himself as a healer, empowered to heal the spiritual wounds of the believer—in these two approaches to a penitent, there is an abyss of difference. One who recognizes that God loves him, despite his being a sinner, or that he can come to God as he is, feels different from one who mistakenly thinks that he must first purify and prepare himself with his own efforts before approaching Christ. The first approaches without hesitation and receives the gift of forgiveness, while the second, in order to approach God worthily, struggles anxiously to achieve his own deliverance from evil, which is unobtainable through human means; thus, the second remains constantly estranged from God.

These are some examples of how dogmatic truth influences positively or negatively the life of the believer. And surely there are many more such examples. So we are not speaking here of particular dogmatic teachings but of dogmatic truth, which has direct bearing on the human psyche and forms the believer's attitude to various issues in life. Stressing, for instance, the love of God as His supreme righteousness, which constitutes a dogmatic truth, places at rest many souls that find themselves before the gates of despair because of a great fear stemming from awareness of their sins. If this fear is not dispelled by the certainty of divine love and the forgiveness granted through repentance and confession, it changes man into an atheist, the result of fruitless individual efforts to overcome that fear. For in this case man thinks that, if he is to believe in a God who punishes and live with the anguish of being rejected by this judgmental God, then it is preferable for him not to believe in God at all, so that he might avoid the prospect of divine punishment.

We can indeed say that the basic reason for the widespread establishment of atheism in the West is the erroneous doctrine of God as judge, punisher, and oppressor, a doctrine propagated by some circles and theologians in the Roman Catholic Church in the past. It is necessary, then, that we Orthodox project our faith—articulated in all doctrinal teachings—concerning God's love and saving intervention through Christ in history. Without this foundation of faith, the simple, virtuous life deteriorates into humanism—that is, into secularized faith—and is transposed to the lower level of man-centered social ethics. It is evident that, in most cases, when the Orthodox faith is rightly expounded and presented, it gives rest to man's soul, when he is well disposed, and he feels joyful and comforted on hearing this truth.

Indeed, on hearing this Orthodox (that is, in the sense of *right*) doctrine and faith, the soul of the listener usually comes to realize the freedom that truth offers. The bonds of anxiety and the inner reactions against a lie that tries to impose itself as truth are dissolved and cease to operate, because the innermost divine origins of human consciousness recognize Orthodox truth as being in harmony with what human existence seeks to hear, even without knowing it.

Therefore it behooves us, in every case that our doctrine provokes some negative reaction, to search whether this results from our transgression from what is right or from personal reasons on the part of the one who is reacting, reasons that make that person unwilling to accept the truth. Unfortunately, much Orthodox literature in recent centuries has been infiltrated by the influence of those who studied in countries and schools where Roman Catholic and Protestant thinking prevail. Sometimes doctrines deviating from the Orthodox faith even dominate and are believed by many clergymen who accept them in good faith as Orthodox.[48] As a result, the return to the sources—to the mind of the recognized Orthodox Church Fathers[49]—is necessary and far preferable to the study of dubious contemporary books and scholarship. A wide selection of contemporary publications has made available the writings of the Holy Fathers, while many modern scholars point out various errors of earlier or contemporary theologians who unquestionably accepted as Orthodox certain erroneous doctrines of others.

ORTHODOX AND HETERODOX: SPEAKING THE TRUTH IN LOVE

In addressing the above dilemmas, we come to the third of our subthemes concerning doctrinal sensitivity and its successes and deficiencies. The middle way and royal measure is indicated by the Holy Fathers as leading to the truth in reality—that is, to thinking and acting rightly. Nevertheless, every day we witness cases where deficiently trained members of our Orthodox Church take extreme positions, either denying the significance of doctrine in the life of our Church and of the faithful, and standing only on the their own good reputation, or treating as doctrinal those issues that have no dogmatic significance whatsoever—issues such as the calendar issue, cooperation on practical and social matters between the various churches and religions, social relations between local ecclesiastical leaders and those of the heterodox, and so on.

Indifference to doctrine undermines interest in the truth. But the excessive treatment of minutiae in doctrinal issues, which demand special training and the inspiration of the Holy Spirit for right understanding and proper articulation, entails the danger that the believer might put aside what directly concerns his salvation and instead try to become an expert and judge on issues in which he is not competent to pass judgment

---

48. See John Zizioulas, *Being as Communion: Studies in Personhood and the Church* (New York: St. Vladimir's Seminary Press, 1997); and Christos Yannaras, *The Freedom of Morality*, tr. Elizabeth Briere (New York: St. Vladimir's Seminary Press, 1984).

49. For more on the "return to the sources" and "the mind of the Fathers," see the Georges Florovsky, *The Collected Works of Georges Florovsky* (Belmont, Mass.: Nordland, 1972–90), especially vol. 1 *Bible, Church, Tradition*.

and does not understand. Unfortunately, daily experience has supplied many examples of those who assert that doctrine has no importance or others, especially theologians or "theologizers," who search for doctrinal errors in ecclesiastical speeches and texts, projecting their knowledge as superior to that of others. And of course, whenever this is a matter of a suggestion being made in good faith, such intervention is praiseworthy and desirable. But when it is an attack launched in bad faith, perhaps with great passion, or when it is a matter of personal disputation and name-calling, we find ourselves in the presence of something unhealthy, which we ought to expose with meekness and kindness in order to help and heal those affected.

The last and more specific theme of our synaxis is related to the discovery of the golden line of demarcation in relations that members of the Orthodox Church have with members of other confessions or religions. The problem of course assumes a different form in lands where the Orthodox are the majority than in lands where they constitute a minority.

In lands where Orthodox Christians prevail, contact and courtesy between Orthodox and heterodox often meet with protest or are characterized as compromising with Christian doctrine or comprising interreligious syncretism. In lands where the Orthodox constitute a minority, frequent and inevitable contact of Orthodox with heterodox and other fellow citizens of other religions, together with the increase in professional collaboration or in the context of social and even family relations, deflects such criticism, so that social relations and collaboration between religious leaders on matters of practical and common interest becomes acceptable and inevitable.

The basis of the protests of those who disagree is, on the one hand, the instruction of the Apostle Paul to Titus: "As for a man who is a heretic, after admonishing him once or twice, have nothing more to do with him, knowing that such a person is perverted and sinful being self-condemned" (Titus 3.10–11). On the other hand, in the sacred canons, we have the prohibition regarding common prayer between Orthodox and heretics or between Orthodox and members of other religions.

However, we must understand this admonition of the Apostle Paul in the context of the conditions under which it was pronounced and of the pastoral problems that St. Paul faced at that time. This is indeed in accordance with the instructions of St. John Chrysostom and St. Basil the

Great,[50] who stressed that the right understanding of the Word of God and of the Church Fathers is always related to the historical circumstances under which it was pronounced.

At that early point, then, in the history of Christianity, when the Epistle to Titus was written, the appearance of a heterodox teacher or heretic was an isolated phenomenon for the Church, and the attempt to bring such a person back to the right faith of the Church was an action that related only to one of her members that was ailing. Therefore, the abandonment of this attempt was justified whenever it became apparent that the member who had been deceived by heresy remained unrepentant.

Today, outside the Orthodox Church there are many people of goodwill who have never consciously chosen heresy but were simply born within heterodox confessions. Surely, it is not possible for us to approach each one of them and explain to them once or twice the sound Orthodox doctrine and faith; and it is not reasonable for us, if they refuse to be persuaded, to abandon our effort with them and turn toward another. And so we engage in open dialogues with representatives of various Christian confessions.

These dialogues are conducted with specific persons, but they are not pursued for their own sake and only with the goal that our partners in dialogue be persuaded and converted. Rather, the dialogues take place with all those whom the specific persons represent. Hence, given that we do not know how the word of God, which is sharper than any double edged sword, operates in the hearts of heterodox who are unknown to us and of the many others who will experience the results of our discussions with the representatives of their faith, we are obliged to bear witness to the truth continually, without counting how often we spoke or whether we were heeded by our interlocutors. Beyond these, there are thousands of other indirect interlocutors who are in dialogue with us. Many of these, caught by the net of the word of God, which is cast out through these dialogues, embrace the Orthodox faith and Church, which would have remained unknown to them had we not spoken.

---

50. Basil the Great (330–79) was bishop of Caesarea in Cappadocia, a remarkable theologian of reconciliation, a prominent ascetic leader, and an extraordinarily compassionate pastor.

The way in which St. John of the Ladder[51] interprets this particular apostolic admonition is significant in this regard. In his discourse "On Discernment," he observes: "In the case of unbelievers or wrong-believers, who malevolently dispute with us, we should cease to engage in dialogue after a first and a second admonition; but in the case of those who desire to learn the truth, we do nothing wrong by being good to them always; however, we consider both these options according to the stability of our heart."[52] This distinction proposed by St. John is very wise and spiritual.

If a heretic or heterodox is of bad faith, then the order to abandon any further discussion after a second admonition is clearly applicable. If, however, such a person truly desires to learn the truth, then we must be in dialogue with him "always," without weariness and without counting either labor or sacrifice. In both cases, our attitude must be commensurate with the strength and endurance of our soul. Therefore, if anyone runs the risk of being led astray by the erroneous doctrines of his interlocutor, he must interrupt this dialogue; but if there is no such danger, he can continue his pursuit.

It is in a similar way and with great discernment that this Holy Father deals with the matter of sharing of meals with heretics. In his *Letter to the Shepherd*,[53] he writes: "The weak should not share meals with heretics, as ordered by the canons; only those who are strong in the Lord, if invited by unbelievers in good faith and wishing to go, should go for the glory of the Lord."[54] Therefore, sharing meals with heretics is left to the discernment and spiritual endurance of those invited. Here again the pinnacle of virtues—namely, discernment—will provide the fitting solution, leading the faithful to seek the spirit of the canon and not the letter, which, according to the Apostle, kills.

On the other hand, we are obliged, in order to avoid scandalizing the weaker brethren, to pay special attention to relations with the heterodox,

---

51. Also known as St. John Climacus, seventh-century abbot on Mt. Sinai and influential author of *The Ladder of Divine Ascent*.

52. See *Ladder*, Step 26, ii, 11.

53. An appendix to the *Ladder*, addressed to a fellow abbot, and sometimes considered the Thirty-First Step, this letter or treatise describes the role and responsibility of a spiritual elder within a community.

54. Paragraph 65.

because it often happens that this is not rightly understood and our free-dom in Christ is misinterpreted or even condemned. This is indeed the spirit of the well-known patriarchal encyclical of 1952,[55] in which avoiding common prayer with heterodox is recommended. Surely, the interpreta-tion given by the zealots, who are lacking in full knowledge, to the term "common prayer," which is characterized as any prayer offered by us in a place and a time where heterodox are present, is excessively broad, because it ignores the spiritual element—that is, the will to address a common petition to the same God. When such a will does not exist, then there is merely synchronization of prayers offered separately by each party engag-ing in prayer to their own God. This is what happened during the sailing of the ship that carried the prophet Jonah, when each of the passengers cried out to his own God for the salvation of the ship, while Jonah was asked to cry out to his own God too. This was not a case of prohibited common prayer but of prayers offered simultaneously despite their being clearly separate from each other, inasmuch as they were addressed to dif-ferent persons.

On all these themes, however, we will have the joy and satisfaction to hear the detailed communications from experts who have been sum-moned here to introduce them. This is why we will not elaborate further at this point. We fervently thank the standing sacred synod of the Most Holy Church of Greece, led by its president, His Beatitude Archbishop Christodoulos of Athens and All Greece, for readily responding to our invitation and petition by sending two select and dear brethren in Christ to participate in our present sacred synaxis—their Eminences Metropoli-tans Anthimos of Alexandroupolis and Vasileios of Elasson, representing also the hierarchs of the Throne in Northern Greece, whose eparchies the prefecture has ceded in tutelage to the said sister Church. We are certain that our spiritual sharing and mutual fellowship during these days in the courts of the Mother Church will be to the benefit of both parties.

We express our deep sorrow and the sorrow of our entire brotherhood in Christ for the illness that, over the last eighteen months, has seized our

---

55. Issued on January 31 by Ecumenical Patriarch Athenagoras (1886–1972) following the creation of the World Council of Churches. See *Guidelines for Orthodox Christians in Ecumenical Relations*, prepared for the Standing Conference of Canonical Orthodox Bish-ops in America, New York, 1973.

brother, His Eminence Metropolitan Damaskinos of Switzerland, and for the subsequent and more grievous illness of our brother, His Eminence Geron Metropolitan Meliton of Chalcedon. Their illnesses deprive us of the joy of their presence in our midst and of their invaluable contribution, from different and crucial junctures and frontline bastions, to the work of the Church. Let us pray, brethren, for their safe return in health to the active life of the Church; "what is impossible for us is possible for God!"

At the same time, however, we express the joy and satisfaction of the Mother Church for the recent decisions of the Great Turkish National Council to adapt the legislation of this land to the European prototypes and to do this in view of the effort to facilitate Turkey's induction into the European Union. This means greater democratization and increased respect for human rights, including the rights of minorities and especially the right of religious freedom, with all that this implies for the Mother Church and the *omogeneia* residing here. The mechanism has already been established for returning to our communities and the various charitable institutions the properties that had been arbitrarily and unjustly confiscated from them. A special committee, under the presidency of our brother the metropolitan of Philadelphia, has been summoned for following up on and promoting these vital matters of immediate concern to us. But what is of primary interest for us here is that, in the context of these positive developments, we hope that it will become more and more possible to have our brother hierarchs who are outside Turkey participate in the administration of the Ecumenical Patriarchate.[56] Indeed, it was with this hopeful prospect in mind that a special committee was constituted for the study of this matter, a committee under the presidency of His Eminence Metropolitan of Perga and of their Eminences Metropolitans of Elioupolis and Thirai, Tyroloe and Serention, Pergamon, and Philadelphia. We express the wish that in the near future we may enjoy the possibility that, through the worthy recruitment of the wisdom and

---

56. This historical proposal by His All Holiness came to fruition in September 2004, when the Holy and Sacred Synod invited and included six (of a total of twelve) members from the various eparchies or churches within the direct jurisdiction of the Ecumenical Patriarchate, with representatives from various regions, including one from the United States, one from the autonomous church of Crete, one from the Dodecanese islands in Greece, one from Western Europe, and two from Canada, South America, or Australasia and Asia.

experience of all our most honorable and very dear hierarchs from every part of the world, this work will benefit the Mother Church and lead to its greater efficacy as well to the efficacy of its ministry and mission.

THE MINISTRY OF THE MOTHER CHURCH

At this point, we wish to mention the enrichment of the Ecumenical Patriarchate by means of an additional eparchy, the sacred metropolis of Arkalochorion, Kastellion and Viannon in Crete, whose first arch-shepherd is our brother Andreas, who is present in our midst and one of the speakers at this synaxis.

We also express the joy and honor that we all feel as a distinguished hierarch of our Mother Church, Metropolitan John of Pergamon, occupies and honors during the current year the chairmanship of the Academy of Athens. We congratulate him and thank him for giving our Church this satisfaction and pride, and we wish him health and long life.

Furthermore, we announce to this sacred gathering that:

Two months ago, we offered hospitality here privately to His Beatitude the Pope and Patriarch Peter of Alexandria, with whom we fraternally exchanged views on various matters of Orthodoxy and of a more general nature, but not in the spirit and content of a related article published in an Athenian ecclesiastical newspaper.

A month ago, their Eminences the Metropolitans of Perga and Philadelphia were sent to Tirana, bearing the congratulations of the Mother Church to His Beatitude Archbishop Anastasios on the completion of ten years from his election by our holy and sacred synod and from his enthronement as first hierarch of the unsettled and grievously suffering Church of Albania. It was he who reconstituted and reorganized this Church in an amazing way, so that, as we said on another occasion, it has been transformed from a problem to a source of pride for the Ecumenical Patriarchate, which, having the duty and responsibility to support the sister churches in times of trouble, attempted and was able to assist effectively this Church as well.

During the first five days of this next November, we will receive an official visit of peace by His Beatitude Archbishop Nicholas of the Czech Lands and Slovakia, whose church and flock were lately tested by floods and other natural calamities that befell most of central Europe.

The delegations of the Churches of Constantinople and Moscow will soon meet anew to continue at this time their cooperation in the task of finding a solution for the Ukrainian ecclesiastical problem and of the reunification of the Orthodox dwelling there as a unified canonical church.

As for the Estonian ecclesiastical problem, it appears that it is proceeding toward a final solution and arrangement after the cooperation of the two same patriarchates on this matter and with the involvement of the Estonian government.

We would also like to announce to your love that an attempt was made to publish in Greek all the discourses of our Modesty—the texts delivered during our various pastoral visits to the eparchies of the Throne and to other churches as well as in other circumstances. The first volume of this series has already been circulated and will be distributed to you as a token of honor and love. Future volumes may be secured by your editorial departments for your libraries.

At this point, we remind you that there is in operation in Geneva, at the Center of the Ecumenical Patriarchate there, a department of postgraduate studies in Orthodox theology, and we kindly ask you to direct there any competent postgraduate students who can discern the differences between the Orthodox doctrine and deviating views, so that a fuller Orthodox self-consciousness, which we will discuss in our synaxis, might be created.

In the context of the dialogue between the monotheistic religions—Judaism, Christianity and Islam—which has been promoted for some years now by the Ecumenical Patriarchate, we visited Bahrain two years ago this past January, and we intend to respond to a similar invitation by the state of Qatar for a visit there around the middle of next October. At the same time, as you know, brethren, we have summoned in Brussels, last Christmas Eve, the Feast of Peace par excellence, in collaboration with the president of the European Union, His Excellency Mr. Romano Prodi, a meeting of high-ranking representatives of the three monotheistic religions. The signing of the Statement of Brussels ensued, a copy of which can be found in the envelope before you. We announce to you in this connection that, after the illness of the metropolitan of Switzerland, we have handed over the responsibility for the dialogues with Islam and Judaism to His Grace Bishop Emmanuel of Region, director of the Office of the Orthodox Church in the European Union, who has in turn laid the groundwork for us to convene here in Istanbul, at the beginning of October, the new phase of bilateral dialogue with Judaism and, in Bahrain during the same month, the bilateral dialogue with the Muslims.

Concluding our address, we embrace you once again with our whole-hearted salutation and fervent prayer for a pleasant stay here and for the successful completion of the proceedings of this synaxis, so that, with God's grace, our present assembly may gradually assume the official character of a synod of the hierarchy of the Ecumenical Throne. These historic developments offer us hope that this desire will become an achievable reality. May God so grant.

International Clergy–Laity Congress, Ecumenical Patriarchate, November 27, 2000

THE PARISH AS NUCLEUS OF CHURCH LIFE

We welcome all the participants of this Clergy–Laity Congress with warm paternal and brotherly greetings: Their Eminences the hierarchs, the reverend fathers, distinguished presenters, and select participants. We express our joy for the realization of this event as well as our hope that beneficial and practical conclusions will ensue.

The Holy Great Church of Christ, the Mother Church, convened this representative clergy–laity gathering of its holy metropolitanates and parishes from all over the world in order to reexamine existing parish practices for the improvement of relationships among all parishioners, including parish priests. The Mother Church does not desire to impose any views or organizational systems, which she might recommend for application. It does, however, desire that certain improvements may result from a careful awareness of existing situations, from a detailed study of ideal models, and from a prayerful exploration of existing possibilities.

That each of us belongs to some parish, and that we have some experience in how a particular parish functions, does not mean that we are fully aware of how it should indeed function. The same applies, for instance, to the fact that, while we each have a soul and body, together with some experience of its inner workings, we may not necessarily have full knowledge of our soul and of our bodies. We do not always recognize, nor are we always aware of, precisely how or what affects our psychological circumstances and our bodily health, the reason we feel sad or happy, or what changes we must endure in order to improve our lives.

Certainly, however, we are not completely ignorant in this regard. Undoubtedly, we notice that some of our actions, or certain foods, habits, and relationships, may either harm us or benefit us. We recognize these things either from personal experience or through study and an exchange of opinions. We may also recognize some things from intuition, while others through divine enlightenment. But this knowledge is not sufficient in itself. We are continuously advised either by specialists, by people who are more experienced, or else by our friends, about other experiences when we converse with them and experiment in an effort to improve our general health.

It was precisely for this reason, then, that we decided to convene this conference in which participants from all around the world may deliberate together, over the course of several days, about our greater "body" (namely, the Church as the body of Christ) and our collective "soul" (namely, the parish as the living cell in that divine organism). Around the sacred sacrificial altar, all faithful gather and join together in the body and blood of Christ, which creates unity in Christ and transforms all members into one body. This body contains the totality of the fullness of the Church inasmuch as it has a head and body and blood, comprising the fullness of the body of Christ. The members of the parish gather around the entire body of Christ. By virtue of the bishop's authority, the priest assumes the position of the bishop, which is necessary for the existence of the Church. It is for this reason that the parish, together with its bishop (or its priest acting in the name of the bishop), fully constitutes the one, holy, catholic, and apostolic Church.

Consequently, the Church as body of Christ serves as the ideal prototype for the flawless organization and administration of the parish. If we recognize how Christ wants His Church to function, and if we compare today's existing parish to the ideal, then we will become aware of any existing deficiencies as well as of any possibilities for change. It is not always appropriate for us to proceed with abrupt leaps toward perfection; for the body cannot tolerate abrupt changes. Our Lord taught us discernment in many ways. He informed His disciples that He had much to tell them, but He did not convey everything at once, because it was not possible for them to bear all that He had to tell them at that particular moment. He also often spoke in parables so that those listening could gradually advance in wisdom and understanding. His transfiguration occurred before only three of His disciples, because the others were not yet sufficiently mature for this revelation. Many miracles were performed before these same three but were not always confessed to the others. He enlightened the Apostle Paul to introduce the faithful gradually to deeper truths and to say, "I fed you milk and not solid food; for you are still spiritually infants" (1 Cor. 3.1–2). Consequently, with an understanding of the existing situation and with an awareness of the ideal with regard to parish life, we will be able to determine what must be done, who must do it, what means are required, what means are available, and how we may discover what is in fact missing.

LIVING EXPERIENCE AND CONTEMPORARY CHALLENGES

As we know, originally the parish did not always exist in today's form. The first local churches were small in membership and constituted a community under a bishop. As the number of Christians increased in the Church and there were insufficient means to serve them, the bishop ordained priests and established other spaces as churches so that the Holy Eucharist could be celebrated in the name of the bishop. The local bishop also set the boundaries of the region within which Christians of that area would be served by priests in a specific church building. These parishes[57] developed *within their boundaries*, defined by local areas or regions within which Christians would be ministered to in each church building and by the priest or priests serving there.

At the time, no distinction was made with respect to the ethnic origins of the faithful. The specific location of each resident, and not his or her race or ethnicity, determined the parish to which he or she belonged. In this way, various pastoral needs were met, although with some exceptions. For example, our predecessor on the Throne of Constantinople, St. John Chrysostom, assigned a special church for the liturgical purposes of the Goths in Constantinople, because of the linguistic difference. From these historical facts, two conclusions may be drawn: first, that the organization of today's parish must arise from local conditions; and second, that this rule, or canon, allows exceptions on a parish level for pastoral reasons. Exceptions on the levels of bishop, archbishop, or metropolitan were unknown in Church history until the recent phenomenon of the so-called Diaspora, where the application of sacred canons was suspended (namely, those canons that specifically prohibit the existence of two hierarchs in one and the same area).

---

57. *Enoria*, the Greek word for "parish," literally means "within boundaries."

Each of today's parishes of the holy archdioceses, metropolitanates, and dioceses of the Ecumenical Throne may, on the basis of the linguistic composition of the *omogeneia* within their congregations, be assigned to one of four categories: 1) existing areas where the element of the *omogeneia* constitutes almost the entire congregation, which, for example, would also include parishes in Crete and the Dodecannese, and so on; 2) existing areas where the element of the *omogeneia* constitutes the majority, but the parish also contains Orthodox from other ethnic backgrounds, because there are no specific parishes that might cater to their pastoral needs; 3) existing areas where other ecclesiastical jurisdictions have developed their own parishes; and 4) areas where those Orthodox from other ethnic backgrounds in fact constitute the majority of the congregation. Clearly, it is for pastoral reasons and not, of course, for ecclesiological purposes that the distinctions between these categories are actually made.

With regard to the size of parish membership, two distinctions may be drawn: 1) those parishes with small membership, such as those in villages and towns; and 2) those with large membership, such as in large cities. With regard to organization, two further groups may be distinguished: 1) those parishes organized on a purely ecclesiastical basis—in other words, without the political community becoming involved in ecclesiastical issues; and 2) those parishes organized in relation to the communities of the *omogeneia*, where the Church participates directly in all matters—such as education, philanthropy, or other community activities—that are not purely ecclesiastical; otherwise, the community may participate in ecclesiastical matters, such as, for example, financial expenses of the community, and so forth.

All of the above show the Church's flexibility with respect to local conditions and circumstances, the Church's purpose being to serve the faithful. At the same time, these provisions also lead to a great deal of diversity, such that identical approaches to parish life, approaches that are at the same time authentic, cannot easily be executed. Still, this variety, together with the accompanying richness of experience, leads to new ideas and to their practical application, ideas that would suit the conditions of each parish individually. Consequently, we would like to express certain general thoughts, rather than those pertaining to specific practical matters, since it is the parish priest and parish council who would determine the questions of how and why a specific parish would take a particular direction. We believe, then, that the fundamental pastoral and spiritual guiding principles for every parish are as follows.

ATTRACTING THE DEDICATED WITHOUT NEGLECTING THE LUKEWARM

As is known, in every parish, Orthodox Christians of varying degrees of zeal and instruction may be found. It sometimes happens that the parish priest and parish council direct their interest to those few who are least connected with the Orthodox Church, and, in order to attract them, the priest and council sometimes secularize the affairs of the Church. We consider this method to be wrong. The parish must direct the weight of its attention to the more devout among its faithful, who also are more willing to help in parish work by accepting different tasks and gladly offering their financial contribution, even from whatever little they might have. For it is these parishioners who will also be the basic support of the parish and constitute its daily congregation. This does not mean that the parish priest and parish council should be indifferent toward other parishioners. Nevertheless, the *typikon*[58] given to us by our forefathers, for example, should not be changed in order to satisfy those who are less connected to the parish, a move that would otherwise alienate the more devout—namely, the faithful who would be liable to turn away and perhaps fall victim to various schismatic groups that supposedly profess zeal and commitment to tradition. All of you know that these schismatic groups gather many devout people and grow with despite financial problems and regardless of their small number. Of course, we are not focusing on financial factors here, but we do consider it a fundamental pastoral error for the parish to try, by means that displease and repel those who are more dedicated in faith, to attract those who are less religious.

Perhaps the essential methodology of a parish priest becomes clearer in the following examples. If, on the one hand, conditions are such that the ecclesiastical music during Sunday's Divine Liturgy becomes Western in style (for instance, by introducing chanting in four-part harmony), repelling those who prefer the traditional Byzantine style, then the parish priest

---

58. Greek for "rule of life" or "rule of prayer" within a particular parish or monastic community.

should regularly conduct evening Divine Liturgies with traditional Byzantine chant to attract those who prefer this form of music. If, on the other hand, conditions demand the celebration of certain anniversaries with purely secular events (such as a lunch at a hotel or other such festivities), then the parish priest should also organize the celebration of the Divine Liturgy, vespers, or an *artoklasia*,[59] to be followed by a reception in the church hall, where there could be refreshments or perhaps speeches and songs. This creates a spirit of familiarity, uniting the entire parish, while at the same time dispelling accusations that the Church is being secularized, or that it shows little concern for its devout faithful.

ADHERING TO TRADITION: LITURGY AND PARISH

This guiding principle concerns mainly those parishes in multi-denominational societies, which influence Orthodox parishioners and lead them to imitate customs that may appear impressive. As is known, most Orthodox in the direct jurisdiction of the Ecumenical Patriarchate have immigrated to various countries throughout the world, becoming established there, sometimes without sufficient knowledge of their Orthodox tradition, without fully being aware of its liturgical richness, and without always understanding the mystery of divine grace, which deigns to descend to the devout assembled for the holy services. Another important issue concerning parish members, and specifically those members of the second and third generations, is that, lacking in liturgical and catechetical formation, experiencing barriers between two different languages, and being influenced by the environment where they live, they are often confronted with difficulties in understanding the Orthodox rites, the deeper symbolism inherent within Orthodoxy, and the total spiritual and bodily participation of the faithful in the services, where vision, hearing, smell, taste, touch, mind, heart, word, standing, kneeling, crossing oneself, movement, gestures, and melody are all coordinated into a single and sober albeit enthusiastic doxology in praise of God.

---

59. A service normally held at the end of a festive or anniversary vespers, where five loaves are blessed, together with wheat, oil, and wine. Afterward, the loaves are broken—the term *artoklasia* literally signifies "the breaking of bread"—and distributed to the entire community as a blessing.

And so parishioners sometimes prefer the simple hymns of Protestant groups, who only worship God "in spirit," or else prefer the pompous rituals of the other Western Churches, which they endeavor to incorporate into parish life. We believe that if the wealth and purpose of each ritual practice in the Orthodox *typikon* were properly analyzed and understood, then they would in fact come to appreciate and even love it just as do those Western scholars who study it themselves. This fidelity to tradition, when properly explained to our faithful, will also have the advantage of retaining the more traditional parishioners, as we have already observed, and of relieving the parish from any—sometimes justifiable—criticism of secularization. We must of course make it clear that the Eucharistic assembly, like every other liturgical assembly of the faithful, must never be turned into a spectacle or display of emotion. The assembly is the prayer and teaching as well as the preparation of souls and bodies to accept divine grace. The parish priest and chanters are merely agents who guide the faithful to God; they do not simply provide entertainment or pleasure.

With regard to personal relationships among parishioners, and specifically between priest and parishioners, it is well known that there is a great difference between parishes in small towns and villages or between the *omogeneia* and those parishes of the Diaspora and in large cities. In smaller parishes, the priest knows each of the faithful by name and enjoys familiar, personal Christian relations with each of them; by contrast, in more populated cities, the priest must make a systematic effort to know each of his parishioners in order to develop a personal Christian relationship with all of them. This personal acquaintance of the parish priest with the faithful is necessary and must serve as the starting point of personal acquaintances and connections among the parishioners themselves. This is because the Christian parish must not be simply a numeric total of the faithful who gather together in Church on great celebrations or Sundays only to depart afterward; rather, a parish comprises a community of faithful who, as far as possible, are concerned for one another, above and beyond the limited time they spend in church.

In the development of these personal relationships, some practical applications that are found among non-Orthodox groups, properly transformed to Orthodox standards and not simply mimicked slavishly, may also be adopted in Orthodox parishes. With regard to cultivating personal relationships within the parish, we can use whatever is good from what we see around us, while avoiding blind imitation of non-Orthodox sources tainted with non-Orthodox ethos. Consequently, as declared by St. Basil the Great concerning classical yet non-Christian education, bees are able to draw whatever is good from every flower and ignore the rest. The same is true with regard to interpersonal relationships within other Christian groups: We must choose the good and reject the rest.

ORTHODOX OF DIVERSE ETHNIC BACKGROUNDS

It is well known that mixed marriages between Orthodox and non-Orthodox are increasing in number and that the children of these families, sooner or later, come to face the dilemma of which church they will belong to. Moreover, these marriages bring the non-Orthodox spouse, or people from the non-Orthodox side of the family, into contact with the Orthodox Church. Their friends as well may become acquainted with the Orthodox environment. However, unfortunately, the image presented by the Orthodox community to those who approach it is not always the best, inasmuch as it sometimes emphasizes the ethnic element over the Christian truth. Here, the need arises to achieve a proper balance of weight for each element of human identity. Those who ascribe importance to the ethnic element accuse the Church of not doing enough to preserve it; those who ascribe importance to the Christian Orthodox element accuse the Church of dealing too much with ethnic elements and of neglecting its principal work, the Christian message and Orthodox life. There are still others who cannot distinguish at all between Orthodox life and ethnic traditions or cultural elements. In this way, the Orthodox faith appears to those outside of it as divided, not unified—as something that depends on one's ethnic descent, whether Greek, Russian, Romanian, Serbian, Antiochian, and so on.

As a result, a non-Orthodox person interested in becoming Orthodox feels that he or she is receiving a strange and confusing message: namely, that in order to become Orthodox and join the Orthodox Church, one must simultaneously change one's ethnicity and become either Greek and Orthodox, or Russian and Orthodox, or else Serbian and Orthodox, and so on. This situation calls to mind those ancient times during which Christians of Jewish origin demanded that those of other ethnic backgrounds should follow the Mosaic law—that, in today's terminology, those Christians from other ethnicities should become Jewish. However, the synod of the Holy Apostles ultimately relieved them of the obligation to follow the Law of Moses. This means that, in today's terms, Orthodox Christians from different ethnicities are obliged to relieve those Orthodox from other ethnic backgrounds of the obligation to follow our own specific ethnic traditions. These traditions are to be loved and respected by all members of the Orthodox Church inasmuch as they derive from the specific nation to which each member of the faithful and their specific Mother Church belong; however, they cannot and must not be imposed on Orthodox who come from other traditions.

The pastoral treatment of those Orthodox that do not come from the *omogeneia* requires special attention, because often they have different—though not always wrong—perceptions on certain issues. Of course, we are not talking about their eligibility to join the Church. We consider their admission to our Church as their Christian duty. And we recognize that, sometimes, albeit subconsciously, there are certain fears or hesitations that arise. Here, we might recall the words of the Lord: "Him who comes to me I will not cast out" (John 6.37). Consequently, the parish is obliged by its Christian duty to find a way of accepting and accommodating those who seek to become its members. Certainly, some arrangements will be needed, such as, perhaps, special liturgies in certain languages; the publication of multilingual books with the liturgical text in order to facilitate participation in the Divine Liturgy; and so on. Or perhaps there will be another solution that parishes may be inspired to adopt, depending on the specific conditions and needs of the newly admitted faithful. However, our basic intention and goal must be that new members will always be accepted into the parish with love and warmth, with a willingness to meet their needs through appropriate arrangements and accommodations.

FOCUS ON THE SPIRITUAL LIFE

The Orthodox Church cares deeply about the entire life of the human person, including all his or her material and spiritual needs; however, the Church's primary interest is clearly centered on the holiness of the faithful. This holiness is expressed in the language of the Orthodox Church in diverse ways. We speak, for example, of the salvation of the soul, communion of the Holy Spirit, spiritual life, life in Christ, and experience of divine grace. All of these expressions imply that the faithful person lives not within himself and in the world around him but in spiritual relationship and communion with the human and divine person of Christ and with the Holy Spirit and, through them, with God the Father—in other words, with the uncreated Trinitarian Godhead. This communion is the distinctive characteristic of the Orthodox Church and its special concern within parish life. This communion also presupposes the following commandments—of repentance, purification, humility; for, without these, as it is said about holiness, "no one will see the Lord" (Heb. 12.14).

The invitation extended by the Orthodox Church to participate in the life of the Holy Spirit for communion with the uncreated Trinitarian Godhead is directed to all people and must be directed by the parish to all its members. The parish is a community of worship, a Eucharistic assembly, an eschatological community. Without ignoring the present world, and without disregarding the problems of the present life, the parish leads its members to the uncreated reality of eternal life and to the final end of the world, the recapitulation of all in Christ. We must never forget or lose sight of this goal. For if the parish forgets its primary mission as a worshipping assembly, it is reduced to a human organization with purely worldly activities and aims. In other words, it is secularized. And the secularized parish does not have any reason to exist, because it does not offer humanity the unique gift that no other institution can offer—that is, the grace (or gift) of God, which is precisely God's uncreated energy that gives life, sanctifies, and transforms.

We will not add any other fundamental principles to the abovementioned. The four points proposed and expounded here are, we believe, the mission of each parish and the characteristic of all parish activities. Most of these issues will be developed by speakers to follow. In summary, however, let us remind you that, through the first guiding principle, we emphasize the need to preserve a higher level of parish life, lest this disturb those with limited vision or those who believe that a rudimentary Christian life is sufficient. Through the second guiding principle, we stress the danger of imitating foreign, albeit impressive models, which may distance us from tradition and grace; instead, the use and appreciation of inspired models may be used to develop and nurture interpersonal relations within the parish. Through the third guiding principle, we underline the universality (not in the form of some "ecumenistic" syncretism but rather in terms of Orthodox catholicity) of the Orthodox parish. Finally, through the fourth guiding principle, we urge the characteristic of holiness, that it may always dominate the life and ministry of the parish as a place of communion with the uncreated energies of God. Let this be succinctly articulated in the four-part motto "noble, traditional, universal, and holy," which should inspire all parishioners during the transformation of parish life as it comes to realize its identity as the one, holy, catholic, and apostolic Church. In this four-fold ministry and with these four words, which are so easy to remember—noble, traditional, universal, and holy—we conclude our address and extend our blessing to all of you. We wholeheartedly wish to each of you and to all your parishes every success in your development and progress toward the unending perfection of the glory of God.

Millennial Youth Conference, Ecumenical Patriarchate, June 18, 2000

YOUTH BEFORE THE THIRD MILLENNIUM

> We praise and bless the Lord!
> Let all the earth praise His Holy Name.
> Blessed is Christ our God!

We are gathered here today in the name and by the grace of God. We have come together because two thousand years ago "the fullness of time" (Gal. 4.4) occurred and a "new child" was born to us who was "the God before all ages," "the one who opened the heavens and descended on earth for the life of the world." We have come together also because on the great and holy day of Pentecost the promise of our risen Lord was fulfilled, when He comforted the disciples with the words: "I will not leave you orphans" (John 14.18). In the name of Christ, God the Father sent the Comforter, the Spirit of Truth. And He continues to send the Comforter forever to renew our life and our world. The same Spirit raises up and leads human beings to each other in the life of the Church. In His name as well have we gathered here today. To Him be all glory, honor, and thanksgiving to the ages of ages!

Our intent and fervent desire is to speak about our youth but also to speak with our youth—that is, with you. For you worthily represent the young people of our Orthodox Church throughout the world. To all the Orthodox youth, then, we convey our paternal prayer and patriarchal blessing as well as our message of hope, courage, conviction, and unshakable faith, "for God is with us!" Directing our gaze to the past, we certainly do not forget the myriads of young people who became the innocent and tragic victims of wars and holocausts, particularly in the closing years of the twentieth century. However, the theme of this conference calls us to turn our gaze predominantly to the future, in order that we might sketch a vision of young people in the Church, a vision based on our hopes for the coming third millennium.

The content of the third millennium is unforeseeable today. For the first time in world history, humankind is subject to a suffocating perplexity about what tomorrow will bring. Many things that in the past were self-evident are now disputed. Many institutions are crumbling. Expectations are being dashed. Unforeseen events take us by surprise. Paradoxical things claim acceptance. What is beyond imagination becomes reality. What was unseen only a little while ago becomes conspicuous today. What is brighter than the sun becomes darkened. The order of all things is troubled and overturned. Nature's forces are explored and exploited in ways unsuitable to the harmony of the natural order. Nature itself is assaulted by human egocentric will and greed. The uniqueness and sanctity of the human person is directly threatened. And all of humanity, coerced by uncontrolled powers of haughty reason and an incurable failure of moral and spiritual conduct, is moving along a precipitous edge that overlooks a yawning abyss.

In view of such changes and developments in the face of the unforeseeable future, it is necessary for us to seek out the prophetic charisma of the Church through the invocation of the Holy Spirit, the Comforter of our life and of the entire world. However, we do so not in order for us to disclose whatever human beings may be planning or to forecast their consequences and make known what only God has set by His authority (Acts 1.7). Rather, we do so in order to remember and recall whatever the Lord our Almighty God has promised and commanded, so that we may speak and promote "edification, encouragement, and consolation" (1 Cor. 14.3).

Having, therefore, yourselves become partakers of the charismata through holy baptism and through your spiritual life in general, you are called to increase your talents in order to become worthy of a more abundant divine grace. You will be inspired by this grace to participate consciously and courageously in the prophetic mission and witness of the body of the Church, so that you preach and promote this "edification, encouragement, and consolation." Moreover, by conducting yourselves in this God-pleasing manner, you will become for future generations an example and prototype of the athletes of Christ and of the servants of peace, love, and hope.

THE CHALLENGE OF UNEMPLOYMENT

We know that in many countries unemployment is rampant, while at the same time there is an increasing abundance and prosperity for the few. This situation exists despite the sincere efforts of many well-intentioned people. Yet the marginalization and disillusionment of young people because of unemployment is the most glaring failure of our economic and political condition even in the most developed societies. This extremely deplorable phenomenon presents an added reason for despair on the part of less developed countries. Unemployment is the result of many factors. One of them is the difficulty that workers have in adapting to demands made on their skills by technical developments. Another is the reluctance of workers to engage in certain types of labor below their level of education. Still another is the inability of the social system to provide jobs for all, even though jobs do exist or could certainly be created.

Young people can successfully respond to these problems in two ways. The first is on the individual level—that is, by cultivating personal versatility and adaptability while continuing their education and their diligent search for employment. The second is at the social level—that is, by promoting ideas, programs, and various solutions that would increase job opportunities, as young people themselves successfully achieve positions of leadership in society. There are many things to be done for humanity, and the resources are definitely available. We need goodwill, ideas, love for the unemployed, coordination of efforts, and vigilant zeal. Since assuming our responsibilities as head of this Church of the First Throne, we have in various ways emphatically expressed to many leaders of nations worldwide and other appropriate persons in positions of leadership the conviction that the problem of unemployment cannot be effectively solved without mutual social trust and above all without a community of justice and social responsibility. Young people must become agents of such a mobilization for the benefit of all humanity.

SOCIAL JUSTICE AND HUMAN RIGHTS

The word of God commands, "Learn justice, you who dwell on the earth" (Is. 26.9). God envisions social justice, which is also secured by respect for human rights. The correlative sensibilities connected to this profoundly serious issue at the local, national, and international levels are well known to all of us. Known, too, are the complex causal factors behind both social injustice and the violation of human rights. Against this deplorable reality, Christian young people must remember the incomparable value of the human person, including the least of the Lord's brothers and sisters. The Christian teaching concerning the value of the human person constitutes a pioneering historical principle of universal validity. It serves as the foundation of legislation concerning human rights. However, Christian young people should not limit themselves to the claim of respect for human rights. They should also advocate another aspect of what is right—namely, human responsibility and duty. For without the latter the former proves equally inhuman—indeed, just as much as the blatant violation of justice does. Therefore, they should advocate both the notion of justice as mercy and the restoration of all things to a condition of harmony—that is, they should advocate the transcendence of a legalistic sense of justice by a justice that combines collectively all virtues.

WAR AND PEACE

How beautiful is that verse of the Psalmist that speaks of the meeting of mercy and truth, the embrace of justice and peace. "Mercy and truth are met together; justice and peace have kissed" (Ps. 84.11). Ultimately, neither social justice nor human rights are comprehensible without mercy and truth. Indeed, without the latter, there can be no true peace. Young people, who are the first victims of war, have a right to a peaceful life in truth, justice, and love. Anxieties about the planet's future, which arise out of the potential destructiveness caused by modern weapons as well as by the greed and ambition of certain irresponsible leaders in nations and societies—these demand that young people should remain always alert and enlightened, never swayed by war-loving sirens.

THE ENVIRONMENTAL CRISIS

Finally, young people and future generations have a right to a peaceful enjoyment of the natural environment, whose integrity is cruelly violated to the great detriment of humanity and the planet. Environmental disasters, biological transformations and changes, and many other forms of abusive conduct of humankind over divine creation and order menace the very survival of humanity and as well as of the animal and plant kingdoms. For this reason, our Ecumenical Throne has long taken numerous initiatives pertaining to the environmental crisis, with the aim of disseminating information and alerting those who are primarily responsible. In this endeavor, we always also include young people, who, on being informed about the seriousness of the issue, become heralds of veneration for God, reverence to human beings, and respect for all creation.

Second International Youth Conference, Ecumenical Patriarchate, July 7, 2007

MEMBERS OF THE CHURCH

It is with great emotion and much fatherly joy that we welcome all of you, our beloved youth, to this historic city, which has been for centuries the sacred center of the Mother Church and See of the Great Church of Christ. As you know so well, our patriarchate is not a "national" Church but rather the fundamental canonical expression of the ecumenical dimensions of the gospel message and of its responsibility within the life of the Church. This is precisely the reason that the Church Fathers and the Councils have given it the title and name "Ecumenical." For the loving care of the Church of Constantinople exceeds barriers of any kind, whether linguistic, cultural, or ethnic. It embraces all without regard to any such considerations. So let it be understood by all of you here at this gathering that you should rightly feel at home; for you are in your own house. Indeed, this is what we would say—that this city and the Phanar are truly your home, the house of your father.

The convocation of this conference, under the general title "Members of the Church—Citizens of the World," constitutes the fruit of the fervent love of the Mother Church for you, its younger members. However, it is also the result of the vigilant attentiveness of the Ecumenical Patriarchate for all matters that pertain to your spiritual needs and concerns.

My beloved children, the Church is not merely an institution—some kind of organization or association. It is a body, one wondrously depicted by the Apostle Paul—a life-giving and life-bearing body—the theanthropic body of our Lord Jesus Christ. Listen to what the Apostle, endowed with the wisdom of God, says in his Epistle to the Ephesians: God the Father has given His Son "to be head over all things in the church, which is His body, the fullness of Him that fills all in all" (Eph. 1.22–23). Our predecessor on the Throne of Constantinople, St. John Chrysostom, emphasizes the truth that Christ, when He became incarnate, "took upon Himself the flesh of the Church"[60] and that Christ Himself has become the firstfruits as well as the head of the Church. All of the faithful, as members of the Church, are also members of the body of Christ, even as St. Paul emphasizes in another place in the same Epistle to the Ephesians: "For we are members of his body" (Eph. 5.30). In his Epistle to the Colossians, the same divine Apostle affirms: "And He (Christ) is the head of the body of the church" (1.18). Again, in First Corinthians, he writes: "For just as the body is one, and possesses many members, and all the members of that one body, being many, are one body; so also is Christ. For by one Spirit we are all baptized into one body, whether we are Jews or Gentiles, whether we are slaves or free. . . . Now you are the body of Christ, and members in particular" (1 Cor. 12.12–13, 27). And again, in the Epistle to the Romans, he states: "For just as we have many members in one body, and all members have not the same function, so we, being many, are one body in Christ, and each of us members one of another" (Rom. 12.4, 5).

Therefore, in perfect concord with these affirmations, we experience a wondrous reality—one body, which has as it its head the hypostasized[61] only-begotten Son and Logos of God, whose members are all those who have believed in Him, have been baptized in His name, and have become

---

60. *Homily before the Exile* 2, in PG 52.429.

61. A theological term, signifying the distinct divine personhood of Christ.

partakers of His life-giving body and precious blood, His body broken and His blood shed for the life of the world and its salvation. The Lord has offered this gift as much for us who find ourselves struggling in this world as for those who have finished their course and find themselves in the heavenly Jerusalem. And so we are the living cells, the members of the eternally living and glorified body of Christ! One of us is the foot, another the hand. One is the eye, another the tongue, another a lung, still another a bone, then another the skin, and so on—each one in proportion to his or her position and responsibility in the Church and in proportion to the grace that each has received from God. Each and every one of us is in constant communion with the head of this body, which is our Savior. This communion, signified in the sacred mysteries[62] and by obedience to the traditional Faith, and in the love that is the ontological bond between the all-holy head and the body of the Church, secures our life and health—that is, our salvation and sanctification. At the same time, as the great Apostle Paul has said, we are members of one another. As all of us conform to the will of the divine head, and as our mutual love and respect for the personality and gifts of each other increases, the balanced and healthy function of the body is assured.

We are aware of how cancer grows in the human body, and we know its catastrophic consequences. It is when one member, or more precisely one cell, begins to grow in a way that is not in proportion to or in harmony with the rest—without regard to its relation to the other members. This is why in the body of Christ no member is allowed to behave in an individualistic way or to develop in a way unrelated to and separated from the rest, with selfish disregard for a pious and faithful conformation to the commandments of the head. Otherwise, the healthy function becomes infected, as do the genuine communion of love and the unity of the faith of the other members. And by either ignorance or malice, the cancers of disorder, disarray, strife, schism, and heresy result ultimately in severance from and division within the body of Christ, a condition that implies eternal death.

Therefore, the Apostle Paul insists with great emphasis:

And truly, the body is not one member, but many. . . . The eye cannot say to the hand, I have no need of you: nor again the head to the feet, I have

---

62. In the Orthodox Church, the word for sacraments is in fact "mysteries."

no need of you. Much more those members of the body, which seem to be weaker, are necessary; and those members of the body, which we think to be less honorable, upon these we bestow more abundant honor. . . . God has tempered the body together, having given more abundant honor to that part which was lacking, so that there should be no schism in the body; but that the members should have the same care one for another. And when one member suffers, all the members suffer; when one member is honored, all the members rejoice. Now you are the body of Christ, and members in particular.

1 Cor. 12.14, 21–23, 24–26

MEMBERS OF ONE BODY

As members, then, of the Church, beloved young friends, you are also members of the body of Christ. Each one of you, regardless of gender, has a personal role and a personal responsibility in the theanthropic body, in proportion to the grace and talent that God has already given you or that He will entrust to you in the future. What is necessary is for you to become aware, in timely fashion, of your talents and spiritual gifts so that you will be able to assume the role and fulfill the obligations that God expects of you as members of the body of the Christ. And there is a way to be certain of these things—by saying from the depths of your heart, as you respond willingly to your feelings of responsibility: "Behold! Here am I, Lord! Speak, Lord! Your servant is listening!"

As for the interpersonal relations that you enjoy with other members of the Church, the Lord expects that you should walk in the communion of love, with mutual respect, replete with every sentiment of brotherly and sisterly solidarity. Walk in such a way that their joy is your joy! Their problems—their struggles, sorrow, anxiety, and pain—let these problems be yours! Not out of social convention or in a condescending manner but with fervent and genuine love! Consider this story from the *Gerontikon*, also known as the *Sayings of the Desert Fathers* [and Mothers]. When someone asked a hermit what really signified love, that man of God answered: "Love is this: if I see a leper on the road and I say to him, 'Come, brother! Take my healthy body and give me yours!' This is true love!"[63]

---

63. See Saying 26 of Abba Agathon, a renowned hermit and one of the founding fathers of the desert tradition in Egypt. See Benedicta Ward, ed., *The Sayings of the Desert Fathers: The Alphabetical Collection* (Mowbrays: London, 1975), 20.

When you think of this measure of love, then you will understand how much work lies ahead of us in order to achieve such love! But do not lose heart! Diligently fight the fight within the framework that the Lord and the Fathers have established. Then the love of God will come on you as a gift that crowns your efforts.

Contemporary people, as you already know, suffer from inconsolable loneliness. Without a conscious church life, there awaits only the cry: "I am alone. . . . Alone! Indeed, opposed even to myself." People who experience this kind of tragic existence are clearly shut off in self-imposed isolation. This individualistic, egocentric way of life has no desire even to try to move beyond the ego and make some sacrifice or suffer self-deprivation for the sake of another human being. This kind of life is already the worst torment, in which one could repeat, along with the atheist existential philosopher, "Hell is other people."[64] However, dearly beloved spiritual children, the person of faith has other presuppositions, other possibilities, and other horizons. These are based on our brotherhood in Christ; they are what binds us together with our fellow Christians.

Consider, if you wish, the tradition that we have lived through the ages to this very day—namely, the tradition of *Romiosyne*[65] and Orthodoxy—as much in this place as in the rest of the world! The parish, or the community, was traditionally the common ground of our brotherhood centered on the temple, on the holy altar and Divine Liturgy, as an axis around which not only personal and family life but also communal and social life revolved. The Church bell, whether tolling in joy or in sorrow, stirred and moved everyone, as all gathered together to share in the collective emotion. Whether it was a celebration of a happy occasion, a wedding or baptism, or a sad occasion such as a funeral—all were drawn to the Church and around the Church.

At the same time, leaders of the Church community, both clergy and lay, were vigilant over all people in the community, and all people were respectful toward them, considering their opinion respectfully and taking their counsel seriously. You may say that things have changed a great deal with regard to the realities of community life. The growing numbers of parishioners in church communities, the divergence and distance experienced in large cities—all these make the realities we have described appear

---

64. Jean-Paul Sartre, in *Huis Clos* (1944), a play translated as *No Exit*.

65. I.e., related to the history and culture of the Eastern Roman Empire.

to be obsolescent. We cannot deny that this is a serious problem. But problems exist for us to confront and resolve on the basis of our personal intentions and abilities but mostly of our Almighty God, His only-begotten Son as head of the body, and in the Holy Spirit as the soul of the Church.

This image of the Church as body of Christ, and of us as its members, is especially revealed, rendered tangible, and experienced most wondrously in the Divine Liturgy. Again, we derive illumination from St. Paul. In the First Epistle to the Corinthians, he writes: "The cup of blessing which we bless, is it not the communion of the blood of Christ? The bread which we break, is it not the communion of the body of Christ? For we being many are one bread and one body; for we are all partakers of that one bread" (1 Cor. 10.16, 17).

When we commune of the one cup and partake of the mystery of our master's body and blood, not only are we joined to the body and blood and soul of the God-Man Jesus Christ. Above and beyond this, we also become joined to the body and blood and souls of one another! We become living members of the eternally living Lord, who rose from the dead. Yet, we also become members of one another! All who partake of the table of the Lord have in their own bodies the treasure of the very body of Christ! In their veins runs the very blood of Christ! In their hearts is found the very faith in Christ! And in their souls flows the very grace of Christ, who brings sanctification!

Everyone equally tastes Christ's holy love; all hold in common the expectation of our blessed hope in Jesus. This is why the Divine Liturgy is the preeminent manifestation of the great ontological truth that we Christians are brothers and sisters. We are not alone, bereft of siblings! When we confess God to be our Father and His Church to be our Mother; when we commune by partaking of the chalice of life—namely, of the body and blood of the only-begotten Son of God, who was incarnate and crucified for us and rose from the dead—we possess not only a larger circle of brothers and sisters, a larger family; we become part of His greater and only true life-giving body! Indeed, this body grows with the addition of every human being who becomes a member of the Church. And it is the desire of its head that it should grow unceasingly in accordance with the commandment given to His holy disciples and Apostles: "Go and teach all nations, baptizing them in the name of the Father, and of the Son, and of the Holy Spirit, teaching them to observe all things that I have commanded you" (Matt. 28.19, 20). This is the one obligation that weighs on the shoulders of all Christians.

CITIZENS OF THE WORLD

And here, beloved daughters and sons in the Lord, we must conclude the first part of our address, satisfied that we have at least hinted at the profound mysteries that lie before us as members of the Church and at our attendant responsibilities and obligations. Now we must move on to the second part of our conference theme: "Citizens of the World." There can be no doubt that for, those of us who bear the name of Christ, "our citizenship is in heaven; from whence also we look for the Savior, the Lord Jesus Christ" (Phil. 3.20), as once again St. Paul, the teacher of the Churches, underscores. And it is abundantly clear that "here, we have no lasting city; instead, we seek the city which is to come" (Heb. 13.14). Beyond this, however, with the exception of monastics and hermits, the rest of us Christians—and we constitute the vast majority—live and move among the organized societies of the world: in cities, cultures, and nations with distinct conditions and self-understood obligations. All of us have a passport; we all receive certain protections from worldly authorities as well as many shared benefits and services. We are citizens of particular countries that convey certain obligations and privileges.

Of course, the world is no paradise, and the condition of the world is not ideal for Christians, as we learn from the unequivocal and diachronic message of the Evangelist John—namely, that "the whole world lies in evil" (1 John 5.19). We know that the world has not accepted Christ as its ruler; it has another ruler, hinted at by the Lord shortly before His Passion when He said, "Now the ruler of this world is cast out" (John 12.31)—that is to say, the devil. Consequently, it is expected that in the world we will have tribulation, that we will face unjust hatred. Our Lord Himself made this known to us: "In the world you will have tribulation, but take courage, I have conquered the world!" (John 16.33). And again: "If the world hates you, know that it hated me before you. If you were of the world, the world would love its own; but because you are not of the world, but I have chosen you from the world—this is the reason that the world hates you" (John 15.18, 19).

Now this reality does not force us to retreat from the world—this is a special grace bestowed on very few, who are called to monasticism—but it should give us a critical stance vis-à-vis the world. Let us be in the world, but let us not be in line with the evil purposes of the world. Think of the fish, which are not made of salt even though they live and swim in the salt-filled sea. Besides, as our Lord Christ said in addressing His heavenly Father during His high-priestly prayer at the Last Supper: "I have given your word to them, and the world has hated them, because they are not of the world, even as I am not of the world. I do not ask that you take them out of the world, but that you preserve them from the evil one" (John 17.14, 15).

Moreover, the quality of being a Christian impels us, while abiding in the world, to be law-abiding citizens, unless the law comes into direct conflict with the will of God. If some demand of the state should completely contravene the will of God, then let us stand firm with the word of the chief Apostle, St. Peter, who said, "We must obey God, rather than human beings" (Acts 5.29). Did not Christ pay the tax of the half shekel, the tax for the temple in Jerusalem, as recorded by the Evangelist Matthew? The Lord told Peter to catch a fish; and there, in the midst of the fish's belly, were sufficient coins for the Lord and for Peter (Matt. 17.24–27). Similarly, the Lord declared, "Render unto Caesar the things that are Caesar's, and unto God the things that are God's" (Matt. 22.21). Foolish anarchy is foreign to the spirit of the gospel. Beyond this, however, it must not escape our attention that the world, and everything in the world, bears the mark of transience, as the Apostle Paul emphasized: "The form of this world passes away" (1 Cor. 7.31).

Therefore, our stance toward the vagaries of life and the insecurities of the world ought to be informed by these words of the Apostle: "But this I say, brethren, the time is short: it remains that both those who are married be as though they were not; and those that weep, as though they wept not; and those that rejoice, as though they rejoiced not; and those that purchase, as though they possessed not; and those that use this world, as not abusing it: for the fabric of this world is passing away" (1 Cor. 7.29–31).

THE WORLD AS VILLAGE

In our day, beloved young friends, every Christian finds himself or herself facing challenges from the world that are more overwhelming than those of the past. Today, the world has become a "large village," a single neighborhood. Distances have been reduced to virtually nothing. In a twenty-four hour span, one can travel from one end of the earth to the other—from our city to Africa; from London to New Zealand; from St. Petersburg to the Egyptian desert; from Beijing to New York. And by means of the mass media and telecommunications—television, radio, the internet, and telephone—one corner of the world can instantly speak with another. When else have human beings had such convenient and instantaneous access to information? There are tremendous dimensions to this reality. And when else have human beings had the entire world at the tips of their fingers? Truly, however, this is a double-edged sword. There is good and there is bad; and it seems worse when one considers how daily news streams into our homes.

Likewise, the formation of international coalitions, associations, and unions, like the European Union—which we hope and pray will not delay the accession of Turkey—limit the significance of national boundaries, with the consequence that the movement and migration between various countries can happen without all of the bureaucratic paperwork of the past. On the other hand, the collapse of the system that stretched an "iron curtain" between East and West has opened wide pathways of communication between two formerly estranged worlds.

In light of all this, it may be asked: What is the position of Christians, and indeed of younger Christians, before this new reality? Should one shut oneself off, indifferent to what is happening all around? One might say: "Let the world go its own way; I am okay within my own small world." But this is desertion and denial of one's responsibility to other human beings! Jesus Christ is "the Lamb of God that takes away the sin of the world" (John 1.29), as St. John the Baptist testified. Christ came as light for the whole world, to save the entire world. "I have come as light for the world, so that every person who believes in me might not remain in darkness. . . . For I did not come to judge the world but to save the world" (John 12.46, 47). And not only this, but He delivered His own flesh up to death "for the life of the world" (John 6.51), "so that every person who believes in him should not perish, but possess eternal life" (John 3.16). All of this operates within us in proportion to our responsibilities to the world; for we, too, have been called to be "the light of the world" (Matt. 5.14). We have received this commandment from the Lord:

"Let your light so shine before other people, that they may see your good works and glorify your Father who is in heaven" (Matt. 5.16).

Let us, therefore, maintain a strong sense of responsibility to the world. We will not become secularized. We will not conform to or identify with the world and its sin. We will not become the world, but we will employ a gracious use of the world, and a discriminating and logical use of this world's tools, which may be placed, as Western Christians say, *ad majorem Dei gloriam*, "to the greater glory of God," and which can assist in drawing many people to Christ; for many are still ignorant of the Savior and the gospel. Let us not forget that most of humankind really does not have even an idea of Christ and the gospel. Is it not tragic that the so-called "golden arches" of McDonalds have more relevance in the modern world than the sign of the Cross? Let us be aware that Christians today constitute only one-third of the world's population.

So there is no justification for us to forget our spiritual obligation to millions of souls. Likewise, we should be interested in the earthly problems of our neighbors, making them at least the subjects of our prayers. Often we will be able to help in material ways, as in relief efforts after a natural disaster. It is very moving how, after the catastrophic tsunami of 2004, funds were collected through radio and television—through radiothons and telethons—in many countries around the world, and these funds were distributed to those in need. Using the media, and having information about the environmental crisis wreaking havoc throughout the creation of God, we are in a position to work with various activists in order to halt—or, at least, reduce—the evil of climate change and global warming. We know that television, radio, the press, and the internet do not by definition always serve what is evil and sinful. Thus, we can use them as pulpits of the Christian truth and as trumpets heralding the gospel of love. Through telephone and technology, we can stay in close contact with many of our brothers and sisters, bringing them comfort and strength, even when they live far away.

It is worth noting the love that a contemporary saint, the Elder Porphyrios of Kavsokalyvia[66] and of Athens, had for radio and the telephone. He built a radio by himself in his monastic hut in Malakasa, so that he

---

66. Fr. Porphyrios (1906–91) was a monk of Mount Athos, known for his spiritual discernment. He spent many years living as a hermit outside Athens.

might listen to the programs of the Church radio station of Greece. And what of him as the spiritual shepherd by telephone? Whenever the Holy Spirit urged him, through some spiritual vision, he would call a spiritual child in need of encouragement, calling at anytime during night and day! How many souls were spared falls and shipwrecks! How many were saved from dangers and severe problems, because of the sacrifice of his tranquility, as he took time to call, even at the expense of his own fragile health. This is an example of how we can use worldly things in a way that demonstrates divine love for the sake of our brother and sister.

Well, we desire to burden you no longer, beloved children. We believe that we have offered some points for further and deeper discussion about the dual quality of being both "members of the Church" and "citizens of the world." As for the rest, we pray that you should be "taught by God" (John 6.45), so that the Holy Spirit might inform your hearts unto salvation. We wholeheartedly thank all of you for your attention and express the praise and esteem of the Mother Church for all those who contributed visibly or silently to the organization and success of this conference. "The Grace of our Lord Jesus be with you. My love in Christ Jesus is with you all!" (1 Cor. 16.23, 24).

Pastoral Address on the Eighteenth Anniversary of Enthronement as Ecumenical Patriarch, Annapolis, Maryland, November 2, 2009

> Address during a banquet in his honor on the occasion of the eighteenth anniversary of his enthronement as Archbishop of Constantinople, New Rome, and Ecumenical Patriarch. Held at the Saints Constantine and Helen Greek Orthodox Church in Annapolis.

HONORING PAST AND PRESENT

God is love. Eighteen years ago today, with these simple yet most profound words, the words of the holy Evangelist John (1 John 4:8), we inaugurated our apostolic ministry as Ecumenical Patriarch. Today, our heart is full of gratitude as we share this special occasion in our life as Ecumenical Patriarch with you, the blessed spiritual children of the Mother Church Constantinople.

From the outset, we wish to recall the historical ministry of our exceptional predecessors and to pray for the repose of their souls—namely, of the great visionary Athenagoras, who also served this archdiocese so faithfully, as well as of the meek and spiritual Dimitrios, whom we accompanied during his official visit to this country in the year before our election and enthronement. We also remember our beloved Archbishop Iakovos,[67] who came from the Mother Church to guide you for nearly four decades.

This official visit to the sacred Archdiocese and the esteemed Metropolis of New Jersey in this unique nation of the United States of America, combined with this generous event and gracious feast for the anniversary of our enthronement, is undoubtedly the most appropriate way of celebration. We have already concluded the eighth international and interdisciplinary environmental symposium on the Mississippi River and in the city of New Orleans, where we gathered theologians, scientists, and leaders of the religious and the political world as well as media representatives from throughout the world and nationally, to explore the ecological problems of the "great river" and their impact on regional and global climate conditions.[68]

We have also concluded our visit to New York, where we had the opportunity to meet with religious, political, and academic leaders as we shared our concerns about the crucial issues that plague our world, such as violations of religious tolerance and of human rights as well as the battle to overcome poverty. Throughout, we have had the overwhelming joy of meeting with faithful of our archdiocese, recognizing the extraordinary ministry of our parishes in this land, and extending to them our patriarchal and paternal blessing. Therefore, we admit that we could not imagine a more fitting way of remembering and rejoicing on this day, and we are sincerely grateful to you for this evening.

Nevertheless, celebration in our Orthodox tradition and spirituality is never disconnected from the way of the Cross. Ours is a spirituality of "joyful sorrow" (*charopoion penthos* or *charmolype*), as St. John of the

---

67. Archbishop Iakovos (1911–2005) served as archbishop of North and South America from 1959 to 1996.

68. The principal purpose of the Ecumenical Patriarch's visit to the United States was the eighth international, interdisciplinary, and interfaith symposium of the Religious and Scientific Committee of the Ecumenical Patriarchate. It was held in New Orleans on the Mississippi River, October 18–25, 2009. Afterward, His All Holiness visited New York City, Atlanta, and Washington, D.C., where he was also received at the White House by President Barack Obama.

Ladder reminds us.[69] We do not, for example, rejoice without recalling and sharing in the suffering of others. And, at the Ecumenical Patriarchate, we can certainly never experience joy without remembering that we embody the tradition of a Church that has known both glory and martyrdom through the centuries.

THE BISHOP AS FATHER AND SERVANT

More important, however, in celebrating the anniversary of our enthronement today, as your spiritual father and patriarch, there comes to mind something else to which we would like to draw your attention. A celebration for a spiritual father and bishop is also a remembrance that the bishop too is a child of God and a son of the Church. For there is only one father, whom all of us have, in heaven. The bishop—whether an assistant bishop, a metropolitan, an archbishop, or an Ecumenical Patriarch—is also, first and foremost, a servant of the Church and not a just a leader. Indeed, insofar as the bishop is a genuine servant, he is also an inspiring leader; insofar as the bishop submits entirely to the will of God, he is also able to direct others safely in the will of God; insofar as he is a devoted son of the Church, he is also able to be a compassionate father of the Church.

Therefore, as we stand before you this evening, celebrating—somewhat like a child might celebrate a birthday—we are humbly grateful to God our Father and personally grateful also to you as our spiritual children for giving us this opportunity to remember that we, too, are a child committed to a ministry within the Church, committed as your spiritual guide and as Ecumenical Patriarch. May our Triune God Who is worshipped—Father, Son and Holy Spirit—bless all of you and your families, this beloved parish of Saints Constantine and Helen, the Holy Metropolis of New Jersey, and the Greek Orthodox Archdiocese of America.

Our mission is love. Our message is love. Our heart is filled and blessed with love for all of you; for truly, God is love.[70]

---

69. St. John of the Ladder in fact coined the term *charmolype* to describe the dual aspect of joyful sorrow, which characterizes the spiritual life.

70. These phrases echo the conclusion of Ecumenical Patriarch's enthronement address in 1991.

Patriarchal Greetings and Paternal Reflections Addressed to the Inter-Orthodox Commissions for Bilateral Dialogues

Committee for Theological Dialogue with the Roman Catholic Church, Ecumenical Patriarchate, September 12, 2005

ONE VISION, ONE PURPOSE

It is with great happiness and fraternal love that we welcome you here today, at this sacred center of Orthodoxy, the see of the Ecumenical Patriarchate. We have gathered here from the four corners of the earth in order to discuss the course of the dialogue between the Orthodox and Roman Catholic Churches.[71] We wish to conclude this meeting with one common position concerning its course and direction, so that we may all proceed in a common understanding. This tradition of ongoing meetings with the members of the inter-Orthodox committee for theological dialogue with the Roman Catholic Church was established many years ago and is just a sample of our wish that our love and cooperation be further cultivated. We are certain that the discussions among yourselves will also prove to be very useful.

The goals of our gathering here are mainly twofold. First, the clarification of some questions regarding procedural and practical matters in view of the reestablishment of the official theological dialogue of the Orthodox Church—represented by you and the rest of the representatives of the local Orthodox churches who were unable to be present—with Rome. Second, the exchange of views and thoughts on the substance of this dialogue, so that a common line of thinking and acting may be formed by the Orthodox representatives on issues to be discussed.

As for the first goal, according to the valid tradition and establishment of all theological dialogues, the body of the representatives of the Orthodox churches—in this case, our gathering—is called to formally accept, according to the custom at this point, the representative of the Church of Constantinople, the first Orthodox see, as the Orthodox co-president of the theological dialogue. Therefore, in accordance with our synodal decision, His Eminence Metropolitan John of Pergamon has already been

---

71. The official theological dialogue between the Roman Catholic and Orthodox Churches commenced on the islands of Patmos and Rhodes on May 29, 1980.

appointed as the representative of the Ecumenical Patriarchate in this dialogue, after the resignation of His Eminence Archbishop Stylianos of Australia from this position. Metropolitan John, together with His Grace Bishop Kallistos of Diokleia, and with the Most Reverend Metropolitan Gennadios of Sassima acting as secretary, will serve as representatives of the Ecumenical Patriarchate. You know, brethren, the theological knowledge and prestige of His Eminence, the metropolitan of Pergamon, in theology—indeed, not only in Orthodox theology but more broadly. He is also a member of the Academy of Athens, having served as its president. In all this, he honors the name of the Church as well as the role of the academic theologian and teacher.

Another practical issue to be addressed is the forthcoming hosting of both the plenary and the preparatory committees of the dialogue commission. The Roman Catholic side has kindly offered to host the preparatory committee, which should be summoned sometime this November. However, it is an obligation of one of the Orthodox churches to host the plenary, which should be summoned within the coming year; it should be borne in mind that the Roman Catholic side hosted it in Baltimore, during its last session.[72] Therefore, it would be very useful, from a practical point of view, to know which Orthodox Church is willing to host the plenary of the dialogue commission next year.[73]

As for the second goal of our gathering, the substance of the meetings that will be held during the new phase of the dialogue concerns the problem of ecclesiology, with special reference to the issue of primacy in the Church. Under this heading also falls the issue of Uniatism, which detained the dialogue in the past decade, and so it will be added to become the primary theme of discussion. All Orthodox churches have agreed on this after visits conducted by the metropolitans of Pergamon and Sassima. Therefore, this gathering cannot review or reconsider this inter-Orthodox decision. However, you are called to exchange thoughts on the best way for us to contribute to future discussion of the timely issue of the unification of the Church. We are confident that this gathering will prove useful and beneficial in this regard.

---

72. The commission met in Baltimore, Maryland, July 9–19, 2000, after an interruption in the theological dialogue following its meeting in Balamand, Lebanon, in 1993.

73. Subsequent meetings were held in Belgrade in 2006, Ravenna in 2007, and Nicosia in 2009.

The Ecumenical Patriarchate always desires that the rapprochement of these two most ancient Churches and traditions will be realized and that all obstacles of unity among Christians will be overcome. Nevertheless, the Ecumenical Patriarchate does not accept the opinion that this unity, for which we are all working, will be realized through any common acceptance of a minimum standard of common faith, through a decision to ignore differences and difficulties or to embrace all differences as a kind of acceptable variety. In this dialogue, there are also issues that touch neither on the faith nor on issues that the ecumenical synods have decided. These issues may be dealt with in different ways by various local Christian communities. However, in matters of faith, unity is mandatory and must be pursued within the framework of the undivided Church— that is, the Church before the Schism. Furthermore, even if there are among our interlocutors some who pursue purposes other than the revelation of the fullness of truth, our attitude and position must be directed, dispassionately and without faltering, toward the immovable goal— namely, the witnessing of the truth. For, although we seem to be discussing only with a certain group of people, the reality is that we are discussing with the entire Roman Catholic world. And within this Roman Catholic world there are certainly many honest people searching for the truth. These people are our real interlocutors, even though we do not know them, even though we do not have direct contact with them. Let us not forget that through this dialogue we are responsible before God and history.

We trust the judgement of the new president[74] as well as of all the members of the inter-Orthodox committee of the dialogue. However, more than anything, we trust the Holy Spirit, whose enlightenment and power we invoke. We wholeheartedly thank the representatives of the holy Orthodox churches who are present, as we thank those who have sent them here. We fervently pray that this cooperation will prove prosperous and productive for the glory of God and for the revelation of His truth. We also wish you all a pleasant stay here. May the grace of God be with you.

---

74. His Eminence Metropolitan John (Zizioulas) of Pergamon. The first president of this dialogue was His Eminence Archbishop Stylianos (Harkianakis) of Australia, who resigned in 2003.

Committees for Orthodox Bilateral Dialogues with Other Christian Confessions, Ecumenical Patriarchate, September 3, 2008

THE INSPIRATION OF PENTECOST

It is with great joy that we greet your arrival here in the sacred courts of the venerable Mother Church. We welcome all of you to the holy Protaton[75] of Orthodoxy and our race, the paternal residence of us all. Both our Modesty and the rest of the reverend brother hierarchs residing here embrace you with deep love and much honor as we welcome you joyfully and warmly. May God reward you for the long distances you have traveled to come here, in response to our patriarchal and synodal invitation, so that we might convene this sacred meeting. We will, of course, have other such opportunities in the future, because we recognize that they are especially useful, as you will personally ascertain during the process of our deliberations. After all, as you will recall, such gatherings have taken place in the past, normally following a more general synaxis of the hierarchy of the Throne; and they always proved very fruitful.

All of you are well aware, beloved brothers, that the will of our Lord Jesus Christ for those who believe in Him has indeed been clearly articulated—namely "that all [His disciples] may be one" (John 17.11): That we may be one among ourselves, one with Him, and, through Christ, one also with the Father and the Spirit. The very name of the Church[76] is a name of unity and gathering "in one and the same place." Yet the enemy of our salvation has in the past sought to sow tares of deceit, division, and schism within the Lord's field. The result was that many of the sons and daughters of the Kingdom unfortunately found themselves outside of the salvific boundaries of the Church—some closer and others farther, but all of them without participation in the soul-nurturing and life-giving altar table of the "one" and "sure" (to adopt the terminology of St. Ignatius of Antioch) Eucharist, being deprived, as a result, of the sanctifying and saving uncreated light of those being deified.

---

75. The Protaton is a large tenth-century basilica in the administrative capital of Mount Athos. It serves as the central seat of the monastic communities. The term is used symbolically here to denote the Phanar as the central liturgical and spiritual see of the Orthodox world.

76. I.e., *ekklesia*, meaning "the calling [or invitation] to gather in one place."

Perhaps the most expressive image of the Church is, as you know, dear brothers, the icon of Pentecost. There, the holy Apostles are depicted seated in a semicircle, at the head of which is Christ. At the other end is an empty space, sometimes with the gospel as the image of Christ's presence in paper and ink. However, a semicircle is incomplete. Fullness is symbolized and depicted by a circle. The circle, then, is what we seek. Moreover, the semicircle represents a wide embrace. For the Church resembles the wide embrace of God's love, which awaits the inclusion, if possible, of all people. And so our obligation to obey the will of our Lord—the will that we have practical love for our separated Christian brothers and sisters but also that we demonstrate fundamental adaptation and conformation to the nature and purpose of the Church—imposes on us the importance of dialogue with all people in the hope of a fruitful end.

Under these conditions, the Church has over the ages entered into dialogue with various schismatic and heretical groups. Even the ecumenical councils as well as many local councils were essentially efforts for dialogue by the Church with those separated from "the faith once delivered to the saints" (Jude 3) on one or another issue. In more recent times, the Ecumenical Patriarchate, in its primary and coordinating responsibility within the Orthodox world, has assumed the historical initiatives for dialogue with other Christian churches and confessions. Indeed, at the Third Preconciliar Pan-Orthodox Conference held in 1986 at the Patriarchal and Stavropegic Center of Chambésy, in light of the forthcoming Holy and Great Synod, it was unanimously decided to establish theological dialogues. As a result, all individual autocephalous Orthodox churches were thereby committed to dialogue.

And so we have official theological dialogues with the Roman Catholic Church, with the non-Chalcedonian churches,[77] with the Anglican Communion, with the World Lutheran Federation, and with the World Council of Reformed Churches as well as with the Old Catholic Church. Most reverend brothers, you are the ones who have graciously assumed in our time this relative burden, responding to this sacred task with a noble sense

---

77. Also known as the Oriental Orthodox churches, these include a number of ancient churches, such as the Coptic, Syriac, Armenian, and Ethiopian churches, which endorsed the Fourth Ecumenical Council of Ephesus (431) but for various reasons did not formally accept allegiance to the Fifth Ecumenical Council of Chalcedon (451).

of responsibility by chairing the specific dialogue committees in the name of the Mother Church. For our part, we take this opportunity to express to all of you our heartfelt patriarchal gratitude and praise (much deserved) on behalf of the holy and sacred synod, for your many efforts, labors, patience, and holy zeal. Alongside these dialogues, we also have bilateral discussions on a regional level, such as the conversations with the Evangelical Church of Germany, with the Roman Catholic Church in the United States, with the Uniting Church in Australia, and so on. Each of these discussions has its own history, which is more or less familiar to all those present here.

THE MATHEMATICS OF LOVE

It is self-evident, dear brothers, that we always carefully and closely follow, both personally and synodally, this work wherein you hold leadership roles. We are informed both through your formal reports as well as by means of the corresponding synodal committees at the Ecumenical Patriarchate. Thus, we are aware of how each of the dialogues is proceeding and what is more or less expected from each of them. In some, of course, there is justifiably greater optimism, while in others less. In yet others, unfortunately, we do not discern any light at the end of the tunnel. This is not a particularly hopeful reality, especially if we take into consideration that the final and ultimate purpose of theological dialogues is, from the very outset, a common cup. Nevertheless, we must continue; we must persist. And we must proceed without ignoring St. Paul's words: "After a first and second admonition, have nothing more to do with anyone who causes divisions" (Titus 3.10)—a message that possibly refers more to the difficult character of the ancient Cretans, whom Titus was called to shepherd.

Yet we also have in mind other "mathematical principles" of the gospel, such as the phrase "seventy times seven" (Matt. 18.22). In this respect, the phrase "first and second admonition" does not necessarily imply one or two interviews, discussions, or conversations. If we are certain about our belief and firmly grounded on the rock of our faith, if we consciously experience the gospel together with the patristic tradition of the ecumenical councils and have perfect Christian love in our hearts, then we do not fear dialogue, regardless of how many difficulties, barriers, and hurdles we may encounter along the way. After all, "perfect love casts out fear" (1 John 4.18).

Therefore, we proceed despite any difficulties, because we also believe that we do not have the moral right to place the lamp of our pious dogma, of our spirituality, and of our ecclesiastical tradition under the bushel, remaining selfishly enclosed within ourselves or resting on the certainty that we possess the fullness of truth and grace. We have surely and undoubtedly been blessed by the Lord with this truth and grace! And certainly our holy Orthodox Church, and she alone, bears all the characteristic elements of the "one, holy, catholic and apostolic Church" of Christ. This is our identity, self-awareness, and conviction; and it is from this starting point that we commence every contact, all communication, and each dialogue. However, this should in no way create within us any pharisaic sense of self-sufficiency or self-complacency. We can never feel self-sufficient or self-complacent as long as people who invoke the same God and call themselves Christian lie outside full ecclesiastical communion and do not participate in the same cup of life. It is helpful once again simply to recall the icon of Pentecost.

Inasmuch as we are Orthodox, we recognize that Orthodoxy is not our own achievement but instead a perfect gift, an invaluable blessing and a precious deposit, which we owe to the boundless mercy of God and not to our own worth or work. Furthermore, we do not overlook that "we have this treasure in an earthen vessel, so that it may be made clear that this extraordinary power belongs to God and does not come from us" (2 Cor. 4.7). Nor do we ignore the imminent danger of arrogance and of claims to "the primacy of truth," where we are often led by the pietism and religious fanaticism that frequently lurk in the heart of certain Orthodox churches, a condition that inevitably condemns those tempted by this error with "the wickedness of those who by their wickedness suppress the truth" (Rom. 1.18). The feeling of unworthiness, humility, godly fear, love, sincerity, and respect for the human person, "for whom Christ died" (Rom. 14.15) are, and should always be, the necessary prerequisites and features of our dialogues with non-Orthodox Christians, who, after all, share with us spiritual roots and a common focus on sacred revelation and the divine-human person of Christ!

Nonetheless, dear brothers, we must also confess with sincerity that we too have certain things to learn from our Christian brothers and sisters of other confessions, with whom we are in dialogue. These are lessons that we perceive with difficulty when we stand in halls mirrored with self-sufficiency, self-admiration, and self-congratulation. Of course, we are not referring here to lessons that are related to the fullness of our theological doctrine, the nucleus of our "logical worship," or the purity of our prayer and experience of ascesis inherited from the Church Fathers. Rather, we mean lessons related perhaps to outward forms of worship informed by superstitious notions that have stealthily been introduced and to outward forms of administration, ritual, and appearance as well as to the presentation of the gospel message to the "global village" of the modern, secular world that we inhabit. So the benefits of dialogue are by definition mutual and, we repeat, it is our intention to proceed with and persist in dialogue as much as possible, entrusting the results of our dialogue to God Himself. May He increase the seed; and may He bring about in abundance the fruitful illumination and salvation of all people.

Brothers, we are also aware that some of those with whom we are in dialogue sometimes attempt to initiate separate conversations with individual autocephalous Orthodox churches; some of these even act out of a senseless competition with the Church of Constantinople for the role of being first-in-responsibility. This is an extremely sensitive matter, which demands careful and concerted attention on the part of all of us, and we will be discussing various aspects of this issue. Clearly, there is a formal inter-Orthodox commitment that all forms of theological dialogues with other Christians be conducted not separately but always collectively under the direct coordination and responsibility of the Ecumenical Patriarchate. It is a matter that we should all remind ourselves and underline unswervingly at all times.

These fundamental introductory thoughts of our Modesty are sufficient to open the meeting. Each of the most reverend brothers will be invited to offer an appropriate introduction at the proper scheduled time. Once again, we thank you for your willing participation and pray for the generous illumination of the Paraclete. At this time, we ask His Eminence Metropolitan John of Pergamon to share his thoughts and insights, his experiences and recommendations from the important theological dialogue with the Roman Catholic Church, a dialogue that the Mother Church has placed under his responsibility for some years now, recognizing together with all the other Orthodox churches his wisdom, experience, and skillfulness.

3

Ecumenical Addresses

Presentations at Ecumenical Gatherings

ENCYCLICAL FOR SUNDAY OF ORTHODOXY 2010

The Responsibility of Dialogue

Our most holy Orthodox Church today commemorates its own feast day,[1] and, from this historical see of the Ecumenical Patriarchate, which has been touched by the suffering of martyrdom, the Mother Church of Constantinople directs its blessing, love, and concern to all of its faithful and dedicated spiritual children throughout the world, inviting them to concelebrate in prayer.

Blessed be the name of the Lord! Those who over the ages endeavored to suppress the Church through various visible and invisible persecutions; those who sought to falsify the Church with their heretical teachings; those who wanted to silence the Church, depriving it of its voice and witness—they all proved unsuccessful. The clouds of martyrs, the tears of the ascetics, and the prayers of the saints protect the Church spiritually, while the "Comforter and Spirit of Truth"[2] leads it to the fullness of truth.

---

1. Celebrated annually on the first Sunday of Great Lent, this feast commemorates the restoration and veneration of icons in the Orthodox Church through the triumph of the iconophiles (who supported the significance and role of icons) over the iconoclasts during the Seventh Ecumenical Council (Nicea, 787). It is also considered a celebration of the Orthodox faith: "This is the victory that overcomes the world, our faith" (1 John 5.4). The service concludes with the solemn chant, "This is the faith of the Apostles; this is the faith of the Orthodox; this is the faith of the Fathers; this faith has established the foundation of the world."

2. From an ancient and popular Orthodox prayer to the Holy Spirit.

With a sense of duty and responsibility, despite its hurdles and problems, as the First Throne Church of Orthodoxy, the Ecumenical Patriarchate is concerned about establishing and protecting the unity of the Orthodox Church, so that with one voice and one heart we may confess the Orthodox faith of our fathers in every age and even in our times. For Orthodoxy is not a museum treasure that must be preserved; it is a breath of life that must be transmitted in order to invigorate all people. Orthodoxy is always contemporary, so long as we promote it with humility and interpret it in light of the existential quests and needs of humanity in each given historical period and cultural circumstance.

To this end, Orthodoxy must be in constant dialogue with the world. The Orthodox Church does not fear dialogue, because truth is not afraid of dialogue. On the contrary, if Orthodoxy is enclosed within itself and not in dialogue with those outside, it will fail in its mission and cease to be the "catholic" and "ecumenical" Church. It will become instead introverted and self-contained, a "ghetto" on the margins of history. This is why the great Fathers of the Church never feared dialogue with the spiritual culture of their age—indeed, they even welcomed dialogue with pagan idolaters and philosophers. In this spirit, they influenced and transformed the civilization of their time and offered us a truly ecumenical Church.

Today, Orthodoxy is called to continue this dialogue with the outside world in order to provide witness and the life-giving breath of its faith. However, this dialogue cannot reach the outside world unless it first passes through all those who bear the Christian name. And so first we must converse as Christians among ourselves, to resolve our differences, so that our witness to the outside world may be credible. Our endeavor in the cause that all Christians be united is the will and command of our Lord, who before His Passion prayed to His Father "that all [namely, His disciples] may be one, so that the world may believe that You sent me" (John 17.21). It is not possible for the Lord to agonize over the unity of His disciples and for us to remain indifferent about the unity of all Christians. That would constitute criminal betrayal and transgression of His divine commandment.

It is precisely for these reasons that, with the mutual agreement and participation of all local Orthodox churches, the Ecumenical Patriarchate has for many decades conducted official pan-Orthodox theological dialogues with the larger Christian churches and confessions. The aim of these dialogues is, in a spirit of love, to discuss whatever divides Christians both in terms of faith as well as in terms of the organization and life of the Church.

These dialogues, together with every effort for peaceful and fraternal relations between the Orthodox Church and other Christians, are unfortunately challenged today in an unacceptably fanatical way—at least by the standards of a genuinely Orthodox ethos—by certain circles that claim for themselves exclusively the title of zealot and defender of Orthodoxy. As if all the patriarchs and sacred synods of the Orthodox churches throughout the world, who unanimously decided on and continue to support these dialogues, were supposedly not Orthodox. Yet, these opponents of every effort for the restoration of unity among Christians raise and regard themselves above episcopal synods of the Church to the dangerous point of creating schisms within the Church.

In their polemical argumentation, these critics of the restoration of unity among Christians do not hesitate to distort reality in order to deceive and arouse the faithful. They are silent about the fact that theological dialogues are conducted by the unanimous decision of all Orthodox churches, and so they attack the Ecumenical Patriarchate alone. They disseminate false rumors that union between the Roman Catholic and Orthodox churches is imminent, while they know well that the differences discussed in these theological dialogues remain numerous and require lengthy debate; moreover, they overlook that union is not decided by theological commissions but by Church synods. They assert that, because the Orthodox "submit" to dialogue with the Roman Catholics, the pope will supposedly subjugate the Orthodox! They condemn as "heretics" and "traitors" of Orthodoxy those who conduct these dialogues—and condemn them purely and simply because they converse with non-Orthodox, with whom they share the treasure and truth of our Orthodox faith. The critics of these dialogues speak condescendingly of every effort for reconciliation among divided Christians and for restoration of their unity, dismissing them as "the pan-heresy of ecumenism" without providing the slightest evidence that, in its contacts with non-Orthodox, the Orthodox Church has in any way abandoned or denied the doctrines of the ecumenical councils and of the Church Fathers.

Beloved children in the Lord, Orthodoxy has no need of either fanaticism or bigotry in order to protect itself. Whoever believes that Orthodoxy has the truth does not fear dialogue, because truth has never been endangered by dialogue. By contrast, when in our day all people strive to resolve their differences through dialogue, Orthodoxy cannot proceed with intolerance and extremism. You should have utmost confidence in your Mother Church. For the Mother Church has over the ages preserved and transmitted Orthodoxy even to other nations. And today, the Mother Church is struggling, in difficult circumstances, to maintain Orthodoxy as a vibrant and venerable worldwide body.

From the Ecumenical Patriarchate, this sacred center of Orthodoxy, we embrace all of you lovingly and bless you paternally, praying that you may journey in health through the holy period of contrition and asceticism known as holy and Great Lent, so that you may become worthy of celebrating the pure Passion and glorious Resurrection of our Savior Lord with all faithful Orthodox Christians throughout the world.

GREETINGS TO THE PAPAL DELEGATION, ECUMENICAL PATRIARCHATE

The addresses that follow were delivered in the Patriarchal Church of St. George.

November 30, 2001

BREAKING THE SILENCE THROUGH LOVE

Your Eminence Walter Cardinal Kasper and our other brethren in Christ, who constitute the delegation from the Church of Rome:[3] It is with great joy that we welcome you, as the delegation from the Church of the Senior Rome,[4] in the joyous celebration of the thronal Feast of our

---

3. The formal salutation is otherwise omitted in the following addresses. On all occasions, with the exception of November 30, 2006, when the pope was personally present, the head of the papal delegation to the Ecumenical Patriarchate was Cardinal Walter Kasper, president (1999–2010) of the Pontifical Council for Promoting Christian Unity.

4. "Senior Rome" or "Old Rome" are phrases referring to the Church of Rome and distinguishing it from "New Rome," which refers to the Church Constantinople as the

Church of Constantinople–New Rome,[5] conveying to us its love and greeting. We request of you that, on your return home, you convey to His Holiness, our beloved brother, Pope John Paul II of Rome, our heartfelt greetings, the expression of our love and our warm gratitude.[6]

Our heart rejoices at the prospect of reconciliation of unity in spirit and unity in faith in the bond of peace, as recommended by the Apostle Paul (see Eph. 4.3, 13) and as prayed by the Lord (see John 17.21). The degree to which our heart rejoices at this prospect is also the degree to which it is also in sorrow and pain in ascertaining that the dialogue of love and of truth, which began with such promise among our churches, is currently passing through a critical phase and risks discontinuance because of reactions to issues on which there exists a theoretical congruence of opinions but also the practical difficulty of acceptance, a difficulty resulting from long-standing conditions.

However, the Apostle who recommends unity to us also reveals to us that hope, together with faith and love, constitute a supreme gift, which we are obliged to pursue. By the grace of God, we have been granted the hope to realize His petition that those who believe in Him through the preaching of the Apostles "may be one." Guided, therefore, by this hope, just as a farmer sows his seed, we too sow proposals for dialogue and await their harvest. Of course, we do not ignore the gospel parable according to which "some seed fell on the path and was trampled on, and the birds of the air ate it up; some fell on the rock, and as it grew up, it withered for lack of moisture; and some fell among thorns, and the thorns grew with it and choked it" (Luke 8.5–7). However, we await and pray that at least part of the seed will fall on good soil and yield fruit a hundredfold.

---

church of the city established by Constantine the Great in 324. They were used in the Second Ecumenical Council of Constantinople (381) and the Fourth Ecumenical Council of Chalcedon (451) in order to define the authority of the Archbishop of Constantinople, who was granted "equal privileges" in 451 to the Pope of Rome.

5. The patronal, or thronal, feasts of the two churches mark the festive day commemorating their foundation by St. Andrew (November 30, in the case of the Church of Constantinople) or Saints Peter and Paul (June 29, in the case of the Church of Rome). The term "patronal" refers to patron saints; the term "thronal" refers to the Throne (or see) of Constantinople.

6. The exchange of formal annual delegations at the respective patronal feasts of the two churches was first established in the late 1960s by Ecumenical Patriarch Athenagoras and Pope Paul VI.

Anticipating this hundredfold result with hope, and fervently praying to God who increases the harvest, we sow the seed of dialogue in every direction, irrigating it and greatly rejoicing at every response while also standing with hope in case of silence. More particularly, in reference to the dialogue of love and of truth with the Roman Catholic Church, a dialogue that was begun by our ever memorable predecessors[7] and that has advanced favorably up to a point, though it is now passing through a critical phase, we repeat the words of St. John Chrysostom: "We cannot bear to remain silent before you, but always wish and desire to speak to and be in dialogue with you, as is the custom of those who love one another."[8]

We declare these things because we sincerely love you and every fellow human being, "descending from the throne of teaching, and entering into dialogue with brethren and friends who are our peers," to paraphrase our predecessor, the same St. John Chrysostom.[9] "Just as God is in dialogue with us each day,"[10] we too desire to be in dialogue with our brethren. "For what the embrace of hands is for the body, the exchange of words is for the soul."[11]

Dialogue does not merely gladden the heart as it extends to one's brethren (see 2 Cor. 6.11), but it also produces harvest, even when the word that is sown bears fruit only after a long time. For spiritual deliberations, which are the presupposition for entering the proposals for dialogue with us, demand much time, like the cultivation of the seed that is sown on good soil and produces fruit at the time of harvest.

PARTNERSHIP IN DIALOGUE

At any rate, in dialogues between churches comprising many thousands of members in their human dimension—members who, for centuries, have appropriated certain views as being true—we cannot expect any

---

7. The "dialogue of love" was initiated by Ecumenical Patriarch Athenagoras and Popes John XXIII (in 1959) and Paul VI (in 1963–64). The "dialogue of truth" was established by Ecumenical Patriarch Dimitrios and Pope John Paul II (in 1979–80).

8. PG 60.491.

9. PG 60.969.

10. PG 49.171.

11. PG 61.491.

rapid or universal acceptance of refined views that result from a dialogue in good faith. Nevertheless, even when the entire body appears unconvinced, some of its members intimate the views of their partners in dialogue, even accepting them or at least relinquishing their rigidity and persistent opposition, thereby becoming forerunners of a broader reconciliation.

We do not know which members are influenced by such dialogue or to which of the parties in dialogue any of these belong. Yet we believe that the word of truth, irrespective of its origin, is positively received by those who love truth. "Everyone who belongs to the truth listens to my voice" (John 18.37), says the Lord. And so we believe that dialogue is eventually beneficial, even if for a time it appears fruitless. "God is in dialogue with us each day; and when we do not listen, He does not desist from dialogue."[12] So we, too, ceaselessly repeat the divine invitation addressed through the Prophet Isaiah: "Come now, let us talk together" (Is. 1.18).

We consider that dialogue is realized not only among the few members who participate in the respective delegations of the churches but also among the members of each Church in their entirety. And so we also recognize benefit in the influence that dialogue has on the faithful whose numbers and identity remain indefinite. Moreover, given the wider publication of the statements that have issued from the dialogues, attentive seekers of truth will, like honeybees, be able to glean all that is truthful in these and to construct an image of truth, being transformed from glory to glory, until with unveiled faces they discern the glory of the Lord. Then, reflecting His image, they will henceforth have Him as their guide and model, from personal experience and not from theoretical learning, moving through His power "as if through the Spirit of the Lord" (2 Cor. 3.18).

Ultimately, this is what we regard as the goal of dialogue—namely, the formation within us of that spiritual condition through which we will be able, by the grace of God, with pure minds and selfless intentions, to see truth itself in person, our Lord Jesus Christ, in His actual glory. When we have achieved this, we are filled with ecstasy and wonder at the vision of Mount Tabor, and all mortal flesh is silent, standing with fear and trembling. For then the soul stands in the presence of the king of glory, whom it has desired. In His presence, many of the problems dividing us

---

12. PG 49.171.

imperfect human beings, and especially those issues bearing on personal conditions and distinctions, are minimized and become as nothing. Indeed, we too wonder how we could attribute such significance to these problems.

Come, then, beloved brethren representing the Senior Rome, let us converse. Come, let us talk about the hope that is in us and about the image of Him whose name we bear and whose image we reflect, so that we may be transformed according to His pattern. Jesus Christ is, as all of us accept, the same yesterday and today and for the ages. He is our head, and we must act in accordance with His mind, for everything that is ours is recapitulated in Him. Consequently, as we have stated on another occasion, the primary object of our dialogue concerns how we have beheld Him, how our hands have touched Him, how His grace has been showered on us, and what changes it has wrought in us. "We are in dialogue with you in all things and in all boldness, as with those whom we love, neither constraining nor concealing anything," in the words, again, of our predecessor St. John Chrysostom.[13]

Yet, our dialogue is also mandatory for another reason. Today's world experiences great stress stemming from insufficient human communication. Uncertainty and suspicion prevail with respect to the sincerity, intentions, and aspirations of various human societies that rally against each other. The Church of Christ, as bearing His message of love, peace, justice, solidarity, reconciliation, and in general the kingdom of heaven, which includes every virtue and fulfills every good heart, must become an instrument of communication, of efficient dialogue, stability, and peace. This will better be achieved if we convince our fellow human beings that we are able to be in dialogue and in concord within our own territory. Then the world will believe that God sent Christ, as Christ said of Himself (John 17.21), and it will lend a listening ear to Him as sent by the Father. We must not, through our conduct, prevent the world from approaching the king of peace and reconciliation.

We say these things in great love and with fervent heart. "For I do not greet you only by word of mouth," says St. John Chrysostom, "but my heart too concurs. This is why I speak to you in boldness, with the lips of my mouth and the depth of my mind."[14] These words of our saintly

---

13. PG 61.491.
14. Ibid.

predecessor fully express our feelings and those of this most sacred Ecumenical Throne, as we conclude this greeting and express once more our warm gratitude for your fraternal participation, in the name of the Church of Rome, on the feast of the Church of this New Rome. May God's grace be with you all.

November 20, 2002

THE PAIN OF DIVISION

We welcome you to the courts of the Church of New Rome with much love and joy, and thank you on behalf of our Church for your participation, both personally and as a delegation from the most holy pope of Rome and the Church of Rome, on the feast of the Apostle Andrew, the first-called Apostle and founder of our Church. The yearly participation of a delegation from one of our respective churches to the patronal feast of the other began some years ago and continues to this day. It is an indication of the goodwill toward the ideal of closer acquaintance and cultivation of love and cooperation between our two churches.

This year is indeed worthy of special exaltation because a century has been completed since our ever memorable predecessor Patriarch Joachim III[15] addressed his celebrated encyclical of the year 1902.[16] Through this encyclical of historic import, all Christian churches were invited to participate in the establishment of a dialogue so that they might be more closely acquainted with each other cooperate more closely in practical matters. They were also invited to prepare themselves for closer relations and, in time, for the restoration of unity, so long as they would seek and achieve this difficult target of unity through commitment to the faith of the first undivided Church.

The pain of the division of the Church's believers into many parts, which are deprived of communion and to a large extent are not in touch with one another or perhaps express hostility toward one another, is one that seized the author of that encyclical and, unfortunately, continues to

15. Joachim III (1834–1912) served as Ecumenical Patriarch from 1878 to 1884 and 1901 to 1912.

16. This encyclical addressed the issue of unity within the Church as well as the importance of relations between Orthodox, Catholic, and Protestant Christians.

bring sorrow to our hearts. Certainly progress has been made. Relations between the various churches today are friendlier, and substantial collaboration has been achieved. The steps being taken toward fuller realization of these relations and toward restoration of unity in faith are, however, still very timid. This is perhaps because of the different ways of life observed by different churches over the centuries. The development during this period of divergent doctrines also inhibits the movement toward full unity, which the heart yearns for and the mind approves of.

Indeed, the hearts of both our Modesty and of all pious Christians are in deep sorrow at seeing the divisions in the body of Christ. We are seized by acute pain as we hear, repeated for so many centuries but never heeded, the cry of grief of the Apostle Paul: "Is Christ divided?" (1 Cor. 1.13). This sorrow and pain, however, do not diminish the love, because love never fails. The aforementioned encyclical of our ever memorable predecessor Joachim III was precisely the product of this love of the Ecumenical Patriarchate for all and especially for those who share the same faith. It is because of such love that this hundred-year-old encyclical has not lost its relevance. Rather, it confirms the necessity that it be studied it once again and the necessity of accepting the invitation, extended to all who bear the name of Christ, to become more acquainted with each other and engage in closer collaboration. Surely, when we examine the situation that exists today and compare it to what ought to exist in accordance with the commandments of our Lord Jesus Christ and of the holy Apostles, commandments pertaining to the unity of all believers, we find that, over history, as Christendom, we fall short of this ideal by a large measure. We also find that we have far to go in order to reach the center of our common ground and to undo our separation from each other, a circumstance that our centrifugal and divisive manner of life for many centuries has fostered.

The Ecumenical Patriarchate always wishes and prays that this rapprochement is accomplished and that all obstacles inhibiting the unity of Christians are lifted. It does not, of course, hold the view that this unity will be achieved through any minimalist acceptance of common faith or obliteration of existing differences. There are some matters that do not pertain to the faith or the holy canons promulgated by the holy ecumenical councils and that each local Christian community may deal with differently. For those matters that pertain to faith, however, unity is necessary and must be sought in the context of the undivided Church before the Schism.

SELF-CRITICISM AND SINCERE DIALOGUE

The seemingly indissoluble nexus of all those differences, disagreements, and historical commitments, which have been inherited from the past, cannot be dissolved except through sincere self-criticism and honest dialogue. This is what produces the need for dialogue and what determines the grounds of its success—namely, individuals studying and sincerely contributing to clarification of the points where divergent doctrines have been developed in the various Christian communities. This need is at the same time a duty of love, deriving from each one's obligation to inform his brother about his faith and hope. This mutual exchange of information, which takes place in dialogue, transmits not only mere knowledge but also the heartfelt warmth of love and other feelings that the participants in a dialogue exchange with each other.

This transmission is a spiritual communion, a kenosis that aspires to the enrichment of the other. It is not a contest aiming at scoring victory over the other but rather an offering of the overflow of experience in participating in the truth of Christ. It is precisely for this reason that it is an unselfish and sacrificial offering. What is sacrificed, however, is not truth—for the sake of a supposedly fraternal avoidance of confrontation—but rather he who offers himself according to the example of our Lord Jesus Christ, who came into the world to bear witness to the truth and became a martyr for it through His sacrifice on the cross.

According to our saintly predecessor John Chrysostom, God is always in dialogue with us. Indeed, God carries on dialogue even "by a silent voice," according to St. Gregory of Nyssa.[17] He carries on dialogue through His creation and through inspiration in the hearts of those of us who are receptive. He carries it on also through prophets and apostles but chiefly and primarily through His incarnate Word and through His Spirit, the Paraclete, who institutes the entire constitution of the Church.

This is why the premise for the success of our dialogue concerning our Triune God and His Church is the participation of the Word of God through the Holy Spirit. At the first apostolic synod, the holy Apostles who participated assured us that they and the Holy Spirit codetermined

---

17. The younger brother of St. Basil the Great and close friend of St. Gregory the Theologian, St. Gregory of Nyssa (335–94) was one of the most prominent theologians of the fourth century.

the decision taken: "It seemed good to the Holy Spirit and to us" (Acts 15.28).[18] If we human beings are alone when we engage in dialogue, then the results of our efforts would be impoverished. Christ must always be invited and must be present in our dialogues, and we should desire to speak as He would speak. With such consciousness and direction, most of our difficult problems would find their solution much more easily.

This is the dialogue in which we so strongly desire to participate. Looking toward its accomplishment, we always address a wholehearted invitation to all. Even when its outcome is not immediately visible, its effect is useful and beneficial. This is because the specification of the differences and difficulties alone, and the realization of the distance that separates the perceptions of one party from the other, constitute a most useful component in the further development of dialogue.

We have before our eyes the hope of recommencing the dialogue. However painful the treatment of certain matters may be, it is nonetheless necessary and redemptive. Without approaching these matters in the light of the cross, the separation is prolonged and those who hesitate to take up the necessary responsibilities bear the heavy accountability of timidity in the act of bearing witness with the crucified Christ to the truth. It is with friendliness, love, and sincerity, without criticism or bitterness about the past, that we again call all Christians to carry on a dialogue about the hope that is in us. By discussing with one another in truth, we honor our brother in dialogue most deeply, recognizing his value and God-given freedom.

Heeding the commandments of the Apostle, who says, "Owe no one anything, except to love one another" (Rom. 13.8) and "Outdo one another in showing honor" (Rom. 12.10), we welcome with all honor and love everyone who participates in this festal joy of our Church. We express to all the deepest thanks of our Modesty and of our holy and sacred Synod, of the sacred clergy and of the Christ-loving laity, and we invoke on all the grace and the rich mercy of our Lord and Savior Jesus Christ through the intercessions of the holy first-called Apostle Andrew, founder of the holy and great Church of Christ of Constantinople, whose memory we celebrate with exceeding joy.

---

18. It is also the opening phrase of decisions made through the centuries by ecumenical councils in the Orthodox Church.

November 30, 2003

HISTORICAL RESPONSIBILITY

We express our warm thanks and those of our holy and sacred Synod for your support in the spiritual work of the Ecumenical Patriarchate. This support is demonstrated today by your participation at our patronal feast once again. We especially thank His Holiness, our brother the pope of Rome, John Paul II, for sending representatives, present here in our midst. We ask them to communicate to him our warm wishes for the strengthening of his health.

The Ecumenical Patriarchate is the coordinator and communicator of the unity of the most holy Orthodox churches. It has performed its mission for one and a half millennia and in a special way during the past millennium, particularly since the Schism between East and West, sometimes under very difficult circumstances for the Orthodox Church. On this day, during which we celebrate the sacred and venerable memory of the founder of the church of our city, St. Andrew, the first-called Apostle of our Lord Jesus Christ, we remember its historic course and the important role it has played throughout the centuries. This city, which has been the see of our church, developed in its political aspect to become the capital of an empire, which endured for an entire millennium. Its church became the center of the most significant events of this historical period.[19] Even when the empire fell, the church of Constantinople was charged with the spiritual leadership of the Orthodox Christian population in many nations, which were governed by a state authority under the influence of a different religion.

Throughout this period of sixteen centuries of historical ecumenical and ecclesiastical responsibility, the Ecumenical Patriarchate experienced the unity of all faithful in Christ as an ontological reality. The unity of citizens of a multiethnic society is a political reality, wherein differences among people may be veiled but the absolute unity of soul and spirit is by no means assured. And so the appearance of divisions and conflicts

19. On the "principle of apostolicity" (the importance of a church being founded by an Apostle) and the "principle of accommodation" (the notion of a Church's importance being grounded in the political influence of its home city), see Francis Dvornik, *The Idea of Apostolicity in Byzantium and the Legend of the Apostle Andrew* (Washington, D.C.: Dumbarton Oaks, 1958), esp. 1–38.

between political regimes as well as their fragmentation and their ultimate fall comes as no surprise. Rather, what causes surprise and gives the appearance of divisions within the Church of Christ herself, which, according to the creed, is the fact that it remains "one, holy, catholic, and apostolic." The Apostle Paul in his Letter to the Galatians points out that, within the Church, there is no difference between Jew and Greek, free person and slave, man and woman: They are all one in Christ. This is simultaneously an ontological reality and a duty assigned to the faithful. It is also at once God's gift and God's commandment.

Therefore, the divisions that have been known from the earliest centuries of Christianity mean that the ontological transfiguration of the faithful into one body of Christ has not yet been achieved. This is not because God has denied His grace but rather because humanity has not accepted the conditions of that grace. God wills all to be saved and to come to the knowledge of truth. God knocks on the door of everybody's heart and, when the heart responds freely and positively, God makes it His permanent dwelling. The failure to reach unity signifies a more general failure in the spiritual life in Christ.

In his Letter to the Ephesians, the Apostle Paul, that deep explorer of the recesses and processes of the human soul, in a moment of spiritual exaltation poetically declares the presuppositions of the unity of the faithful in Christ:

> I therefore, the prisoner of the Lord, beseech you to walk in a way worthy of the vocation to which you are called, with all lowliness and meekness, with longsuffering, forbearing one another in love, endeavoring to preserve the unity of the Spirit in the bond of peace. There is one body, and one Spirit, even as you are called in the one hope of your calling; one Lord, one faith, one baptism, one God and Father of all, who is above all, and through all, and in you all.
>
> Eph. 4.1–6

One body, one Spirit, one hope, one Lord, one faith, one baptism, one God and Father of all: These are the conditions for the unity of all the faithful in Christ. Wherever even one of these conditions does not exist, disunion and individualism among the faithful are the inevitable consequences, with the obvious and painful result of division that we experience today. Many ecclesiastical bodies, many spirits, many hopes, many "lords," many faiths, and many opinions about the Christian God: All of these make people wonder if Christians, who in their creed confess their belief in one God, really do believe in one God or if, having different understandings of the one and only God, they think and act as if they believe in many different gods.

REPENTANCE AND UNITY

The saddest part of the great Christian division is that most Christians do not see it as a failure and a call to repentance or reunification but rather accept it as natural, proposing theories and arguments to legitimize the division, reminding us of the words of the Psalmist who declares, "I find excuses for committing my sins" (Ps. 143). Christians are very comfortable with how they are and how they live—that is to say, they excuse their division into many confessions, many faiths, many baptisms, many spirits, and many hopes. This is clearly evident when one compares the often passive and sometimes self-complacent attitude of each Christian to the painful prayer of the Lord before the last moment of His earthly life, when He asked His Father and God that all who will believe in Him "may be one" (John 17.21).

Many who assert belief in Christ neglect the commandment, found in His prayer, "that they may be one." They endeavor to justify their faith, which diverges from the faith of other Christians, with theories whereby that attempt to legitimize this division and differentiation. This means that they set forth their own perceptions about unity instead of accepting what Christ commanded in that regard. Such perceptions are to be found either in the unified structure of the established churches under one ecclesiastical administration, even if under this same ecclesiastical administration there exist believers with different faiths, as happens, typically, in the case of Uniatism within Roman Catholicism;[20] or else in the generalized faith in Christ, interpreted individually, as happens with numerous Protestant confessions. Such perceptions are also to be found in the theory

---

20. A term signifying the Eastern Catholic churches, which have maintained full communion with the Roman Catholic Church while preserving liturgical traditions of the Orthodox Church. Uniatism has been the source of contention and controversy in certain Orthodox churches as well as within Orthodox–Catholic discussions.

that unity is ultimately achieved through diversity, albeit a diversity of faiths and beliefs and not of external expressions of faith. The union of diverse faiths, however, is not the unity that the Apostle Paul experiences, endorses, and encourages to us as unity in the one and same faith in Christ and His body that is His Church.

All of these theories aimed at legitimizing present divisions are examples of the human way being set above the divine will and of the self-satisfaction of each individual being elevated above obedience to God's commandments. People do not want to lose their autonomy by belonging to the one body and one Spirit of Christ, and so they do not seek unity outside the scope of their own beliefs and choices. On the contrary, they are convinced that their own choice of faith is the correct one, believing that all others should belong to it. Therefore, they refuse to be a part of another Christian faith. As a result, division is perpetuated and becomes legitimized as if in accordance with the will of Christ, in spite of His agonized prayer that all Christians may be one, after the pattern of His own unity with the Father.

Non-Orthodox Christians who listen to these words might well say that, for the sake of unity, the Orthodox Church, too, is obliged to accept some of the positions supported by other churches. This opinion ignores that the content of the Christian faith does not fall under the authority of each individual and that it cannot be dealt with or disposed of as if it were a personal possession. The faithful are obliged to keep the deposit of faith not as an ideological and intellectual fossil but as a living way of life. A different faith implies a different way of life; yet, as already noted, it does not lie within the individual authority of the faithful to determine the Christian ethos and the content of the Christian commandments.

This determination was made by the Lord and transmitted through the Apostles orally, sometimes even being recorded in their letters. The rejection of the living tradition by the faithful of Protestant confessions has resulted in their total reliance on faith and their ultimate legitimatization of individual opinions as the unique criterion of truth. It is obvious that such a perception about truth, expressed in various contradictory opinions and attitudes, is unacceptable from both a rational and an ecclesiastical point of view. On the contrary, the truth is one, just as the Apostle Paul says that there is one faith, one baptism, and one Lord. Therefore, we faithful must aim to see the one icon of Christ and be transfigured according to this unique icon. If each one sees the icon of Christ in a different way, and if each tends to imitate or resemble what one sees, the result is many faiths and many lords, each differing from one another, according to individual choice.

However, we have the ability to be one in Christ by the grace of God, although we have to realize that, in the words of the Apostle Paul, we must endeavor "to keep the unity of the Spirit in the bond of peace" (Eph. 4.3). In order to achieve this, we should not put forward our own opinion about the Lord and about the content of faith as being correct. Instead we should investigate which is the faith of the ancient Church, as experienced and expressed by the Apostles and Holy Fathers.

This search for the common fundamental Christian faith in our time, especially when we have been divided into many Christian confessions, can take place only through a dialogue in love and truth. For this reason, the Ecumenical Patriarchate fearlessly carries on dialogues with all who are willing. It is prepared to understand the reasons for the historical divisions and explore ways of bringing all back to the one faith, one baptism, and one Lord. This is why our Church is opposed to every action that tends to stabilize existing divisions or promotes methods of unity that deviate from the apostolic ideal, promising human and administrative-ecclesiastical unification without a simultaneous return of all to the one faith, one baptism, the one icon of Christ, to which all must look and imitate. We would include so-called Uniatism among these methods of unification within the Christian Church—methods that we categorically reject. However, we support the efforts of the World Council of Churches as well as of all other interchurch and inter-Christian organizations in which the faithful of various Christian confessions are able to participate. We consider these organizations not to be promoting a kind of unity that cannot be achieved owing to differences of faith. Rather, we regard them as an opportunity for dialogue and for witnessing to our hope

> until we all come in the unity of the faith and of the knowledge of the Son of God, unto a perfect man, unto the measure of the stature of the fullness of Christ. That we henceforth be no more children, tossed to and fro, carried about with every wind of doctrine, by human deception, and cunning craftiness, whereby people lie in wait to deceive. But speaking the

truth in love, we may mature in all things into him, who is the head, even Christ.

Eph. 4.13–15

The solution to the problem of unity among Christians lies in these words from Paul's Letter to the Ephesians—namely, in the unity of knowledge and in the maturity of growth in the Son of God. Everything else follows naturally. However, without this unity in the knowledge of the Son of God, nothing else can achieve unity of faith or unity of the churches.

We wholeheartedly and fervently pray that our Lord Jesus Christ will reveal to all those invoking and bearing His name the true icon of His face, so that we may all reach the unity of His knowledge, which will bring unity among all Christian churches. Yet, until we arrive at this point, we must conduct dialogues with all people in a spirit of reconciliation and understanding, "speaking the truth in love" and witnessing our hope as the only hope of the whole world, whether it knows or ignores this. May the grace of God and His abundant mercy be with you all.

November 30, 2004

RELICS OF THE SAINTS

The feast of St. Andrew, the first-called and founder of the Church of the once small town of Vyzas, which subsequently became the great city of Constantine, is the occasion for us to gather here today in an encounter where the longing for unity is vivid and manifest. The feast is all the more illustrious, and the longing for unity all the more urgent, by reason of the exceeding joy we feel on this occasion, as the senior Church of Rome returns and restores to the Church of Constantinople–New Rome the venerable relics of our holy predecessors Gregory the Theologian and John Chrysostom.[21] It takes but little effort to sense resonating about us the words of the St. Gregory, words uttered sixteen centuries ago in this city: "As for me, my tongue is loosened and my voice raised like a trumpet before the present benefaction and before this most beautiful sight of the

---

21. On the return of the relics of Saints Gregory the Theologian and John Chrysostom, see Introduction, 9.

children of God who, formerly dispersed, are now gathered into one, taking rest under the same wings and in the house of God, progressing in concord, and joined in one covenant of good and of the Spirit."[22]

At this hour of jubilation, then, we express again the warm thanks of our Church, together with our personal thanks for this invaluable gift, first of all to God and then to the most holy pope of Rome as well as to the curia for their decision, so well disposed, so imbued with brotherly love, and so very just, to authorize the return of these sacred relics to our Church, to which they formerly belonged and from which they were unfortunately removed. As we know, these relics were removed eight hundred years ago, during a period of tumultuous ecclesiastical dispute and secular tension, whose divisive consequences continue to this day and will assuredly continue in the future if we of the present generation do not resolve to reverse the course on which we have been embarked for centuries, a course that places a great distance between us, in order to direct the course instead into one that leads to our convergence.

More than eight decades ago, in its noted encyclical letter, the Ecumenical Patriarchate proposed that a tactical course of conflict that had been followed up to that point be transformed into a course of rapprochement.[23] This is a proposal that has on the whole been accepted and borne fruit, of which this occasion that so gladdens us today is an example—namely, the restoration of the venerable relics of the aforementioned saints, the several dialogues that are being held, albeit not without occasional difficulties, and, generally, the creation of a climate in which awareness of the need for unity as a universal obligation incumbent on all Christians prevails.

---

22. *First Theological [or Irenic] Oration* 7. See F. Williams and L. Wickam, *On God and Christ: The Five Theological Orations and Two Letters to Cleidonius* (Crestwood, N.Y.: St. Vladimir's Seminary Press, 2002).

23. Referring to the historical 1920 synodal encyclical of the Ecumenical Patriarchate issued "to the churches of Christ everywhere." In this encyclical, the Ecumenical Patriarchate proposed a "league of churches" and declared that the Orthodox Church "holds that rapprochement between the various Christian churches and fellowship between them is not excluded by the doctrinal differences which exist between them. In our opinion such a rapprochement is highly desirable and necessary. It would be useful in many ways for the real interest of each particular church and of the whole Christian body, and also for the preparation and advancement of that blessed union which will be completed in the future in accordance with the will of God. We therefore consider that the present time

Of course, those who would regard all efforts at rapprochement with mistrust or timidity are never entirely absent. However, we believe that, with the passage of time, all will be persuaded that rapprochement is sought and achieved not by sacrificing the fastidiousness of our faith—not, in other words, through concessions on matters of truth with a purpose of securing a minimum of commonly acceptable truths, as some who are unfamiliar with how matters actually stand have proposed. Rather, it is sought actually within truth itself—that is, through the experience of the whole truth by all and sundry in the Holy Spirit, the truth that is the unity with Him who said, "I am the way, and the truth, and the life" (John 14.6). It is within this experience alone that a secure and indissoluble unity may be attained. For any external unity, which relies on the suppression of differences through inclusive formulations of the articles of the creed, cannot be maintained for long; nor can it satisfy the demand of the Lord's intercessory prayer that all who believe in Him "may be one."

In actual fact, the unity that the Lord desires is spiritual, personal, and absolute; it is not merely administrative, organizational, or ideological; moreover, it is hard to achieve because of our human frailty. Nonetheless, it is the goal toward which we must look perseveringly and unwaveringly "till we all come to unity of the faith and to knowledge of the Son of God" (Eph. 4.13). The vision of a single Christian fold and of a single shepherd, being our Lord Jesus Christ rather than any mere human being, must not for a moment be absent from our minds, while the proliferation of Christian sects and differentiated groups should never be gratifying to us.

LEARNING FROM THE SAINTS

Nobody would deny that ecclesiastical unity must be prepared through common acceptance and mutual understanding of the articles of faith, which the aforementioned dialogues pursue and serve. In this respect, in the same first *Irenic Oration* that we have already cited, our predecessor St Gregory the Theologian adds that "nothing so strongly urges concord within those who are genuinely disposed toward God as the agreement

---

is most favorable for bringing this important question and studying it together." This encyclical is credited with inspiring the modern ecumenical movement and the creation of the World Council of Churches.

regarding God; and nothing so leads to disunity and discord as disagreement regarding God." Nevertheless, ecclesiastical unity must be considered and experienced more profoundly than as mere organizational or administrative union, as mere coincidence of opinions and convictions, or even simple agreement on the formulation and intellectual conceptualization of doctrinal truths as a whole. A theological and intellectual agreement certainly helps and can pave the way to unity, but it is not in itself the end; it does not in itself constitute unity. The "unity of the acknowledgment of the Son of God" spoken of by the Apostle is the communion of an ontological nature with Christ, in whom alone can unity be achieved. This becomes particularly apparent when we note that schisms and divisions exist also among Christian groups that do not disagree on basic doctrinal principles of faith.

It has indeed been noted in history that certain doctrinal differences are promoted so as to be exploited as a means of fomenting political alienation and crushing the spirit of cooperation among peoples. Doctrinal contention is used to rationalize or defend a preexisting psychological estrangement. The words of our Lord Jesus Christ about His relationship with the Father—"If you had known me, you would have known my Father also" (John 8.19); "whoever that has seen me has seen the Father" (John 14.9); and many other scriptural passages of similar nature, including, in Christ's intercessory prayer, the phrase "that they may be one," followed by the words "even as we are" (John 17.11)—all these imply a unity whose nature resembles the unity of the three persons of the Holy Trinity. This unity is indeed difficult for human beings to conceive or achieve, which is why St. John Chrysostom, when interpreting the Lord's words "where two or three are gathered together in my name, there am I in the midst of them" (Matt. 18.20), considers sameness of opinion and an absolute agreement of spirit and heart as something extraordinary.

Such agreement presupposes an ontological union of the gathered faithful with Christ—the ability for each of them to say, "Nevertheless, I live: yet not I, but Christ lives in me" (Gal. 2.20). Then, certainly, those gathered in the name of Jesus Christ not only feel but truly are one in Christ, in whom all live. Consequently, the unity of the faithful with Christ and with one another is the ultimate and utmost achievement, the final step of their spiritual evolution and progress; by the same token, it is also their primary and most essential concern.

Given all this, the attitude of all must be positive before we make any effort that benevolently and sincerely tends toward the unity we seek and desire. And so we will remain in dialogue with all those who desire unity, even if we are divided by difficulties and disagreements, which we will remain in dialogue in order to overcome through consultation. This course is encouraged by St. John Climacus, who undertook the good struggle in the seventh century, well before the Schism; for, as he writes in his discourse *To the Shepherd,* those pastors who are strong in faith, when they are invited by heretics in a spirit of trust and goodwill, should respond positively.[24] He also emphasized in his *Ladder of Divine Ascent* that, to all those who desire to learn the truth, we should never refrain from doing good "to the end of time"—that is to say, with inexhaustible patience and love—even though they lack faith or are heretical.[25] Nonetheless, he adds, our comportment should also be commensurate with our spiritual strength and endurance. The command of Apostle Paul that we abandon heretics after a first and second admonition is more pastoral than doctrinal. A strong shepherd, one who knows the full truth in Christ, is entitled and obligated to seek the stray sheep and to debate with them until they are gathered into the one fold of the one Christ, as we read in the parable of the good shepherd, who left the ninety-nine sheep in search of the one who was lost.

Naturally, no Christian would accept the term *heretical* as applying to oneself. Yet, in fact, it is obvious to all that Christians today are divided into numerous groups, some of which accept as truth views that others reject, so that one of those in disagreement must surely be in error about the faith. The revelation as to who is in the right and who in the wrong is, on a human level, a matter of sincere, painstaking, and unremitting dialogue in good faith; on the divine level, it is a matter of divine revelation to pure hearts that unceasingly strive for and sincerely seek after the true person of Christ. Certainly human beings alone are incapable of acquiring the living truth; for, as Christ assured us, "No person can come to me, except it be given to him by my Father" (John 6.65). For this, however, to be granted "from on high," certain prerequisites must be

---

24. Paragraph 65.
25. See Step 26, ii, 11.

fulfilled, the first of which is that the quest must remain unselfish, unsullied by any historical or personal prejudice. We do not a priori cast any doubt on the sincerity of anyone with whom we are in dialogue; and we hope that we will be vindicated for our trustfulness. However, we cannot ignore the contentions that have accrued and that constitute an onerous, problematical heritage not only in themselves but also in terms of their psychological implications.

Our Lord Jesus Christ promised that, when two or three people on this earth agree on everything they would ask from God, their request would be granted; for, when two or three are gathered in His name, He assures us that He is among them. And so Christ too is making the same request to the Father, who accepts the requests of the Son. Yet, though it may seem easy, it is quite difficult for two or three to agree people on any request; moreover, it is quite difficult to gather in His name—in other words, "in the presence of the very person" of Christ—when they disagree as to His person. Who or what is Jesus Christ for each of the Christians engaged in dialogue? What constitutes His Church? Whose head is He? What exactly is His will? Such are the questions to which a single answer, agreed on and grounded in experience, must be rendered for any gathering truly to exist in the common name of the same Christ. Until such unity of spirit is achieved, we must overcome many hurdles, while at the same time we must not be overwhelmed by pessimism in the face of our having not yet achieved this desirable perfect unity. Thus, we embark on the course that leads toward this unity, and the Lord is so good as to supplement what is lacking among us. As our predecessor St. John Chrysostom stated so succinctly in his beautiful *Catechetical Homily*, his well-known Easter sermon, the Lord is so good as to reward us, though we come at the eleventh hour, even as He rewards those who have worked from the first hour.

With such optimism and hope, with faith in Christ's love for all and with a benevolent, fraternal disposition, we sincerely expect that the words of our Lord Jesus Christ about the one fold and the single shepherd will ultimately be realized—even if at the eleventh hour. Therefore, we cordially greet the delegation of elder Rome, along with His Holiness Pope John Paul II,[26] who dispatched it, for graciously participating in the

---

26. This was the last time that the papal delegation was commissioned by Pope John Paul II, who died on April 2, 2005.

patronal feast of our Church. We also greet all those who share in our joy
for the feast of the founder of our Church, St. Andrew, and for the return
of the venerable relics of our predecessors St. Gregory the Theologian and
St. John Chrysostom. It is our fervent hope that this doubly illustrious
day will mark a new period of more concerted progress toward the unity
that we desire for all Christian churches and all people in Christ.

November 30, 2005

STAGES OF DIALOGUE

In celebrating today the blessed memory of St. Andrew, the first-called
Apostle and founder of our Church, we first express our admiration and
joy, because it is through his intercessions and blessings that our Church
grew and was glorified, survived though persecuted, and still lives to this
very day. The little leaven of the first few believers, through the uncreated
energy of the Holy Spirit, affected such a multitude of individuals and
peoples, cultivating to such great spiritual depth and width the ferment
of the most holy Church of Constantinople, that their successors were
able to carry on their shoulders the great responsibility of the Church
commissioned through the decisions of the ecumenical synods. Therefore,
we would like to express our gratitude to God that for making us worthy
of ministering to this Church which has been persecuted for centuries,
undergoing many trials and tribulations. However, throughout, the words
of God to the Apostle Paul have also proved to be true: "My strength is
perfected in weakness" (2 Cor. 12.9).

In such a joyful state of wonder, gladness, and gratitude, we are deeply
aware of your brotherly love, Your Excellency Cardinal Kasper, as well as
the love of our very beloved brother His Holiness, Pope of Rome Benedict
XVI,[27] who has sent this official delegation, and we would like to thank
all of you wholeheartedly for coming here today in order to celebrate with
us. Our brotherly feelings, however, are permeated by sorrow that we
have still not succeeded in partaking from the one bread and drinking
from the same cup so that, in accordance with the sentiment of the Apostle, we who are many might be one body (1 Cor. 10.17). To be sure,

---

27. Pope Benedict XVI was elected successor to Pope John Paul II on April 19, 2005.

we experience both ontologically and existentially this intense sorrow of spiritual separation, a separation more painful than any other. We pray fervently for the achievement of this desired unity of all in Christ, but we also urge all to maintain a productive dialogue of goodwill.

Our Lord Jesus Christ is knocking unceasingly on the door of the hearts of all people, waiting for them to open so that He may enter and bring life, freedom, the knowledge of truth, and the peace that surpasses all understanding. Our prayer is in harmony with His work. We pray that He may always invite all people to Himself, to joy and freedom, to life and eternity. By the same token, our invitation for dialogue addresses all people, regardless of faith or standing. The final goal we desire is that we may learn the truth that is in Christ and taste the great delight that derives from knowing Christ. This can be attained only if we take the division that is in our hearts and replace it with the purpose of uniting with all people in Christ, a unity that is the fullness of love and joy.

Certainly, the course for the unity of all has various levels and stages of progress; it is also an issue that plays out over a period of time that exceeds the lifespan of most individuals. First, there is a need to ameliorate human adversity, which is so widespread, and gradually to foster relations of mutual acceptance and tolerance, even trust. The anticipated goal of this dialogue is not a personal victory of one side over another; the goal is to discover a ray of truth and accept this truth in common. The discovery and acceptance of the first ray of truth should therefore lead to a discovery of yet another ray, and so on. The more the mind of a human being is enlightened, the more one discovers that peaceful coexistence with one's fellow human beings is ultimately beneficial to all.

The fullness of the truth, however, cannot be obtained or ensured only through accuracy in expression, because it is chiefly an ontological reality. It is an experience in Christ; indeed, it is Christ. Living in Christ cannot be achieved simply by means of the intellect. It also requires a genuine grafting onto Him, as in the case of a well-cultured olive tree (Rom. 11.23) and in the communion of His body and spirit (1 Cor. 10.16) as well as in the ascent to Mount Tabor and in participation in His Transfiguration (Matt. 17.2–6), so that we may be enlightened by the uncreated divine light and recognize Jesus walking among us under a different guise, knowing Him "in the breaking of the bread" (Luke 24.35). All this does not in the end depend on accuracy or correctness in the formulation of truth. It is an indication that the formulation of truth cannot fully express reality or substitute for it. The formulation of truth are the palisades, the boundaries beyond which truth ceases to exist; but the full knowledge of truth—that is, the ontological participation in it—is not given only to those who understand its formulation and can analyze it.

Still, the Holy Fathers formulated, with much zeal and attention to detail, the dogmatic definitions of the holy ecumenical synods, in an effort to protect us from inadvertently overstepping the boundaries of truth and falling into the realm of error or deception. And so the definitions or terms simply denote or indicate the truth; they do not exhaust or embody it. Even so, they are necessary and useful, inasmuch as their understanding helps—especially if combined with love, faith, prayer, and other virtues—in the preparation for the acceptance of the great event that is the real encounter of the soul with Christ and the soul's incorporation into His body. Then the truth is lived experientially and all discussions concerning this issue become superfluous. Once the truth is lived, it transforms the one who experiences it into a herald of the gospel of peace and salvation—into one who declares, together with the Apostle, "Woe to me, if I do not preach the gospel" (1 Cor. 9.16).

UNITY IN CHRIST

With regard to this, one of our contemporary ascetics confirms through experience the long tradition of the Church when he says:

> The Christian . . . once he finds Christ, once he knows Christ, once Christ enters his insignificant soul and he feels Him, then he will want to call out and shout from the mountaintops, he will want to talk about Christ and about who Christ is. For once you love Christ, you prefer nothing else to His love. Christ is everything. He is the source of life. Everything beautiful and good exists in Christ.

Our effort to develop dialogues is, therefore, an effort that aims in the final stage to know the person and the love of Christ. First, however, it has to pass through the earlier stages of getting to know and love our neighbors, finding common ground and points of commonality that we share with them, just as the Apostle says that he "has become all things to all people in order that he might by all means save some" (1 Cor. 9.22). Our effort in this, while naturally pleasing in the eyes of God, who wants the unity of all in Christ, is nevertheless judged and criticized in manifold ways.

Some, who already belong to the Church, fear that an invitation to unity, if extended in the interest of peaceful coexistence to the heterodox and to those of different faiths, invariably conceals some concession of the truth. They believe that this somehow entails an acceptance of syncretism or even that this unity is pursued within the framework of abandoning certain truths in order to agree on others purely and simply for the sake of unity. However, their perception is not true; the unity of Christians cannot possibly be achieved outside the one and only Jesus Christ, who does not accept contradictory or different accounts and descriptions. He is the personal and sole expresser of truth; He is self-truth. It is not possible for us to be united if we ignore the face of Christ and all that it entails.

Therefore, if we try to find human expressions of the truth that, inasmuch as they are concise or perhaps obscure, give the impression that we are in agreement with all, we will not be successful in our unity. For we will simply be deceiving ourselves by creating an apparent unity, which would only cover and conceal our disagreement and division. It is simply impossible for a hidden disagreement to remain forever in secret. Sooner or later, the time will come when it will surface and reveal the decayed and decrepit nature of a hollow unity.

Some others, moreover, doubt the sincerity of those in dialogue. They suspect our collocutors have somehow set traps in order to ensnare us. We cannot of course rule out the possibility that a collocutor might be dishonest. However, we set our hopes in God, who knows our sincerity, that He will not allow us to injure the truth by becoming victims of insincere collocutors.

Still others refer to cases in the past when similar dialogues failed, claiming that this failure will be repeated in dialogues of our own time. And so they come to the conclusion that all new dialogues are in vain. If, however, even one soul benefits from these dialogues and returns from its erroneous path to the truth of Christ's way, then surely our hard work has been worthwhile, because one soul is worth more than the entire world.

There are, furthermore, those who support the idea that dialogues are nothing but the devil's deception, his way to seduce us through argumentation. Many who begin with the purpose of countering the enemy's arguments are indeed tempted, drawn into his promises, and are finally overtaken by him. Thus, it is true that in the course of history such incidents have occurred. Still, we are not afraid, for we do not depend on our own strength in order to hold fast to the truth. Rather, we hold on to the irresistible power of God. It is Him whom we beseech to protect and safeguard our collocutors, who are characterized by right and sound knowledge, from being seduced into the errors of their brothers. After all, "greater is the one that is within us, than the one that is in the world" (1 John 4.4).

Thinking along these lines, then, we follow the counsel of St. John of the Ladder, who advises us never to grow tired of conversing with those of good faith who ask the reason of the hope that we have within us. We have as our role model the one whom we celebrate and honor today, our patron saint, Andrew, the first-called Apostle, as well as all apostles through the centuries, who courageously conversed with our idolatrous forefathers and with those who held heterogeneous beliefs, calling them to knowledge of Christ.

Being aware of all these reservations, we nevertheless persist in our desire of dialogue with all—both with Christians who belong to the same denomination and those who are heterodox, with people of the same faith and those of a different faith. We hope to reach a better understanding of one another and develop peaceful relations so that, one day, we may realize the much desired peaceful coexistence of all humanity. If, then, we are asked to provide an individual with the opportunity to meet Christ, inviting that person to see Him living in the Church, we will definitely do so with joy. The manner and goal of each dialogue differs, of course, according to the situation, but the disposition is always peaceful and personal, while the goal is always encounter with and unity in Christ.

DIALOGUE OF TRUTH

As for the theological dialogue with our respected and beloved sister Roman Catholic Church, we sincerely desire to continue it, having overcome, with the fraternal intervention of the new Primate of the Church of Rome, the obstacles that have arisen in the recent past. The honorable and beloved pope of Rome, His Holiness Benedict XVI, also desires the cultivation of good relations between our two churches together with the promotion of cooperation and ultimate unity of our churches. We anticipate his visit here with honor and joy, once his obligations and responsibilities permit him.[28]

We also express our joy at the mutual lifting of excommunications, an event that took place on the seventh of December 1965,[29] almost exactly forty years ago, bringing about a radical change in the climate of the relations between Roman Catholic and Orthodox Christians, while allowing the restoration of peace between us. We also express our joy at the commencement and continuation of the theological dialogue, the obstacles encountered along the way notwithstanding.

A dialogue that is dispassionate and unprejudiced can only be beneficial, despite the hesitations of some, whose fear is grounded in memory of tensions in the past that led to the anathemas lifted in 1965. In any case, there is no doubt that a deviated course of a thousand years cannot be righted overnight and transformed into a course of convergence and unity. Nevertheless, we ought to preserve that convergence toward unity as our vision and we ought to labor for its realization. It is for this purpose that representatives of one church participate in conferences and celebrations of the other church. Besides attendance at our respective patronal feasts, another example of this is the recent conference of the bishops of the Roman Catholic Church, which convened to discuss the topic of the Holy Eucharist. That conference was attended by our representative, His Eminence Metropolitan John of Pergamon, who also serves as Orthodox co-president in the Joint International Commission for Theological Dialogue. Such was also the case when Your Eminence Cardinal Kasper attended our recent interreligious conference here on the topic of "Peace and Tolerance."[30]

---

28. Pope Benedict XVI formally responded to the invitation of Ecumenical Patriarch Bartholomew and officially visited the Phanar in November 2006.

29. The excommunications, or anathemas, dating to the Schism of 1054 were jointly lifted on December 7, 1965, by Ecumenical Patriarch Athenagoras and Pope Paul VI, in simultaneous services held at the Patriarchal Church of St. George and the Basilica of St. Peter, as a symbolic gesture of repentance for the divisions of the past and of reconciliation in the future. This gesture did not heal the schism between the two churches; however, it publicly demonstrated their sorrow and regret at unfortunate actions of the past as well as their goodwill and sincere desire for unity in the future.

30. The Second International Peace and Tolerance Conference, cosponsored by the Ecumenical Patriarchate and the Appeal of Conscience Foundation, took place in Istanbul in November 2005.

We wholeheartedly thank His Holiness Pope Benedict XVI of Rome for participating in our joy through his delegation. We thank as well as all those who participate in the celebration of this thronal Feast of the Ecumenical Patriarchate, and we invoke on all the grace and abundant mercy of God, through the intercessions of St. Andrew, the first-called of the Apostles.

November 30, 2006

REMEMBRANCE AND ANTICIPATION

By the grace of God, Your Holiness,[31] we have been blessed to enter the joy of the Kingdom, to "see the true light and receive the heavenly Spirit."[32] Every celebration of the Divine Liturgy is a powerful and inspiring concelebration of heaven and of history. Every Divine Liturgy is both an *anamnesis*[33] of the past and an anticipation of the Kingdom. We are convinced that during this Divine Liturgy we have once again been transferred spiritually in two directions: toward the kingdom to come, where angels already celebrate, and toward the historical celebration of the liturgy through the centuries. This overwhelming continuity with heaven as well as with history means that the Orthodox liturgy is the mystical experience and profound conviction that "Christ is and ever shall be in our midst!" For in Christ there is a deep connection between past, present, and future. And so the liturgy is more than merely the recollection of Christ's words and acts. It is the realization of the very presence of Christ Himself, who has promised to be wherever two or three are gathered in His name.

At the same time, we recognize that "the rule of prayer is the rule of faith" (*lex orandi lex credendi*), that the doctrines of the person of Christ and of the Holy Trinity have left an indelible mark on the liturgy, which comprises one of the undefined doctrines, "revealed to us in mystery," of which St. Basil the Great so eloquently spoke. This is why, in liturgy, we are reminded of the need to reach unity in faith as well as in prayer.

---

31. In the presence of Pope Benedict XVI, who attended the celebration of the Divine Liturgy at the Ecumenical Patriarchate during his official visit to the Phanar.

32. From a hymn chanted after the congregation has received Holy Communion.

33. Greek for "remembrance."

Therefore, we kneel in humility and repentance before the living God and our Lord Jesus Christ, whose precious name we bear and yet at the same time whose seamless garment we have divided. We confess in sorrow that we are not yet able to celebrate the holy sacraments in unity. And we pray that the day may come when this sacramental unity will be realized in its fullness.

And yet, Your Holiness and beloved brother in Christ, this concelebration of heaven and earth, of history and time, brings us closer to each other today through the blessing of the presence, together with all the saints, of the venerable predecessors of our Modesty—namely, St. Gregory the Theologian and St. John Chrysostom. We are honored to venerate the relics of these two spiritual giants, whose sacred relics were solemnly restored to this holy church only two years ago, when they were graciously returned to us by the late Pope John Paul II. Just as, during our thronal Feast, we welcomed and placed their saintly relics on the patriarchal throne and chanted, "Behold your throne!" so today we gather in their living presence and eternal memory as we celebrate the Liturgy named in honor of St. John Chrysostom.

And so our worship coincides with the same joyous worship in heaven and throughout history. Indeed, as St. John Chrysostom himself affirms, "Those in heaven and those on earth form a single festival, a shared thanksgiving, one choir."[34] Heaven and earth offer *one* prayer, *one* feast, *one* doxology. The Divine Liturgy is at once the heavenly kingdom and our home, "a new heaven and a new earth" (Rev. 21.1), the ground and center where all things find their true meaning. The Liturgy teaches us to broaden our horizon and vision, to speak the language of love and communion, but also to learn that we must be with one another in spite of differences and even divisions. In its spacious embrace, the Liturgy includes the whole world, the communion of saints, and all of God's creation, which becomes "a cosmic liturgy," to recall the teaching of St. Maximus the Confessor. This kind of liturgy can never grow old or outdated.

The only appropriate response to this showering of divine benefits and compassionate mercy is gratitude (*eucharistia*). Indeed, thanksgiving and glory are the only fitting response of human beings to their Creator. For

---

34. PG 56.97.

to Him belong all glory, honor, and worship: Father, Son, and Holy Spirit, now and always, and to the ages of ages. Truly, our hearts are filled with particular and wholehearted gratitude toward the loving God; for today, on the festive commemoration of the Apostle founder and protector of this Church, the Divine Liturgy is attended by His Holiness our brother and bishop of the elder Rome, Pope Benedict XVI, together with his honorable entourage. Once again, we gratefully welcome and greet this presence as a blessing from God, an expression of brotherly love, an honor bestowed on our Church, and evidence of our common desire to continue—in a spirit of love and faithfulness to the gospel truth and in the common tradition of our Fathers—the unwavering journey toward the restoration of full communion among our churches, a unity that is His divine will and command. May it be so.

November 30, 2007

THE RELICS OF ST. ANDREW

It is with particular joy that we welcome you today to this historical center of Orthodoxy on the occasion of the joyous feast of the Ecumenical Throne. Your presence here both strengthens and seals the bonds of love and trust between our churches, bonds that have been cultivated in recent decades and that have been especially established by the visit here last year of His Holiness, our most beloved brother in Christ, Pope Benedict XVI of Rome, and by his fervent participation in the thronal Feast of the Ecumenical Patriarchate.

We are particularly moved today because, this year, we enjoy the distinct blessing and spiritual pleasure of honoring the founder and patron of the Church of Constantinople, the glorious and first-called among the Apostles, Andrew, whose sacred relics were generously and graciously permitted by the love of His Holiness to be donated to us during our recent visit to Naples, being returned from Amalfi to the Throne of this Patriarchate[35] in order to remain here for the sanctification of our faithful

---

35. In October, 2007, during an interfaith conference organized in Naples by the Community of Sant Egidio, a relic of St. Andrew, previously preserved in the Roman Catholic Cathedral of St. Andrew in Amalfi, was presented to Ecumenical Patriarch Bartholomew.

and as a sign of communion with the Apostle, whom we commemorate today. The relics are a sign as well of the fraternal unity of Christians throughout the world. Thus, it is with fond memories that we recall our recent meeting with His Holiness in Naples and our constructive and brotherly conversation there. This encounter contributed to the cultivation of an atmosphere of friendship and cooperation between our two churches, strengthening yet further the relationship between us. We always believe that the peaceful coexistence of Christians, in a spirit of unity and concord, must be of fundamental concern to us all.

This is precisely what, during his visit here last year, we confirmed jointly with His Holiness in the Common Declaration, which we cosigned, stating that "we share the same emotions and the same intentions of brotherhood, cooperation, and communion in love and truth."[36] In an age when, as we once again jointly emphasized last year, we observe "the rise of secularism and relativism, or even nihilism, especially in the western world,"[37] we must take inspiration from the example of the Apostle Andrew, who "endured many trials in every land and spoke of numerous difficulties . . . and yet remained upstanding through the strength of Christ and for the sake of the faithful."[38]

CHRISTIAN UNITY: THE ROOTS OF WESTERN CIVILIZATION

The feast of this Apostle provides the appropriate occasion for us to pray together more intently for the restoration of unity within the Christian world. The fracture of this unity has been the cause of so much trouble in human affairs, and its consequences have proved tragic. The philosophy of the Enlightenment in the West and the French Revolution sparked a truly cultural revolution aimed at replacing the Christian tradition of the Western world with a new, non-Christian concept of man and society. This revolution gave rise in many ways to the practical materialism of contemporary societies but also to diverse forms of militant atheism and totalitarianism, which, over the past two centuries, have, it is sad

---

36. From the Common Declaration by Pope Benedict XVI and Patriarch Bartholomew, issued at the conclusion of the official papal visit to Constantinople on November 30, 2006. See Chapter 5, "Messages and Declarations," 417.

37. Ibid.

38. See the *Life of St. Andrew*, according to the *Synaxaristes* of Constantinople.

to recall, claimed the lives of millions of innocent victims. Those who remained faithful to Christian values were led to this new cultural environment by means of various processes and to the loss of the concept of mystery relating to God, to the loss of the concept of the living worship of Him—a sense of mystery that is genuinely preserved in the East—and to the reduction of religious life to a humanistic ethic through the importation of relativism into doctrinal formulations.

Today, then, it is our obligation more than ever to reclaim the Christian roots of Europe as well as the sacramental and doctrinal unity that it enjoyed before the Schism of our two churches. The re-evangelization of our peoples is "today, more so than ever before, timely and necessary, even within traditional Christian lands," as we admitted and confessed in common here exactly one year ago.

And so we believe that Western and Eastern Europe must stop regarding themselves as foreign to one another. Contact among Christians of the Latin tradition and the Orthodox faith could become most productive for both sides. For the feast of the Apostle Andrew, whom we commemorate and celebrate today, is a call for all Christians of the world to return to the fullness, youthfulness, and purity of the Christian tradition as found in the early Church. The example bequeathed to us by the Apostle Andrew, who remained faithful to His teacher throughout even the most grueling circumstances, preferring the Cross of Christ to any compromise, invites us to uncompromising resistance to the destructive consequences of the consumer culture we live in today, to the increasing relativism that characterizes our doctrine and faith, to "the diverse forms of exploitation of the poor, migrants, women, and children," as we declared again last year. He invites us as well to "joint action to preserve a respect for human rights in every human being created in the image and likeness of God." The first-called among the Apostles, St. Andrew, when threatened by the governor of Patras, could have modified the demands of his preaching to avoid a horrible death. Instead, he preferred eternal glory to the fleeting comfort of compromise, "considering the abuse that he suffered for Christ to be greater wealth" (Heb. 11.26). It is he who today calls all Christians, and especially ecclesiastical leaders and shepherds, "to choose rather to share ill-treatment with the people of God than to enjoy the fleeting pleasures of sin" (Heb. 11.26).

Today's celebration is an invitation extended to both our churches to embrace the unity of the Cross. Just as our Lord Jesus Christ stretched out His arms on the Cross, uniting what was formerly divided, so also His Apostle, in imitation of his Master, stretched out his arms, gathering us all today and calling us to stretch out our arms on the cross spiritually so that we might achieve unity.

Elder Rome has the foremost St. Peter as its Apostle and patron. New Rome, Constantinople, has the brother of St. Peter, the first-called of the Apostles, Andrew. Both invite us to the fraternal unity that they shared with each other and that can be acquired only when the Cross becomes our point of reference, the object we approach. Let us, therefore, beseech these two brothers and greatest of Apostles that they may grant peace to the world and lead everyone to unity, in accordance with today's very timely *troparion*[39] of St. Symeon Metaphrastes,[40] archbishop of Thessalonika:

> You, Andrew, were first called of the Apostles;
> Peter was supremely honored among the Apostles.
> Both of you endured the Cross of Christ,
> Proving imitators of Your Lord and Master,
> And one in mind and soul. Therefore, with Him,
> As brothers, grant peace to us.

November 30, 2008

DIALOGUE OF LOVE AND TRUTH

With great joy and jubilation in the Lord we welcome your presence and participation in the annual celebration of the memory of the glorious St. Andrew, the first-called disciple, founder of our Holy Church of Constantinople. We wholeheartedly thank our very beloved brother Pope Benedict XVI, head of the Church in Rome, who was well disposed to send you here as the bearer of his brotherly message with feelings of love

---

39. I.e., hymn.

40. Also known as Symeon Logothetes, St. Symeon was a renowned Byzantine hagiographer who authored the tenth-century *Menologion* (or collection of saints' lives, organized according to monthly commemoration).

and honor. These feelings we return wholeheartedly, wishing him and the holy "sister Church"[41] of Rome every blessing and grace from God.

Decades ago, a holy practice was established: visitation by representatives of our churches at each other's thronal feasts. The ever memorable heads of our churches, Patriarch Athenagoras and Pope Paul VI, established the first such event. It was animated by the living desire that our churches, which had been separated for a whole millennium and occasionally found themselves in an opposition that was beneficial to neither, finally entered a period of a dialogue of love and truth. This dialogue would have as its end the full restoration of complete unity, just as in the first millennium after Christ.

Today, those who have been entrusted by the mercy of God with the leadership of our churches possess this same deep desire to continue this bilateral dialogue of love and truth, leaving the results to the All-Holy Spirit, who leads to "all truth" (John 16.3) and to God who multiplies our seed (1 Cor. 3.6–7). Continuing to observe vigilantly from this sacred center the course of this double dialogue, we rejoice in its continuation and progress. For, on the one hand, the dialogue of love cleanses our relations from every hint of proselytism or other activity contradicting the spirit of mutual respect and love; on the other hand, the dialogue of truth, entrusted to the Joint International Committee, continues its difficult and painful task under the co-presidency of your beloved Eminence, for which we congratulate and thank you.

THE APOSTLES PETER AND ANDREW

In today's reading from the holy Gospel of John during the celebration of the Divine Liturgy, we heard how strong the bond was between the Lord and the brothers Andrew and Peter. Since Andrew with another disciple, most probably John, spent a whole day conversing and remaining with the Lord in His lodgings—what a great privilege indeed!—Andrew

---

41. A traditional phrase coined in apostolic times to denote churches united in Christ, it was used in medieval times to signify Orthodox churches in communion with each other. In recent times, it was adopted by Ecumenical Patriarch Athenagoras in his correspondence with Pope John XXIII and, later, in formal exchanges and declarations between Patriarch Athenagoras and Pope Paul VI. The phrase is reserved exclusively for Orthodox–Catholic relations.

hastens and announces to Peter that they have found the Messiah. This scene is indeed moving and decisive for what would occur in the future. Peter and Andrew, brothers according to the flesh, at that moment also became brothers in Christ, united by imperishable bonds not only with Him but also with one another.

After the Ascension of the Lord into the heavens, and the descent of the Holy Spirit on the day of Pentecost, the two Apostles went out evangelizing the peoples, bearing witness to the resurrected Christ. Peter went as far as Rome, sanctifying the Church there through his blood; and, according to ancient tradition, Andrew came to Byzantium, founding the Church there, the place that, by divine providence, would become New Rome, the City of Constantine. And so the two brothers, Peter and Andrew, while they may have followed separate geographical routes in bearing witness to the gospel, nevertheless remained united in history through the bond of our two churches, Rome and Constantinople. This union between the two Apostles, which began as a biological bond, became a spiritual bond in the Lord Himself and concluded as a bond of our churches, which we are called to bear in mind unceasingly as we proceed toward the restoration of the full union of our churches. Today, in honoring the Apostle Andrew, we also honor his brother Peter, and, just as it is not possible for Peter and Andrew to be thought of separately from one another, it is not proper that the churches of Rome and Constantinople should continue to journey in division.

We are therefore obligated to remove from our midst the thorns that have accumulated for a millennium in the relationship between our churches in matters of faith as well as on issues touching on the structure and governance of the Church. In this matter, we have as a most valuable guide our common tradition of the seven ecumenical councils and the first millennium after Christ, from which we should draw out the basic beliefs in order to remove what that the millennium of our separation from one another contributed to the increase of the distance between us.

We are called to this, as we said earlier, out of respect to the sacred memory of the two first-called Apostles, from whom our churches draw their very being. We are called to this also by reason of our responsibility to the contemporary world, which is shaken by a variety of conflicts and is in urgent need of the message of reconciliation brought by the founder of the Church through His Cross and Resurrection. It is evident that, if this message is not respected by us Christians, its influence on contemporary humanity will remain weak. The Church must always be in a position to repeat to everyone the words of Phillip to Nathaniel, which we heard in today's Gospel passage: "Come and see" (John 1.47). Only then will its message be convincing, when it is able to give itself as the first example of reconciliation and love.

In this spirit, and with these thoughts and feelings, we again greet the presence of the venerable delegation of the elder sister Church of Rome and His Holiness, its head, our beloved brother Pope Benedict, asking the Lord to bless and direct the course of our churches to the fulfillment of His holy will.

November 30, 2009

THAT THE WORLD MAY BELIEVE

It is with great joy that we welcome you once again to the courtyard of the Church of New Rome to concelebrate the sacred memory of its founder and protector, St. Andrew, the first-called of the Apostles. We express our heartfelt gratitude to our beloved brother in the Lord, His Holiness Pope Benedict XVI, who deigned to delegate his representatives to the thronal feast of our Church, following the custom established decades ago for an exchange of visitations during the patronal feasts of our two ancient and apostolic churches. This custom serves as confirmation of their desire to lift the impediments that accumulated over a millennium and prevented the fullness of communion among them. We attribute great symbolic significance to your presence here inasmuch as it also reveals—in a deeply formal manner—the desire of the most holy Church of Rome to do whatever it can to contribute to our joint effort to rediscover our unity in the same faith and sacramental communion according to the will of Him who has called us to unity "so that the world may believe" (John 17.21).

As is well known, St. Andrew, the first-called of the Apostles, whom we celebrate today, was the brother of St. Peter, the chief among the Apostles; together, they knew Christ and believed in Him. The two brothers held this faith in common; the two churches, which they founded and sanctified by means of their preaching and martyrdom, also hold this faith in common. This same faith was proclaimed as doctrine by the Church Fathers whom we recognize in common, the Fathers who gathered from east and west in ecumenical councils, where they transmitted the faith as an invaluable treasure to our churches so that on this we might build our unity in Christ. It is this same faith, preserved intact for an entire millennium in both east and west, that we are again called to establish as the basis of our unity, cleansing it from any chance addition or alteration, so that "with one soul and one mind" (Phil. 2.2) we may proceed to communion in the divine Eucharist, wherein lies the fullness of the unity of the Church of Christ.

This journey toward achieving full communion, as enjoyed by our churches in common during the first millennium, has already commenced with the dialogue of love and truth, and it continues by God's grace despite occasional difficulties. It is with vigilant concern and unceasing prayer that we follow the process of the ongoing official theological dialogue between our two churches, which is co-chaired by Your Eminence and is now embarking on the examination of critical ecclesiological issues, such as the question of primacy in general and that of the bishop of Rome in particular. Everyone is aware that this thorny issue proved a scandalous contention in the course of relations between our two churches, and that is why the eradication of this impediment from among us will surely greatly facilitate our journey toward unity. We are, therefore, convinced that the study of Church history during the first millennium, at least with regard to this matter, will also provide the touchstone for the further evaluation of later developments during the second millennium, which unfortunately led our churches to greater estrangement and intensified our division.

In a world shattered by contrasts and conflicts, the exchange of peaceful and constructive dialogue is the only way of achieving reconciliation and unity. In the apostolic passage read during this morning's Divine Liturgy, the Apostles are promoted as an example of utter humility in imitation of the crucified Lord: "When reviled, we bless; when persecuted, we endure; when slandered, we speak kindly. We have become like the rubbish of the world, the dregs of all things, to this very day" (1 Cor. 4.12–13). If this ethos of humility must prevail in the relations of the faithful toward the persecutors of the Church, how much more so should it prevail in the relations among Christians themselves! The peaceful resolution of existing differences in inter-Christian relations by no means implies estrangement from truth. For truth does not fear dialogue; on the contrary, truth employs dialogue as a means of finding acceptance and favor even among those who for various reasons rejected it. Hatred and fanaticism provoke the defensive entrenchment of each side in blind persistence on its own positions and opinions, while consolidating differences and obliterating all hope of reconciliation. Such an attitude is absolutely unrelated to the spirit of Christ's gospel and the apostolic example. For only by "speaking the truth in love" (Eph. 4.15) do we truly speak the truth, just as only by loving truthfully (2 John 1) do we truly love. A dialogue imbued by a sincere spirit of humility guarantees this blessed combination, which is the only divinely inspired way for all those who wish to be imitators of the Apostles (1 Cor. 4.16).

It is this spirit of sincere and loving dialogue that the Church of Christ itself is today called to implement in its relations among divided Christians. At the same time, it is called to proclaim this spirit to all persons of goodwill, wherever they happen to be. We know from bitter experience that religion can easily be misused as a banner of fanaticism and conflict. We have personally emphasized on numerous occasions that war in the name of religion is war against religion. This is why interfaith dialogue, dialogue that does not entail any compromise of one's religious convictions, is particularly mandatory in our age. It is this dialogue that is encouraged and cultivated by our Ecumenical Patriarchate, which contributes in this way to the consolidation of peace in our contemporary world.

Your Eminence Cardinal Kasper and your honorable entourage, through the order established by the holy ecumenical councils, divine providence has assigned to the church of this city the ministry of serving as the First Throne of the Orthodox Church, bearing responsibility for coordinating and expressing the unanimity of the local holy Orthodox churches. With this responsibility, then, we are now working diligently in preparation for the Holy and Great Council of the Orthodox Church, by activating the appropriate preconciliar instruments. Only last June, we successfully convened the Fourth Pan-Orthodox Preconciliar Consultation, which dealt with the question of the Orthodox Diaspora; soon, we will convene the preparatory commission for the study of other issues to be examined at the Great Council. The purpose of this entire endeavor is to forge the unity of the Orthodox Church, so that "with one mind and one heart" it may contribute to the witness of the gospel in our modern world. In this important effort and, on the whole, difficult service, the Church of Constantinople always considers the support of the Old Church of Rome as invaluable, and so with great love we also direct our thought there at this moment.

Greeting you and, through you, him who sent you here—namely, our beloved brother in the Lord, Pope Benedict—with a sacred embrace, we pray that the Lord our God, through the intercessions of the holy glorious and first-called Apostle, Andrew, will protect His Church from all evil, guiding it to the fulfillment of His divine will. Welcome here among us, beloved brothers!

The World Council of Churches (WCC)

Homily at the Sixtieth Anniversary of the WCC,
St. Pierre Cathedral, Geneva, February 17, 2008

APOSTOLIC INSPIRATION

> I appeal to you, brothers and sisters, by the name of our Lord Jesus Christ, that all of you should be in agreement and that there should be no divisions among you, but that you should be united in the same mind and the same purpose.
>
> 1 Cor. 1.10

St. Paul was exasperated by the internal quarrels and divisions in the church at Corinth, which he had founded some years earlier. So, in this first letter, sent to the members of that young fellowship, he made the appeal that we have just heard. The Apostle to the Gentiles took that step, because he realized that in an environment dominated by pagan culture—as was that Greek city, where several schools of thought flourished—the Christian faith that he had revealed to them ran the risk of being reduced to human philosophical wisdom, if each of them claimed to belong to one or another master and not to *the* Master, Jesus Christ. He therefore asked them the crucial question: "Is Christ divided?" In so doing, he wished to remind the Corinthians that division in the Church contradicted its very nature, damaged its fundamental witness, and caused its essential mission in the world to fail.

It is precisely this gospel truth that, at the beginning of the twentieth century, served as the inspiration for the mobilization of our churches, which, confronted with the scandal of division, focused their attention on the pressing question of Christian unity, by establishing bonds of fellowship between divided churches and by building bridges to overcome their divisions. One of those significant bridges was without doubt the World Council of Churches, whose sixtieth anniversary we are, with due solemnity, celebrating today. It is, dear sisters and brothers, with great joy and deep thankfulness to our Triune God that our church, the Ecumenical Patriarchate, is taking part in this anniversary. It is an anniversary that provides the World Council of Churches, its member churches, and its governing bodies with an opportunity to review the work done so far. However, more than this, it also gives us, above all, a unique opportunity to turn together to the future and provide new impetus, new vision, and a renewed mandate to this fellowship, which is precisely what our sixty-year-old council is.

ECUMENICAL INSPIRATION

Who would have imagined at the time that one day the appeal by the Church of Constantinople in 1920, "Unto the churches of Christ everywhere," inviting them, after the fratricidal First World War, to form a "league of churches," would assume such concrete form? It would be a "koinonial/communion of churches," after the pattern of the League of Nations (founded, that same year, in this welcoming city of Geneva), with the aim of overcoming distrust and bitterness, drawing the churches together, creating bonds of friendship among them, and thereby fostering cooperation. As was noted in that encyclical, "Love should be rekindled and strengthened among the churches, so that they should no more consider one another as strangers or foreigners, but as relatives and part of the household of Christ and 'fellow heirs, members of the same body and partakers of the promise of God in Christ.'"

Forty-one years ago, our predecessor Ecumenical Patriarch Athenagoras paid an official visit to the World Council of Churches and the Protestant Church of Geneva. On that occasion, Dr. W. A. Visser 't

Hooft[42] offered an eloquent address from the pulpit of this historic cathedral of the Reformation, stating that "the Church of Constantinople was one of the first in modern history to remind Christianity that it would be being disobedient to the will of its Master and Savior if it did not seek to demonstrate to the world the unity of the people of God and of the Body of Christ." He added that, by means of the encyclical of the Patriarchate, "Constantinople sounded the clarion call to bring us together."

Far be it for us, obviously, to claim, by quoting the words of Visser 't Hooft, a great personality and pioneer of the ecumenical movement, that our Church alone fathered the World Council of Churches! It is, however, a historic fact that the resolute action by Constantinople coincided with similar initiatives undertaken by Anglican and Lutheran leaders in the United States and Northern Europe, in particular by Bishop Charles Brent[43] and Bishop Nathan Söderblom,[44] who on their part initiated an almost simultaneous process to bring Christians closer together and encourage them to engage in dialogue with one another: Bishop Brent in order to stimulate theological reflection within "Faith and Order," and Bishop Söderblom to promote social action by the churches within "Life and Work." And so it can be said that the concerted action by Orthodox, Anglican, and Reformation churches in the 1920s laid the foundations for the modern ecumenical movement and that they were among the originators of the formation of the World Council of Churches thirty years later. This fellowship remains to this day indisputably the most representative institutional expression of the ecumenical movement, now on its way to celebrating its centenary.

Sixty years (to within a few months) have passed since Monday, August 23, 1948, when the archbishop of Canterbury, Geoffrey Fisher,[45] during a plenary session of the first assembly at Amsterdam, formally opened the World Council of Churches. This interchurch platform has since been at

---

42. Willem Adolph Visser 't Hooft (1900–85) was a Dutch reformed theologian, who served as first general secretary of the World Council of Churches. See his *Memoirs*, 2nd ed. (Geneva: WCC Publications, 1987).

43. An American Episcopal bishop, Brent (1862–1929) served in the Philippines and Western New York.

44. The Lutheran archbishop of Uppsala, Söderblom (1866–1931) received Nobel Peace Prize in 1930.

45. Geoffrey Fisher (1887–1972) served as archbishop of Canterbury from 1945 to 1961.

the service of its member churches, dedicated to increasing the spirit of the gospel, seeking Christian unity, and encouraging cooperation by the churches in their social and diaconal work as they confront the acute pressing problems of humankind.

Those familiar with the history and development of the council will acknowledge that the first two years after that inaugural assembly were a time of exploring what actual character this interchurch forum should take. While the aims of the council were clear in the eyes of its founding members, its nature and role in the community of churches remained undetermined. The famous 1950 Toronto Statement[46] was able to provide assurance that it was not the intention of the council to become a substitute for the churches or to compel them to adopt positions contrary to their ecclesiological convictions. It must be emphasized that only after such assurance had been given were the member churches able to determine a framework for their future work in performing the tasks they had set for themselves two years earlier.

Once the legitimate question of its nature had been resolved, the council, particularly after its amalgamation with the International Missionary Council and the World Council of Christian Education in the 1960s, entered a prosperous and productive period for the next thirty years. During that time, it performed invaluable work in numerous areas—admired and praised by some, challenged and criticized by others—in theological research, mission and evangelism, Christian education, diaconal service, sustainable development, social justice, protection of the environment, defense of human rights, the eradication of poverty, and the removal of racial discrimination. In the course of those years of intensive work and abundant harvest, two very distinct trends became evident in the council's life. One, which could be described as "ecclesiastical" in nature, was to consider that the ecumenical task was to concentrate on the concern to reach doctrinal and organizational unity among existing individual churches as soon as possible. Emphasis was laid on the content of faith as well as on church order and structure. The other trend involved realization of the real difficulty in arriving at doctrinal unity and was more

---

46. An effort to define "the ecclesiological problem" of membership in the World Council of Churches. Orthodox churches have traditionally regarded this statement as justifying their continued membership in the WCC.

pragmatic. The essential element in ecumenism was considered to be action by churches in the world and for the world as they mobilized their faithful to become aware of Christ's presence in social, scientific, and political activity.

However, in the course of those endless animated discussions between the supporters of these two schools of thought on the nature and mission of the council, other voices were also raised, particularly from the Orthodox East. They pointed out that an ecumenism that chose one of those two trends to the exclusion of the other would betray the fundamental principles of ecumenical work and would be making no essential contribution to the churches on their way toward unity. They underlined that unity was not an end in itself but was intended to serve both the churches and the world, drawing no distinction between sacred and profane, eternal and temporal. True ecumenism, they declared, should strive for Christian unity and persist in concern about the evils afflicting today's world. As our own Church of Constantinople stressed thirty-five years ago on the occasion of the twenty-fifth anniversary of the Council:

> The World Council of Churches, an instrument involved not only in theological dialogue but also in solidarity and mutual love . . . must persist in its efforts to enter into a more open and real encounter with humankind, which is today suffering in so many ways. In this way, the Council, by visible and invisible means, in word and deed, in its decisions and actions, is able to proclaim Christ, and Christ alone.

CRISIS OF ECUMENISM

In fact, in the course of the sixty years of its life, the council has provided an ideal platform where churches, with different outlooks and belonging to a wide variety of theological and ecclesiological traditions, have been able to engage in dialogue and promote Christian unity, all the while responding to the manifold needs of contemporary society. However, it must be recognized that during these sixty years, and especially during these last twenty, the life of the council has often been turbulent as a result of the great number of differences—theological, ecclesiological, cultural, and ethical—that have poisoned friendly relations between its members. This gradually surfaced in the form of a painful crisis ten years ago, on the eve of the fiftieth anniversary of the WCC and only months before its eighth assembly at Harare, Zimbabwe.[47] That crisis was initially attributed to differences between Orthodox and Protestant members of the council, but it was in fact a crisis between those representing different theological and ecclesiological traditions as well as between the various churches, each of which had its own distinctive interpretation of holy scripture and a different perception of moral, social, and political issues.

It was, nonetheless, a healthy crisis that enabled us to engage in sincere and humble dialogue, with no ulterior motives. It helped us to surmount chronic difficulties that had been poisoning our friendly relationships. At the same time, it gave us a new impetus to continue our common journey along the path to unity. So a special commission was established, and we are all aware of its results after so many years of intense dialogue and fruitful work in a spirit of fellowship and mutual respect. Thus, freed from tensions of the past and determined to stay and act together, two years ago, at the ninth general assembly at Porto Alegre, Brazil,[48] we laid down markers for a new stage in the life of the council, taking account of the present situation in interchurch relations and of the changes gradually taking place in ecumenical life.

We are certainly glad that the council still has at the center of its work the vision of its member churches to achieve, by God's grace, unity in the one faith and around the same eucharistic table. Hence the paramount importance and leading role of the World Council of Churches, and in particular of its Faith and Order Commission, in the detailed study of ecclesiological issues that affect the very being of the council and the quest for Christian unity. It is a task that still remains difficult to fulfill. It is a way that must be traveled in love, responsibility, and mutual respect for the tradition and doctrine of the Church of our Savior, Jesus Christ. We are also pleased that the same ninth assembly confirmed the calling that the World Council of Churches has with respect to the Church's presence in society, recognizing the council's role as catalyst for establishing peace in the world, promoting interfaith dialogue, defending human dignity, combating violence, protecting the environment, and being in solidarity with those in need. We wholeheartedly bless those diverse activities of our

47. December 3–14, 1998.
48. February 14–23, 2006.

council all the more so because the mission of Christians in the world is precisely to incarnate God's truth and love as fully as possible. For, at the end of time, we will be judged according to whether we have or have not lived in the spirit of Christ.

With regard to the guidance that the ninth assembly provided for the coming years, we cannot fail to mention its decision, so very right and relevant, to enable young adults to participate actively in the life of the council. We firmly believe that this initiative to involve young people cannot fail to prove beneficial and promising for the council. For it will enable a new generation of laborers to flourish in the ecumenical vineyard, which is all the more necessary because, as the older generation, we have not taken care, or perhaps have not had the desire, to train successors to take up the torch. Their presence, we can be sure, will bring a breath of fresh air and renewed dynamism to our council.

As a council, we are always exploring our role today and attempting to discern our proper place in the new ecumenical constellation that is gradually taking shape in interchurch relations. The ninth assembly pertinently recognized that the far-reaching, rapid changes taking place in the life of our churches are forcing the World Council of Churches to reexamine ecumenical relationships and initiate a process of reconfiguring the ecumenical movement. This will give structure to the complex relations between the council and its many partners, thus ensuring greater consistency, clarity, and transparency in our work.

It goes without saying that more than ever we need to clarify the mission and particular role of each partner within the ecclesiastical arena. We wish to say, however, that any sharing of responsibilities must not come at the expense of the council. For we would be stripping it of its substantial role if we gradually reduced it (as is the tendency sometimes today) to the mere role of "animator" in the process of setting up new interchurch alliances, or, again, of establishing parallel "ecumenical" instruments to perform tasks that properly flow out of the council's very raison d'être. That is why it is our firm belief that the three pillars—unity, witness, and service—on which we built the council sixty years ago must be retained and even strengthened, so that the council may be in accord with its constitution and credible in its mission.

In conclusion, paraphrasing a popular expression, "The church must be at the center of village life," we wish to state our firm conviction that the reconfiguration process in the ecumenical movement will give us an opportunity to locate the World Council of Churches at the center of the life of the global ecumenical village. The tenth general assembly of the council[49] will present a great opportunity to do precisely that, and its character and contents are already being discussed at the present meeting of the central committee.

VISION FOR ECUMENISM

Dear brothers and sisters in Christ: Today, a concern that all our churches share is the vision for the future of the council. And we should ask ourselves several questions in a serious, respectful, and responsible manner: Do our churches, sixty years later, still want the council to be a presence in their church life? If so, what do they expect of the council? How do they see its future? Do we envisage a different council? Would this be a different or diversified, a new or renewed council? Would it perhaps be a more pragmatic or effective council? What sort of council do our churches need? Are we prepared as member churches to stand by the conclusions of the special commission, which suggested that the time has come, the *kairos* had to be seized, for the World Council of Churches to bring its member churches together into an "ecumenical space," where trust could be created and built up? It would be a space where the churches will be able to develop, and test against the facts, their own conceptions of the world, and their particular social work as well as their liturgical and doctrinal traditions while retaining their respective distinctiveness one from another and encountering one another at a deeper level.

Are we today prepared, as member churches, to reaffirm the role of the council as a privileged ecumenical space, where the churches will freely create networks for diakonia and for defending or promoting certain values? In this regard, will we place our material resources at one another's disposal? And how, through dialogue, will the churches continue to break down barriers that prevent them from recognizing one another as churches confessing a common faith, administering the same baptism, and celebrating the Eucharist together, so that the community, which is what they now are, may become a communion in faith, in sacramental

---

49. To be held in Busan, Korea, in 2013.

life, and in witness? Are we ready to renew our confidence in this council as a useful and necessary instrument as we attempt to respond to social and ethical questions, thereby enabling churches, despite ecclesiological diversity, to reaffirm that they belong to one fellowship because they confess the Lord Jesus Christ as God and Savior, to the glory of the one God, Father, Son and Holy Spirit, and to renew their determination to stay together in order to let their love grow for one another?

Dear sisters and brothers, we conclude by returning to where we began. The bonds of friendship among divided churches and the bridges by which we can overcome our divisions are indispensable, now more than ever. Love is essential, so that dialogue between our churches can occur in all freedom and trust. Then, we will acknowledge that the divergences originating from different ways in which churches respond to moral problems are not necessarily insurmountable, since churches witness to the gospel in different contexts. We will also recognize that dialogue on ethical and moral questions should proceed on the assumption that churches are not content to "agree to disagree" on moral teaching but that they are prepared to confront their divergences honestly, examining them in the light of doctrine, worship, and holy scripture.

Let us, therefore, proceed with hope along the path that we have trodden these past sixty years. We must not be discouraged when obstacles stand in our way. Our vocation as humans and as icons of the Triune God is nothing less than to reproduce here on earth the movement of shared love that exists eternally in the communion of the divine Trinity. Let us pray that God the Father will graciously endow us with the power of the Holy Spirit, so that we may "know the love of Christ that surpasses knowledge" and "be filled with all the fullness of God" (Eph. 3:19).

Address to the Faith and Order Commission at the Orthodox Academy of Crete, Kolymbari, October 7, 2009

UNITY AS CALLING, CONVERSION, AND MISSION

It is with great joy that we accepted the gracious invitation of our beloved Faith and Order Commission to address this auspicious plenary gathering. We would also like to welcome you all—academics and pastors, ministers and lay leaders from diverse regions of the world—to our Orthodox Academy[50] on this uniquely beautiful island. The theme of this plenary session is "Called to Be One Church: That They May Become One in Your Hand." It should be recalled that it was on this blessed island of Crete that the Faith and Order Commission of the World Council of Churches in June 2005 revised and finalized the statement on ecclesiology, which later was received at the ninth general assembly of the World Council of Churches at Porto Alegre (February 2006). This text constitutes the culmination of a long development and maturing perspective—through numerous phases, stages, and interpretations—of member churches. It began as early as 1927, at the first conference on Faith and Order, in Lausanne, if not earlier, in an earnest search for the visible unity for which we all yearn and to which we are all called. Let us, then, together renew our commitment to dialogue and unity as a way of reflection and renewal. And let our deliberation be a prayerful offering to God in our sincere desire that we "may be one" (John 17.21) in response to our Lord's command and call.

UNITY AS CALLING

In this commitment, let us begin with thanksgiving and praise that impose on us what in Orthodox thought and spirituality we call the "apophatic approach."[51] The teaching on the apophatic way pertains to the conviction that, by nature and by definition, God is beyond human understanding; if we could comprehend and grasp God, God would not be God. This is the teaching of the great mystics, such as St. Gregory of Nyssa in the fourth century and St. Gregory Palamas in the fourteenth century, who underlined the radical transcendence as well as the relative immanence of God. Basing their theology on sound scriptural principles, according to which "no one can see God" (Exodus 33.20; John 1.18, and 1 John 4.12), these Church Fathers proclaimed God as profoundly unknowable and yet personally known, God as invisible and yet accessible,

---

50. An institution of theological and ecumenical reflection within the Metropolis of Kissamos and Selinon and under the spiritual auspices of the Ecumenical Patriarchate, the Orthodox Academy of Crete was founded in 1968.

51. Apophatic, or negative, theology implies that God is beyond human comprehension, description, and definition.

God as distant and yet intensely present—the infinite and incomprehensible God, who becomes intimate and incarnate to the world. God's incomprehensibility and inaccessibility ultimately oblige us to a spirit of humility and worship.

If the apophatic attitude is our starting point, then we may appreciate how the unity of the Church, like the unity of God, is also a never ending search, an ever unfolding journey. As St. Gregory of Nyssa would affirm, even in the age to come, growth in the divine life is without end and with endless perfection; it is, indeed, constant progress through continually refining stages. This mindset demands from us a sense of forbearance rather than of impatience. We should not be frustrated by our human limitations, which unfortunately determine our disagreements and divisions. Our ongoing and persistent pursuit of unity is a testimony that what we seek will occur in God's time and not our own; it is, by the same token, the fruit of heavenly grace and divine *kairos*.

UNITY AS CONVERSION

If unity, as the goal toward which we continually and persistently advance, is indeed a gift from God, then it demands from us a profound sense of humility and not any prideful insistence. This means that we are called to learn from others as well as to learn from time-tested formulations. It also implies that imposing on others our own ways, whether "conservative" or "liberal," is arrogant and hypocritical. Instead, genuine humility demands from all of us a sense of openness to the past and the future. In other words, much like the ancient god Janus, we are called to manifest respect for the time-tested ways of the past and regard for the heavenly city that we seek (see Heb. 13.14). This "turning" toward the past and the future is surely part and parcel of our ecumenical conversation as well of as our evangelical conversion.

It is crucial, then, that we learn from the early Fathers and Mothers of the Church, that we embrace the mind of the early Church by immersing ourselves in the spirit of the Christian classics. In a word, Orthodox theology refers to this as "tradition." This in no way signifies a sentimental attachment to the past or an intellectual fascination with patristic literature. Rather, we should learn from those who, in each generation, maintained the integrity and intensity of the apostolic faith. The Church in our age must be marked by such continuity and consistency with the past, which forms an intrinsic part of the contemporary Church. In this regard, at least for Orthodox Christians, Saints Basil and Gregory are very much alive, vividly present—not only in our liturgy but also in our teaching and practice.

At the same time, we should turn our attention to the future, to the age to come, to the heavenly kingdom. Orthodox theology adopts the term *eschatology* to describe this attitude. *Eschatology* does not imply a sense of escapism or otherworldliness. Focusing on the "last times" or the "last things" is a way of envisioning this world in light of the next. An eschatological vision offers a way out of the impasse of provincialism and confessionalism. It paves the way for radical conversion, urging us to "listen to what the Spirit is saying to the churches" (Rev. 1.10–11). It allows us to believe that God's light is stronger than any darkness in this world and that the Alpha and the Omega is working in us and through us for the salvation of the world and for the unity of the Church. And so we pray with conviction, "Come, Lord Jesus," *Maranatha* (Rev. 22.20).

UNITY IN MISSION

Finally, the sense of calling and the urgency of conversion permit us to discern the areas of our common ministry and united mission. As individual communities we are "fragile sticks," in the words of the biblical passage of our conference taken from the Prophet Ezekiel (37.15–28). Together, however, we can become one people under one God, neither divided among ourselves nor defiling the covenant of the Lord. Indeed, the conditions of this new way are the avoiding of idol worship (37.23) and the making of peace (37.26). In modern terminology, it is the preservation of creation as the proper way of worshipping the Creator. It is also the promotion of tolerance and understanding among religions and peoples in our world. Working closely together on issues of environmental awareness and ecumenical dialogue is a crucial reflection of the "everlasting covenant" (37.25–26) whereby Ezekiel's God proclaims, "I will be their God and they shall be my people . . . forevermore" (37.27–28).

For the Prophets, just as for the apostolic community, justice and peace are closely linked to the preservation and balance of the land as God's creation. This means that our churches are called to a common ministry and mission, proclaiming and promoting a worldview wherein God's authority, the authority of the Kingdom, guides our ways and determines our actions. We must never forget that this world is inherited; it is a gift from above, offered as a means of communion with God. If, then, we are to submit to the authority of God and His kingdom, then we must be authentic and prophetic in our criticism of the world's consumerism. We must remember and remind our faithful that the land and all the fullness thereof belong to the Lord (see Ps. 24.1), that the world's resources must be oriented toward others. We must recall the Lord's beatitude, according to which "the meek shall inherit the earth" (Matt. 5.5). For the meek person reverses the world's attitudes to power and possessions; otherwise, the land becomes a place of division and violence. Meekness is ultimately a way of caring, a way of sharing. And it stands as a contrast and correction to the desecration that we have brought into God's creation.

Beloved brothers and sisters, the unity that we seek is a gift from above, a gift that we must pursue persistently as well as patiently; it is not something that depends solely on us but, again, primarily on God's judgment and *kairos*. Nevertheless, this sacred gift of unity is something that also demands of us radical conversion and reorientation, so that we may turn humbly toward our common roots in the apostolic Church and the communion of saints and that we may entrust ourselves and submit to God's heavenly Kingdom and authority. Finally, however, unity obliges us to a common purpose in this age as we look forward to the age to come; for unity commits us to a sacred ministry and mission in realizing that Kingdom—as we declare in the Lord's Prayer, "on earth as in heaven." Such is the sacred gift that we have inherited. This, too, is the sacred task that lies before us. Therefore, "Let us go forth in peace"[52] to proclaim the good news to the world.

As we conclude, let us remember all those ecumenical pioneers who served this commission with competence and deep commitment in the past thirty years, either as moderators, directors, or staff, and with whom we have had the privilege and opportunity to work with on so many important themes, but who now are no longer among us. In particular, we would like to mention the renowned Greek theologian Professor Nikos Nissiotis and Professor John Deschner, who served as moderators, without forgetting Rev. Dr. John Meyendorff, who had served earlier. We would also like to mention Rev. Dr. Lukas Vischer and Bishop Dr. William Lazareth, who

---

52. Petition from the closing prayers of the Divine Liturgy of St. John Chrysostom.

served as directors, as well as Protopresbyter Vitaly Borovoy, deputy direc-tor. May their memories be eternal and may they continue to rest peace-fully in the refreshing hands of our merciful God. Let us continue to honor their memories by imitating their dedication and zeal.

We would also like to thank Dr. Mary Tanner and Bishop Dr. David Yemba Kekumba, who served as moderators, and the Rev. Dr. Günther Gassmann, Rev. Dr. Alan Falconer, and Rev. Dr. Thomas Best, who served as directors, for their immense contributions to the commission. We also do not want to forget those of the Ecumenical Patriarchate who served the commission as staff for several years—namely, His Eminence Metropolitan John of Pergamon, member of the Academy of Athens, and His Eminence Metropolitan Gennadios of Sassima, who for ten years served as a staff member and later replaced us as vice-moderator and consequently became moderator of Faith and Order. We would like to thank and congratulate both of them for their dedicated service to the commission. May the grace, peace, and love of God be with all of you!

CONFERENCE OF EUROPEAN CHURCHES (CEC)

Opening of the Twelfth General Assembly, Trondheim, June 26, 2003

THE GIFT OF GOD'S WORD

It is for us a joy and a notable privilege to address you at the inaugura-tion of the twelfth assembly of the Conference of European Churches. May He who alone can heal and reconcile, Jesus Christ our Savior, be with us throughout our discussions. May He give us courage, generosity, and imaginative vision. Our task is not an easy one. At a time when the European Union is rapidly expanding, when Europe is seeking to understand and define itself anew—at a time, moreover, when many would wish totally to exclude Christ and the Christian Church from their definition of what constitutes Europe—how shall we succeed in bearing effective witness? How shall we convey to contemporary Europe a message that is humble yet prophetic, kenotic yet challenging? How shall we carry into practice the beatitude "Blessed are the peacemakers, for they will be called children of God" (Matt. 5.9) and yet at the same time be faithful to Christ's teaching that He comes to bring "not peace but a sword"

(Matt. 10.34)? How shall we heed God's warning, spoken through the Prophet Jeremiah: "They have healed the wound of my people carelessly, saying 'Peace, peace,' where there is no peace" (Jer. 8.11)?

At the outset, let us be clear about one thing. Christ says to us, "Apart from me you can do nothing" (John 15.5). It is a striking fact that in *The Philokalia*, the classic Orthodox collection of spiritual texts, there is no verse from scripture that is quoted more often than this. "Apart from me you can do nothing." All is gift; all is grace. If we are to speak to Europe a word of healing and reconciliation, then, that word has to be God's word and not our own. What, as Christian communities, we have to offer to the world is not a program, not an ideology, but a person: the theanthropos (God-Man) Jesus Christ. Healing means salvation, and salvation means Christ the Savior. "My eyes have seen your salvation," Symeon the Elder said to God as he welcomed Christ in the temple (Luke 2.30); to Symeon salvation meant not a set of ideas but precisely and specifically this young child whom he saw before him, this forty-day-old infant whom he held in his arms. "I am the truth," Christ insisted (John 14.6). Saving truth is not a series of propositions but a living person.

Salvation is Jesus Christ the Savior: But what does Christ mean to us? Let us call to mind, as a guiding image to inspire us in our conference, the meeting of the risen Christ with His disciples on the evening of Easter day (John 20.19–20). His first word to them, "Peace be with you," is a word of healing and reconciliation, which brings them joy. But His next action is to show them His stigmata, His wounds, the marks of the Passion that He bears on His hands and in His side. Why should Jesus do this? We may answer: for the sake of recognition, to show the disciples that it is indeed He Himself; to convince them that the one whom they saw shortly before, hanging on the Cross, is now once more alive, present among them in the selfsame body in which He suffered and died.

Yet surely our Lord's action means more than this. These wounds that the risen Christ shows to His disciples are His credentials to a suffering humankind. These same wounds are our healing and hope. They make it plain that, though He has risen victorious from the dead—and though He is soon to ascend into heaven in glory—in His perfect being there is still a place for our pain and anguish. The wounds of the risen Christ underline the truth of what is said in the Letter to the Hebrews (and, in the whole of the New Testament, there is perhaps no Christological text more important than this): "We do not have a high priest who is unable to sympathize with our weaknesses, but we have one who in every respect has been tested and tempted as we are, yet without sinning" (Heb. 4.15).

SALVATION AS TWOFOLD

These words lead us to reflect on the double way in which Christ acts as our healer and Savior. He is our Savior, first, because He is, in the words of the Nicene Creed, "true God from true God." Salvation is a divine act; a prophet cannot be the savior of the world, for the death of a mere man does not destroy death. If, then, Christ is to save us He must be God. He cannot just be one of us. However, in the second place, as the Letter to the Hebrews makes clear, salvation has to reach the point of human need. Christ our God heals us not from a secure distance, not in an exterior manner, but by Himself becoming what we are, by making Himself totally vulnerable, by accepting into Himself all our pain and grief. "In every respect tempted as we are," suffering with us and for us in His compassionate love, He is in very truth the wounded healer. Although He is not one of us, He is one with us.

As St. Gregory of Nyssa affirms in his *Catechetical Oration*,[53] the true greatness and glory of God are to be seen not in any act of overwhelming power—neither in the creation of the universe nor in any cosmic miracle such as the stilling of the storm—but rather in the *kenosis* whereby He has chosen to share in all our fragility and brokenness, becoming obedient to death, even death on the Cross. His total sharing in our humiliation is the true summit of His divine omnipotence. God is never so strong as when He is most weak. Such is the way in which Jesus Christ heals and reconciles. Such is the message that we are called to bring to Europe.

In speaking of Christ as healing and reconciliation, we must add something else. Salvation is personal but it is not solitary. No one is saved alone. We are saved in the Church, as members of it and through communion with all its members. Healing and reconciliation in Christ have an ecclesial dimension. We are saved through our incorporation into the body of Christ by means of the sacraments of baptism and the Eucharist.

---

53. See James Srawley, *The Catechetical Oration of Gregory of Nyssa* (Cambridge: Cambridge University Press, 1956).

Here precisely we are brought face to face with one of the challenges that we cannot avoid at this assembly. Our unity is genuine, but it is still incomplete. Despite all the progress that has been made in our quest for visible unity—and for this we glorify God—we Orthodox remain convinced that the time has not yet come for us to share together at the Lord's table in His sacramental body and blood. There continue to be serious doctrinal questions over which, as churches, we are still in disagreement, and so, according to our Orthodox understanding of the Eucharist, it would be unrealistic, and even untruthful, for us to share together in Holy Communion.

When discussing this painful and disputed issue, all of us need consistently to respect the good faith and spiritual integrity of all who differ from us. Those who believe that the time has not yet come to share in Communion should not accuse the opposite side of treating the Holy Mysteries in a casual or light-minded manner. At the same time, those who believe that at this very moment we can and should receive communion together must not suggest that anyone who says "Not yet" is lacking in openness and love. God alone knows who among us shows the deepest reverence for the Eucharist and who among us feels the greatest love.

THE CALL TO BE PRACTICAL AND PRAYERFUL

We would like to conclude with two final suggestions. Let us be practical, and let us be silent. First, then, in all our deliberations let us seek to be practical and realistic. Healing signifies the removal of specific wounds; reconciliation means the overcoming of particular divisions. It is not enough to formulate theories. We must resolve on concrete action. As we learn from the parable of the sheep and the goats (Matt. 25.31–46), at the Last Judgment you and I will not be asked how strictly we fasted, how many prostrations we made in our prayers, how many books we wrote, how many speeches we made at international conferences. We shall be asked: Did you feed the hungry? Did you give drink to the thirsty? Did you take the stranger into your home? Did you clothe the naked? Did you care for the sick and the prisoners? That is all we will be asked. Love for Christ is shown through love for other people, and there is no other way.

Notice how, concerning everyone who is in need and distress, Christ says "I": "I was hungry, I was thirsty, I was a stranger, sick, naked, and a prisoner." Christ is looking at us through the eyes of all who suffer. Is that not frightening? Almost everywhere in the wealthier cities of Europe our streets are full of the hungry and the homeless, full of young women—all too often from the poorer countries—who have been trapped in vice and prostitution. What are the European churches doing about that?

One of our tasks at this assembly will be to speak to each other about these problems, to tell each other about the projects, of social aid and reconstruction, in which our church communities are engaged. If there were time, we would have liked to tell you today something about the efforts made by the Ecumenical Patriarchate of Constantinople to confront the environmental crisis, to explore the dilemmas of bioethics, and to assist the street children in the district of the Phanar. All of us here at this service have our own stories to tell. Yet, as we listen to each other and learn from one another's experience, let us also search our conscience and repent. How much more there is that we could and should have done?

Let us, then, be practical; and in the second place let us also sometimes keep silent. Let us allow some space in this congress for the dimension of *hesychia*, or creative stillness. "Be still, and know that I am God" (Ps. 46.10). As well as listening to each other, let us also listen to the Holy Spirit. St. Ignatius of Antioch spoke of Christ as "the Word that came out from silence." If our words at this meeting do not spring from silence of heart, then we shall prove to be, in St. Paul's phrase, "a noisy gong or a clanging cymbal" (1 Cor. 13.1). But if the words that we speak to Europe at this congress are indeed words that come our from silence, then by God's grace and mercy they will prove to be words of fire, liberating and life-creating. May God bless you all.

Keynote Address at the Thirteenth General Assembly,
on the Fiftieth Anniversary of the Conference of European Churches,
Lyons, July 19, 2009

A FUTURE OF HOPE

We give honor and glory to the Triune God, who has blessed the work of our Conference of European Churches during its fifty years.[54] Lyons is

---

54. The editor is grateful to the Rev. Aimilianos Bogiannou, of the Liaison Office of the Orthodox Church to the European Union in Brussels, for his assistance in supplying this text.

a highly symbolic place for celebrating this anniversary, since it was to this city that St. Irenaeus[55] came from the East to exercise his ministry as bishop. Thanks to the faith and love of St. Irenaeus, the distance between East and West was bridged, and East and West thereafter journeyed together in a spirit of dialogue, praying the Lord to guide them toward ". . . unity of faith and communion in the Holy Spirit,"[56] so that they could experience in future the fullness of their love and communion in the same faith.

We have often expressed our belief, personally and as Ecumenical Patriarch, as well as at the level of all Orthodoxy, that it is only by engaging in dialogue and by closely cooperating that the churches will prove capable of proclaiming the gospel of Christ to the world in a convincing and effective way. For that reason, as the Church of Constantinople, since our blessed predecessor, Patriarch Joachim III issued his famous Encyclical of 1902, we believe strongly that reestablishing communion between Christians is a prime and urgent duty for us all, inasmuch as it is a commandment given by Christ our Savior in His last prayer. That prayer is a legacy from our Lord Jesus Christ that we must observe to the letter, in order that the world may believe (John 17.21).

It was in that spirit, and by always praying in our liturgies for the union of all Christians, that we Orthodox founded, together with other churches, the World Council of Churches more than sixty years ago. Similarly, more than fifty years ago, together with several other European churches, we also established this Conference of European Churches, whose fiftieth anniversary we celebrate today by giving thanks to God. As joint founders and present members of CEC, we not only enjoy the fruit harvested to this day as we share in the joy of those who rejoice; indeed, we not only share our joy at all that has been done, at the many rich achievements blessed by God, but we also accept our measure of the responsibility incumbent on us for any omissions or failures over the years. We wish deliberately here to emphasize this Orthodox position, wishing thereby to dispel any possible doubts and misunderstandings that

---

55. One of the Apostolic Fathers, Irenaeus (c. 125–202) was bishop of Lyons, disciple of Polycarp of Smyrna (who was in turn disciple of St. John the Evangelist), and author of *Against Heresies*.

56. From the Divine Liturgy of St. John Chrysostom.

may have arisen, both within and outside our Orthodox Church, with regard to what CEC has already achieved.

We wish here to express our happiness that a great number of Orthodox colleagues have made a valuable contribution to CEC at all levels. We owe them an immense debt of gratitude. However, quite apart from the invaluable contribution made by all those colleagues, we cannot ignore our responsibilities and obligations toward CEC and especially those with whom we are enjoined to seek unity according to the commandment of our Lord, who enjoins us to do everything in our power to reestablish full communion between the Christian churches in Europe. That is our hope and unshakeable conviction.

A CHARTER OF UNITY

Dear brothers and sisters, it is in that spirit and with the greatest hope that we look forward to the future of CEC. There is no doubt that, during the past fifty years, CEC has achieved much of great significance. Over those years, countless documents on ecumenical issues have been produced, documents of great theological depth, such as the *Charta Œcumenica*,[57] which is the fruit of joint efforts by all the churches of Europe—namely, our own CEC and the [Roman Catholic] Council of European Bishops' Conferences (CCEE).

Nevertheless, as was emphasized in the message from the Third European Ecumenical Assembly at Sibiu in 2007, our faithful have not become consciously aware of many proposals made in the *Charta*; nor, moreover, have the proposals been implemented by our churches. Unfortunately, the faithful in our churches remain unaware of a great number of its recommendations, which have remained a dead letter, incapable of producing the positive desired effects. The result is that what we have said is not matched by our actions. This damages the credibility of our churches and gives the impression, both within and without, that we are incapable of finding solutions to current problems. I am sure that for all of you these comments are not new, and that is why I strongly recommend and

---

57. A joint ecumenical document of the Conference of European Churches and the (Roman Catholic) Council of European Episcopal Conferences, which promotes increased cooperation among churches in Europe. It was signed in Strasbourg in 2001.

heartily encourage the appropriate bodies within CEC to do everything in their power to promote the reception of this document and increase awareness of what has been agreed on.

We believe that our theological schools and faculties can contribute to this end and that they should assume responsibility in the form of study programs to inform and appropriately guide the students of our churches, so as to convey to them the well-founded spirit of reconciliation and the ecumenical imperative. Moreover, we recommend that scholars in that field and teachers in our faculties of theology together examine the problems that still hinder the prospect of full communion between our churches. We recommend that they examine those problems so as to find appropriate solutions and enable us all, with God's help, to reach unity of faith and communion in the Holy Sprit. The Ecumenical Patriarchate has always stressed the need for cooperation between our theological faculties in Europe[58] and welcomes the commitment made in the *Charta Œcumenica* (section 2, subsection 3). We therefore welcome and view with great favor such initiatives and all steps taken in that direction and duly appreciate CEC's theological contribution as well as its involvement in promoting programs designed to improve cooperation between our theological faculties.

In this regard, we would like to emphasize that cooperation between CEC and the Council of European Bishops' Conferences (CCEE) has been essential and constructive. In order to improve this ecumenical commitment, we are proposing to set up a better-organized and well-structured way of cooperation between our two organizations. We should like to recall that the Church of Constantinople, some time ago during the eighth CEC assembly at the Orthodox Academy in Crete in 1979, proposed that the Roman Catholic Church should in the future become a member of CEC. It is clear that such a step is not a simple matter and would require preparatory work and changes to the relevant rules. However, we are convinced that a conference of *all* the European churches working in harmony will be able to respond better to the sacred command of our Lord to reestablish communion between the churches. It will be able better to serve our contemporaries, confronted as they are with so

---

58. From as early as the patriarchal encyclical of 1920.

many complex problems. It will then be possible more effectively to promote dialogue between the churches of Europe and the European union as well as various European institutions. This dialogue, in which our own church has been involved for many years, is invaluable and essential, not only for the churches but also for the political bodies of the European Union and, above all, for the peoples of Europe.

The future of a new Europe under construction is somber and, indeed, uncertain, being built without Christian spiritual values, which touch on everything concerning the support and protection of human beings and their dignity. That is why we declare that, for Europe, respect for the dignity of each human person as created "in the image of God" must be the foundation for the absolute respect for and protection of the rights of all people, independent "of color, religion, race, nationality and language."[59] These are difficult times, and the conditions of life are critical. Wars and conflicts between nations endure, sadly, as do walls of separation. Social and economic injustice affects all households. Xenophobia, racism, human-rights violations, and denial of religious freedom cause increasing disquiet. Secularization and the crisis in spirituality and Christian values are daily of growing concern for our churches. Our very faith in Jesus Christ is also being called into question. Our young people continue to face unemployment and a shortage of jobs. Businesses, small and large, are closing down every day because of the deep economic crisis. In search of a better future, hundreds of thousands of poor immigrants, victims of trafficking in human beings, seek refuge on our continent. And, finally, the environment itself also suffers from our indifference and incompetence in protecting it, in creating a space for respect of nature and for the economy of creation. For some years now, Christians, Jews, and Muslims have been engaged in dialogue with a view toward promoting peace and reconciliation among the different monotheistic religions. All are desperately seeking hope.

LET US ACT NOW

That is why no procrastination can be justified. On the contrary, the collaboration between our churches and their cooperation with European

---

59. See the Third Pan-Orthodox Preconciliar Conference, held in Chambésy, Switzerland, 1986.

leaders active in the fields of politics, the economy, and society is critical and urgent. We have an obligation to proclaim and witness together to the crucified Christ, who suffered, was buried, and "by death has conquered death," as the Easter *troparion* declares.[60] He has destroyed death and freed the human race "by giving us life."[61] Despite difficulties and setbacks, despite crises and conflicts, despite wars and much suffering, it is today the duty of all Christians and all churches together to communicate this message of resurrection and hope, this message of reconciliation and peace, for Christ is the hope of the world. We do not ignore pain, suffering, or martyrdom, but we are determined to persist in resistance and to proclaim with you all, today, tomorrow, and to all eternity, the words of the Apostle Paul:

> And do this, understanding the present time. The hour has come for you to wake up from your slumber, because our salvation is nearer now than when we first believed. The night is nearly over; the day is almost here. So let us put aside the deeds of darkness and put on the armor of light.
>
> Rom. 13.11–12

Inspired by unshakeable belief, love, and faith, we must proclaim to the oppressed and suffering the strength, courage, and will to resist—all of which come from the optimism and the hope of Christ's message:

> Put on the full armor of God so that you can take your stand against the devil's schemes. . . . Stand firm then, with the belt of truth buckled around your waist, with the breastplate of righteousness in place, and with your feet fitted with the readiness that comes from the gospel of peace. In addition to all this, take up the shield of faith, with which you can extinguish all the flaming arrows of the evil one. Take the helmet of salvation.
>
> Eph. 6.11, 14 –17

It is our firm belief that, in love and communion, the Triune God will guide our steps and the work of the Conference of European Churches and all churches in Europe over the next fifty years, for the good of all and to the glory of God's holy name.

---

60. From the Resurrection hymn of the Orthodox Church.
61. Ibid.

National Council of Churches of Christ in the USA (NCCC)

Address at an Ecumenical Doxology, New York, October 24, 1997

CHRIST IS IN OUR MIDST

We greet you with the sure knowledge that Christ is in our midst.[62] We bring you the apostolic blessing of the Ecumenical Throne. We see in your faces the abiding commandment of our Lord and Savior Jesus Christ to "love one another." We are moved by your generous hospitality and your kind words of welcome. We feel at home among dear friends and faithful believers, for we know many of you personally. We are grateful to Almighty God for this occasion to be together, to speak words of praise to Him who is the author of creation, and to have our hearts burn within while Christ speaks to us. Indeed, this body, its triumphs of common praise and struggles to understand the fractured churches of Christ, meets the Lord, like the disciples on the road to Emmaus. Speaking to one another, we at times do not recognize that Christ is in our midst, encountering us through each other. And then something occurs that reveals the Lord Himself mystically present among us. We can thankfully sense the joy of such wonderful moments from time to time. We feel it now, in the unity of love that you show to our Modesty.

The National Council of Churches of Christ will soon celebrate its fiftieth anniversary.[63] This council has been the preeminent forum for ecumenical witness in the United States. This year, we also celebrate the seventy-fifth anniversary of the Greek Orthodox Archdiocese of America. For two-thirds of its existence in the Americas, it has shared its witness with the member communions of the National Council of Churches. We are proud of our rich association and humbly ask God to continue to show His mercy on our endeavors on behalf of Christ in the world. Our beloved brother in the Lord, Archbishop Iakovos, who led our holy archdiocese so ably for thirty-seven years, has left his mark and name on this blessed house.

---

62. This address was delivered during a pastoral visit to the Greek Orthodox Archdiocese of America for its seventy-fifth anniversary.

63. Ceremonies were held November 9–12, 1999, in Cleveland Ohio, where the National Council of Churches of Christ was founded.

The council has brought together many churches for the sake of restoring not only our visible unity but also our spiritual communion in the mystery of the risen Lord. It has encouraged the churches to engage together in theological discourse. It has assisted the churches in promoting the study of the holy scriptures together as siblings in our Father's house. The council has enabled the churches to share their resources with the needy, as commanded by Christ. The NCCC has encouraged her members to respond together to the challenges of this nation's complex and diverse society.

We especially would like to commend the National Council of Churches for its response to the recent, tragic outbreak of the intentional burning of church buildings. As is well known, the destruction of these houses of God was an expression of hatred and racism. In the past two years alone, more than two hundred churches were destroyed in various parts of this country. The destruction of these churches left thousands of faithful Christians without places to gather for worship. We deplore these acts of violence and hatred. As Orthodox Christians, we weep with our sister churches, having experienced this bitter pain ourselves. Thankfully, the National Council of Churches was able to encourage its members in responding to this crisis. Indeed, the council helped to focus the attention of the entire nation on this tragedy. Because of the efforts of the council, many of the churches have been rebuilt. Through its witness, the NCCC has reaffirmed that "we are members one of another" (Eph. 4.25).

In the difficult road that this house has traveled toward understanding, we are also reminded that our disunity as Christians can have tragic consequences for innocent persons and for society as a whole. We are likewise reminded that, when Christians unite, there can be healing and reconciliation that bears witness to God s love for all. The Ecumenical Patriarchate of Constantinople has always been a principal proponent of the contemporary ecumenical movement. In the historic patriarchal synodal encyclical of 1920, the Church boldly called on the divided churches to seek opportunities for theological dialogue and common witness. This encyclical has proven to be a prophetic document. Just as the Apostle Andrew, founder of the Church of Constantinople, was first called to witness to the Word in flesh, so too our predecessors of blessed memory glimpsed a vision of the united body of Christ in the world.

At a time when contacts between the churches were very limited, the encyclical of 1920 called on the divided churches to end their isolation and work together to overcome their differences. The Ecumenical Patriarchate remains faithful to the fundamental convictions expressed in that encyclical. We believe that divisions among Christians are a tragic contradiction to the gospel of our Lord. Christian disunity is a sin against the icon of God's love for the world as expressed by the Holy Trinity. If Christians are divided over doctrine, how will they speak with authority and integrity about the good news of God's salvation? How can Christians preach the gospel of healing if we continue to wound ourselves in the reality of our divisions? How will we bear witness to faith in the unity of the Holy Trinity if we are divided among ourselves?

However, the reconciliation and ensuing restoration of visible unity among Christian communions must be centered on Jesus Christ and rooted in the truth of the apostolic faith. We will not find unity in falsehood. We must not ignore the doctrinal and ethical issues that divide us. We reject as short-sighted the attempt by some—in an effort to achieve a superficial or cosmetic reconciliation—to relativize the importance of the historic Christian faith. Ultimately, such an approach to Christian unity diminishes our understanding of God, the human person, and the entire cosmos. We earnestly and lovingly seek reconciliation and unity that bears witness to "the faith once delivered to the saints" (Jude 1.3). We further believe that the restoration of visible unity must be fostered by persons truly growing in their relationship with God. Those concerned with the unity of Christians must be persons of prayer, sharing in the life of the community of faith. Our Lord prayed to the Father for the unity of His disciples. With that prayer of His we join our own prayer for unity. For it is through prayer that we are transformed into His likeness. It is within the community of faith that we are nurtured in our relationship with God, with one another, and with the entire creation.

Since the patriarchal encyclical of 1920, much has been accomplished. We have experienced the fruits of the Holy Spirit in our common prayers for reconciliation and unity. Love, joy, peace, and hope have inspired us to strive for greater acts of common experience in the Lord. Prejudice and misunderstanding among Christians of various churches have diminished. We have witnessed hopeful expressions of theological consensus on certain points among the communions. At times, there is a spirit of cooperation and reconciliation evident among Orthodox, Roman Catholics, and Protestants. This must surely be a cause for joyful thanksgiving to God, "the source of every good and perfect gift" (James 1.17).

ACKNOWLEDGING TENSIONS

Our Modesty must also frankly admit that, at times, ecumenical relations among the churches in recent years have undergone serious difficulties in many places. Here in the United States, the relationship between the Orthodox and the Protestant denominations within the National Council of Churches has been greatly strained in these past few years. This has resulted from different perspectives on the nature of the Church and on the purpose of ecumenical dialogue as well from different perspectives on moral questions. In other parts of the world, the Orthodox Church has been deeply vexed as its faithful are proselytized by communions to whom it has shown love and respect in America. In lands where the Orthodox Church is recovering from decades of persecution, a new threat to the Orthodox faith has appeared. Many Protestant missionaries from the West, whose voices were not heard during the decades of oppression, have come not to lend support but to convert Orthodox believers. Orthodox Christians who suffered for generations, expected the prayers, support, and encouragement of their ecumenical partners. Sadly, they were treated like the servant tortured by the fellow servant who himself, however, was treated with mercy by his master. The good achieved by some of our partners has been overshadowed by the evil committed by others. These so-called missionaries claim to be Christians, but they behave as wolves in sheep's clothing. Three hundred million Orthodox Christians seek the very guarantees of love and freedom that other churches have enjoyed in the name of religious freedom. We ask for your love and understanding as we seek to rebuild the house that was shattered by active governmental persecution.

Dear friends in Christ, we are obliged to say these things not to discourage you or to darken this joyous visit. We come here today as a pilgrim, proclaiming our absolute confidence in the gospel of Jesus Christ, who is our light and our life. We say these things to encourage you all the more to be devoted to the genuine and loving reconciliation between the churches. Our movement toward the visible unity of the churches is filled with great joys and with some sorrows. We know that the road to reconciliation is not an easy one. Yet we also know that our Lord is truly with us. He is our way. He is our truth. He is our life. He travels with us as He walked with the disciples on the road to Emmaus. In calling us to be His disciples, Christ calls us to join with Him in His ministry of reconciliation and renewal. Let us lift the veil of division from our faces that we might advance together from glory to glory.

OCCASIONAL ADDRESSES AND MESSAGES

Address at the Millennial Celebrations for the Christianization of Norway, June 4, 1995

A PROUD PAST

Your Majesties, Your Excellency the prime minister, Your Eminence Bishop Andreas Aarflot, Primate of the Church of Norway, distinguished guests: It gives us special joy to have the honor to address greetings of peace during the festive events of this great and historic day. On this occasion, representatives of all of Christendom are assembled here today in an ecumenical celebration of the millennium of Christianity in Norway. The joy of Norwegian Christians brings joy to all Christians who are united in the bond of love. Together we offer up our common doxology to our Lord Jesus Christ. In this peaceful country, He has proven His power to change the hearts of humankind and to transfigure them.

When thinking about the Norwegian nation today, we cannot but think back more than a thousand years ago, at a time when the heroic king Olaf Tryggvason[64] decided to convert his kingdom into a Kingdom of Christ, while the Vikings coming from Normandy terrorized other peoples. Today, the Christian descendants of those seafaring warriors and conquerors constitute an exemplary people. Under the benevolent influence of the teachings of Christ, they have cast away the shortcomings of their ancestors while still retaining their virtue and courage. Consequently, the love that the Vikings had of war has been transformed into love of peace, and the capital of Norway has become the capital of world

---

64. Olaf (960s–1000), king of Norway from 995 to 1000, is said to have founded the first church in Norway (995) and the city of Trondheim (997).

peace, since it is here that the Nobel Prize for Peace is awarded. Their ancestors' love of the sea is maintained to this day. We marvel at the great Norwegian commercial fleet and at the accomplishments of the modern Norwegian seafaring explorers,[65] courageous, worthy successors of those ancient seamen who reached America five centuries before Columbus.

As Christians we feel proud of Christian Norway. On account of its respectability, industriousness, and love of learning, Norway has established itself as an example of economic development and at the same time of social justice and democracy. Of course, we do not have the poetical ability of the ancient skalds[66] to sing praises. However, we can repeat the beginning of Norway's national anthem: "Yes, we love this country." Today's celebration of the millennium of Norwegian Christianity is simultaneously observed by Evangelicals and Roman Catholics as the great feast of Pentecost, when the Church of Christ appeared for the first time in its ecumenical dimension as preordained to unite within itself all of the races and languages on earth. The hymnology of the Eastern Orthodox Church saw in this event the reconstitution of the original unity of man, and it praises Pentecost, contrasted against the Tower of Babel, a symbol of disunity: "When having descended He confounded the tongues, the Most High divided the world into nations; when He distributed the tongues of fire, He called all the world into unity."

THE LIGHT OF PENTECOST AND THE DARK AGES

We regard combining the impending Feast of Pentecost with the celebration of the millennium of Norwegian Christianity as particularly successful and symbolical, not only because Pentecost potentially included the future Christianization of the Norwegian nation but also because, during the period of Christianization, the ecumenical unity that was present at Pentecost was still alive in Europe. The two great ecclesiastical centers, Rome and Constantinople, by now had many differences. They nonetheless felt that they were two parts of a single, undivided Church. We wish, in addition, to remind all of you that the emperor of the Christian West at the time, Otto III,[67] was the nephew of the emperor of the

---

65. Nansen to the North Pole, Amundsen to the South Pole, and Heyerdahl, who sailed the oceans in small vessels.

66. Scandinavian bards.

67. Otto (980–1001) was elected king at the age of three in 983.

Christian East, Basil II,[68] on his mother's side, as well as of the great Prince Vladimir[69] of the newly baptized Christian Russia. It is not, therefore, paradoxical that it was in that unity that the flames of Pentecost shone strongly and that the Holy Spirit called to the one undivided Church of Christ new peoples—the Poles in 966, the Russians in 988, the Norwegians in 995, the Hungarians in 1000. It is also not paradoxical that, in this wondrous unity of peoples, Olaf Tryggvason, who was baptized in England, negotiated in Constantinople the baptism of Vladimir of Russia and organized the Church of Norway with the aid of the German Archdiocese of Hamburg-Bremen. However, within a few decades the tragic schism between the Christian West and the Christian East was completed, and five centuries later the Christian West was divided between the Reformed North and the Roman Catholic South. The very high steeples and domes of the cathedrals of Europe were reminiscent now not of Pentecost but of the Tower of Babel.

Considering the hardships that the divisions among Christians have led to over the centuries—the racial hatred and the religious wars—we perceive with sorrow the disappointing image that a divided Christianity presents to the outside world and how much, as a result of this, the name of the God of love "is blasphemed among the Gentiles" (Rom. 2.24). Today, however, in this ecumenical pan-Christian joy, let us glorify our Lord, because the completion of the millennium of Norwegian Christianity finds all Christians united in the quest for the lost unity of Pentecost, yet united in a common affection for the first one thousand years of existence of the one indivisible Church. "By this all men will know that you are my disciples, if you have love for one another" (John 13.35)—today, these words of our Lord can be better understood, while already there are set in motion actions that unite or complete the different traditions and elements that are actually or apparently divisive are being reinterpreted or reformulated. In the context of this shared affection for the lost unity among Christians and of the common effort and prayer for the unity of all in the future, the pan-Christian contribution in this historic celebration of the millennium of Norwegian Christianity assumes particular significance. Moreover, our personal presence here shows the importance that this event is given by the Ecumenical

68. Basil (958–1025) Porphyrogenitus, or the Bulgar-slayer, reigned from 976 to 1025.

69. Vladimir (958–1015) was prince of Kiev and converted to Christianity in 988, baptizing all the Kievan Rus.

Patriarchate, the center of unity of all the independent Orthodox churches. It is the Mother Church who gave birth in Christ, through baptism, to the Russians, Serbs, Bulgarians, and other Orthodox peoples.

Today we fulfill another sacred historical duty, to the person of the first Christian king of Norway. After more than a thousand years, we are reciprocating the visit to Constantinople in 986 of the then young Prince Olaf Tryggvason, representative of his close friend and protector the Grand Prince Vladimir of the Russians. Olaf participated in the negotiations that led to the great event of the baptism of the Kievan Russians in 988. As the Icelandic sagas already relate, Olaf returned to Kiev bringing with him a certain Bishop Paul.[70] Certainly, he had met with our predecessor Patriarch Nicholas II,[71] and assuredly he attended a patriarchal liturgy, which is described with admiration in later narrations of the baptism of the Russians. Finding ourselves here today, we honor the glorious King Olaf Tryggvason for the Christianization of Norway, and we also honor him for his contribution to the preparations for the Christianization of the Russians. In this regard, we propose that he is one of Christianity's truly ecumenical pioneers and personalities.

In the year 995, wars, instability, and inquietude prevailed throughout Europe. A vast many Christians expected the Second Coming in the year 1000. In fact, the tenth century is described by historians as the "dark century" (*seculum obscurum*) of Medieval Europe. And yet, within this darkness the light of Christ shone on many new peoples—the Poles, the Russians, the Norwegians, and the Hungarians. One millennium later, in the year 1995, humanity looks on with great unrest at reports of regional wars, new international threats of environmental catastrophes, and the rise of religious fanaticism. The twentieth century, which faced two world wars and the threat of nuclear war, is also the century during which many Christian churches underwent the long tyranny of atheist dictatorship. This century is ending in instability and uncertainty about the future. For us Christians, however, there is Christ, the hope of the world. There is faith that always triumphs. Our Lord, who recently demolished the powerful fortresses of atheistic arrogance, has the power to resolve "those

---

70. See N. de Baumgarten, in *Orientalia Christiana* 24, no. 33 (1931); and in *Orientalia Christiana* 27 (1932): 68–71.

71. Patriarch of Constantinople from 984 to 995.

things impossible for human beings" (Matt. 19.26) and to bring to the world the peace so greatly desired. We pray that His light, which in the year 995 illuminated the land of Norway for the first time, will illuminate all the earth and unite all peoples in a common doxology of His name.

The Constantinople Lecture, Westminster Abbey, London, December 4, 1995

VISIBLE UNITY FOR THE NEXT MILLENNIUM

From this holy church of the glory of God, of the pride that its founders took in the Lord, and of all those who acknowledge it as a visible sign of their own glorious heritage and identity, we address a greeting of peace, love, and honor to all—to Your Grace, dear brother Dr. George Carey,[72] archbishop of Canterbury, to those who accompany you, and to all our beloved friends here present, to you all, beloved sisters and brothers in the Lord, who have gathered here today. We thank you for the heartfelt welcome, for the kind words and many demonstrations of your love— and, above all, for the opportunity to address glory and honor to God, who is worshipped in Trinity in the midst of this assembly. We also offer glory and gratitude for the treasure that we possess in His saints, and among them Edward the Confessor,[73] the devout king who reigned in England from 1042 to 1066, adorned by God with many gifts of divine grace, before whose sacred shrine every faithful person repeats the Psalmist's song: "God is wonderful in His saints" (Ps. 67.36).

We thank all of you for the sacred sentiments to which this our common assembly invites us. Of itself, it completes a visible expression, if not of the full unity of the Church, then, at any rate, of the earnest desire for the attainment of this unity—or, to speak more precisely, for the preparation of our hearts and consciences for the reception and acceptance of the great gift of unity, as the author of the Church and our Lord Jesus Christ wished it and as the Holy Spirit gives it, to the glory of God the Father.

We have been invited to formulate some ideas about this unity in the context of the Constantinople Lecture, organized under the auspices of

72. George Leonard Carey was archbishop of Canterbury from 1991 to 2002.

73. Edward (1003–66) was canonized in 1161 by Pope Alexander III.

the Anglican–Eastern Churches Association, which was founded as long ago as 1864. In October we had the pleasure of meeting members of this association, led by their Anglican president, Bishop Michael Manktelow, during their pilgrimage to Constantinople and Cappadocia. We thank them most warmly for their kind invitation this evening. The name of the lecture permits a certain ambiguity, allowing the question, "Who is expected to speak here—the Patriarch of Constantinople or Constantinople itself?" We are grateful for the license granted by this ambiguity. And we hasten to explain from the start that, consonant with the faith and character of our tradition, it is always the Church that speaks. We are merely its humble and unworthy mouthpiece, continuously in need of God's grace, so that we may expound at every moment and in every place the experience and witness of the Church. Consequently, as the visible sign and center of the unity of the most holy autocephalous Orthodox churches throughout the world, Constantinople must, as it has been invited to, lay before you at this hour its witness to the particular theme of the lecture—namely, the Orthodox perspective on visible unity and ecumenism in the coming millennium and in relation to the Apocalypse of St. John on the island of Patmos as well as in relation to the natural environment. In the dimensions of time, and place, and thought, the questions posed are great. Who can dare to approach them without fear and trembling? Fortunately, as has already been stated, we are called to articulate today the voice of the Church. And we hear it saying the following.

The first topic is visible unity. The elements of the problem are well known from the ecumenical movement in general and from the particular programs, studies, proposals, and activities of all on the subject, particularly in the context of the activities of the World Council of Churches. These elements have also been clearly established during the Second Vatican Council,[74] within the official theological dialogues, and in ecumenical endeavors in general.

All of us who speak on the present question invoke the prayer of our Lord, "Holy Father, keep them in your name . . . that all may be one" (John 17.11, 21). But we do not always remember that this prayer concludes with a categorical injunction for all those who believe in Christ:

---

74. Second Vatican Council, 1962–65.

"And I have given them the glory that you have given me, that they may be one even as we are one" (John 17.22). The glory of God, which is imaged and revealed for the unity and through the unity of the Church, is not hidden. Where it truly exists and lives, it shines on all things and persuades all human beings. And the world believes and glorifies God and is saved!

Visible too, however, and unhidden is the disgrace, "shame," and "dishonor" of division—precisely because this reveals the harsh contradictions of word and deed. Yet, as the Apostle said, God is dishonored and His Holy Name blasphemed when those who boast of the law break it (Rom. 2.23–24). Sadly, we Christians are entering the third millennium as children and bearers of this "shame" and "disgrace." And instead of unity what is visible is division, separation, and, in some instances, confusion as well as proselytism and open conflict, as they are handed down to the first generation of the coming millennium.

This spectacle grows even more painful when we consider that the twentieth century, which is drawing to a close, although it was a period of fearful conflict in political, ideological, and military terms, was—as no other epoch of the second millennium—a century of active and, as is believed, sincere ecumenical endeavor for the reestablishment of the anticipated visible unity of the churches. What then? Is our failure the only harvest of this toil? Have we passed by and lost the only opportunity given by divine providence to the churches? Did we make our aim a mechanical understanding of unity, one of domination or perhaps one openly pluralistic and wholly foreign to the basic principles of ecclesiology, on which the ancient undivided Church had in many ways relied to preserve her unity? Does that Church, with which our Orthodoxy believes and confesses that it finds itself in uninterrupted succession and identity, persevere in proposing itself as a foundation and model of visible unity both in the present and in the future?

Unfortunately, it is becoming more certain that we Christians will not have prepared a crown of glory, worthy of our compassionate God's grace and loving kindness toward us, a crown with which we might distinguish, with visible unity, the last year of the second millennium and the first of the third millennium. For not only have the stated aims not been attained, but also some of what has been attained ecumenically has either been lost or relegated to the sidelines, while new signs of friction have appeared and new obstacles have been placed on the road to unity. As we call to mind great and sacred moments of previous ecumenical events and the attitudes associated with the loving association of Christians, we feel that what was said to the angel of the Church in Ephesus applies also to us: "I have this against you, that you have abandoned your former love!" (Rev. 2.4). That first ecumenical love, where it has not yet fled, indicates the right road toward visible unity and preserves genuine hope.

AN ORTHODOX PERSPECTIVE ON THE BOOK OF REVELATION

We observed earlier that the word at this moment belonged not so much to our Modesty as Patriarch of Constantinople as to the Church of Constantinople itself. In other words, it belongs to the collegial conscience of Orthodoxy. We think it wise, therefore, to recall that, as leaders of the most holy autocephalous and autonomous Orthodox churches in different places, we have considered together, both at our first meeting in our see at the Phanar on the Sunday of Orthodoxy in 1992 and also at our second meeting this past September on the sacred island of Patmos, the various problems that preoccupy our world. On these questions, we jointly decided the following.

There is a pressing need for the visible unity among Orthodox to be stressed and strengthened. From the point of view of the subject of today's address, this means that, when the unity of one of the Christian families is strengthened, the unity of the whole body is strengthened. And where existing unity is more distinctly established, that serves as a model of a wider unity among Christians. The subsisting unbroken internal unity of the Orthodox churches in different places offers a promising ecumenical perspective. We emphasize this because, as shown in numerous instances, the spectacle of ecumenical unity has become a nightmare for some believers otherwise well-disposed. It is also an instrument for an internal terrorism of the churches at the hands of the distrustful. And for this reason there is an obvious need for linking together ecumenical and pastoral care.

Moreover, we note in the same spirit that the most holy Orthodox Church throughout the inhabited world, sojourning in the world and being inevitably affected by the changes taking place in it, finds herself today confronted with particularly severe and urgent problems which she desires to face as a unified body, adhering to St. Paul, who said, "If one member suffers, all suffer together" (1 Cor. 12.26). One of these problems is that of internal upheavals in the life of some of our sister Orthodox churches. These upheavals have become manifest principally since the recent and unexpected political changes in the countries of Eastern Europe that are predominantly Orthodox. Such dissension leads to tension and even schism. Because of this, as leaders, we have pointed out—in the words of St. John Chrysostom—that "the blood of martyrdom cannot wipe out the sin of schism" and that "to tear the Church asunder is no less an evil than to fall into heresy." It is necessary, then, indeed urgent, that, after the failures and disappointments, we pursue the restoration of the unity of Christians, envisaging at the same time the unity of the whole of humanity. In this spirit, we have clearly emphasized in the past, and we repeat today, that the participation of Orthodoxy in the ecumenical movement was and is the fulfillment of a sacred obligation, whereby our Church may establish her witness, giving a reason for the hope that is in us (1 Pet. 3.15) in humility, love, and confidence.

Our hope flows from the firm conviction that Orthodoxy, adhering to the witness of the one, undivided, Church of the Apostles, the Fathers, and the ecumenical councils, shows the way not to the past but to the future! This conviction is greatly encouraged by evidence of the more general revival of the spirit of the Fathers of the Church. As noted during our meeting, this creative revival "has not only helped the contemporary theological and ecclesiastical world to renew the life of our local churches in general, but also offered to the various organizations of the contemporary ecumenical movement and the connected bilateral and multi-lateral theological dialogues the witness of 'the one holy catholic and apostolic Church.'" Sadly, this witness has not succeeded in averting phenomena that overshadow the vision of unity. For this reason, the crises and deviations observed during the last decades in the bosom of the ecumenical movement impose on the Orthodox Church the need to resist such deviations.

We will certainly disappoint all those who expect that from this resistance will follow the declaration of confessional warfare. Nothing is more foreign or abominable to Orthodoxy than this, notwithstanding the violent and utterly non-fraternal assaults, proselytism, and other such attacks, which it suffers today at the hands of ancient and newfangled "saviors of humanity." The resistance of Orthodoxy, considered as a counterattack of love, has been for the most part a martyr's witness of faith and endures as an exercise in silence, prayer, and patience. We are doing everything in our power on behalf of reconciliation and peace "in accordance with the measure of the gift of Christ" (Eph. 4.7). We need this endurance and love even more in view of the very probable eventuality

> that the coming millennium will bring humanity face to face with "a clash of civilizations" in which the religious element will be dominant. Such a possibility obliges all religious leaders to use wisdom, prudence and courage so that every element of fanaticism and hatred may be averted and eliminated, thereby safeguarding peace in a world which has been tried so severely in wars and conflicts during the century that is drawing to its end.

Furthermore,

> in a world confronted by all kinds of sects and terrifying interpretations of the Book of the Apocalypse, all of us, especially the younger generation, are called to learn and bear witness, in word and deed, to the fact that only the love of God, of our fellow human beings, and the whole creation offers meaning and salvation to our lives, even during the most difficult periods of history.

In proclaiming these words from Patmos, the leaders of the Orthodox churches stressed, in addition, that, "in spite of the dramatic presentation of the events, the book of the Apocalypse contains in its depths the same gospel of Christ and reveals to us that human sin and the demonic destructive forces have been, and will be, defeated by Jesus Christ, the Lord of history, who is 'the Alpha and the Omega . . . the One who is and was and is to come, the Almighty' " (Rev. 1.8). In saying this, we find ourselves already in the spiritual atmosphere of the Book of the Apocalypse. Those who proposed the subject of the Constantinople Lecture expressed the wish that we also say something about this sacred book in relation to global anxiety over the natural environment. Clearly, this was also dictated by the desire to learn more about the celebration of the Year of the Apocalypse, proclaimed by our Church on the completion of 1,900 years since the writing of the Apocalypse, the last book of holy scripture, by John, the servant of God, who "was on the island named Patmos for the Word of God and the witness of Jesus Christ" (Rev. 1.9). In fact, it pleased

Almighty God that we should celebrate this anniversary in Patmos last September.[75] There, we had the opportunity, in the context of an organized scientific international symposium, of studying topical and supremely important and urgent questions relating to the environment and of announcing conclusions and proposals, which, we hope, will attract the interest of responsible parties throughout the world but also of all people, who need to become more conscious that the destruction of the natural environment is equivalent to the suicide of humanity.

This anxiety of the Ecumenical Patriarchate for the protection and preservation of the natural environment and the integrity of God's creation is a fruit of sound biblical and theological principles, which we have received from our Fathers and understand in relation to the destructive distortions of the thought and behavior with respect to the environment. Our Church has undertaken concrete initiatives in recent years on an inter-Orthodox, inter-Christian, and interfaith level as well as on an intercultural and interdisciplinary level, in terms both of our individual responsibility and also of cooperation with other churches, foundations, and organizations. Among the latter, we especially think of the Worldwide Fund for Nature (WWF), which is surely well known to you, while we also express from this podium our sentiments of honor, love, and gratitude to its international president, His Royal Highness Prince Philip, Duke of Edinburgh, who deeply honors us with his friendship and cooperation.

Bearing all this in mind, the leaders of the Orthodox churches included in our message from Patmos the following statement: "The Orthodox Church considers humankind to be a steward and not the owner of material creation. This perception is particularly expressed in the tradition and experience of the ascetic life and of worship, and above all of the

---

75. The first of (now) eight environmental symposia organized by the Religious and Scientific Committee of the Ecumenical Patriarchate was held in the Aegean Sea and concluded on the island of Patmos on September 20–27, 1995. Organized under the aegis of the Ecumenical Patriarch, His All Holiness Ecumenical Patriarch Bartholomew, and the international president of the Worldwide Fund for Nature, His Royal Highness Prince Philip, duke of Edinburgh, the symposium brought together about two hundred scientists, religious leaders, philosophers, economists, artists, and policymakers to examine the nexus of religion and the environment. Participants included representatives from thirty-two countries as well as representatives of the Christian, Muslim, Jewish, Hindu, Buddhist, and other religions.

Eucharist. It is imperative today that we all display love and keep an ascetic attitude toward nature." However, this ascetic stand before the material creation presupposes spiritual training and discipline for the great aims and great visions that our God, incarnate in Christ, revealed and that He entrusted to His Church and set as a further goal and as the final realization of human history. These spiritual insights and divine visions have been and are darkly overshadowed by two errors of Christians— namely, by two "di-visions." Christian peoples have placed greater hope in military division than in God's vision for the life and salvation of humankind. Christian churches have neglected the vision of unity and have been dragged into "di-vision" or separation resulting from the error of self-satisfaction and self-reliance.

It is now time that, at the dawn of the third Christian millennium, we definitively throw away the prefix *di* from the word *division*. For us Christians, vision is sufficient: It is enough and more than enough. For it is a portrayal of the God of peace, of reconciliation, and of love. As is well known, the churches of our continent are preparing the Second European Ecumenical Assembly in 1997 at the city of Graz in Austria, and its theme, "Reconciliation: Gift of God, Source of New Life," supports this vision. We Christians are justified by the grace of God; indeed, we can and must be, so that we can dedicate the third millennium in hope.

And just as we say "yes" to life, we confidently say "yes" to the vision of unity. And as we look forward to the one who is coming, the bridegroom of the Church, we cry out: "Amen. Yes, come, Lord Jesus" (Rev. 22.20).

ROME AND CANTERBURY

Homily delivered in St. Peter's Basilica, the Vatican, June 29, 1997

CONFESSION OF THE HEART

Your Holiness,[76] the grace of the Holy Spirit, whose supreme triumph the Church experienced in history through the event of Pentecost, which we celebrated once again in similar fashion a few weeks ago in both our

---

76. Pope John Paul II.

liturgical traditions, has gathered us together in this historic Basilica of St. Peter to glorify with spiritual hymns the Lord of power and mercy, who out of extreme love for humankind makes possible all things that happen in our world and especially this fraternal encounter of ours.

It is a privilege that for years we have met, through one another's official delegations, on the occasion of our churches' respective patronal feasts, but at the same time it is a trial, inasmuch as, because of our continuing division, we have not yet been rendered worthy to receive the grace of the common cup to which, nevertheless, all Christians seeking and professing the Lord—in both the East and the West, the North and the South—continue ardently to aspire. At this sacred moment, then, we relish to a greater degree the spiritual purification of this privilege as well as of this trial, particularly as we meet personally this year, in order to celebrate the venerable memory of Peter, chief of the Apostles, and Paul, who was martyred together with Peter in the same gospel truth and in the same blood of martyrdom.

The first and fundamental matter for Christ, a matter that cannot be repressed, concealed, or, still less, abolished by any worldly force, is without doubt both the profession of our immaculate faith, "delivered once for all to the saints" (Jude 3), and the obedience that throughout history corresponds and conforms to with this unshakeable faith. The apostolic saying that "because I believed, therefore I proclaimed" (2 Cor. 4.13) is neither rhetorical self-satisfaction nor mere justification. It is a law of life and a measure of truth in the Church. Fortunately, theology in the East and West alike has long emphasized, even through contemporary Protestant theologians, that, "just as Christ is always proclaimed Lord, so faith, at the same time, is always obedience."[77]

For this reason, all the Church's vicissitudes—whether arising from within or without, due to our sins—occurring from time to time in history are related directly or indirectly to the profession of and obedience to this faith. This is why there is so much persecution of the world's faithful; and this is also the reason for the heresies and divisions among the faithful. It is, then, reasonable and proper at this historical moment

---

77. See Emil Brunner, *Dogmatik*, 3:59 (English translation of volume 3: *Dogmatics III. The Christian Doctrine of the Church, Faith, and the Consummation* [Cambridge: James Clarke, 2003]).

not merely to call to mind but rather for all, both near and far, to recall in our conscience and memory the indispensable and indissoluble unity between *the mere profession of the lips* and *the deepest expression of the spirit* with respect to the substance of our faith. We are, moreover, reminded of this more than ever before by the gospel reading, which we have just heard, about Peter's profession of faith at Caesarea of Philippi (see Matt. 16.20).

A PRIMACY OF SERVICE

The unparalleled importance of this passage has been recalled more than amply, as everyone is well aware, whether in exegetical or polemical theology, in an effort to identify or interpret the primacy sought among the Apostles. Fortunately—with God's assistance, albeit through numerous afflictions and humiliations—today we have reached the maturity of true apostolic awareness that seeks *primacy not so much among specific persons but rather among ministries of service*. And we know how many urgent ministries of service confront us in the world at every moment, at least if we are truly concerned not with "being admired by men" but with "being pleasing to God." Today, as we learn once again, the principal and queen of Christian virtues, the only virtue that can truly transform and save the world, is humility coupled with repentance. This is surely the most courageous of virtues and, consequently, the most convincing profession of our faith. It is not possible to believe and truly profess on the one hand that "You alone are holy, You alone are Lord, You alone are most high, Jesus Christ, with the Holy Spirit, in the glory of God the Father" and on the other hand to seek other sources of power and glory in the Church and in the world.

And so great humility and constant repentance are necessary for pastors and faithful alike. Nevertheless, even among the faithful, it is not easy to ignore or uproot the spirit of the world. In order for us to be worthy of acquiring "the mind of Christ," we must first reach "the measure of the stature of the fullness of Christ" (Eph. 4.13). For, if, according to the undeniable words of the Lord, "the whole world lies within the power of the evil one" (1 John 5.19), then we should also remember the Lord's verdict about the evil one—that "this kind cannot be driven out by anything other than prayer and fasting" (Matt. 9.29).

It is only with these spiritual coordinates that the integrity of our faith can be preserved in history; it is only in this manner that our faith can be authentically professed and honored as the power that "overcomes the world" (1 John 5.4). It is obvious that, as presuppositions of the integrity of faith, these spiritual coordinates clearly demonstrate that *orthodoxia* (true faith and true worship) without *orthopraxia* (true living and true practice) is intolerable hypocrisy but also that theological reflection on works and faith is merely sterile academic verbiage. However, in asserting this, Your Holiness and my beloved brothers and sisters, we do not at all wish to disrupt our meditation on this solemn occasion. Instead, it is our intention to declare boldly to the Christian world today, with sincerity and fear of God, our conviction about the need for self-criticism and ongoing repentance.

What, then, should be sought in the first place—at least, according to a Christian sense of self-criticism and repentance—is an identification neither of those who erred first or last, nor of those who erred most or least. This would be a cowardly and worldly inquiry, which even the pre-Christian *eranes* and *thiases* of Athens considered an inferior occupation for a spiritual person. Indeed, the fundamental issue before us is to identify how, by serving our neighbor, we may save our brother and sister; and how, through our neighbor alone, we too may be made worthy of salvation.[78]

In this regard, unfortunately, we Christians have misunderstood and misinterpreted St. Paul's golden rule—"Bear one another's burdens, and so fulfill the law of Christ" (Gal. 6.2)—as constituting simply a mutual solidarity of a worldly nature. Early on it was necessary for the Neptic Fathers of the East to complete or complement—indeed, to correct—the meaning of these words by St. Paul with the famous self-awareness and self-reproach that they practiced and promoted throughout their vigilant lives. For this is truly the only possibility of "fulfilling the law of Christ." And so, according to the concepts of self-awareness and self-reproach as described in *The Philokalia*, all sins and errors of our brothers and sisters—all transgressions, with the exception of erroneous beliefs and heresies[79]—weigh not on others but on ourselves.[80] We are to spontaneously

---

78. See Anthony, Saying 9. See *The Sayings of the Desert Fathers: The Alphabetical Collection*, trans. Benedicta Ward (London: Mowbrays, 1975), 2.

79. See Agathon, Saying 5, 18.

80. See Anthony, Saying 4, 2.

render ourselves personally responsible for these errors without grumbling or blaming. This is the only sincere method of "fulfilling the law of Christ," if we truly desire our brothers and sister, our wretched selves, and the entire world to be saved.

Just as the incarnate God became "like us in every way except sin," so too we are called to become like our brothers and sisters in every way "except heresy." If, out of profound love for humanity and the world, our Lord—who alone was without sin—was able to say of His disciples to the Father and to us, "And for their sake, I sanctify myself" (John 17.19), how much more so should we, as wretched human beings, purify, consecrate, and sanctify ourselves ceaselessly for the world through constant *kenosis*.[81]

Finally, Your Holiness, as we congratulate and embrace you on the occasion of this great feast commemorating the supreme Apostles Peter and Paul, may we also be permitted to declare in truth that only when *the primacy of a kenotic ethos* prevails convincingly in the historical Church will we be able not only to reestablish our deeply desired unity in faith but also to render ourselves immediately worthy of experiencing all that God's revelation has promised to those who love the Lord—namely, "a new heaven and a new earth."

Address before the Twelfth Ordinary General Assembly of the Roman Catholic Synod of Bishops, the Vatican, October 18, 2008

THE DIVINE FACULTY OF PERCEPTION

Your Holiness,[82] beloved synodal Fathers: It is at once humbling and inspiring to be invited by His Holiness to address the Twelfth Ordinary General Assembly of this auspicious synod of bishops, an historical meeting of bishops of the Roman Catholic Church from throughout the world, gathered in one place to meditate on *"the Word of God"* and to deliberate on the experience and expression of this Word *"in the Life and*

---

81. Greek term for "self-emptying" or "humility." See Foreword, viii.

82. Delivered at the invitation of Pope Benedict XVI. This was the first occasion that an Ecumenical Patriarch—and, indeed, any Orthodox hierarch—addressed such a gathering. The theme of the assembly was "The Word of God in the Life and Mission of the Church."

Mission of the Church." This gracious invitation is a gesture full of meaning and significance—we dare say, an historic event in itself. For it is the first time in history that an Ecumenical Patriarch is offered the opportunity to address a synod of the bishops in the Roman Catholic Church and thereby to be part of the life of our sister Church at such a high level. We regard this as a manifestation of the work of the Holy Spirit leading our churches to a closer and deeper relationship with each other, an important step toward the restoration of full communion.

It is well known that the Orthodox Church attaches to the synodal system fundamental ecclesiological importance. Together with primacy, synodality constitutes the backbone of the Church's governance and organization. As our Joint International Commission for Theological Dialogue between our churches explained in the Ravenna document,[83] this interdependence between synodality and primacy permeates all levels of the Church's life: local, regional, and universal. Therefore, in having today the privilege to address your synod, our hopes are raised that the day will come when our two churches will fully converge on the role of primacy and synodality in the Church's life, a goal to which our common theological commission is devoting its study at the present time.

The theme to which this episcopal synod devotes its work is of crucial significance not only for the Roman Catholic Church but also for all those who are called to witness to Christ in our time. For mission and evangelization remain a permanent duty of the Church at all times and places; indeed, they form part of the Church's nature, as she is called "apostolic" both in the sense of her faithfulness to the original teaching of the Apostles and in that of proclaiming the Word of God in every cultural context and in every age. The Church needs, therefore, to rediscover the Word of God in every generation and make it heard with a renewed vigor and persuasion even in our contemporary world, which deep in its heart thirsts for God's message of peace, hope, and charity.

This duty of evangelization would have been, of course, greatly enhanced and strengthened if all Christians were in a position to perform it with one voice and as a fully united Church. In his prayer to the Father a little before His passion, our Lord has made it clear that the unity of the

---

83. Produced on October 13, 2007, the document examined ecclesial communion, conciliarity, and authority in the Roman Catholic and Orthodox churches.

Church is inextricably linked with her mission, "so that the world may believe" (John 17.21). It is, therefore, most appropriate that this synod has opened its doors to ecumenical fraternal delegates so that we may all become aware of our common duty of evangelization as well as of the difficulties and problems of its realization in today's world.

This synod has undoubtedly been studying the subject of the Word of God in depth and in all its aspects, theological as well as practical and pastoral. In our modest address to you we will limit ourselves to sharing with you some thoughts on the theme of your meeting, drawing from how the Orthodox tradition has approached the Word of God throughout the centuries and in the Greek patristic teaching in particular. More concretely, we would like to concentrate on three aspects of the subject—on *hearing and speaking the Word of God through the Holy Scriptures,* on *seeing God's Word in nature and above all in the beauty of the icons,* and, finally, on *touching* and sharing *God's Word in the communion of saints and in the sacramental life of the Church.* For all these are, we think, crucial in the life and mission of the Church.

We seek to draw on the rich patristic tradition, which dates to the early third century and in which a doctrine of five spiritual senses is expounded. For listening to God's Word, beholding God's Word, and touching God's Word are all spiritual ways of perceiving the unique divine mystery. In reference to Proverbs 2.5, where we read about "the divine faculty of perception," Origen of Alexandria[84] writes:

> This sense unfolds as sight for contemplation of immaterial forms, hearing for discernment of voices, taste for savoring the living bread, smell for sweet spiritual fragrance, and touch for handling the Word of God, which is *grasped by every faculty of the soul.*

The spiritual senses are variously described as "five senses of the soul," as "divine" or "inner faculties," and even as "faculties of the heart" or "mind." This doctrine inspired the theology of the Cappadocians (especially Basil the Great and Gregory of Nyssa) as much as it did the theology of the Desert Fathers (especially Evagrius of Pontus and Macarius the Great).

---

84. A creative Christian thinker, Origen (185–254) was one of the most distinguished and influential writers of the early Church.

HEARING AND SPEAKING THE WORD THROUGH SCRIPTURE

At each celebration of the Divine Liturgy of St. John Chrysostom, the presiding celebrant at the Eucharist intones, "That we may be made worthy to hear the Holy Gospel." For "hearing, beholding, and handling the Word of life" (1 John 1.1) are not first and foremost our entitlement or birthright as human beings; they are our privilege and gift as children of the living God. The Christian Church is, above all, a scriptural Church. Although methods of interpretation may have varied from Church Father to Church Father, from "school" to "school," and from East to West, nevertheless scripture was always received as a living reality and not a dead book.

In the context of a living faith, then, scripture is the living testimony of a lived history about the relationship of a living God with a living people. The Spirit, "who spoke through the prophets" (Nicene–Constantinopolitan Creed), spoke in order to be heard and to have an effect. It is primarily an oral and direct communication intended for human ears to benefit from. The scriptural text is, therefore, derivative and secondary; the scriptural text always serves the spoken word. It is not conveyed mechanically but rather communicated from generation to generation as a living word. Through the Prophet Isaiah, the Lord vows, "As rain and snow descend from heaven, watering the earth . . . so shall my word go from mouth to mouth, accomplishing that which I purpose" (Isaiah 55.10–11).

Moreover, as St. John Chrysostom explains, the divine Word demonstrates profound consideration for the personal diversity and cultural context of those hearing and receiving. Adaptation of the divine Word to the specific personal readiness and the particular cultural context defines the missionary dimension of a Church called to transform the world through the Word. In silence as in declaration, in prayer as in action, the divine Word addresses the whole world, "preaching to all nations" (Matt. 28.19) without privilege or prejudice to race, culture, gender, or class. When we carry out that divine commission, we are assured, "Behold, I am with you always" (Matt. 28.20). We are called to speak the divine Word in all languages, "becoming all things to all people, that [we] might by all means save some" (1 Cor. 9.22).

It is today more imperative than ever, then, that, as disciples of God's Word, we provide a unique perspective—beyond the social, political, or economic—on the need to eradicate poverty, to provide balance in a global world, to combat fundamentalism or racism, and to develop religious tolerance in a world of conflict. In responding to the needs of the world's poor, vulnerable, and marginalized, the Church can leave a defining mark on the space and character of the global community. While the theological language of religion and spirituality differs from the technical vocabulary of economics and politics, the barriers that at first glance appear to separate religious concerns (such as sin, salvation, and spirituality) from pragmatic interests (such as commerce, trade, and politics) are not impenetrable, as they crumble before the manifold challenges in the realms of social justice and globalization.

Whether dealing with environment or peace, poverty or hunger, education or healthcare, we feel today a heightened sense of common concern and common responsibility. It is felt with particular acuteness by people of faith as well as by those whose outlook is expressly secular. Our engagement with such issues does not of course in any way undermine or abolish differences between various disciplines or disagreements with those who look at the world in different ways. Yet the growing signs of a common commitment to the well-being of humanity and to the life of the world are encouraging. It is an encounter of individuals and institutions that bodes well for our world. And it is an involvement that highlights the supreme vocation and mission that the disciples and adherents of God's Word have to transcend political or religious differences in order to transform the entire visible world for the glory of the invisible God.

SEEING THE WORD OF GOD—THE BEAUTY OF ICONS AND NATURE

Nowhere is the invisible rendered more visible than in the beauty of iconography and the wonder of creation. In the words of the champion of sacred images, St. John of Damascus: "As maker of heaven and earth, God the Word was Himself the first to paint and portray icons." Every stroke of an iconographer's paintbrush—like every word of a theological definition, every musical note chanted in psalmody, and every carved stone of a tiny chapel or magnificent cathedral—articulates the divine Word in creation, which praises God in every living being and every living thing (see Ps. 150.6).

In affirming sacred images, the Seventh Ecumenical Council (Nicea, 787) was not concerned with religious art; it was the continuation and confirmation of earlier definitions about the fullness of the humanity of God's Word. Icons are visible reminders of our heavenly vocation; they are personal invitations to rise above our trivial concerns and menial reductions of the world. They encourage us to seek the extraordinary in the very ordinary, to be filled with the same wonder that characterized the divine marvel in Genesis, when "God saw everything that He made; and, indeed, it was very good" (Gen. 1.30–31). The Greek (Septuagint) word for "goodness" is *kallos*, which implies—etymologically and symbolically—a sense of "calling." Icons underline the Church's fundamental mission to recognize that all people and all things are created and called to be "good" and "beautiful."

Indeed, icons remind us of another way of seeing things, another way of experiencing realities, another way of resolving conflicts. We are asked to assume what the hymnology of Easter Sunday calls "another way of living." For we have behaved arrogantly and dismissively toward the natural creation. We have refused to behold God's Word in the oceans of our planet, in the trees of our continents, and in the animals of our earth. We have denied our very own nature, which calls us to stoop low enough to hear God's Word in creation if we wish to "become participants of divine nature" (2 Pet. 1.4). How could we ignore the wider implications of the divine Word assuming flesh? Why do we fail to perceive created nature as the extended body of Christ?

Eastern Christian theologians always emphasized the cosmic proportions of divine incarnation. The incarnate Word is intrinsic to creation, which came to be through divine utterance. St. Maximus the Confessor insists on the presence of God's Word *in all things* (see Col. 3.11); the divine Logos stands at the center of *the entire world*, mysteriously revealing its original principle and ultimate purpose (see 1 Pet. 1.20). This mystery is eloquently described by St. Athanasius of Alexandria: "As the Logos, He is not contained by anything and yet contains everything; He is in everything and yet outside of everything . . . the first-born of the whole world in its every aspect."

The entire world is a prologue to the Gospel of John. And when the Church fails to recognize the broader, cosmic dimensions of God's Word, narrowing its concerns to purely spiritual matters, it neglects its mission to implore God for the transformation—always and everywhere, "in all places of His dominion"—of the whole polluted cosmos. It is no wonder that on Easter Sunday, as the Paschal celebration reaches its climax, Orthodox Christians sing, "Now everything is filled with divine light: heaven and earth, and all things beneath the earth. So let all creation rejoice."[85] All genuine "deep ecology" is, therefore, inextricably linked with deep theology: "Even a stone," writes Basil the Great, "bears the mark of God's Word. This is true of an ant, a bee, and a mosquito, the smallest of creatures. For He spread the wide heavens and laid the immense seas; and He created the tiny hollow shaft of the bee's sting." Recalling our minuteness in God's wide and wonderful creation only underlines our central role in God's plan for the salvation of the whole world.

TOUCHING AND SHARING THE WORD OF GOD:
THE COMMUNION OF SAINTS AND THE SACRAMENTS OF LIFE

The Word of God persistently "moves outside of Himself in ecstasy" (Dionysius the Areopagite),[86] passionately seeking to "dwell in us" (John 1.14), that the world may have life in abundance (John 10.10). God's compassionate mercy is poured and shared "so as to multiply the objects of His beneficence" (Gregory the Theologian). God assumes all that is ours, "in every respect being tested as we are, yet without sin" (Heb. 4.15), in order to offer us all that is God's and to render us gods by grace. "Though rich, He becomes poor that we might become rich," writes the great Apostle Paul (2 Cor. 8.9), to whom this year is dedicated. This is the Word of God; gratitude and glory are due to Him.

The word of God receives His full embodiment in creation, above all in the sacrament of the Holy Eucharist. It is there that the Word becomes flesh and allows us not simply to hear or see Him but to *touch* Him with our own hands, as St. John declares (1 John 1.1), and to make Him part of our own body and blood, in the words of St. John Chrysostom.

In the Holy Eucharist the Word that is *heard* is at the same time *seen* and *shared* as communion (*koinonia*). It is not accidental that, in the earliest eucharistic documents, such as the Book of Revelation and the

---

85. From the matins canon of the Easter vigil.

86. Anonymous theologian, most probably from Syria of the fifth to sixth centuries, whose mystical writings were influential among later Church Fathers, particularly St. Maximus the Confessor in the seventh century.

Didache,[87] the Eucharist was associated with *prophesy* and the presiding bishops were regarded as successors of the prophets (as, for example, in the *Martyrion Polycarpi*). The Eucharist was already described by St. Paul (1 Cor. 11) as "proclamation" of Christ's death and second coming. As the purpose of scripture is essentially the proclamation of the Kingdom and the announcement of eschatological realities, the Eucharist is a foretaste of the Kingdom and, in this sense, the proclamation of the Word par excellence. In the Eucharist, Word and sacrament become one reality. The Word ceases to be "mere word" and becomes a *person*, embodying in Himself all human beings and all creation.

Within the life of the Church, the unfathomable self-emptying (*kenosis*) and generous sharing (*koinonia*) of the divine Logos is reflected in the lives of the saints as the tangible experience and human expression of God's Word in our community. In this way, the Word of God becomes the body of Christ, crucified and glorified at the same time. As a result, the saint has an organic relationship with heaven and earth, with God and all of creation. In ascetic struggle, the saint reconciles the uncreated Word and the created world. Through repentance and purification, the saint is filled, as Abba Isaac the Syrian insists, "with compassion for all of God's creatures,"[88] which is the ultimate humility and perfection.

This is why the saint loves with a warmth and generosity that are both unconditional and irresistible. In the saints, we know God's very Word, since, as St. Gregory Palamas declares, "God and His saints share the same glory and splendor." In the gentle presence of a saint, we learn how theology and action coincide. In the compassionate love of the saint, we experience God as "our father" and God's mercy as "steadfastly enduring" (Ps. 135). The saint is consumed with the fire of God's love. This is why the saint imparts grace and cannot tolerate the slightest manipulation or exploitation of society or nature. The saint simply does what is "proper and right,"[89] always dignifying humanity and honoring creation. "His words have the force of actions and his silence the power of speech" (St. Ignatius of Antioch).[90]

---

87. An anonymous Christian treatise, part of the collection of apostolic writings and dating to the late first or early second century.

88. *Mystic Treatises*, Homily 48.

89. From the Divine Liturgy of St. John Chrysostom.

90. One of the Apostolic Fathers, Ignatius (35–117) authored a series of letters as he traveled to Rome for his martyrdom.

And within the communion of saints, each of us is called to "become like fire" (*Sayings of the Desert Fathers*),[91] to touch the world with the mystical force of God's Word, so that, as the extended body of Christ, the world too might say, "Someone has touched me!" (see Matt. 9.20). Evil is eradicated only by holiness, not by harshness. And holiness introduces into society a seed that heals and transforms. Imbued with the life of the sacraments and the purity of prayer, we are able to enter the innermost mystery of God's Word. It is like the tectonic plates of the earth's crust: The deepest layers need shift only a few millimeters to shatter the world's surface. Yet for this spiritual revolution to occur, we must experience radical *metanoia*—a conversion of attitudes, habits, and practices—for ways that we have misused or abused God's Word, God's gifts, and God's creation.

Such a conversion is, of course, impossible without divine grace; it is not achieved simply through greater effort or stronger willpower. "For mortals, it is impossible; but for God all things are possible" (Matt. 19.26). Spiritual change occurs when our bodies and souls are grafted onto the living Word of God, when our cells contain the life-giving blood-flow of the sacraments, when we are open to sharing all things with all people. As St. John Chrysostom reminds us, the sacrament of "our neighbor" cannot be isolated from the sacrament of "the altar." Sadly, we have ignored the vocation and obligation to share. Social injustice and inequality, global poverty and war, ecological pollution and degradation—all these result from our inability or unwillingness to share. If we claim to retain the sacrament of the altar, we cannot forgo or forget the sacrament of the neighbor—a fundamental condition for realizing God's Word in the world within the life and mission of the Church.

Beloved brothers in Christ: We have explored the patristic teaching of the spiritual senses, discerning the power of hearing and speaking God's Word in scripture, of seeing God's Word in icons and nature, and of touching and sharing God's Word in the saints and sacraments. Yet, to remain true to the life and mission of the Church, we must personally be changed by this Word. The Church must resemble a mother, who is both sustained by and nourishes through the food she eats. Anything that does not feed and nourish everyone cannot sustain us either. When the world does not share the joy of Christ's Resurrection, this is an indictment of our own integrity and commitment to the living Word of God. Before

---

91. Joseph of Panephysis, Saying 7. See Benedicta Ward (ed.), *Sayings*, 88

the celebration of each Divine Liturgy, Orthodox Christians pray that this Word will be "broken and consumed, distributed and shared" in communion. And "we know that we have passed from death to life when we love our brothers" and sisters (1 John 3.14).

The challenge before us is the discernment of God's Word in the face of evil, the transfiguration of every last detail and speck of this world in the light of Resurrection. The victory is already present in the depths of the Church whenever we experience the grace of reconciliation and communion. As we struggle, in ourselves and in our world, to recognize the power of the Cross, we begin to appreciate how every act of justice, every spark of beauty, every word of truth can gradually wear away the crust of evil. However, beyond our own frail efforts, we have the assurance of the Spirit, who "helps us in our weakness" (Rom. 8.26) and stands beside us as advocate and "comforter" (John 14.16), penetrating all things and "transforming us," in the words of St. Symeon the New Theologian, "into everything that the Word of God says about the heavenly Kingdom: pearl, grain of mustard seed, leaven, water, fire, bread, life and, mystical wedding chamber." Such is the power and grace of the Holy Spirit, whom we invoke as we conclude our address, extending to Your Holiness our gratitude and to each of you our blessings:

> Heavenly King, Comforter, Spirit of Truth, present everywhere
> and filling all things;
> treasury of goodness and giver of life:
> Come, and abide in us; and cleanse us from every impurity;
> and save our souls. For you are good and love humankind.[92]

POPE JOHN PAUL II

Homily on the Return of the Relics of Saints Gregory the Theologian and John Chrysostom, Ecumenical Patriarchate, November 27, 2004

LONG-AWAITED RETURN HOME

Today, all of us honor the return from exile of the twice exiled St. John Chrysostom and the return to his see of St. Gregory the Theologian, who

---

92. An ancient and popular prayer to the Holy Spirit, often recited at the beginning of liturgical services.

willingly resigned from his position of leadership for the sake of peace in the Church.[93] Beloved children in the Lord, awaiting the blessings of the saints: It is with great emotion and joy that we return from Rome to our venerable see, accompanying the sacred relics of our holy predecessors, Saints Gregory the Theologian and John Chrysostom, who, with their Christ-like virtue, theological brilliance, and zealous apostolic work, illuminated the Archdiocese of Constantinople. For eight hundred years, these relics have been in exile, though in a Christian country—not of their own will but as a result of the infamous Fourth Crusade, during which this city was sacked in 1204.

Once again, from here, we would like to express our gratitude to His Holiness the Pope of Rome and his curia for their generous decision to return these holy relics to the Church of Constantinople, where they belong. This gesture differentiates them from the deed of their predecessors eight centuries ago, who accepted the spiritual and material treasures that had been taken from our city and our Church. That, albeit eight centuries later, these saints are returning where they have always belonged, and justice has been restored, is a joyous event and worthy of special exaltation.

On the occasion of this historic event, the blessed spirits of the saints are undoubtedly rejoicing at their return home. And, together with them, in the same spirit, the chorus of our city's saints rejoices, from Andrew, the first-called Apostle and founder of our Holy Mother the Great Church of Christ, and Stachys, to Photius the Great and Ignatius, Proclus, and Alexander, and Tarasius; from Gennadios Scholarios and Gregory V, to Theodore and the other Studites, to the martyrs and confessors, and to all the saints of the past. Also rejoicing is the congregation of the Church of Constantinople all over the world, in Western Europe, past Cadiz and in the Far East, even to the antipodes. However, those who especially rejoice are the members of the small flock remaining here, who will have the daily consolation, refuge, strength, and blessing of the presence of their blessed great archbishops through their holy relics.

The bodies of the saints, as dwelling places of God's grace and of all the gifts of the Holy Spirit, are holy, as are their souls. Their holiness and

93. The relics were returned by Pope John Paul II to Ecumenical Patriarch Bartholomew in November 2004. They are currently treasured in the Patriarchal Church of St. George.

grace were not left behind after their sleep in the Lord but reside in their holy relics. That is why they emit a sweet fragrance, perform miracles, heal illness, exorcise demons, and abolish the power of evil spirits. And so, when we approach and venerate the holy relics with piety, we become participants in divine grace and in the gifts of the Holy Spirit. Our soul is calmed, our heart becomes peaceful, the agitation of evil and unclean thoughts ceases, we are consoled, we are supported, we come to contrition, we gain strength to continue with patience our Christian struggle for repentance, purification, and union with our theanthropic Lord Jesus Christ. For we have before us the "tangible" example of the saints whose holy relics we venerate. For they believed, loved, hoped, struggled, persevered, gained, were united, were sanctified, were crowned, and became the "extension" of Jesus Christ to the present time and forevermore. This is exactly the case with Saints Gregory and John, who became archbishops of Constantinople.

So, with deep emotion, our hearts once again exclaim words of filial love, infinite respect, and pious supplication. We all unanimously cry out once more to St. John Chrysostom to assume "your throne," as the lords and people rightly did when his holy relic, on being returned for the first time to Constantinople from its exile in Komana, Armenia, where, unjustly exiled, it slept in the Lord, was placed on the episcopal throne in the church, as an expression of sorrow for the injustice by which he was exiled. Certainly, none of us feel responsible for the second exile of this holy relic from our venerable see. Nevertheless, we need to explore to what degree we have kept alive in our hearts the treasures of his immortal teachings and salutary exhortations. Have we perhaps been led astray by the confusion of ideas and beliefs in our time and forgotten the only truth, which St. John Chrysostom and all the saints proclaimed, that "there is no salvation but in Jesus Christ"?

To St. Gregory the Theologian, who literally restored the Orthodox faith to this city at a time when the Arian heresy[94] had almost completely prevailed, we cry out with one voice that "we welcome him with prayers," refusing to repeat the phrase "you dismissed us with prayers," which he requested in his farewell speech before one hundred fifty bishops as he

---

94. The fourth-century teaching of Arius (250–356), a presbyter from Alexandria, on the relationship of the persons of the Trinity and the precise nature of the Son of God.

resigned from the throne. The few Christians remaining in the city today welcome the holy relic of St. Gregory, as it was welcomed in the past, when it first returned here, by the few who remained loyal to the Orthodox faith, having preserved the purity of their faith when thousands followed the heresy of Arius. He restored the faith miraculously long ago. We earnestly pray to him to undertake that task once more, as in his second arrival in this city he finds it once again, although for different reasons, in a critical state.

With the arrival of these holy relics, two more saints are added to the chorus of saints manifest in our city through their sacred relics, strengthening us in our difficult work. Let us all ask them to show each one of us what we should do, to give us courage and forbearance, unshaken faith and peace in the Church in the midst of secular disorder, the illumination and grace of God, repentance and mercy, so that, walking with God, we may reach the haven of peace, love, mutual understanding, tolerance regardless of cultural differences, and cooperation for the good of all people.

And may the God of peace and love, who, according to St. John Chrysostom in the *Catechetical Oration* on the night of Easter, "accepts the works, embraces the opinion, honors the deed, and praises the intention," and "grants rest to him who has worked from the eleventh hour just the same as to him who has worked from the first"—may this God accept each one of us as well, even the least, just as He accepts those who work from the first hour, granting us His great and rich mercy. This we ask through the intercession also of St. Gregory the Theologian.

On the First Anniversary of the Repose of Pope John Paul II

SYMBOL OF STABILITY

It is with great pleasure and solemn reminiscence that we gladly respond to the gracious invitation of the honorable Lech Walesa to offer a brief personal testimony, for publication, on the anniversary of the passing of the late Pope John Paul II into the paternal embrace of our heavenly Lord one year ago this April.[95] For more than a quarter of a century, His

---

95. This address was written in 2006 at the invitation of Lech Walesa, former president of Poland (1990–95).

Holiness Pope John Paul II[96] shepherded the Roman Catholic Church, standing as a symbol of firm stability and unrelenting hope in an age of widespread turmoil and despair. The diverse ministerial efforts of the late pope were a reflection of his conviction and commitment to follow and to imitate the Prince of Peace and to care for the poor of this world.

More especially, we would succinctly describe the ministry of the late pope as one of solidarity, reconciliation, peace, and dialogue. The term that is perhaps most characteristic of the vision and action of Pope John Paul II is surely *connections*. He was a man who could make and realize connections in the world. He was, first of all, able to discern the inner unity of all people and all things in God and, second, willing to strive toward realizing and manifesting that inner unity so as to render it visible and tangible.

Man of Solidarity

Mercy and righteousness, justice, and peace are the essential characteristics of God's kingdom. Deeply cognizant of his unique pastoral responsibility to preach God's kingdom to millions worldwide, His Holiness' tenure as the chief shepherd of Western Christendom was undoubtedly inspired by his abiding faith as well as by the difficult circumstances in which his home country of Poland had suffered for so many years under totalitarian oppression. This is an experience of martyrdom, with which the Orthodox Church can most certainly identify, having itself experienced so much suffering through the centuries. After decades of repression, the people of Poland continued to yearn for freedom and demonstrated in a nonviolent manner against oppressive tyranny. Is it any wonder, then, that *solidarnosc* became a household word all over the world, wherever lovers of freedom symbolically joined hands and hearts in a profound act of solidarity?

From the first moments of that powerful protest in the late 1980s, His Holiness understood that the mission of the Church was linked to the liberation of men and women from tyranny. He brought their struggle into his own embrace, transforming it into a holy endeavor worthy of

---

96. John Paul II (1920–2005) was pope of Rome from 1978 to 2005.

every human effort and of all God's blessings. It was as a result of this initial victory of the human spirit, so eloquently articulated through his voice and encouraged through his support, that the walls that had so long imprisoned Eastern Europe came tumbling down in a mighty roar of thunder.

When His Holiness visited his homeland some ten years later, in 1999, true to his role as a priest and pastor, he urged his countrymen and women never to take the gift of freedom for granted, noting that it "requires constant effort in order to be consolidated and lived responsibly." Moreover, he encouraged them to have the "determination to build together the civilization of love, which is based on universal values of peace, solidarity, justice, and freedom." These words surely remain an exhortation to all people in every nation on earth.

MAN OF RECONCILIATION

The same zeal for peace that led to His Holiness' leadership in this solidarity that transcended political, cultural, and geographic boundaries also motivated his profound desire to establish avenues for reconciliation across the boundaries of historical time, religious discrimination, and cultural bigotry. We are referring of course to the outreach of His Holiness to the Jewish people through manifold expressions but especially through his moving and historical visit to the Holy Land in the year 2000.

As has been painfully and repeatedly recorded throughout the past millennia, the Jewish people have suffered at the hands of their diverse enemies. Sometimes, many who would identify themselves with the Church of Jesus Christ were, lamentably and deplorably, counted among those enemies and persecutors. The contradiction, seen with the clarity of hindsight, could not be more glaring. After all, how could any follower of the Prince of Peace ever be so prejudiced against the very people through whom their God had chosen to be revealed? How could the adherents of the gospel of love ever become such cruel perpetrators of criminal hatred and hurt?

Pope John Paul II saw that, at the start of a new millennium, this contradiction could no longer stand or be tolerated. With aching heart and remorseful tears, he fervently prayed among the Jews in the city of

Jerusalem that this hatred would be no more. Indeed, His Holiness potently observed at a solemn ceremony held at the Yad Vashem[97] memorial museum—a place of profound revelation and of painful memory, one that we still recall from our own pilgrimage there[98]—that "to remember is to pray for peace and justice, and to commit ourselves to their cause. Only a world at peace, with justice for all, can avoid repeating the mistakes and terrible crimes of the past." To this cause of peace and justice, therefore, in a moment of regret and hopefulness at once, His Holiness enjoined the entire Roman Catholic Church. There was not a single Christian of any tradition who remained unmoved by this compassion and love. There was not a single human being in the world who remained untouched by this commitment and repentance.

On the same day that His Holiness made this vow among the Jews in Israel, he pointed out at a gathering of Christian, Jewish, and Muslim faithful that each of these three great monotheistic faiths rooted in the City of Peace, Jerusalem, share a common view of human dignity and of human responsibility toward one another. This common view is based on the shared reverence that all three faiths have for the one God who created human beings in the divine image and likeness. It is also grounded on the common desire for love and justice, expressed through the pursuit of peace.

Man of Peacemaking

His Holiness repeatedly highlighted the universal ramifications of this shared belief, emphasizing:

> Religion is the enemy of exclusion and discrimination, of hatred and rivalry, of violence and conflict. Religion is not, and must not become, an excuse for violence, particularly when religious identity coincides with cultural and ethnic identity. Religion and peace go together! Religious belief and practice cannot be separated from the defense of the image of God in every human being.

How much more relevant are His Holiness' words today than they were just a few years ago! The entire region surrounding the Holy Land

---

97. The Holocaust Museum in Jerusalem.
98. In 1999.

has today become a hotbed for religious and political fundamentalism, extremism, and terrorism. The war in Iraq has, it is regretful to say, led to an unprecedented outbreak of anarchy, tribal conflict, and ethnic strife. At a time when all of us should have been celebrating the failure of the theory of inevitable and ultimate "clash of civilizations," with visions of 9/11 burned in our memory, we all now fear its destructive impact on the whole world.

While religious extremists on both sides of the divide would have us believe that this clash is divinely inspired or humanly inevitable, we all know that it is the very antithesis of the truths found and propounded in Christianity, Judaism, and Islam alike. This is precisely why we jointly proclaimed, with leaders of other religious faiths, in the Bosphorus Declaration, at a Conference on Peace and Tolerance organized here in Istanbul in 1994, that "a war in the name of religion is a war against religion." Similarly, bearing these words in mind, on the eve of the war in Iraq, we also declared: "The basic prerequisite of peace is the respect for the sanctity of the human person and his freedom and dignity. From this respect are born all other prerequisites for the peaceful coexistence of all human beings on earth in the love of one God and Father, who is not a God of war and battle but of reconciliation and peace."

On the World Day of Peace in 2003, His Holiness Pope John Paul II celebrated the fortieth anniversary of Pope John XXIII's encyclical *Pacem in Terris*[99] and called on all people to "resolve to have the same outlook: namely, trust in the merciful and compassionate God who calls us to brotherhood, and confidence in the men and women of our time because, like those of every other time, they bear the image of God in their souls. It is on this basis that we can hope to build a world of peace on earth."

MAN OF DIALOGUE

It is this same motivation that directed the steps of His Holiness to our patriarchal seat here in Turkey only one year after his elevation to the see of Rome, as he came to visit our predecessor of blessed memory, the late Ecumenical Patriarch Dimitrios. Together, the two leaders solemnly proclaimed the opening of the official Joint International Commission

---

99. Translated as "peace on earth."

for Theological Dialogue between the Roman Catholic and Orthodox Churches. Following and based on the "dialogue of love"[100] established by their predecessors, Pope Paul VI and Patriarch Athenagoras in the 1960s, the "dialogue of truth"[101] was the commencement of an historical conversation and expression of goodwill between the two "sister churches" in an effort to begin the process of healing the tragic wounds of schism and division. In the face of its triumphs and failures, the continuation of this dialogue and its progress was always a high priority in the heart of His Holiness, who shared with us the deep conviction that the churches who lived together in full unity during the first thousand years of the history of the Christian Church should once again be able to recover their full ecclesial communion through an open and sincere dialogue in our time.

In 2004, just one year before his repose in the Lord, Pope John Paul II consented to our humble request and endorsed the formal return to Constantinople of the sacred relics of St. Gregory the Theologian and St. John Chrysostom, our venerable predecessors on the Ecumenical Throne and formative teachers of the early Church. And so, on June 29, 2004, we personally attended the patronal feast of the Roman Catholic Church, accepting an invitation, extended annually, to an event where we are traditionally represented by an official delegation. That year also marked the fortieth anniversary of the inception of the "dialogue of love" established in Jerusalem in 1964 as well as the eight hundredth anniversary of the Fourth Crusade. In June 2004, in our presence, Pope John Paul II officially apologized for the tragic events of the Fourth Crusade.

In 2001, during an official visit to the Church of Greece, Pope John Paul II had already extended an apology for the past offenses, including the sacking of Constantinople during the Fourth Crusade, perpetrated against the Orthodox Church by the Roman Catholic Church. Thus, in the official ceremony of 2004, we formally responded that no material compensation would ever be appropriate but that the rightful return of the sacred relics of the two archbishops of Constantinople would constitute a spiritual restoration of that Church's legacy. The return of their

---

100. The period of ecumenical communication and fraternal exchange that began in 1963–64.

101. The period of formal conversation and theological dialogue that began in 1980.

relics would be a tangible gesture of the acknowledgment of past errors, a moral restoration of the spiritual legacy of the East, and a significant step in the process of reconciliation.

These two splendid and courageous gestures on behalf of the late pope—the visit to the Phanar for the opening of the theological dialogue, and then the return of the sacred relics—stand out in our mind and in our heart as superb symbols of the vision and ministry of unity that the late Pope John Paul II both embraced personally and practiced publicly. They are a testimony of the integration of theory and practice, of faithful theology and pastoral ministry, and ultimately of traditional history and contemporary reality.

Such a deep conviction for the unity of all Christians also led His Holiness during his pontificate to visit the various historic centers of Christianity as well as to issue encyclicals urging the divided Christians to work for their unity. His dedication to the sacred cause of unity was openly expressed in his memorable encyclical *Ut Unum Sint.*[102] There he recognized the difficulties that his own ministry historically caused to the unity of the Church, urging all Christians to express their views of the ministry of papal primacy and to suggest ways in which such a ministry might be more acceptable and more appropriate as a service to Church unity.

A REMARKABLE MODEL

The ministry of the late Pope John Paul II spanned but a short time in the history of the Christian faith. Nevertheless, what His Holiness was able, with the grace of God, to accomplish during those few decades was nothing short of remarkable and historic. It will long remain a milestone in the journey of the Roman Catholic Church. And it will long serve as a model for committed leadership in the world.

We fondly recall the warm words of welcome with which His Holiness received our patriarchal delegation to Rome on the patronal feast of Saints Peter and Paul in June of 2002. In his address, the late pope stated:

Much still remains to be done so that a greater brotherhood may reign on earth. The desire for revenge often prevails over peace, especially in the

---

102. Translated "that they may be one."

Holy Land and in other regions of the world struck by blind violence. This gives us a sense of the precariousness of peace that obliges us to unite our forces and so that we may be together and act together so that the world may find in our common witness the strength required to make the changes that are indispensable. This path of collaboration will also lead us to full communion following Christ's will for his disciples.

His stature as a moral, religious, and indeed prophetic leader, not just for all Catholics throughout the world, and in fact not just for all Christians of our time, but for all people of all faiths, was deeply rooted in his personal faith and conviction that this faith must be lived in such a way that others may see truth, understand justice, and find peace. It must be realized in acts of solidarity with all human beings, reconciliation of all religious faiths, peace across all national and cultural boundaries, and dialogue with all Christian denominations and churches. He left behind the indelible legacy of his personality and ministry.

He was indeed a man of great connections. May his memory be eternal!

On the Theological and Spiritual Insights of Pope John Paul II, Ecumenical Patriarchate, November 30, 2005

BROTHERLY EXCHANGE

It is with great pleasure that we have accepted and hereby respond to the gracious invitation of the rector of the Pontifical Lateran University and editor of *Nuntium*,[103] Bishop Rino Fisichella, that we contribute an article for the special issue in memory of our beloved brother, the late pope, His Holiness, "John Paul II: Christ, Man, History." We have been asked to provide a commentary, within the section entitled "The Ecumenical Dialogue," on the message that the late Pope delivered at the Phanar on the occasion of the Feast of St. Andrew (November 30), the patronal feast of the Ecumenical Patriarchate, and that was signed at the Vatican on November 22, 2001. The papal delegation was led by His Excellency Walter Cardinal Kasper, president of the Council for Promoting Christian Unity, who also read the message on that occasion.

---

103. First delivered as a lecture at the thronal feast of the Ecumenical Patriarchate and subsequently published in *Nuntium* 25 (2005). *Nuntium* is the official theological journal of the Pontifical Lateran University.

THE MESSAGE AS MESSAGE

While a message in itself may not always appear significant to many observers in the wider Church, it is critical to recall that, before the courageous initiatives and historical steps of Ecumenical Patriarch Athenagoras as well as of Popes John XXIII and Paul VI, such messages between our two churches were unprecedented and unheard of. Relations between the two churches were frozen from the eleventh century, with only brief moments of a release of that tension during the thirteenth and fifteenth centuries. A message from the head of one church, in this case the leader of the Roman Catholic Church, to another is a powerful—indeed even a profoundly liturgical—symbol of the unity to which both leaders aspire. It also represents the mind of a wider community, both clergy and laity, who supports these leaders. And it should guide the thinking and determine the priority of faithful members of our churches on all levels of the hierarchy.

More than a mere formality, such messages reflect the hopes and trials alike of the ongoing bilateral discussions between our churches. They preserve the primacy of faith held by the Church while at the same time proclaiming the importance of patience and perseverance in dialogue. These messages, therefore, are the "dialogue between the dialogue," constituting the formal contacts between churches during periods when the official theological dialogue is either not in session or else in suspension—as has unfortunately been the case in recent years, although steps have been taken toward resuming this dialogue. Sometimes, such messages even encapsulate and clarify the essence of the dialogue itself.

DIALOGUE AND DOCTRINE

The late Pope John Paul II speaks of "the mystery of the Christian vocation." Indeed, there is a depth of mystery to the vocation of all Christians to dialogue and cooperation. Called by Christ Himself to be one, even as He and the Father are one (see John 17.22–23), we recall at once the awesome nature and the dominical command for unity and reconciliation. The divisions that have beset the relations between our two churches over the last millennium should never overshadow the unity that defines the Christian Church for the first millennium. Pope John Paul II underlines, in the very next sentence, the importance of "the recognition of the

Messiah." The quest for truth must occur in the spirit of love; both, in turn, must also be accompanied by a spirit of humility and prayer.

It is in this spirit and context that our churches initiated "the dialogue of love" in the 1960s and 1970s, later also instigating "the dialogue of truth" (see 2 John 1.3) in 1979 when they established, on a global level, the Joint International Commission for Theological Dialogue. To date, this commission has produced four significant statements: On the Sacramental Understanding of the Church (1982); On the Relationship between Faith, Sacraments and the Unity of the Church (1987); On the Meaning of the Ordained Ministry (1988); and On the Methodological Problem of Uniatism (1993).

TRADITION AND REALITY

While a radically new and dramatically different relationship has characterized our two churches in recent decades, especially in the wake of both the Pan-Orthodox conferences (1961–68) and the Second Vatican Council (1962–65), this relationship has not been without its trials and tensions. This, however, should come as no surprise to those who study and respect history. Just as the estrangement between our two churches was a gradual phenomenon and not a sudden occurrence, the steps toward reconciliation and healing can themselves only be gradual. Reconciliation and restoration can be neither forced nor imposed; it is a process that cannot be either hurried or undermined. The healing of wounds—doctrinal, cultural, and institutional—always takes time and involves pain. It demands both toil and tears. It requires both communication and prayer, which is the ultimate source and form of communication.

This is why Pope John Paul II refers to the reality of "difficulties" that sometimes characterize the relations between the two churches. One reason for these difficulties is that the traditions we embrace are diverse, as are the doctrinal divisions that sometimes ensue. The late pope also emphasizes the "common desire to pass on the apostolic faith together to our contemporaries." The Christian message is doubtless strengthened when its adherents are united, and it is endlessly weakened when its adherents are divided. We are obliged not only to work toward visible unity but also to collaborate in certain critical actions in a suffering world. Nonetheless, centuries of divergence have inevitably led to differences in our appreciation of traditional elements and dimensions of our faith. These differences can neither be ignored nor underestimated. Otherwise, we are not faithful to "the faith once delivered to the saints" (Jude 17).

Despite sincere intentions and positive initiatives, it is inevitable that an honest and authentic dialogue will encounter changes and challenges. We must persist in faith and in hope. Our vision of unity is one that is filled with great joy as well as some sorrow. We recognize that the road to reconciliation is not easy. Yet we are also aware that our Lord accompanies us on this journey. He is our sure way, our faithful companion, and our living hope. He walks with us as He walked with His disciples on the road to Emmaus after His resurrection. And He invites us to join Him in this ministry of restoration. By accepting this divine mandate, we are committing ourselves to the light of the Resurrection and professing that the light of the risen Lord is greater than any darkness within us or around us.

"FOR THE LIFE OF THE WORLD"

Finally, in the conclusion to his message, the late Pope John Paul II observes the reality of "terrorism and war" while at the same time underscoring the priority of "fasting and prayer." The historical occasion of this address coincides with the tragic events of September 11, 2001, which shocked the entire world with the inhumane destruction of life in the United States. The ugliness of fear can be overcome only by the hopefulness of dialogue.

This is why, just as fear and death are not abstract concepts but tragic, unfortunate realities in our world today, their antidotes, love and life, must also become tangible, incarnate, practical, and manifest. Every Christian is called to take visible steps to manifest and materialize the love that we have been commanded by Christ to extend toward our human neighbor as well as toward our natural environment. For how we respond to people (especially those in need) and how we treat creation (especially through the lifestyle we lead) in turn reflect how we worship our Creator God.

Our fasting, too, should not be disconnected from our liturgy. The truth is that we respond to nature with the same delicacy, the same sensitivity and tenderness, with which we respond to a human being in a relationship. Whatever we proclaim and profess in His name is closely related to and has immediate consequences for the life of the world. All religious activity is judged by its impact on the world (and especially the environment), while all activity affecting the environment is measured by its effect on people (and especially the poor).

Fasting stands in direct contrast to the demonic ways of fear and death. It is a loud protest against the negative forces of destruction and consumption in this world. The one who fasts is free, uncontrolled by attitudes that violate and abuse. The purpose of fasting is always service, never selfishness. It is not about self-absorption or even about self-control but primarily about sharing and communion. It is about breaking down barriers with our neighbor and our world. This, of course, is precisely the purpose of dialogue, which seeks to discern the living Word of God in all people and the unmistakable traces of God in all places of His dominion.

Homily at Chevetogne Monastery, Belgium, November 15, 1994

DOM LAMBERT BEAUDUIN

Today we are filled with particular joy and emotion inasmuch as we regard our presence in the midst of your fraternity as a fact of exceptional significance. Your brotherhood has played a leading role in the recent peaceful relations between Western Catholicism and Eastern Orthodoxy. Indeed, the brotherhood of Chevetogne constitutes a sincere voice of peace between the West and the East in general.

We feel, moreover, that today the soul of Dom Lambert Beauduin,[104] of blessed memory, prophet of unity among Christians and founder of your brotherhood, who in recent decades has been watching from heaven the vindication of his actions—we feel that today he surely rejoices. We are not aware of any other publication that caused so many waves as did his daring and pioneering article "L'Occident à l'école de l'Orient: Mystère Pascal," published in 1926 in the first issue of your journal *Irénikon*, immediately after the founding of the brotherhood in the first monastery of Amay. We are now experiencing a new period of peace, inaugurated thirty years ago by the epoch-making meeting in Jerusalem between the forerunners of this reconciliation, Pope Paul VI and Ecumenical Patriarch

---

104. A Belgian monk, Dom Lambert Beauduin (1873–1960), in 1925 founded the monastery now known as Chevetogne Abbey. He was a renowned liturgical reformer and ecumenical pioneer.

Athenagoras. So it is difficult for us today to comprehend what a grand revolution that article constituted. There for the first time a Roman Catholic monk and scholar expressed admiration for the Christian East, which at the time was generally despised. His advice for the West to become an apprentice at the school of the East was addressed to people whose view of Orthodoxy was entirely negative.

Gallantry is usually proved in times of war. Lambert Beauduin proved gallant in the struggle for peace. It seems that the peaceful land of Belgium produces people who are peaceful and at the same time brave. We wish to remind you of the example of another great Belgian, one who fought for religious freedom and peaceful coexistence long ago, when relations between Roman Catholics and Orthodox were at their worst. Just a few years after the deplorable events of the Fourth Crusade, Henry II, Latin emperor of the Orthodox East and count of Flanders and Hainaut, clashed with Cardinal Velagio, the papal legate, in an effort to save the oppressed Orthodox clergy of Constantinople from the cardinal's excessive zeal. He also saved the monasteries of the Holy Mountain Athos from persecution and looting. When he passed away, many Orthodox mourned his death; indeed, the monks of Great Lavra on Athos preserved his memory as a benefactor for a long time afterward.

The examples of these two admirable Belgian Christians prove that it is possible to "preach the gospel of peace" (Rom. 10.15) when others preach the way of war, to love when others hate, and to call brothers those whom others see as enemies. Of course, the work of Emperor Henry was forgotten over the centuries. Yet the peaceful work of Lambert Beauduin still lives and bears fruit. In fact, you, as his beloved children and brothers in the Lord, continue his work, and we pray that you will continue with his daring and dynamism, without heeding any of the apparent difficulties that might disappoint you.

Today, relations between Christians of the East and Christians of the West differ from those in 1926. During the last three decades, tremendous progress has been made with respect to the fraternal rapprochement of our churches. Not only were the anathemas of 1054 lifted, but today relations between the churches of Rome and Constantinople are much more fraternal than even during the period before the Schism, when the Church was one and undivided, although Latin and Orthodox Christianity had great difficulty understanding each other because of geographical distance and linguistic or cultural differences.

THE PROBLEM OF UNIATISM

There definitely exist many more obstacles. The recent revival of the clashes in areas where Uniatism[105] has been revived is the most characteristic example of a major contemporary problem. It is a fact that Uniatism constitutes a traumatic experience for the East, as it has resulted in a tragic hemorrhage to the body of the Orthodox Church. An equally traumatic experience in the past was the catastrophic invasion of the Byzantine Empire during the Fourth Crusade.

It seems, however, that God chose those ways so painful for the East in order to bring the West into living contact with Orthodoxy and its treasures. After the sad events of the Fourth Crusade against the Orthodox East, we experience a real conquest of the West by means of the art of Byzantium. The marvelous mosaics, which during the thirteenth century decorated the basilica of Santa Maria Maggiore in Rome as well as the baptistery of San Giovanni in Florence, are true copies of Byzantine patterns of that time. It was also during the same period that the Greek Fathers become known to the West and, by the end of the thirteenth century, the four great Eastern Fathers—Athanasius the Great, Basil the Great, Gregory the Theologian, and John Chrysostom—were added to the list consisting of the four Western ecclesiastical teachers, Ambrose of Milan, Jerome of Rome, Augustine of Hippo, and Gregory the Great.

In the same way, the more recent hemorrhage of Orthodoxy caused by the Uniates has brought about a transfusion of Eastern blood into the Western Church, which was called to abandon its isolation within the Latin world. It is a fact that the existence of Uniatism and the efforts for its expansion have been the primary motive for the study of the Greek Fathers by theologians of the West. It is also a fact, of course, that this study was initially aimed at the discovery of patristic arguments against Orthodoxy. Yet the study of the Fathers of the East as well as of its liturgical texts ended in the discovery of previously ignored treasures of the Orthodox Church and in the conclusion that there is a great deal for the West to learn from the school of the East.

---

105. A controversial and bitter point of division and discussion—both in former centuries and in contemporary theological dialogue—between East and West, Uniates are also known as "Eastern Rite Catholics," recognizing the supremacy of the pope while retaining Eastern traditional and liturgical practices.

We believe that God, in His infinite wisdom, uses mysterious ways to realize His plans. And so we are confident that whatever might now seem like an obstacle will in the end prove to be a means for the accomplishment of the divine cause for salvation. We pray to our Lord "for the peace of the world" and "for the union of all." The pain that Orthodoxy feels as a result of the division of Christianity is greater than the pain of any wounds inflicted on it during its tormented course through the centuries.

As Lambert Beauduin was fond of noting, "Orthodoxy lives more in the joy of the Resurrection than in the pain of the Cross." The truth is that the pain of the Cross is constant in Orthodoxy, which, however, always looks forward to the triumph of the Resurrection. Likewise, we live and confront all difficulties in the firm belief that God will give rise to better days, days of peace and unity among Christians, when all problems will simply be historic reminiscences.

THE ARCHBISHOP OF CANTERBURY

On the First Official Visit of Dr. Rowan Williams, Archbishop of Canterbury, to the Phanar, Ecumenical Patriarchate, November 17, 2003

A HISTORY OF MUTUAL RESPECT

Your Grace, the Most Reverend and Right Honorable Dr. Rowan Williams, Metropolitan, Archbishop of Canterbury and Primate of All England, beloved brother in Christ: It is with great joy and deep satisfaction that we welcome Your Grace to the see of the Church of Constantinople on your first official visit here since your elevation to the historic see of Canterbury and to the office of Primate of the Anglican Communion.[106] We offer thanks to God for the gift of your presence among us today. We regard it as a great blessing and a sign of the bond of love that unites our two churches in the name of our common Lord.

It is, indeed, a remarkable gift of divine grace that there has never been any cause of conflict or bitterness between Anglicans and Orthodox in

---

106. Rowan Williams is the 104th archbishop of Canterbury, enthroned on February 27, 2003. A poet and theologian, he was bishop of Monmouth and archbishop of Wales.

the course of history. Our relations have always been marked with mutual respect, while there have been occasions when the Anglican Church supported and assisted the Ecumenical Patriarchate during difficult times. We acknowledge this with deep appreciation.

In the context of this long history of fraternal relations, our two churches have also engaged in official theological dialogue from as early as the nineteenth century, before the appearance of the ecumenical movement, of which they have been founders and supporters ever since. This official theological dialogue was revived in the sixth decade of the previous century and continues to function fruitfully to this day under the co-chairmanship of Bishop Mark Dyer on the Anglican side and Metropolitan John of Pergamon on the Orthodox.[107] The active participation and personal contribution of Your Grace in this dialogue until your appointment to the present high office in your Church has been invaluable and is deeply appreciated by all members of the relevant commission. We should like to express also our own thanks to Your Grace for this contribution.

In the person of Your Grace we recognize with great satisfaction the Church leader who combines profound theological knowledge and scholarship with remarkable openness and pastoral sensitivity to all human beings. Your deep knowledge of the Orthodox tradition and theology makes the Orthodox in particular look on Your Grace as a bridge between West and East in the Christian world. We regard this as a great gift of God to His Church in our time. It is commonly recognized that the times in which we live are accompanied by serious challenges to the Christian Church. The rapid advance of science along with the ethical dilemmas it creates, the environmental crisis with its alarming consequences for the natural environment, the domination of technology accompanying and sustaining tendencies of globalization at the expense of cultural diversity, the social and economic injustice that widens the gap between rich and poor countries as well as between rich and poor people. It exacerbates discrimination against minorities, the outbreak of unjust wars, and, above

---

107. The present Anglican–Orthodox dialogue commenced in 1973, when the first meeting of the Anglican–Orthodox Joint Doctrinal Discussions was held in Oxford. It resulted in the Moscow Statement in 1976. The Dublin Agreed Statement concluded the second phase of this dialogue, which was reconstituted in 1989 as the International Commission for Anglican–Orthodox Theological Dialogue.

all, the use of religion as an instrument of national and racial conflict—all these invite the Christian churches to reconsider their theological and pastoral priorities and to regard their confessional differences in a new light. The quest for Christian unity appears to be imperative in the present circumstances. All of us should avoid taking initiatives and proceeding to innovations that may create obstacles to this unity. Christian unity is necessary today more than ever.

Your Grace, brotherly love has led your steps to this ancient and historic city, where there resides the first in rank of the Orthodox churches as well as the first in service to them. The Ecumenical Patriarchate has experienced in the course of its long history what St. Paul describes as "strength in weakness," and it continues its mission in the world with faith and hope, deriving strength from the grace of God. We are truly glad to welcome Your Grace and your entourage to our Patriarchate, and we wish you a pleasant stay in our city.

Reflections on the Focolare Movement

Chiara Lubich, Founder of the Focolare Movement, March 14, 2008

EMBODYING THE DIALOGUE OF LOVE

There are some people whose lives touch other lives so universally that, on their passing, they remain an indelible inspiration and grace. One such life—a life worth living and well worth remembering—was that of Chiara Lubich,[108] founder of the Focolare movement.[109] While we mourn with profound and sincere sorrow her falling asleep in the Lord, at the same time we recognize that she has not left a void but in fact has motivated millions of people across the world. Throughout her life, Chiara Lubich established communities of love and nurturing in accordance with Christ's first command and principal calling to "love one another as [He] loved us" (John 13.34). And, of course, the fruits of such love will never pass away; they long outlive any single individual.

---

108. Chiara Lubich (1920–2008) was a Roman Catholic activist in Italy and founder of the Focolare movement. She died on March 14, 2008.

109. An international organization that promotes unity and dialogue, the Focolare movement was founded by Chiara Lubich in a bomb shelter in 1943 and currently operates in hundreds of nations throughout the world.

Chiara Lubich was committed to the word of the gospel and to the unity of the Church as well as to the promotion of brotherhood among all people. In this respect, her work not only touched tens of thousands of core members and millions of active adherents or friends within the Focolare movement itself; it also encouraged numerous people, of all confessions and all faiths, to embrace one another in a spirit of true humility and love.

Whether welcoming a head of church or greeting a head of state, whether receiving a prize for progress in religion or a doctorate in the field of education, whether addressing a beloved member of her wider community or standing before an auspicious gathering of the United Nations, Chiara was both filled with and exuded the fire of God's Spirit, always sharing and forever smiling. Personally, we will never forget how, at her beckoning and following her example, the Focolare community would always generously welcome us with flowers in every city of the world where we visited and where her community flourished.

Chiara deservedly gained the high regard and profound respect of the Great Church of Constantinople for her monumental work in promoting ecumenical relations through the "dialogue of love." To this end, she worked closely with Pope Paul VI; indeed, the late Ecumenical Patriarch Athenagoras affectionately called her "Thekla," after the apostolic collaborator of St. Paul.[110] We recall with affection her many visits to the Ecumenical Patriarchate, whether under the tenure of Patriarch Athenagoras, our immediate predecessor Patriarch Dimitrios, or even during our own humble tenure. Most especially, we will never forget our meeting with her during our most recent visit to Rome, in early March of this year, just days before her passing, which God truly blessed.

Just as the life in the risen Lord emerges from the reality of the Cross, and just as the Christian Church is built on the blood of martyrs, so also it comes as no surprise that Chiara Lubich created her movement from the destruction and depression of the Second World War. Her lifelong mission was to alleviate human suffering, whether in the form of pain or poverty, and to incarnate the "good news" of peace and reconciliation in every corner of our planet.

---

110. In Acts 14.

May her soul find rest where the righteous repose, in that place where there is no sorrow, grief, or mourning. We are certain that Chiara's memory will be eternal. And may the Lord of the living and the dead bring comfort to all those that love her and survive her.

OCCASIONAL GREETINGS TO INTERNATIONAL MEETINGS OF ORIENTALE LUMEN

Istanbul, May 12, 2004

THE LIGHT OF CHRIST AND THE LIGHT OF THE EAST

Christ is risen! We give thanks to our loving God, the Father, the Son, and the Holy Spirit, for the opportunity to welcome you warmly to our historic city. It is a joy to greet you during this sacred season when we celebrate the glorious Resurrection of our Lord and Savior Jesus Christ. This year, we are grateful that all Christians can observe together Pascha, the feast of feasts, as well as the Feast of the Ascension and the Feast of Pentecost.

We recognize the presence of many eminent speakers, and we thank them for their contribution. We also express our appreciation to Mr. Jack Figel for organizing this important meeting of Orientale Lumen in Istanbul.[111] We have followed with great interest the deliberations of your conferences since they began in Washington D.C., in 1997. From the outset, these conferences have expressed a special appreciation for the "light of the East." In the spirit of the apostolic letter *Orientale Lumen* by His Holiness Pope John Paul II,[112] the conferences have examined the rich spiritual and theological treasures of the Christian East. We firmly believe that this is a noble and necessary endeavor, which serves the cause of reconciliation and unity. Many of our hierarchs and theologians have contributed to the Orientale Lumen conferences over the past seven years, but we are especially grateful for the contributions of His Excellency

---

111. Orientale Lumen meetings are annual conferences organized in various parts of the world in response to the the apostolic letter *Orientale Lumen* ("light of the East"), promulgated by Pope John Paul II in 1995.

112. Issued on May 2, 1995, to mark the centenary of the apostolic letter *Orientalium Dignitas* by Pope Leo XIII.

Archbishop Vsevolod of Scopelos and His Grace Bishop Kallistos of Diokleia. These distinguished hierarchs of the Ecumenical Throne are present with us and are also presenting papers at this conference.

The rich heritage of the Christian East is truly "lumen," a light for all who wish to appreciate the richness of the historic Christian faith. However, this heritage has often been neglected by many in the Christian West, both Roman Catholics and Protestants. The Christian faith is often identified only with the Roman Catholic and Protestant expressions, especially in North America and the Western nations in general. Now, more than ever, the "Light of the East" is recognized as a valuable inheritance that Christians worldwide would do well to better appreciate. This inheritance provides spiritual and theological perspectives pointing us to Christ, the true "Light of the world." This inheritance can help us heal the wounds of our Christian divisions. It can help overcome the divisions among peoples and nations. Orthodox Christianity faithfully embodies the "Light of the East" and is a treasure offered to all who seek spiritual wisdom and guidance.

For many years, the Orientale Lumen conferences have also expressed a concern for the restoration of the visible unity of the churches. The conferences have provided a valuable opportunity for members of the Roman Catholic Church and Orthodox Church to meet together, pray together, and study together. The Ecumenical Patriarchate is committed to the movement to restore visible unity among the churches. This conviction is deeply rooted in the gospel of our Lord Jesus Christ. As the good shepherd, our Lord came to heal and to reconcile us with the Father. On the night that He gave himself up for the life of the world, our Lord prayed for the unity of His followers. As members of His Church, we too have a profound obligation to share in the divine action of reconciliation. In celebrating the Resurrection, we proclaim the divine victory over all forces of division and alienation. Together with the Apostle Paul, we declare, "God was in Christ reconciling Himself to the world and has given us the ministry of reconciliation" (2 Cor. 5.18).

Mindful of its historic obligations, the Ecumenical Patriarchate has assumed a role of leadership in the contemporary ecumenical movement. Indeed, from the earliest days of the twentieth century, the Ecumenical Patriarchate issued a number of encyclicals, which dealt with the topic of the unity of the Church. Since that time, it has consistently reminded all of the tragedy of Christian disunity, which is contrary to the will of our Lord. Our disunity is a scandal, which weakens our witness to the gospel of Christ and our mission in the world. Our disunity does not give glory to our God of reconciliation.

For this reason, then, the Ecumenical Patriarchate has been an ardent proponent of genuine efforts among Christians to overcome animosity and misunderstandings. It has called on the churches to come out of their isolation and enter into dialogue for the sake of reconciliation and the restoration of visible unity. The Ecumenical Patriarchate has reminded the followers of Christ of the Lord's passionate prayer for their unity, "that they may be one even as you, Father, are in me and I in you, may they also be one in us, so that the world may believe that you sent me" (John 17.21). We all need to hear clearly this powerful prayer of our Lord today.

Your conference this week makes us especially mindful of our obligation to advance reconciliation between the Orthodox Church and the Roman Catholic Church. We remember with much joy that this dialogue began forty years ago in Jerusalem, where, on the Mount of Olives, in 1964, our predecessor Ecumenical Patriarch Athenagoras, of blessed memory, met with Pope Paul VI, of blessed memory. Coming from West and East, from Old and New Rome, these humble servants greeted each other as pilgrims and brothers in Christ. Mindful of our Lord's prayer for unity, they prayed together; they exchanged the kiss of peace; and they vowed to begin, with God's help, a new process of reconciliation, which would lead to the restoration of community between the Orthodox Church and the Catholic Church. There Patriarch Athenagoras declared, "May this meeting of ours be the first glimmer of dawn of a shining and holy day, in which the Christian generations of the future will receive communion in the holy body and sacred blood of the Lord from the same chalice, in love, peace, and unity, praising and glorifying the one Lord and Savior of all."

This historic encounter between Pope Paul VI and Patriarch Athenagoras in Jerusalem opened up a new era in the relations between our two churches. The meeting of our two Primates eventually led to many new contacts between Rome and Constantinople. It led in 1965 to the historic "lifting of the anathemas of 1054." It led to the development of formal theological dialogue. And, yes, their meeting in 1964 also provided the foundation for your conference this week. Thus, we give thanks to God for these holy and faithful bishops. They were inspired by our Lord's prayer for the unity of His disciples and followers. May their words and actions be a powerful example for us now and in the days ahead.

THE DIFFICULT ROAD TO CHRISTIAN UNITY

We know that the process of reconciliation is not always easy. The division between the Orthodox Church and the Roman Catholic Church has persisted for centuries. Nevertheless, we firmly believe that, with the guidance of the Risen Lord, our differences are not beyond resolution. Moreover, we believe that we have a solemn obligation to our Lord to heal our painful divisions. For this reason, we must be equally persistent in our prayer. We must increase our expressions of love and mutual respect. We must strengthen our theological dialogue.

Our reconciliation will not take place without fervent prayer for unity. Through prayer, we open ourselves up to the healing presence of our heavenly Father. By praying together for the unity of the churches, we profess our willingness to participate in God's reconciling activities both in our churches and in our societies. Our reconciliation will not take place without countless acts of love, forgiveness, and mutual respect. Through such actions, we unite ourselves consciously with our Lord, who manifested God's mercy and love. By expressing our love together, we become the persons through whom Christ continues to work in our world today. And, finally, our reconciliation will not take place without theological dialogue. Through our exchanges, we seek the guidance of the Spirit, who will lead us in all truth. By speaking to one another with love and respect, the Spirit can guide us today to express together the apostolic faith in a manner that is life-giving and healing.

We can never accept a superficial unity that neglects the difficult issues that separate us at the table of the Lord. With prayer and love, we must examine fully and honestly all the theological issues that divide us. The unity, which our Lord desires for us as Orthodox and Roman Catholics, must always affirm the faith of the Apostles and sustain the good order of the Church. The division between our churches is not simply the result of theological differences. This division has been compounded by political, economic, and cultural factors over the centuries. The division also has been aggravated by historical acts that have had tragic consequences both for the churches and for the world.

During this year, we recall with profound sadness the sack of the city of Constantinople in 1204. Eight hundred years ago, Western Crusaders entered this city and plundered it. This tragedy reflected the complex political, cultural, and commercial realities of the day. However, the event also profoundly aggravated relations between the Church of Rome and the Church of Constantinople. Some historians have expressed the opinion that the Fourth Crusade and the temporary establishment of a Western hierarchy by Rome in the East may truly mark the beginning of the actual Schism between our churches. There is no doubt that the tragedy of that Fourth Crusade deepened the animosity between the Christian West and the Christian East, especially among the laity.

We deeply appreciate that His Holiness Pope John Paul II has recognized the disastrous consequences of the Fourth Crusade in 1204. During his visit to Greece in 2001,[113] His Holiness Pope John Paul II declared that the Crusaders "turned against their own brothers in the faith." His Holiness asked the Lord for forgiveness for the sins, "by action or omission, of members of the Catholic Church against their Orthodox brothers and sisters." We are deeply moved that His Holiness Pope John Paul II made this plea for forgiveness. It is yet another expression of his desire to heal the division between our churches. With gratitude to our Lord, we recognize the pope's sincerity and honor his request for forgiveness. To his prayer, we also add and declare: May our good and merciful God forgive all who sin against the unity of the Church, and may He guide all believers on the path of reconciliation.

Avoiding Errors of the Past

Now, we must resolve not to undertake actions that further divide the Orthodox Church and Catholic Church. Today, let us not repeat the mistakes of history. If we recall the tragic events of the past, we do so with the conviction that similar actions must not be repeated today. Because of this conviction, we lament that the Catholic Church has formally established four new dioceses in Russia. We are deeply disturbed that groups

---

113. The pope's visit to Greece in May 2001, at the invitation of the Church of Greece, marked the first time a pope had visited that country since 1291.

within the Catholic Church continue to proselytize in Eastern Europe. We strongly oppose the move by some to establish a Catholic patriarchate in Kiev. We have stated elsewhere that such action could "carry the risk of returning [us] to the climate of hostility that existed until only a few decades ago." We express these things with great pain. For we believe that these actions do not contribute to the reconciliation of our churches. These unfortunate actions disturb relations between our faithful and prevent genuine theological dialogue in some places. These actions are contrary to the affirmation that a relationship of "sister churches" exists between the Orthodox Church and the Catholic Church.

Many of you have come to this conference from the United States. We recognize that there exists in your country a close relationship between the Orthodox Church and the Roman Catholic Church. Bishops from the two churches meet each year to discuss issues of common concern. This formal theological dialogue began in 1965. Since then, theologians have produced twenty-two statements. The most recent report deals with the topic of the *Filioque*. Theologians have provided a number of valuable recommendations to our churches for the resolution of this historic point of difference. We propose that these significant recommendations be studied formally by our churches so that this issue can be finally resolved.

To advance the cause of reconciliation, we have decided to undertake another official visit to Rome, and so we have accepted the invitation of His Holiness Pope John Paul II to join with him for the celebration of the Feast of Saints Peter and Paul on June 29. We will have the opportunity to pray to the princes of the Apostles as well as to speak with His Holiness and his brother bishops about the issues that continue to divide our churches. We will also officially open the church of St. Theodore, which His Holiness Pope John Paul II has graciously offered to the Orthodox community of Rome. This gesture is a further sign that there are bonds of faith and love between us that are not broken.

Distinguished and beloved participants, guided by the risen Christ, you have come as pilgrims to this city and to the Ecumenical Patriarchate. Over the centuries, many pilgrims have preceded you. Now, you too are making your pilgrimage to this ancient and venerable center of Christianity because of your love for our Lord Jesus Christ. You undertake this journey because of your desire to advance the unity of the churches. You engage in this pilgrimage to deepen your appreciation of the "Light of the

East." This week you will truly find that here, in this sacred place, the "Light of the East" is bright, a faithful witness to our Lord and Savior in this city and this Church.

Here, in this region, the Apostle Andrew, the first-called, preached the gospel of Christ. Here, martyrs such as St. Euphemia[114] gave their lives for the sake of the "good news" of salvation. Here, Fathers of the Church, such as St. John Chrysostom, taught the apostolic faith. Here, bishops such as St. Gregory the Theologian gathered to proclaim the faith in the ecumenical councils. Here, great missionaries such as St. Cyril and St. Methodius began their journeys.[115] Here, you will pray in the churches where pious men and women have prayed for centuries. And here you will see that faithful believers continue to pray today. They continue to treasure this heritage and to serve our Lord with love and devotion. Let your pilgrimage be a special time when the risen Christ can touch your lives, strengthen your faith, and deepen your love.

"May the God of steadfastness and encouragement grant you to live in harmony with one another in accordance with Jesus Christ so that together you may with one voice glorify the God and Father of our Lord Jesus Christ" (Rom. 15.5). To Him be glory now and forever and unto ages of ages.

On the Tenth Anniversary of Orientale Lumen Meetings, San Diego and Washington, D.C., June 2006

GRASSROOTS ECUMENISM

It is with great pleasure and paternal joy that, on behalf of the Mother Church of Constantinople, we humbly greet the blessed tenth anniversary of the Orientale Lumen conferences, scheduled to be held in San Diego and Washington, D.C., in June of this year. While in the past we have

---

114. The Great Martyr Euphemia died in 304–7 in Chalcedon, where she is credited with a miracle during the Fourth Ecumenical Council (451). Her relics are treasured in the Patriarchal Church of St. George at the Phanar.

115. Born in Thessalonika, Cyril (or Constantine, 827–69) and Methodius (815–84) were brothers and Byzantine missionaries of Christianity to the Slavic peoples, credited with developing the Glagolitic alphabet that formed the basis of Old Church Slavonic. They are venerated as "equals to the apostles."

been present in spirit and in letter, this year we are especially grateful to have the opportunity to be with you both in image and in word.[116]

Indeed, it is most fitting that, on this particular occasion, we are conveying this personal and paternal greeting to you by means of a living image and of words. As you know, religious icons and the theological word are at the very heart of encounter and rapprochement between our two sister churches. Even the emblem of your conferences depicts the image of apostolic reconciliation, revealing an embrace of the great pillars of the early Church, Saints Peter and Andrew. Moreover, your gatherings aim at the education, information, and formation of clergy and laity alike on central and essential elements of our respective traditions. In this, they comprise at once an experience and an expression of a sincere dialogue carried out in love and in truth.

Since their inception in Washington, D.C., in 1997, your pioneering ecumenical gatherings have indeed provided an exceptional forum for people of Eastern Orthodox, Eastern Catholic, and Roman Catholic backgrounds throughout the world—in the United States, in Great Britain, and in Australasia but also in the remarkable city where the Ecumenical Patriarchate historically resides—namely, Constantinople, Turkey. Participants have been privileged to meet in one and the same place in order to explore one and the same ecclesiastical origin and to worship one and the same loving God, whose incarnate Word prayed in earnest, and with tears, "that they may all be one," *ut omnes unum sint* (John 17.21). Your sacred intent, therefore, is blessed from within and from above by the very nature of your initiative. For, while your effort may be, as you describe it, "grassroots," we are convinced that it is at the same time rooted in heaven.

In recent decades, we have learned very well that the unity of the Church is a common vision, responsibility, and task. In this regard, it requires faithfulness to fellowship, commitment to conversation, and dedication to dialogue. Its conditions include patience in overcoming prejudice, understanding and appreciation of differences, and the grace to discern doctrine. Each of us, from his or her own particular position and unique perspective, is called to engage in formal and informal discourse

---

116. On this occasion, the message of the Ecumenical Patriarch was transmitted by video to the participants.

in order to examine the roots of our divisions and to explore ways of overcoming barriers and achieving visible, sacramental unity.

It is at once a divine command and a human obligation that we make every effort and at the same time take gradual steps toward such unity. This endeavor brings us closer to our Lord and Savior. Moreover, it brings us closer to one another as members of the body of Christ. And, finally, it brings us closer to the world itself, where we are able to confess a shared faith in a global society torn by division and crying out in distress. Inevitably, there will be many and manifold challenges—and we have experienced some of these, even within the official theological dialogue between our churches. Yet the fruits that we reap are equally numerous and diverse—and you have experienced some of these in your conferences over the past ten years.

Of course, it is critical and reassuring for us to remember that, while formal discussions and informal gatherings have taken place in recent years, many of the difficult and sensitive points of difference in doctrine and practice reach back many centuries. We should not, therefore, expect the results of our efforts to be immediate. Nevertheless, already our churches have been drawn out of isolation and separation and brought into closer association and conversation. Today, ecclesiastical hierarchs and theological leaders are able to exchange views, face to face, on crucial theological and spiritual issues. Lay leaders, both men and women, are able to engage with each other in substantial and meaningful gatherings, such as your blessed Orientale Lumen conferences.

It is, therefore, with great pleasure that we are communicating with you today to convey to all of you—organizers, speakers, and participants alike in the sessions to be held in California and the District of Columbia—our heartfelt patriarchal greeting and paternal blessing, together with our sincerest wishes for successful deliberations and interactions in prayer, plenary, and fellowship. "May the grace of our Lord Jesus Christ, and the love of God the Father, and the communion of the Holy Spirit, be with all of you."

4

Academic Discourses

Occasional Lectures at Scholarly Institutions

ONE HUNDRED FIFTIETH ANNIVERSARY OF THE
THEOLOGICAL SCHOOL OF HALKI

Heybeliada-Halki, August 29, 1994

GRADUATES OF A HISTORICAL SCHOOL

Glory to the Father and the Son and the Holy Spirit, the holy and one
in essence, the life-giving Trinity, for the joy and excitement of this
blessed congregation today, of all the alumni of this sacred school from
the west, and the north, the south and the east, in the glorifying Christ
unto the ages. With one mouth and one mind, and with hearts throbbing
with justified emotion, we have gathered to celebrate the completion of
one and a half centuries since the renowned holy Theological School of
Halki, our mother school, opened its doors and began its momentous,
priceless contribution to the Church and the nation, to humanity and the
world.

What if during the past twenty-three years the school has ceased opera-
ting "due to misfortunes of our times"?[1] We are nevertheless obliged to

---

1. The theological school of Halki sits on the hilltop of one of the "islands of the
princes," Heybeliada (in Turkish) or Halki (in Greek). While the institution's function
was diminished both as a secondary school and as a graduate seminary since the late 1950s,
it was officially closed by Turkish authorities in the early 1970s. The magnificent nine-
teenth-century building contains a library of forty thousand books and historical manuscripts, classrooms filled with old wooden desks, as well as spacious reception and

remember the beginnings of its historical undertaking. . . . From the outset, Halki was destined to become a beacon emitting "the light of Christ" to the ends of the earth, wherever all of you, beloved friends and brothers, "fully decorated with ecclesiastical ranks," from your many positions and bastions, are doing the work of an evangelist.

Today we are not here as patriarchs, archpriests, priests and teachers; today, we are the school's students, graduates who emigrated abroad and now return to the bosom of the mother, to our natural home. This moment of reunion between teachers and students, both living and deceased children of the school, would undoubtedly be much more significant had the school not been forced to close its doors for nearly a quarter of a century. During this time, the Church has taken successive steps that to date, unfortunately, have borne no effect. We are now in the process of preparing a meeting with His Excellency the minister of education of Turkey in order to inform him about the new perspectives and proposals of the Ecumenical Patriarchate. We hope that this will facilitate a solution to the problem.

AN APPEAL TO TURKISH AUTHORITIES

Permit us to convey to you what we said in this very room a few days ago on the occasion of the opening of the Fifth International Conference of Orthodox Theological Schools:

We pray and hope that the honorable and democratic Turkish Government will soon issue the required permit for the reopening of our school. It is inconceivable, on the one hand, to accept the active presence of the First Throne of Orthodoxy in the territory of our country and not provide this Throne with the potential and means to educate its members and renew its blood as a living organism. Such a thing is an inconsistency, incompatible with the notion of religious freedom. . . . We hope therefore that the existing legal and bureaucratic obstacles will soon be overcome and that

---

dormitory rooms. It is the dream and desire of Ecumenical Patriarch Bartholomew that the Patriarchal Theological School will be reopened. He persistently underlines the 1923 Treaty of Lausanne and Turkey's obligation both to recognize the legal status of the Patriarchate as being ecumenical in scope and nature and to respect its right to educate clergy and leaders.

this beautiful building will again become a living beehive, which will produce the sweet honey of the wisdom of God and prepare preachers of peace, universal love and reconciliation.[2]

Today, then, on behalf of the Ecumenical Patriarchate and the Greek Orthodox community living here, all of you Halkites have gathered for this anniversary, together with our Modesty. And so we add with emphasis that we are extending an appeal to the honorable government of the Turkish Republic so that it may allow the reopening of this historical theological school, the admission of students, and the invitation of visiting professors from abroad.

Knowledge, the sciences, ideas, wisdom, and letters must circulate freely and without restrictions. It is inconceivable that this school was allowed to operate during the Ottoman Empire and is deprived of this right in modern cemocratic Turkey, the Turkey of the great reformer Kemal Atatürk,[3] the Turkey that is cosignatory to all human-rights declarations of the United Nations. The opening of the school will not cause any harm or damage to our country; on the contrary, it will be beneficial inasmuch as it will produce ambassadors of goodwill. Turkey is the bridge between Asia and Europe, between East and West, between Islam and Christianity. From this perspective, since Turkey is a secular state where religion and state are separate, all religions and dogmas must be offered the same potential to prepare and educate their leaders, according to the needs and demands of our times, on the verge, as we are, between the twentieth and twenty-first centuries.

How is it at all possible for the numerically superior religion in this country to have a multitude of theological schools and ecclesiastical seminaries while, at the same time, our sole theological school and the respective school of the Armenians are not allowed to operate? "Have we not power—for the same applies to us—to eat and drink?" (1 Cor. 9.4) Here, we should mention the conclusions (paragraph 6.2) of the European Council Presidency, which convened in Brussels last December, according to which "the variety of civilizations, languages, religions, traditions

---

2. Held at the Theological School of Halki (August 14–20, 1994) on the topic "Let Your Light Shine: Orthodox Theological Education in the Modern World."

3. Mustafa Kemal Atatürk (1881–1938), founder and first president of the modern republic of Turkey.

and descent should be regarded as a source of enrichment and a factor of unity, and it should cease constituting a cause for tensions and antagonisms."

We, too, have repeatedly declared that the Patriarchate, together with the Orthodox minority that surrounds it, should and could be a bridge and bond between Turkey and Greece—not a cause for division, friction, and antagonism. A religious and spiritual foundation, rooted in this great and holy city over seventeen centuries now, can in many ways prove useful in the building of peace, stability, reconciliation, and prosperity for humanity. And so it should be given every opportunity and means to fulfill its political and spiritual mission rather than be subjected to restrictions or attacks on the part of the Press or of a few terrorists. It most certainly deserves better treatment, since it has, by general consent, inestimably and immensely contributed to world civilization.

PERFECTED IN WEAKNESS

Nevertheless, according to today's epistle reading, "being reviled, we bless; being defamed, we entreat" (1 Cor. 4.12–13). "Our strength is made perfect in weakness" (2 Cor. 12.9). More specifically, with respect to the reopening and free operation of our school, we will continue to pray and work without ceasing "until the day dawns, and the day star arises in the hearts" (2 Pet. 1.19) of the state and its political rulers—until they provide us with the permission we seek. Then, together, we will ascend this holy hill to glorify our Father in the heavens, offering the opening benediction and blessing the pure and youthful "beehive" of Orthodoxy.

We have the feeling—or, rather, the conviction—that this will happen in the not too distant future. Justice will triumph! Reason will prevail! And the saying that "enmity does not know how to appreciate what is beneficial" will no longer be valid. Once again, the school will serve as the "capital of true glory of the Ecumenical Throne." Then, we will proclaim, "Glory to the righteous and saving God." And a prayer of doxology to the Triune God of our Fathers for this ancient monastery will once again be uttered by thousands. At the left aisle of the church, there is the chapel and icon of the Theotokos *Glykophilousa*,[4] also known as the *Paphsolypi*.[5]

---

4. Greek for "sweetly kissing one" or "mother of tenderness."

5. Greek for "cease all sorrow."

This *Panagia Paphsolypi*[6] will put an end to our sorrow and change it into joy. "Great joy shall come to all people" (Luke 2.10) of God, to all Orthodox and all Christians, to the whole civilized world. For spiritual foundations and centers like our school cannot be monopolized; they belong to the many, they belong to all.

We bring to mind the words of the celebrated Belgian Byzantinologist Henri Grégoire about the universal radiance and the beneficial effect of our school: "The school of Halki is not just the theological school of the Ecumenical Patriarchate; it is the theological school of all of Orthodoxy. It is not just the theological school of all Orthodoxy; it is the theological school of all Christianity. It is not just the theological school of all Christianity; it is the school of the Oikoumene." May God save the Church and the school!

University Lectures and Academic Awards

City University, London, May 31, 1994

ANCIENT WISDOM AND WESTERN CIVILIZATION

We are deeply grateful for the honor bestowed on us today, which we accept not as an individual but on behalf of the Ecumenical Patriarchate and the entire holy Orthodox Church, in whose rich vineyard we are privileged to labor. We may toil in this vineyard, we may plant seeds here, we may harvest its fruits, but it is ultimately God's vineyard; they are God's seeds, and it is God's fruit. Therefore, all glory is due to Him.

The joy that we feel on receiving this degree is increased by the company in which we receive it: His Royal Highness Prince Philip; our brother in Christ, the Archbishop of Canterbury; the Lord Bishop of London; the Lord Mayor of London; and, of course, the administration, faculty, and students of this extraordinary university, which serves and enriches London, the largest city in Europe. Moreover, we warmly thank His Lordship, the Bishop of Stepney, for his kind and generous introduction.

Our joy is further multiplied because this honorary degree is conferred on us on the momentous occasion of the centenary of City University.

---

6. Panagia, Greek for "all-holy mother."

One hundred years is indeed a landmark, an achievement worthy of praise and recognition. We are deeply touched that you have chosen to include us in your celebrations. To you, the esteemed administration and faculty as well as the beloved students, we extend our heartfelt congratulations and paternal prayers that God, the giver of light, will continue to illuminate your hearts and minds as you grow in knowledge and wisdom. May God bless you with yet another centenary!

The ancient Greeks believed that human beings could rise to their full potential only within a city. This great university and its talented students are proof of that ancient wisdom. Nevertheless, increasingly these days we see another, darker aspect of life in our cities: children without clothing, food, or shelter; people without jobs; brothers killing brothers; broken families, broken lives, and broken dreams. So we ask ourselves: Why? What went wrong? How can this be?

Our first instinct is to doubt the wisdom of the ancients; but our better instinct is to believe it all the more. For if we truly believe that cities offer great opportunities, we will be driven to discover why so many are not finding those opportunities. What is missing? What is lacking? The answer, we feel, lies in faith—not knowledge, wealth, or political action, but simply faith. Knowledge expands minds, but faith open hearts. Wealth builds houses, but faith moves mountains. Politics achieves the possible, but faith can achieve the impossible.

Western civilization has brought about the greatest human achievements, from medical miracles to man on the moon; from stable democracies to high standards of living. Yet these achievements have not come without a price, and that price is most evident on the streets of our cities. Politicians and professors alone cannot heal the problems of Western society, be they pornography, pollution, drugs, poverty, crime, war, or homelessness. Religious leaders have a central and inspirational role to play in bringing the spiritual principles of brotherhood, tolerance, morality, and renewal to the fore.

We consider this degree such a unique honor because it is bestowed by a secular university on a spiritual institution, thereby demonstrating that one is not antithetical to the other. Beyond this, it also brings our two worlds closer together, and for this we are truly grateful to God. We are convinced that our mission today—namely, bringing the healing power of the Holy Spirit to all the children of God—is more vital than ever.

The spirituality of the Church offers a different sort of fulfillment than that offered by the secularism of modern life. Here, too, there can be no antithesis.

The failure of anthropocentric ideologies has left a void in many people's lives. The frantic pursuit of the future has sacrificed the inner peace of the past. We need to regain our religious outlook. We must urgently counter the effects of secular humanism with the Church's teaching about the human person and the world, elevating the pursuit of the temporal toward a healthy respect for the eternal by bringing one into harmony with the other. Beyond this, we must repair the torn fabric of society by reminding ourselves daily that the misfortune of some affects the fortune of all.

Our society resembles the lawyer who asked Jesus, "Teacher, what must I do to inherit eternal life?" And Jesus said, "What is written in the law?" The lawyer replied, "You shall love the Lord your God with all your heart, and with all your soul, and with all your mind; and your neighbor as yourself" (Luke 10.25–27). This led to a further question, one that is extremely relevant to our world today, namely: "And who is my neighbor?" (Luke 10.29). Jesus answered with the story of a man robbed and beaten on the road from Jerusalem to Jericho. A priest encountered him and, just as we might step over a homeless person today, crossed to the other side of the road. Then a Levite arrived; he, too, avoided the situation by crossing the road. Now, a Samaritan traveling down the road was moved to bind up the man's wounds, take him to the closest inn, and care for him. Jesus asked, "Which of these three, do you think, proved to be a neighbor to the man who fell among robbers?" (Luke 10.36) When the lawyer said it was the Good Samaritan, Jesus said, "Go and do likewise" (Luke 10.37).

Today there is hardly any more important question than this, "Who is my neighbor?" The future of humankind rests on how we respond; sadly, however, we do not always respond as we should. In Bosnia, where warfare still rages, too many, like the priest in Jesus' parable, have chosen to "cross the road" rather than confront the situation. In Los Angeles, London, and St. Petersburg, too many of our children have been abandoned to the urban warfare of the streets. On the other hand, in South Africa, we have seen millions of our fellow human beings behave like the Good

Samaritan. The South Africans are proving themselves to be true neighbors to their own.

If God would grant us the power to plant just one idea, as though it were a seed, in the fertile minds gathered within this great cathedral today—thereby returning the favor for this degree by offering to a secular institution a simple yet profound spiritual exhortation—it would be this: "Go and do likewise." Know that *every* human being is your neighbor, and behave accordingly. Above all else, "love your neighbor as yourself" (Luke 10.27). Thank you; and may God bless you.

University of Bucharest, Romania, October 26, 1995

THE MYSTERY OF LOVE

> Many members, yet one body . . . and whether one member suffers, all the members suffer with it; or one member be honored, all members rejoice with it.
>
> 1 Cor. 12.19, 26

From this podium of the historical and glorious University of Bucharest, we extend our warm feelings of love and honor, both personally as well as in the name of the Holy Mother and Great Church of Christ, to all of you who constitute this distinguished assembly—and more particularly to you, the honorable dean, tutors, students, and staff at this temple of education—but also, on this joyous occasion, to the entire academic community of Romania. Moreover, we extend our deepest gratitude for the honor of this invitation and the cordial reception extended to us and our entourage.

We have opened with the words of the Apostle concerning the multitude of faithful but also concerning the unity of the body's members, the solidarity among them in co-suffering and co-rejoicing; that is, we began with words about the mystery of love, the majestic hymn of which follows in the verses of the thirteenth chapter of the First Epistle to the Corinthians. Today, we are witnesses to this love, a love that we experience and share. For our Holy Ecumenical Throne has co-suffered with the noble people of Romania over many centuries, and more especially during this century, which has so impudently denigrated the picture both of the human person and of God. In the same manner, our Church has also rejoiced in watching the glorious moments of this nation, its periods of peace, freedom, and progress.

This is especially true because of the relations of our Church of Constantinople with the Church of Romania, which she has supported incessantly from the very beginning, according to the historical circumstances as well as the human distractions during different periods, the final judgment of which may only come from God, the righteous judge. As for the present occasion, our predecessors offered us a unique opportunity for one Church to participate in the joy of the other by recognizing the ripe time for granting autocephaly to the Church of Romania one hundred ten years ago and, later, seventy years ago, for granting the same Church a patriarchal value and honor. Those truly great events are causes for enormous joy for all of us and constitute a significant reason for this festive assembly. In good conscience, then, we partake in this joy, precisely because we happen to constitute one body. "And whether one member suffer, all the members suffer with it; or whether one member be honored, all members rejoice with it" (1 Cor. 12.26).

Our joy is increased because, beyond the events mentioned, at this festive assembly, the Primate of the Church of Romania[7] is also being honored with an honorary doctorate. Thus, we congratulate your beloved Beatitude for this deserved honor. Moreover, we congratulate our sister Church of Romania for the memorable historical moments in its life. We also congratulate this university and spiritual seedbed for the award of its highest honor, which through its recipient, His Beatitude our brother, reaches and affects the entire Church of Romania, the venerable hierarchy, the pious clergy, and the faithful people. Moreover, we feel that, in the person of our brother, it is precisely the Orthodox flock—embellished in the past with so many "stigmata" for the glory of God—that is being honored. For all this, therefore, we rejoice and we congratulate both our honored brother and those honoring him. We also recognize, from the bottom of our heart, the respect that this university reserves for the Church of Romania, a respect demonstrated through this act as well as through the good relations that this Church enjoys with the academic and intellectual community of this country.

---

7. Patriarch Teoktist, who served as patriarch of Romania (1986–2007).

This festive moment further prompts us to express certain thoughts in the hope that we are not burdening your hospitality. To begin with, we wish to underline that, as a Church, we honor every higher occupation concerned with spiritual matters. We esteem and respect the servants of the spirit and of the sciences not only because they cultivate the mind and the heart but also because they contribute to the examination and understanding of the entire creation of God. They approach His glory, and those who have the grace and courage become confessors of the power and witnesses of this divine glory, guiding the youth "in the nurture and admonition of the Lord" (Eph. 6.4). On the other hand, we acknowledge and esteem the many services that science, while surmounting and subduing so many tribulations resulting from various illnesses of the body and the spirit, offers to humanity in its effort to meet its daily needs.

THE FREEDOM OF THE SPIRIT

Finally, we remind you that the Orthodox Church has always respected the freedom of the spirit and the science of research. Spiritual freedom happens to be a common right and common duty. It is in fact a duty for the Church, which should never present obstacles to or oppress this freedom, though, unfortunately, it sometimes does, through excessive zeal or fear that such freedom will lead to error. When fear and impatience become the basis and starting point of human action, there is no possibility for freedom, life, and progress but rather only for decline, darkness, and death. On the contrary, freedom is the precondition for dynamic development and progress of mind.

Yet, the freedom of the spirit is also the duty of those working for science. So we hope that they are guided not only by their reason but also by the spirit of God. For "where the spirit of the Lord is, there also is freedom" (2 Cor. 3.17). We also hope that those preoccupied with science will accept and recognize their spirit as a gift from God, which is beneficial for them, their neighbor, and the entire creation. History has taught all of us—and this is well known and plain for people of goodwill—that when people attempt to act selfishly, thinking that anything can be achieved apart from or without God the Creator, they have wrought destruction for humanity and all creation. This is the message of the closing century, when the subordination of science to causes often alien to the natural environment has been pursued. Today, we have reason to believe that the cultivation of the spirit and the sciences will not be realized without the Spirit of God. This is why we welcome the fact that your university has been enriched with the incorporation of a theological school, which, among others, pursues the development of creative dialogue with all the sciences. This dialogue happens to be absolutely necessary, especially in our days.

In this regard, the Primates of the Orthodox Churches, who gathered in Patmos one month ago, declared in our common message: "Looking forward in faith and hope to the coming millennium, we invite all people to prayer and vigilance in view of the grave problems as well as the great possibilities appearing on the horizon. The achievements of science in most areas, and particularly in biology, entail incredible achievements as well as dangers. The Church cannot remain indifferent to these prospective developments, since the survival of the human person as the 'image of God' is at stake."

Therefore, in discerning these dangers, we welcome the opportunities, we remain in the faith, we retain our hope, and we pursue honest and sincere dialogue with all people in all places, and especially with those who pursue knowledge and love truth. Once more, we congratulate all of you and pray that God may bless you with His infinite mercy.

Georgetown University, Washington, D.C., October 21, 1997

The original title of this address was "*Phos Ilaron*: Joyful Light."

THE GROUND OF UNION

It is a special honor that this distinguished university is conferring the title of honorary doctor on our Modesty. This is an opportunity for us to approach one another and communicate in a spirit of fellowship. Although we proclaim that we worship the one and same Lord Jesus Christ, whose name we bear as Christians, we seek in common the causes of our divergence. In the distant past, great attempts have been made by each side to prove its case, and, motivated by a different spirit, each has judged the other to have diverged from the true faith. This deeply rooted conviction with respect to our divergence has led to a thousand years of our taking separate, independent courses. We confirm not with unexpected astonishment, but neither with indifference, that indeed the divergence between us continues to grow and the final destination of our courses is quite different. Our heart is opposed to the specter of an everlasting separation. Our heart requires that we once again seek our common foundations and the original starting point that we share. In this way, retrospectively, we can discover the points of our divergence and the reasons that led to our separate courses. We will also be able, by lifting all blame, to proceed along the same road and to the same common goal.

Assuredly, our problem is neither geographical nor one of personal alienation. Neither is it a problem of organizational structure or jurisdictional arrangement. Nor again is it a problem of external submission or absorption of individuals and groups. It is something deeper and more substantive. The manner in which we exist has become ontologically different. Unless our ontological transformation toward one common model of life is achieved, not only in form but also in substance, then the realization of unity becomes impossible.

No one ignores that the model for all of us is the person of the theanthropos (God-Man), Jesus Christ. But which model? No one ignores that incorporation into Christ is achieved within His body, the Church. But whose Church? As a result of the diverse responses to these basic questions, we have marched along divergent ways. This is easily understood and perhaps historically inevitable. For whether we comprehend it or not, our existence is ontologically shaped in harmony with our inner self. According to the description of our Lord (see Matt. 15.11), it is not what goes into the mouth that defiles a person but what comes out of the mouth. This means that our essence is in continuous transformation (see Rom. 12.2, 2 Cor. 3.18) "by the renewing of our mind" and in the reflected glory of the Lord.

There is one characteristic detail regarding God's glory that cannot be understood without careful attention is described in the Old Testament, where Jacob succeeded in having his flock bear multicolored lambs by placing before them multicolored rods (see Gen. 30:37–43). In similar fashion, the Apostle Paul wrote to the Corinthians and said that we are constantly being transformed into the likeness of the image of the glory of the Lord, which we reflect. Consequently, the "glory" of the Lord, which we see as in a mirror, is what transforms us. It is to this glory that we are likened. The reflection of the divine glory recreates or regenerates us into something other than or in essence different from our previous nature. Transformation into the image of the Lord and the image of His body becomes the fundamental pursuit of our life, accomplished essentially through the intervention of the Holy Spirit.

As a result, we do not engage in idle talk and discuss intellectual concepts that do not influence our lives. We discuss the essence of Being who truly is, with whom we seek assimilation by God's grace; and because of the inadequacy of human terms, we call this "the image of the glory of the Lord." Based on this image, and in the likeness of this image, we become "partakers of divine nature" (2 Pet. 1.4). We are truly changed, although "neither earth, nor voice, nor custom distinguishes us from the rest on mankind."[8]

TRANSFORMED BY GRACE

This change, bestowed on us by the right hand of the Most High, remains hidden, secret, and mystical to many. And so our life, directed toward Him, is called mystical. What lead us to divine grace are the divine mysteries. The entire transformation of language and intellect that ensues is beyond comprehension; when directed by God, it leads to unspeakable mysteries. However, the change of our essence, *theosis* by grace, is at the same time a tangible fact for all Orthodox faithful. Grace is obtained not only through the transformed relics of the saints, which is totally inexplicable without acceptance of the divine. Grace also radiates from living saints, who are truly in the likeness of the Lord (see Luke 8.46). This change is also obtained through holy baptism, which through grace transforms the neophyte. The transformation may be discerned and grasped by the senses only those baptized, who are receptive to it without any external persuasion. According to the trustworthy testimony of devout Christians, divine grace infuses even the inanimate. This, too, is realized only by those who are sensitive and pure in heart. Grace can be obtained also through the presence of the saints, who have influenced and sanctified, and to a degree transformed, even natural objects and places.

And so the Orthodox Christian lives in a place not of high theoretical speculation and debate but rather of authentic life and reality, essential

---

8. *Letter to Diognetus* 2, in PG 2.1173.

and empirical, as confirmed by grace in the heart (see Heb. 13.9). This grace cannot be affected by questions or doubts based on logic, science, and argumentation. Our conception of Holy Tradition also moves along the same track. For Orthodox Christians, Holy Tradition is not just some collection of teachings, certain texts outside the holy scriptures and based on oral tradition within the Church. It is this, too, but it is much more than this. First and foremost, it is a living and essential imparting of life and grace—an essential and tangible reality, propagated from generation to generation within the Orthodox Church. This transmission of faith, like the circulation of living sap from the tree to a branch, from the body to a member, from the Church to a believer, presumes that one is grafted to the fruitful olive tree (see Rom. 11.23–25) and the embodiment of the members in the body (see Rom. 12.5, 1 Cor. 10.16–17, 12.12–27).

Membership in the Church is not an act of cataloging a person as a member of a group. Rather, it is the true rebirth of this person in a new reality, the world of grace. From that moment onward, he or she is nourished and grows a new body, which is of a different substance to the body of the flesh and is joined with the body of Christ through baptism. The relevant scriptural verse (Gal. 3.27) and baptismal hymn—"Whoever is baptized in Christ has been clothed in Christ"—is not mere symbolism or poetic allegory. It points to a real fact that brings change in the substance of the human being. Those baptized as infants, whose Orthodox parents grafted them into the body of the Church, are unable to express in words the change that occurred; but they know and feel it. However, those present at the moment of baptism, who are endowed with purity of heart, can also see the grace that surrounds the newly baptized. Those baptized at a mature age and with depth of faith are able to express and describe the liberating feeling of renouncing the devil and joining Christ.

This ontological view of the life in Christ constitutes a substantial part of the experience of the Eastern Orthodox Church. The glow of its light illumines all facets of ecclesiastical and personal life in the Church, disposing of the need for pointless inquiries. The Master Himself knocks on the door and desires that we open to Him the door of our heart so that He may enter and break bread with us. This is the foundational issue and posture for the Orthodox Christian. Understanding this opens the door for communication and makes dialogue possible.

DOCTRINE AS LIFE AND LIFE AS DOCTRINE

This ontological position of the Orthodox Church brings us to the difficult issues before us. Let us look at some of these. Regarding dogma, the Orthodox Church maintains an apparently contradictory position. On the one hand, Orthodoxy has never initiated a dogmatic dialogue. On the other hand, the Church has never neglected one. Let us explain what we mean by this. As we have noted, the Orthodox faithful awaits and desires to become the reflection of the glory of God; through the grace of the Holy Spirit, he or she becomes an image of our Lord Jesus Christ. Orthodox Christians, in other words, desire to have direct knowledge of one person of the Trinity, Jesus Christ, and through Him alone of the remaining two divine persons—the unapproachable (except to the Son) person of the Father, and the person of the Holy Spirit. The Orthodox Christian strives toward purity of heart for the visitation of grace; and, having been fulfilled, the Orthodox Christian is able to behold the glory of God. Thus transformed from glory to glory, the Orthodox Christian approaches God.

In this respect, in the spiritual journey, a dogmatic description of the manifestation of the Lord and His Body, the Church, is unnecessary, because our experienced guide at every moment protects us from all deception and allows us to accept the glory of the Lord in whatever appearance it takes. And so experiencing the dogma of the Church is not something taught through intellectual instruction; instead, it is learned through the example of Him who, through incarnation, was joined to us. For dogma is life; and life is the expression of dogma. Mere theoretical discussion on the meaning of life and dogma is superfluous.

However, the evil opponent of humanity tries to interject his own distorted filter—a foreign doctrine, a false glory, a deceptive teaching—between the faithful and the divine glory. In this case, the Church, like a good shepherd, hurries to guide the faithful toward the right glory. The entire body of the Church rises and vigorously warns that the enemy's doctrine is erroneous and that, by embracing it, we are separated from the true glory of God, and, thus led off track, we miss our goal. In order to protect the faithful from "missing the mark,"[9] the Church battles the

---

9. The literal meaning of the Greek word for "sin" (*hamartia*).

distortions, which are continuously planted by cunning spirits, regarding the glory of God. However, this difference in dogmatic theory does not lend itself to systematic analysis. For a systematic exposure of this dogmatic teaching could be understood only spiritually. If the faithful voluntarily accepted any distortions of it, the purity of their pure vision would be harmed. This truth is captured in the recognition that, for those who have an immediate personal knowledge of the Lord, every rational description of Him is needless. For those still on the road to knowing Him, an accurate presentation of the basic elements of His glory is nevertheless useful, as it helps them avoid false beliefs.

Concerning those who have freely chosen to shun the correct glory of God, the Orthodox Church follows the recommendation of the Apostle Paul: "A man that is a heretic after the first and second admonition, reject" (Titus 3.10). The same, of course, does not hold true for those who, with meekness and fear, ask you for a reason for the hope that is in you (see 1 Peter 3.15). Therefore, the Orthodox Church is always open to every dialogue in good faith, but it refrains from participating in planted squabbles, since the danger of being misunderstood always lurks there.

If time and your kindness permit, let us examine one such case, so that you may better appreciate our position. The nature of the Church, viewed in light of the Orthodox faith, is a reality recognized spiritually and not descriptively. Each of us knows the members of his own body not because we have been taught about them or because they have been described in detail by anyone. "We know" them in a unique way because of the direct and living bond that we share with them, even if we do not have a scientific understanding of them. In similar manner, the Church is our body. Since its head, our Lord and Savior Jesus Christ, exists before creation, the Church coexists with Him before all time. The Church is not an imaginary or legal entity, a mere gathering of faithful, or a worldly establishment. The Church is Christ, and those whom He chooses, in one body with Him for all eternity. The full comprehension of this presumes living this reality in full. That is to say, concerning the Word of Life, we must experience what our hands have handled (1 John 1.1), without exception—we must experience a sense of the union of all things in Christ, in whom all things exist, not in a pantheistic but in a Christological sense.

All this leads to the conclusion that the organization, goals, functions, and generally the whole life of the Church are not determined by human judgment but rather by the real and unchanging nature of the Church. And so the steadfastness of the Orthodox Church on ecclesiastical assumptions of every type is the result not of a narrow view but rather of a living ecclesiastical experience. We speak not of an object subjected to free manipulation but of an existence independent of our desires and directed by Him who governs all things and who bestowed on us limited responsibility, or ministry. The starting point of the occasionally misunderstood position of the Orthodox Church regarding ecclesiological matters is rediscovered in the essence of this ministry, within this real body that is directed by its head, the Lord Jesus Christ.

In these few words, your judgment is expected regarding my thoughts about our hope—a hope that starts from a living experience rather than from an intellectual concept. We thank you for your patience and attention. Our love for you is sincere and warm. Let not the simplicity of our words cloud your judgment regarding their truth. For you are able to understand the words of the divine Logos through the uttering of human words. Let us always hear the words of the divine Logos so that His grace may be with us. Indeed, this is our wish for you.

University of Sofia, Bulgaria, November 14, 2007

The original title of this address was "Truth and History."

THE BYZANTINE LEGACY OF LETTERS AND CULTURE

It is a particular honor to communicate with you in this spiritual institute of higher learning in response to your gracious invitation to receive an honorary doctorate from the State University of Librarian Studies and Technological Information. We accept this honor as one bestowed on the Ecumenical Patriarchate, which we humbly lead and by whose ecumenical spirit we are inspired, and which respects the universal and particular values of each nation. A characteristic example of this ecumenical spirit lies in the ministry of Saints Cyril and Methodius, whom the Ecumenical Patriarchate, respecting the local traditions, sent to this region that they might work with great zeal and love. This is precisely why they were honored here not only as saints but as contributing substantially to the spiritual and cultural life of Bulgaria, inasmuch as they "transplanted" the mature Byzantine civilization and "assimilated" it to the life of your people. Indeed, we rejoice that you continue to commemorate these saints and to regard them as patrons of education and letters.

On this occasion, then, we congratulate you all—both teachers and students as well as administrators and staff of this university—on the work that you perform, especially in the field of library science during this age of immense technological development and digital information, and particularly in the field of electronic books, which are expected largely to replace the printed publication of former eras. Much like many of you, as part of an older generation, we have been raised with less familiarity in the rapidly advancing electronic media. It is, therefore, natural that we have a preference for traditional libraries, where illustrious publications are collected, categorized, and catalogued in accordance with scholarly principles in order to preserve and promote written knowledge and information on all matters related to human affairs. At the same time, however, we appreciate and admire the vast possibilities opened up when resources and sources of information are made accessible to people across the globe—when they are made available through electronic libraries and information technology. It appears that the two systems of knowledge will long coexist, and so your university has the unique responsibility and task of studying and developing both alike.

We pray that God will grant you health, strength, and inspiration to continue your work with enthusiasm for the benefit and development of all those who love knowledge and wisdom. As you rightly emphasize, both forms of library science involve the preservation of cultural and historical heritage. This heritage may be variously evaluated, but it cannot be altered. This is precisely why there is an effort to reprint the classical books of history with the purpose of reconciling peoples and serving their peaceful coexistence. Thus, we have elected to explore briefly with you a subject that pertains to your profession and interest in order to draw certain crucial conclusions regarding the development of an ecumenical spirit. Let us, then, outline certain dimensions of the subject "truth and history" to encourage your interest and deliberation. For the preservation of historical and cultural heritage is directly related to truth. This is particularly important because, in our age, there appears to be some confusion, albeit not explicit, between truth and the appreciation of reality. That is, instead of appreciating certain events that occur in certain places, people seek to portray an unacceptable distortion of these events.

THE PRIMACY OF TRUTH

The Old Testament preserves a wonderful account whose conclusion is that truth supersedes all else, including power itself. Zorobabel, the protagonist of the story in question, confesses: "'Truth is greater and more powerful than all else. . . . It remains and prevails forever; it lives and triumphs to the ages of ages. . . . Blessed be the God of truth.' And the people confirmed: 'Truth is great and powerful'" (Ezra 4.35–41). Truth reigns, then, and it is foolish for anyone to try to conceal or change it. Indeed, every institution of higher learning is committed and sworn to serve the truth, as we observe in the graduation ceremony, where each student implicitly declares, "I shall live in accordance with science."

The placing of truth at the very summit of pursuits in an academic institution is an inevitable consequence of its scholarly identity. It is characteristic that, in a certain Japanese university, a column of one of its halls is clearly and manifestly inscribed with the words of Christ in the original language of the Gospel: "You shall know the truth, and the truth shall set you free" (John 8.32). Contrary to the pursuit of truth is the ideology—any ideology or conviction—that leads to fanaticism and the distortion of truth. An ideologue is interested primarily in securing ways of confirming his ideology through argumentation rather than in discovering the truth, especially when the latter jeopardizes his ideology. Naturally, we are neither interested in stirring the passions of the past nor in justifying all the actions of our ancestors, or again in justifying all of our own actions, but instead in preserving history in a way that is uninfluenced by emotions, no matter how noble or good those may be.

And so our theme has two dimensions—history and truth. Let us begin with history, both general and ecclesiastical. Indeed, it is fitting to begin with a definition of history. In Greek, the term for "history" derives etymologically from the word *istōr*, which in turn is a derivative of the verb "to know" and signifies someone who has knowledge, skill, and wisdom. Originally, history implied studying and learning about something, while later it included narrating an event or describing an acquaintance; again, in later centuries, it also signified the process of depicting or decorating temples, homes, or public spaces.

THE HISTORY OF HISTORY: SECULAR AND SACRED PERSPECTIVES

Nevertheless, in speaking today about history, we mean primarily the reflection and recording of events that occurred in society at a specific time and place. In examining the history of history, we ascertain the existence of numerous forms of history and historians, their differences depending on the era and conviction of each historian. In the beginning, what prevailed was "primitive history," consisting of the simple recording of chronology and general information. Later, "natural history" was developed—namely, the description of events connected by time and place. Then, "cultural history" was emphasized as a way of portraying events connected to peoples and races. Still later, historians developed the concept of "critical history," by which, on the basis of various methods and principles, they judged events that occur in particular places and times.

The ancient Greeks developed three forms of history, identified with three great historians. Herodotus, who is also considered the father of history, introduced "narrative history" as a literary form, a record of the establishment of cities and the sequence of genealogies.[10] Thucydides was concerned with "political history" as a way of discerning the causes of events, which are interpreted in light of the universal human spirit.[11] Polybius was especially interested in "pragmatic history" as a way of examining popular customs and laws as well as religious and social structures.[12] Since then, these three historians have greatly influenced numerous historians through the centuries. Students of history have imitated their ancestors and in turn developed further dimensions of historical research, each building on the contributions of the other. So much, in brief, for the appearance of the science of history in ancient times as well as for its subsequent influence not only on Greeks and Romans but also on all historians through the centuries and throughout the world.

Now, as a hierarch and leader in the Orthodox Church, may we be permitted to say a little about ecclesiastical history, which has certain

---

10. Herodotus, 484–25 B.C.
11. Thucydides, 460–395 B.C.
12. Polybius, 203–120 B.C.

unique characteristics. First, as Orthodox clergy, we speak of "sacred history" inasmuch as this relates to our faith. We believe that human life and history are not directed by invisible or indefinite forces; we are not victims of fate or chance or even of some mechanistic determinism. Rather, it is God who personally directs our life and history. In the Orthodox Church, we do not believe in the phrase "In the beginning, there was an idea" or "In the beginning, there was matter." Instead, we believe and declare that "In the beginning was the Word"—that is, the hypostatic, or Trinitarian, God: Father, Son and Holy Spirit. Accordingly, God directs and supervises history through His divine and uncreated energies. Moreover, in these latter days, the Word of God became human, assumed flesh, taught, suffered, was crucified, arose, and ascended into heaven. In the Orthodox Church, there is no contrast between "the Christ of faith" and "the Christ of history." The Christ in whom we believe and are saved entered history in order to transform it.

And so Christ is revealed in history; the kingdom of God is manifest in history; and adoption in Christ takes place within history. In this way, "sacred history" is identified with "salvation history." This means, among other things, that the interpretation of the holy Bible and of ecclesiastical texts does not occur outside of history; these are not perceived as a code of divine commands. Rather, interpretation of them occurs within history, through the Church, as an expression of divine love for the *transformation* of history. In other words, the Church moves within history and not outside of history. The church lives in historical time and space; it embraces humanity within history and its diverse problems, transforming and sanctifying both time and space while at the same time sanctifying humanity within a particular age and place. And so the Church is not characterized by manicheistic[13] or monophysitic[14] tendencies. For it sees humanity in its entirety, as comprising both body and soul while at the same time facing numerous problems arising from the mortality and corruption of this life.

---

13. Manicheism, an early Gnostic Christian sect, founded by Manes (216–76), articulated a popular cosmology involving a struggle between good and evil, light and darkness, matter and spirit.

14. From the Greek words for "one" (*monos*) and "nature" (*physis*), monophysitism is the Christological teaching that Christ had only one nature, which was divine, with his human nature being subsumed within the divinity.

In any case, in the Orthodox Church, the concept of time is not defined as cyclical or repetitive, as it was in classical Greek thought. Nor is it understood in linear fashion, as being directed toward the end of history and the experience of the heavenly kingdom, as in Hebrew theology. Rather, it is distinguished by the cruciform concept of time, by time in light of the Cross, whereby the kingdom of God approaches us as we live in history and time while at the same time we await the completion of the kingdom in the future. In order to appreciate this cruciform concept of time, we might take the example of the conch (or sea shell), which makes both a circular and a forward movement.

The experience of "sacred history" leads to the "theology of reality," which is none other than the experience of the heavenly kingdom in specific human lives expressed through words and actions. When Moses ascended Mount Sinai to receive the divine commandments; when St. Paul ascended the third heaven and "heard ineffable words, which no human words can utter" (2 Cor. 12.4); when those who have acquired deification through the ages—prophets, Apostles, Fathers, saints, righteous, confessors, ascetics—ascend to divine vision and know God "face to face," they all behold the uncreated light, the light and brilliance of the transfigured Lord; then, whatever these people write and enact constitutes the *theology of reality*. All of the written texts of the Fathers and of the local and ecumenical synods, the liturgical sources as well as the saints' relics—these constitute the "theology of reality." One cannot be a Christian if one is dissociated from history.

On a purely historical level, at least within ecclesiastical history, errors are recorded on the part of human beings replete with passions. Yet, in truth, the Church proceeds in history by means of its saints. This means that certain members of the Church may create schisms and divisions as a result of a spirit of self-centeredness and arrogance; they may question sacred canons established by local and ecumenical synods; they may resort to various secular means in order to disturb peace in the Church; they may distort the truth. Nevertheless, in the end, the Holy Spirit, which acts within the Church and which directs the institution of the Church, prevails through its deified members.

Furthermore, "sacred history" and the "theology of reality" are not only closely interrelated by the all-encompassing circle of time and space; they are also experienced beyond space and time, without at the same time abolishing history. We are speaking here of "eschatological history."[15] For the Church Fathers, history (as time and space) is transcended but not abolished. In the Orthodox Church, we do not speak of the end of history but of its transcendence to a higher plane of perfection. This means that Christ, who assumed human flesh at His incarnation, preserves and deifies this to the ages. Therefore, the body of the risen Christ exists eternally; and, since every human body will rise and the saints will live in paradise, both in body and in soul, history too will never cease to exist. The body of Christ is an indispensable part of history, and the sanctified body of its faithful is a historical reality. And so, the relics of the saints—including, here in your own country, the blessed relic of St. John of Rila,[16] which abundantly contains the grace of the Holy Spirit—imply that history is not abolished but instead transformed, being elevated to a higher plane.

In this way, the terms "sacred history," "theology of reality," and "eschatological history" contain the entire theology of the Church concerning historical *being* and historical *becoming*. However, enough about history. Let us return to our original objective and briefly explore the concept of truth and its relationship to history. From the outset, we have stated that our theme is "history and truth" because existing history is inevitably judged as truthful or false. After all, our whole life is distinguished by these two characteristic features, truthfulness and falsehood. By what criterion, then, are we able to distinguish between truthful and false history?

HISTORY AS TRUTH: FUNDAMENTAL CRITERIA

In speaking of truth, we might consider the etymology of the word. *Aletheia*, the Greek word for truth, derives from the deprivative *a* and the root term *lethe*, which implies a forgotten or concealed reality. And so the word *truth* signifies exemption from obliteration, from the loss of a memory, from the disappearance of that memory. Indeed, since forgetfulness includes also the false interpretation of reality, "historical truth" denotes

---

15. From *eschaton*, the Greek word for "last times," signifying the kingdom of heaven.

16. St. John of Rila (876–946) was the first Bulgarian monk and is the patron saint of Bulgaria. His relics are preserved in the famous Rila Monastery, founded in the tenth century.

the description and presentation of reality and events in their ontological expression. Therefore, truth is whatever has not been forgotten, whatever is preserved alive in the memory, and whatever is restored or removed from forgetfulness.

Of course, whenever history is narrated not so much according to how events took place but instead according to how the narrator, for personal reasons, wishes events to have taken place, this is not history; at least, it is certainly not truthful history. Rather, it is deliberate falsehood, which does not serve truth but only an ideology or prejudice, usually and typically political in nature. This means that we are to judge historical events and condemn unjust or wrongful actions, but we are not to conceal or change events in order to displace or distort responsibility. In this respect, by knowing the truth of people and events, we live freely, "with sound soul," as Pericles would put it.[17] For evil things that occur are corrected by *repentance* and *confession* and not by ignorance or denial. This is precisely why, empowered by such presuppositions about historical knowledge, an ancient sage said, "Blessed is the one who has learned history"—that is, history that is transformed by truth and not distorted for personal expediency.

Modern man struggles to acquire the truth about all things, about science, about politics, about religion, and especially about history, both present and past. The question is how one may discern true history from false history, and this subject is precisely the object of scholarly research. Now, many people claim to express the truth, even as they record various individual aspects of an event. So there must be certain clear boundaries and authentic measures through which the truth of historical reality is ascertained. Allow us at this point to underline some of the more significant criteria for the assurance of truth.

The first is the transcendence of subjectivity and the search for objectivity in the interpretation of historical reality. The historical scholar understands—or, at least, ought to understand—that human knowledge has limitations, which cannot be supersede without risking deceit. So this scholar must negotiate certain hurdles encountered in the search for historical truth—"reliability of sources," which must be objective; an "authentic criterion of interpretation," which must be beyond personal

---

17. Pericles, 495–29 B.C.

ideology; and the "collective subconscious," which is related to each race's cultivation of a sense of cultural superiority at the expense of respecting the achievements of other races, which are thereby undermined or over-looked. In reality, to negotiate these hurdles is to overcome subjectivism and achieve objectivism in historical knowledge.

The second criterion consists of the "hermeneutic keys," or interpreta-tive measures, by which historical knowledge is secured. It is beneficial for us to learn how to study or examine each historical event. In this respect, we feel that it is important that all knowledge embrace the study of three necessary elements—the *narration* (or description), the *explanation*, and the *critical evaluation* of each event and its consequences. The first ele-ment involves the questions "What? Where? When? Who? How?" The second involves the question "Why?" And in the third matter, the person performing the critical evaluation, as well as that same person's social environment, adopts a scale of values. The historical scholar must study what and where a particular event occurred, by means of whom it oc-curred, and how it occurred. An intensive, objective analysis of the event constitutes the surest method of study and evaluation. In the search, then, for truth through the study of past events and historical sources, what assumes critical importance is not only the precise study of the "letter" of an event or phenomenon but especially the careful analysis of the "spirit" or "mind" of the person who recorded it.

In this regard, Athanasius the Great offers a critical insight in his con-frontation of the Arian heresy. In his treatise entitled *Against the Arians*,[18] he develops the idea that, in order to explore and express truth, and in order not to err in the hermeneutic analysis of a scriptural passage, we must comprehend and acquire the knowledge of the "time" in which the specific passage was written, the "person" to whom it refers, and the "reality" or reason, for which the author wrote the particular passage. The words of St. Athanasius are quite expressive: "Therefore, we must reveal the mind [or spirit] of what is said; we must seek to comprehend what is concealed and not simply what is stated explicitly, so that we do not mistakenly wander from the truth." Elsewhere he observes: "We are not simply to conceive the words on the surface, but rather seek to understand

---

18. A series of four discourses against the fourth-century heretical teaching of Arius in Alexandria.

the person to whom it refers, thereby applying our mind [or spirit] with piety." St. Athanasius notes that we must learn how to "return from the letter to the spirit."

These authentic hermeneutic criteria are crucial for the understanding of words, both written and spoken, as well as of events that occurred in particular times. This is what we also emphasized in our doctoral dissertation *On the Codification of the Sacred Canons and on the Canonical Regulations in the Orthodox Church,*[19] where we appropriately stressed that the holy canons of the Church should be examined on the basis of principles formulated by the Church Fathers such as St. Athanasius.

The fourth criterion for interpreting reality is the study of the historical rule known as "heterogeneity of purpose." This phrase implies that a given reality may originate in a particular purpose but, along the way, is also influenced by different motivations and comes to a conclusion in a purpose that is quite different. The scholar must by all means return to the past and search for the cause that precipitated this change in purpose. For example, it is quite possible for an ideologue to develop a certain theory in a disinterested manner; but in its application by other, self-interested people, this theory may nevertheless be transformed and forcefully imposed on others so that, in the end, it becomes a form of bureaucratic authoritarianism. It is clear, then, that the interpretation of historical events and reality must include a distinction between the original purpose and the final result.

As a continuation and consequence of the previous criteria, the fifth criterion implies that the interpretation of reality must be liberated from personal passion, diverse influences, and all forms of nationalism. This criterion is not, unfortunately, to be taken for granted, because, in interpreting historical events, we see them through the lens of various forms of nationalism and political presupposition. And this means that historical research is in fact no longer promoted; instead, we are led to divisions in the name of unilateral and individual perceptions. Christ said, "Know the truth, and the truth shall set you free" (John 8.32). Throughout our life, we must be seekers of the truth—not only of historical but also of existential reality. Then the discovery of truth will set us free from all forms of influences, which are not the truth but only ghosts of the truth.

---

19. See Introduction, 3

THE REALITY OF SUFFERING

By way of conclusion, then, we would like to say that these are existential questions beyond historical reality and events that occur in historical time and space, as well as within the depth of our hearts, causing us profound suffering. They are, moreover, existential questions related to life and death, to the meaning of life and existence, of ecstasy with respect to another being, and of personal encounter with the living God. These existential problems greatly plague the human person. An example of this is found in the life of the late Archimandrite Sophrony Sakharov, Russian in origin, who lived within the ecclesiastical and spiritual jurisdiction of the Ecumenical Patriarchate, first on Mount Athos and then in England.[20] He experienced the events of the First and Second World Wars as well as of the Russian Revolution of 1917. Father Sophrony felt profound sorrow for the shedding of so much blood on the earth; yet, above all else, he felt much pain in his heart for the existential and spiritual problems related to God, problems that he experienced but that he witnessed especially in all those estranged from the God of truth.

Accordingly, then, living in a world filled with such problems, we must study the historical events of the past and interpret them accurately in order to improve the contemporary social conditions of life, to offer meaning and purpose to young people of our age, and, especially, to transform and raise the natural and cultural history of humanity to the level of "sacred history," so that we might discern the meaning of life.

The Ecumenical Patriarchate is the bearer of precisely this spirit, which we have endeavored to expound briefly today. We feel in our hearts a sense of deep sorrow and pain because of the many disturbing realities of our time—the selective interpretation of history, the pollution of our planet, the various religious controversies and divisions, social injustices and inequalities, as well as the material deprivation and the hunger experienced by human beings, but most especially the hunger and thirst among people for righteousness and for an encounter with the Trinitarian God, since, in the formulation of St. Gregory Palamas, "Christ is the truth, the Father is the Father of truth, and the Spirit is the Spirit of truth." In this

---

20. Father Sophrony (1896–1993) was the disciple and biographer of St. Silouan of Mount Athos as well as founder of the Patriarchal Stavropegic Monastery of St. John the Baptist in Tolleshunt Knights, Essex, UK.

way, we work within history from the privilege of the First Throne in the assembly and administration of the universal Orthodox Church—at once a privilege and a service, a witness and martyrdom, for the transformation of the whole world and for the discovery by all people of the living and saving truth.

It is the same purpose of serving the truth that is embraced by schools of library science, such as your own, which are the very archives in which knowledge and historical heritage are safeguarded. And so we feel obliged to congratulate this institute wholeheartedly for your wonderful and beautiful initiative, expressing also our sincerest wishes to all of you, faculty and students alike. We thank you once again for the invitation to us and for the opportunity to speak, invoking on everyone the boundless mercy and love of the Trinitarian God so that we may live in history, move in truth, and proceed toward the eschatological completeness of truth.

Fordham University, New York, October 27, 2009

> The original title of this address was "Discerning God's Presence in the World."

THE ECUMENICAL IMPERATIVE

It is with sincere gratitude that we accept this invaluable honor of being received into the ranks of those who have been awarded doctorates from this esteemed Jesuit school. We welcome this privilege as recognition of the sacred ministry of the Ecumenical Patriarchate, an Apostolic institution with a history spanning seventeen centuries, throughout retaining its see in Constantinople. Yet our Church is no worldly institution; it wields no political authority. Instead, it leads by example, coordinating pan-Orthodox Christian unity by virtue of a primacy of honor—a ministry emanating from its supranational authority. This universal consciousness gave rise to the first seven ecumenical councils, to the articulation of the "symbol of faith" (or Nicene Creed), and to the establishment of the New Testament canon; it also gave birth to churches from the Caspian to the Baltic and from the Balkans to Central Europe; today, its jurisdiction extends to the Far East, Western Europe, Australia, and America.

Of course, this ecumenicity constitutes both an ancient privilege and a lasting responsibility, demanding an open ministry within our own communions and among other Christian confessions as well as toward the world's faith communities. Within our ecumenical initiatives, the international theological dialogue with our "sister Church" of Rome—instituted in the 1960s as the "dialogue of love" and continuing today as the "dialogue of truth"—constitutes our foremost encounter of "speaking the truth in love." A concrete example of this encounter here at Fordham is the Orthodox Christian Minor Studies Program, which is the first of its kind at a major university in the United States. This program complements both the annual lecture series "Orthodoxy in America" and the Orthodox Christian Fellowship, and it demonstrates a practical synergistic spirit, modeling for Orthodox and Roman Catholics everywhere a shared a common purpose based in truth and in love.

Our purpose this evening, though, is not to outline for you how the ecumenical imperative defines our Church but, rather, to inspire in all of you the primacy of ecumenicity, the value of opening up in a world that expects us "always to be prepared to give an answer to everyone that asks us to give the reason for the hope within us" (1 Pet. 3.15). In this regard, we would like to draw your attention to three dimensions of "opening up," or "ecumenical consciousness"—opening up to the heart, opening up to the other, and opening up to creation.

OPENING UP TO THE HEART: THE WAY OF THE SPIRIT

As faith communities and as religious leaders, we have an obligation constantly to pursue and persistently to proclaim alternative ways to order human affairs, rejecting violence and reaching for peace. Human conflict may well be inevitable in our world; but war certainly is not. If the twenty-first century will be remembered at all, it may be for those who dedicated themselves to the cause of tolerance and understanding. Yet the pursuit of peace calls for a reversal of what has become normal and normative in our world. It requires conversion (*metanoia*) and the willingness to become individuals and communities of transformation. The Orthodox Christian spiritual classics emphasize the heart as the place where God, humanity, and the world may coincide in harmony. Indeed, the *Philokalia* underlines the paradox that peace is gained through sacrifice (*martyria*), perceived not as passivity or indifference to human suffering but as relinquishing selfish desires and achieving greater generosity. The way of the heart stands in opposition to everything that violates peace. When one awakens to the way within, peace flows as an expression of gratitude for God's love for the world. Unless our actions are founded on love instead of on fear, we will never overcome fanaticism or fundamentalism.

In this sense, the way of the heart is a radical response, threatening policies of violence and politics of power. This is why peacemakers—whether Jesus Christ, or Mahatma Gandhi (1869–1948), or Martin Luther King Jr. (1929–68)—threatened the status quo. Indeed, the Sermon on the Mount shaped the pacifist teaching of Leo Tolstoy,[21] whose work *The Kingdom of God Is Within You* was influenced by the writings of the *Philokalia* and in turn profoundly influenced both the nonviolent principles of Gandhi and the civil-rights activism of King. Sometimes, the most "provocative" message is "loving our enemy and doing good to those who hate us" (Luke 6.27). Some may announce "the end of faith" or "the end of history," blaming religion for violent aberrations in human behavior. Yet, never was the peaceful "protest" of religion more necessary than now; never was the powerful "resistance" of religion more critical than today. Ours is the *beginning*, not the end of either faith or history.

OPENING UP TO THE OTHER: THE WAY OF DIALOGUE

This is why the interreligious gatherings initiated by the Ecumenical Patriarchate are crucial for paving the way toward peaceful coexistence among the world's peoples. Such dialogue draws people of diverse religious beliefs and cultural traditions out of their isolation, instituting a process of mutual respect and meaningful communication. When we seek this kind of encounter, we discover ways of coexisting despite our differences. After all, historical conflicts between Christians and Muslims are typically rooted in politics, not in religion. The tragic story of the Crusades is a telling example, bequeathing a legacy of cultural alienation and ethnic resentment.

To speaking, then, of an inevitable and inexorable "clash of civilizations" is incorrect and inappropriate, especially when such a theory posits

---

21. Tolstoy, 1828–1910.

religion as the principal battleground on which such conflict is doomed to occur. National leaders may provoke isolation and aggression between Christians and Muslims; or else demagogues may mobilize religions in order to reinforce national fanaticism and hostility. However, this is not to be confused with the true nature and purpose of religion. Christians and Muslims lived alongside each other during the Byzantine and the Ottoman Empires, usually supported by their political and religious authorities. In Andalusian Spain, believers in Judaism, Christianity and Islam coexisted peacefully for centuries. Such historical models reveal possibilities for our own pluralistic and globalized world.

Moreover, any theory about "the clash of civilizations" is invariably naive, inasmuch as it oversimplifies differences between peoples, cultures, and religions. How ironic that religion promotes a more "liberal" position than does the "realism" of a political scientist! The visit by Pope Benedict XVI to the Ecumenical Patriarchate in Istanbul in November 2006 was historical not only for relations between the Eastern and Western Churches but also for Christianity and Islam. The then newly elected pope continued a tradition established by his predecessor, the late Pope John Paul II, who visited the Phanar immediately after his election in 1978.

We affectionately recall how Ecumenical Patriarch Athenagoras (1886–1972), an extraordinary leader of profound vision and ecumenical sensitivity, a tall man with piercing eyes, would resolve conflict by inviting the embattled parties to meet, saying to them, "Come, let us look one another in the eyes." This means that we must listen more carefully, "look one another" more deeply "in the eyes." St. Nilus of Ancyra wrote, "You are a world within the world; look inside yourself and there you will see God and the whole creation."[22] Each of us constitutes a living icon of the divine Creator. And we are, furthermore, always, whether we know it or not, closer to one another in more ways than we are distant—closer than we might ever suspect or even imagine.

OPENING UP TO CREATION: THE WAY OF THE EARTH

Speaking of icons when it comes to God and creation leads us to our final point. For nowhere is the sense of openness more apparent than in

---

22. St. Nilus of Ancyra, a fifth-century Greek ascetic writer. His *Ascetic Discourse* appears in volume 1 of *The Philokalia*.

the beauty of Orthodox iconography and the wonder of God's creation. In affirming sacred images, the Seventh Ecumenical Council (Nicea, 787) was not primarily concerned with religious art but with the presence of God in the heart, in others, and in creation. For icons encourage us to seek the extraordinary in the ordinary, to be filled with the same wonder expressed in the Genesis account, when, as we read, "God saw everything that He made and indeed, it was very good" (Gen. 1.30–31). The Greek word for "goodness" is *kallos*, which implies, both etymologically and symbolically, a sense of "calling." Icons are invitations to rise beyond trivial concerns and mundane reductions. We must ask ourselves: Do we see beauty in others and in our world?

The truth is that we refuse to behold God's Word in the oceans of our planet, in the trees of our continents, and in the animals of our earth. In that, we deny our own nature, which demands that we stoop low enough to hear God's Word in creation. We fail to perceive created nature as the extended Body of Christ. Eastern Christian theologians always emphasize the cosmic proportions of divine incarnation. For them, the entire world is a prologue to St. John's Gospel. And when the Church overlooks the broader, cosmic dimensions of God's Word, it neglects its mission to implore God for the transformation of the whole polluted cosmos. On Easter Sunday, Orthodox Christians chant:

> Now everything is filled with divine light: heaven and earth, and all things beneath the earth. So let all creation rejoice.[23]

The principal reason for our visit to the Unites States this month was the organization of an environmental symposium along the Mississippi River,[24] focusing on its impact on New Orleans; this journey was also a personal pilgrimage after our original visit to New Orleans after the devastation of Hurricane Katrina.[25] The symposium was the eighth in a series of international, interfaith, and interdisciplinary conferences, at which scientists and theologians, politicians and journalists gather in an effort to raise awareness on regional environmental issues that have a global impact on our world. After all, we are convinced that recalling our minuteness in

---

23. From the canon of Easter matins.
24. Held in Memphis and New Orleans, October 18–25, 2009.
25. In January 2006.

God's wide and wonderful creation only underlines our central role in God's plan for the salvation of the whole world.

DISCERNING GOD'S PRESENCE IN THE WORLD

Opening up to the heart; opening up to the other; and opening up to creation. Our age demands no less than openness from all of us. We hear it often said that our world is in crisis. Yet never before in history have human beings had the opportunity to bring so many positive changes to so many people simply through encounter and dialogue. The interaction of human beings and ethnic groups is today direct and immediate as a result of technological advances in telecommunications, mass media, and means of travel. While it may be true that this is a time of crisis, it must be equally emphasized that there has also never been greater tolerance for respective traditions, religious preferences, and cultural peculiarities.

The human heart, the other person, and the natural creation each constitute profound icons of the living God. May you always remain open to the heart, to others, and to creation. This is the only way to discern the presence of God in our world.

Georgetown University, Washington, D.C., November 3, 2009

> This address, "A Changeless Faith for a Changing World," was delivered at Georgetown University in response to an invitation by the Center for American Progress.

A CHANGELESS FAITH FOR A CHANGING WORLD

Thank you very much, Professor James J. O'Donnell, provost of Georgetown University, and John Podesta, president of the Center for American Progress. I am also especially grateful to the students who are present with us today, and grateful for their interest. Progress is often equated with change. So let us acknowledge this: It may appear strange for a progressive think tank to sponsor a lecture by the leader of a faith that takes pride in how little it has changed in two thousand years. The fact is that our first instinct in Orthodoxy is to conserve the precious faith that has been handed down to us in an unbroken line from Jesus Christ through the Apostles—in the case of our Ecumenical Patriarchate, the first See of the Orthodox World, through St. Andrew the Apostle, to whose see we are the two hundred seventieth successor.

But even though our faith may be two thousand years old, our thinking is not. True progress is a balance between preserving the essence of a certain way of life and changing things that are not essential. Christianity was born a revolutionary faith—and we have preserved that. In other words, paradoxically, we have succeeded in not changing a faith that is itself dedicated to change. However, permit us, as lawyers might say, to open with a disclaimer: By calling Christianity revolutionary, and saying it is dedicated to change, we are not siding with progressives—just as, by conserving it, we are not siding with conservatives. All political factions believe God is on their side. As Abraham Lincoln said of the Union and Confederacy, "Both read the same Bible, and pray to the same God; and each invokes His aid against the other."

The only side we take is that of our faith—which today may seem to land us in one political camp, tomorrow another—but in truth we are always and only in one camp, that of our Lord and Savior Jesus Christ. In his book *The Power of Progress*, John Podesta offers a lucid account of American progressivism.[26] Its core beliefs are in boundless opportunity for all, equal access to education, good jobs, fair pay, and the freedom to pursue one's dreams. It also encompasses personal and national security, respect for the environment, and harmony among nations. Although Orthodoxy has never taken up the banner of progressivism per se, over the centuries we have taken up many causes that are progressive by definition—and today we will discuss three of them in particular. First, nonviolence; second, philanthropy, and specifically in the form of healthcare; and third, environmentalism.

PREACHING AND PRACTICING NONVIOLENCE

Let us begin with a Christian concept that has led to some of the most significant changes of the past century that were not delivered at the barrel of a gun—quite the opposite. It is the Christian concept of nonviolence,

---

26. *The Power of Progress: How America's Progress Can (Once Again) Save our Economy, Our Climate, and Our Country* (New York: Crown, 2008).

even and especially in the face of evil. We noted earlier that Christianity is a revolutionary faith. The highest law of all is to love God and one another.

Now we all know the political and theological revolution that followed after the Roman Empire eventually adopted Christianity, which spread like a cleansing fire and rose to dominance in Europe, Asia Minor, Northern Africa, and beyond. However, we do not always pay as much attention to the revolution in thinking that facilitated this dominance. In the early years, citizens of Rome saw Christ's followers persecuted, tortured, brutalized, and murdered in huge numbers throughout the Empire. In most cases, Christians did not resist the evil that was done to them; rather, they went willingly to their painful deaths. Why was this? Of course they had faith—a giant faith, a faith rarely seen in human history. Many in the pagan world had faith but, when threatened, they relented. The world had never before seen anything like the willing martyrdom of these early followers of Christ. The world had never before seen it simply because it was a completely new and radical idea introduced by Jesus and described in Matthew 5:

> You have heard that it has been said: An eye for an eye, and a tooth for a tooth. But I say unto you, resist not evil; but whoever smites you on thy right cheek, turn to him the other also . . . I say unto you, Love your enemies, bless them that curse you, do good to them that hate you, and pray for them which despitefully use you, and persecute you.
>
> Matthew 5:38–39, 43–44

Now if that is not a revolutionary concept, we do not know what is. And the proof lies not only in the rapid spread of Christianity among the Romans who witnessed these martyrs and were awestruck by their example. The proof can be seen in our own time, in the civil-rights revolution that in less than fifty years brought America from Bull Connor[27] to Barack Obama. What made the movement unstoppable by any human force was the doctrine of nonviolence adopted by Dr. Martin Luther King Jr. in the face of evil. It is one of the most powerful ideas known to man—and yet

---

27. Theophilus Eugene "Bull" Connor, 1897–1973.

it did not come from man. In fact for human beings, it is completely counterintuitive—for our first instinct is to strike back, not turn the other cheek.

We Orthodox Christians will forever hold in our hearts the late primate of America, Archbishop Iakovos of blessed memory, who shared the faith, courage, and humility of those early Christian martyrs and joined hands with Dr. King in Selma, Alabama, in March 1965. However, there is another Orthodox link in this chain. Dr. King was extremely conversant with Christian theology, and yet at a critical juncture, early in the civil-rights movement, he began to doubt the power of love to resolve social problems. A chance conversation about Gandhi led King to study the Mahatma's successful use of nonviolence for freedom in India—and that restored Dr. King's belief that love was powerful enough to win civil rights for African Americans.

That story is well known. What may be less known is the fact that Gandhi's inspiration was an Orthodox Christian whose name will also be familiar to you: Leo Tolstoy, who in 1893 wrote a seminal book not about Christian ideas but rather about how to put those ideas into practice, especially the ideas expressed in Matthew 5. His book entitled *The Kingdom of God Is Within You* was translated into English in 1894,[28] and the same year a copy came into the possession of a young Hindu lawyer in South Africa. Gandhi found the book "overwhelming" and, after launching his campaign of nonviolent civil disobedience in India in 1906, would often be seen carrying Tolstoy's writings with him, even into jail. The two men corresponded until Tolstoy's death in 1910; in fact, the last long letter that Tolstoy wrote was to Gandhi.

Tolstoy found his own inspiration not only in the New Testament but also in the works of others, including the American abolitionist William Lloyd Garrison[29] and the pacifist Adin Ballou,[30] who took seriously the injunction of Jesus regarding how to "resist evil." But it is safe to say that, in the hands of Orthodox Christians such as Tolstoy and Iakovos, the doctrine of nonviolence led to some remarkably progressive achievements.

---

28. See the recent translation by Constance Garnett (Lincoln: Bison Books, University of Nebraska Press, 1984).

29. Garrison, 1805–79.

30. Ballou (1803–90) was a prominent proponent of abolitionism.

BYZANTINE PHILANTHROPY AND THE PROBLEM OF HEALTHCARE

Let us proceed to a topic that is extremely timely: healthcare, which epitomizes the concept of philanthropy in its most essential meaning, the word being derived from the Greek for "love of human beings." How many people know that the modern hospital originated in the Eastern Roman Empire, also known as the Byzantine Empire? It is widely acknowledged that the first hospitals were created in Cappadocia, which is now part of Turkey, sometime around A.D. 370 by Basil the Great, bishop of Caesarea. Since antiquity there had been a tradition of maintaining hostels for those without food or shelter or for travelers on a long journey. St. Basil was apparently the first to add doctors and staff to look after the sick.

Later that century, our revered predecessor on the Ecumenical Throne, St. John Chrysostom, opened hospitals in Constantinople, the capital of the Roman Empire. It is important to note that these institutions were funded by the emperor and by the Church, respectively—in other words, they were public institutions, free of charge and created for the public good. By the end of the sixth century, hospitals could be found throughout the empire. They were usually maintained by the Church, in keeping with the parable of the Last Judgment in the Gospel of Matthew:

> For I was hungry and you gave me food, I was thirsty and you gave me drink, a stranger and you welcomed me, naked and you clothed me, ill and you cared for me, in prison and you visited me.
>
> Matt. 25.35–36

Byzantine hospitals began as institutions for the poor, but by the seventh century they also began to service the wealthy, including relatives of the royal family. These were well-organized institutions—doctors made daily rounds of patients, except on Christian holy days; nurses or physicians' assistants looked after patients' needs and carried out doctors' orders, while orderlies carried out general chores such as cleaning and so on. At least one Byzantine emperor, Manuel I Comnenus, was himself a trained physician.[31] During his reign from 1143 to 1180, he personally treated patients in the Empire's hospitals.

---

31. Manuel I (1118–80) was a Byzantine emperor, who reigned at a critical time of Byzantine history.

In summary, it is clear that we owe to the Byzantines the development of the modern institutions we call hospitals. Yet, what may be more important, we owe to them the view that every member of society, from the greatest to the least, deserves the best-quality healthcare available at the time. This is obviously relevant today, and, as the Unites States government debates the best way to provide and proceed with healthcare for its citizens, we hope and pray that the Byzantine-Orthodox approach may provide a model worthy of emulation. However, just as every human life is a gift from God, to be treated with love and respect, so too is all the rest of creation—which is why the Orthodox Church has also been a leading voice for healing the environment.

RESPONDING TO THE ENVIRONMENTAL CRISIS

We have followed with great interest and sincere concern various efforts to curb the destructive effects that human beings have wrought on the natural world. We view with alarm the dangerous consequences of humanity's disregard for the survival of God's creation. Our venerable predecessor, the late Patriarch Dimitrios of blessed memory, invited the whole world to offer, together with the Great Church of Christ, prayers of thanksgiving and supplications for the protection of the gift of creation. Throughout the Orthodox world since 1989, every September 1, the beginning of the ecclesiastical calendar, has been designated a day of prayer for the protection of the environment. Nonetheless, it is fair to ask: Beyond any platitudes, what can Orthodox Christianity contribute to the movement to protect the environment? Fortunately, we have a very specific answer: We believe that, through our unique liturgical and ascetic ethos, Orthodox spirituality can provide significant moral and ethical direction toward a new awareness about the planet.

Our sin toward the world—the spiritual root of all our pollution—lies in our refusal to view life and the world as a sacrament of thanksgiving and as a gift of constant communion with God on a global scale. We believe, therefore, that our first task is to raise the consciousness of adults, who most use the resources and gifts of the planet. Ultimately, however, it is for our children that we must perceive our every action in the world as having a direct effect on the future of the environment. At the heart of the relationship between man and environment is the relationship between human beings. As individuals, we live not only in vertical relationship to God and in horizontal relationships to one another but also in a complex web of relationships that extend throughout our lives, our cultures, and the material world. Human beings and the environment form a seamless garment of existence, a complex fabric that we believe is fashioned by God. As human beings, created "in the image and likeness of God" (Gen. 1.26), we are called to recognize this interdependence between our environment and ourselves. Moreover, in the Book of Genesis, human beings participated in creation by giving names to the things that God created (see Gen. 2.19). There is no escaping our responsibility for the environment.

There is also an ascetic element in our responsibility toward God's creation. This ascesis, or self-discipline, requires voluntary restraint in order for us to live in harmony with our environment. By reducing consumption—in Orthodox theology we speak of *enkrateia*, or self-control—we ensure that sufficient resources are left for others in the world. We must challenge ourselves to align our personal and spiritual attitudes with public policy. *Enkrateia* frees us of our self-centered neediness in order that we may do good works for others. We do this out of a personal love for the natural world around us. We are called to work in humble harmony with creation and not in arrogant supremacy against it. Asceticism provides an example of how we may live simply.

Asceticism is not a flight from society and the world but a communal attitude of mind and way of life that leads to the respectful use, and not the abuse, of material goods. Excessive consumption results from estrangement from self, land, life, and God. Consuming the fruits of the earth unrestrained, we ourselves become consumed by avarice and greed. Excessive consumption leaves us emptied, out of touch with our deepest self. Thus, asceticism is a corrective practice, a vision of repentance. Such a vision can lead us from repentance to return, the return to a world in which we give as well as take from creation in an act of reciprocity and respect.

We are of the deeply held belief that many human beings have come to behave as materialistic tyrants. Those that tyrannize the earth are, sadly, tyrannized themselves. We have been called by God to "be fruitful, increase and have dominion in the earth" (Gen. 1.28). Yet, dominion is not domination; it is an eschatological sign of the perfect kingdom of God, where corruption and death are no more. If human beings treated one another's personal property the way they sometimes treat their natural environment, we would regard that behavior as antisocial. Indeed, we would impose the judicial measures necessary to restore wrongly appropriated personal possessions. It is, therefore, appropriate for us to seek ethical and even legal recourse, where possible, in matters of ecological crimes.

It follows, then, as we have repeatedly observed, that to commit a crime against the natural world is a sin. For humans to cause the extinction of species and to destroy the biological diversity of God's creation; for humans to degrade the integrity of the earth by causing changes in its climate, by stripping the earth of its natural forests, or destroying its wetlands; for humans to injure other humans with disease; for humans to contaminate the earth's waters, its land, its air, and its very life with poisonous substances—all these are sins. Consequently, in prayer, we should ask for the forgiveness of sins committed both willingly and unwillingly. And it is certainly God's forgiveness that we must ask, for having caused harm to His creation.

In this way, we can begin the process of healing our natural environment, which was blessed with beauty and created in love by God. Then we may also begin to participate responsibly, as persons making informed choices both in the integrated whole of creation and within our own souls. It is with that understanding that we have called on the world's leaders to take action in order to halt the destructive changes to global climate that are being caused by human activity. This common cause unites all humankind—just as the waters of the world are all united. To save one river is to save all the rivers and all the oceans. God created heaven and earth as a united whole, and we must assume a holistic view of creation. For us, at the Patriarchate, "Ecumenical" is more than simply a name or label; it is a worldview and way of life.

THE LORD FILLS ALL CREATION

We hope that the three examples we have chosen—nonviolent pursuit of social change; care for the health and welfare of all in the community; as well as respect and love for the environment as God's creation—will serve to illustrate some of the ways in which one of the most conservative members of the Christian family has played a role in some otherwise progressive causes. However, we also hope we have made clear that neither these liberal causes nor any conservative causes that we choose to undertake—none of these things define the Church of God, no matter what any human being may assert. The Church encompasses all of God's creation; indeed, that is our key theme for today—that we are all interconnected and that the connection is God.

The Lord fills all of creation with His divine presence in one continuous connection from the substance of atoms to the mind of God. Let us work together to renew the harmony between heaven and earth as well as to transfigure every detail, every particle of life. Let us love one another and lovingly learn from one another, for the edification of God's people, for the sanctification of God's creation, and for the glorification of God's most holy name.

Scholarly Conferences and Occasions

British Museum, London, November 12, 1993

> The original title of this address was "'*Mnemosyne*' and the Children of Memory."

TRUTH AND MEMORY: THE MUSE OF HISTORY

Thank you, Sir Steven Runciman, for your kind words.[32] We deeply appreciate them, as they come from a great churchman, historian, and scholar of the Eastern Roman Empire—from one who has made the world more aware of the glorious history and legacy of the Orthodox Christian Church. We express our sincerest to Dr. Robert Anderson, director of the British Museum, for offering this great museum, or "seat of

---

32. Sir Steven Runciman (1903–2000) was a British historian and prolific author on the Crusades and the Middle Ages. Many of his seminal works also dealt with the Eastern Church. See, for example, *The Fall of Constantinople, 1453* (Cambridge: Cambridge University Press, 1965), *The Great Church in Captivity: A Study of the Patriarchate of Constantinople from the Eve of the Turkish Conquest to the Greek War of Independence* (London: Cambridge University Press, 1968), and *The Byzantine Theocracy* (Cambridge: Cambridge University Press, 1977).

the muses," for our discussion of *"Mnemosyne* and the Children of Memory." And we extend our greetings to all the children of God who have come together for this conference. In Greek mythology, Mnemosyne, or Memory, had several children—Clio, Euterpe, Thalia, Melpomene, Terpsichore, Erato, Polymnia, Urania, and their leader Calliope. Collectively known as the Muses, they came to be associated with the liberal arts and sciences.

Our own expertise lies not so much in the liberal arts as in the spiritual arts. However, one child in particular of Mnemosyne is no stranger to the Church, and that is Clio, the muse of history. In the Church, Clio appears in two forms: spiritual history, the incarnation of the eternal Logos, the Word of God, revealed in the Bible, expounded in Holy Tradition, and immune to change from the beginning of time; and secular history, the word of man, offered in books, whose interpretation changes from generation to generation. The Church protects and defends its spiritual history. But the Church has somehow been marginalized and excluded from secular history—at great cost not only to Greek Orthodoxy but to the entire human family. This is what we wish to speak to you about today—not just about Mnemosyne but also about its counterpart, Lethe, the river of oblivion, of forgetfulness.

You might be forgiven, after speaking to the average person, for thinking that the history of Christianity starts with Jesus Christ, moves on with St. Paul at Corinth and Ephesus, continues with the bishop of Rome, and ends with the Protestant Reformation. Mnemosyne has certainly forgotten Romiosyne![33] The history and life-giving legacy of Orthodox Christianity have been lost in the waters of oblivion. The reasons for this are complex. They have to do with the miraculous predominance of the West since the Renaissance. We must remember that it is the victor who writes history—and Western historians by and large believe that the Roman Empire fell in A.D. 476. They tend to forget, or pass over in silence, that Constantine the Great moved the capital of the Empire to New Rome, or Constantinople, in 330. How many of us realize, for example, that all seven ecumenical councils of undivided Christianity were held not in Greece or Rome but in the East, in what is now Turkey?

---

33. Here used in the sense of the Greek (or Hellenistic) Orthodox (or Byzantine) ideals, culture, and faith.

WESTERN PERCEPTION OF BYZANTINE HISTORY

What really happened in 476 was that the West was overrun by barbarians, and the Greco-Roman civilization that once extended throughout the Empire was shattered. To give some measure of how distant we grew over the centuries, consider the unusual name Western historians gave the Eastern Roman Empire when they "rediscovered" it in the sixteenth century: Byzantium, the pagan, pre-Roman, and pre-Christian name of what was then Constantinople (and is now Istanbul). This was perhaps a logical step for those historians. For centuries after Rome fell, barbarian kings, whose claim to authority was based on force, grabbed at the glorious mantle of Rome in order to borrow legitimacy. So powerful did the idea of Rome remain in the popular imagination! The Renaissance was supposed to be a "rebirth" of classical civilization, and to some degree it was. Western scholars created a different name for the New Rome that had not only survived but flourished another millennium in the East: Thus was born the term "Byzantine empire." We live in a world dominated by the West and by Western ideas. We admire those ideas and admit to their power. Yet there must be a way for us to do so without betraying our own history. We must summon Clio to speak her truth, which is stronger than any power.

There is another factor at work here. Besides writing history, the West has also long dictated preferences. The interest that Renaissance scholars took in the Eastern Roman Empire and its Church may have been lopsided, even condescending, but at least we were considered a legitimate field of study. But then came the Enlightenment, which made it fashionable to look down on anything "eastern" or "spiritual." Voltaire called Byzantine history "nothing but declamations and miracles . . . a disgrace to the human mind,"[34] while Gibbon described the later Roman Empire as "the triumph of barbarism and religion."[35] The Enlightenment set the stage for the national revolutions of the nineteenth century, and its anticlerical tone influenced all of them. Our Western civilization found it difficult to comprehend the mysticism of the East, which felt the presence

---

34. Voltaire (1694–1778) authored, among other works, *History of the Russian Empire under Peter the Great*, 2 volumes.

35. The classic work by Edward Gibbon (1737–94) is *The History of the Decline and Fall of the Roman Empire*, 6 volumes.

of our Lord Christ, the Theotokos (or Mother of God), the myriads of angels, and thousands of saints.

We must also decry the simplification of Byzantium as "Greek." The Roman Empire was, first and foremost, ecumenical. Whether Latin or Greek predominated in Constantinople, ours was a multiethnic empire, with the Church willing to use the local language to convey the word of God. Thus were the Slavs and others converted to Orthodoxy and brought into the orbit of our Roman civilization. And the ecumenical idea, the notion that held together the diverse Christian communities under the rubric of Rome, was reinforced under the Ottomans—whose own empire, let us remember, was also multiethnic and often tolerant. It was Mehmet II,[36] conqueror of Constantinople, who sought out the greatest ecclesiastical personality of the time, George Scholarios,[37] and enthroned him as Ecumenical Patriarch Gennadios, head of the "Rum Millet"[38] and spiritual leader of the entire Orthodox world.

The Mother Church was the repository of memory, our Mnemosyne, during those difficult centuries, and we who continue that tradition today are her children. Let us be clear about this: The memory preserved by the Church during the Ottoman years was not that of a single ethnic group, whether Greek or otherwise. As shown in Dr. Runciman's great books,[39] the memory preserved by the Mother Church throughout the centuries was in fact the memory of an Orthodox ecumenical civilization. However, in the early nineteenth century, Mnemosyne was smiling on individual ethnic histories, while Lethe was swallowing up ecumenical Orthodoxy. And almost two centuries later, as the chief representative of the Orthodox oikoumene stands here before some of the greatest monuments of ancient Greece, we have yet to reconcile nationalism and orthodoxy. The Mother Church believes that, before this reconciliation can occur, Mnemosyne must reclaim ecumenical Orthodoxy—the wayward child we gave

---

36. 1432–81.

37. Gennadios Scholarios (1400–73) was the first patriarch of Constantinople under Ottoman rule.

38. The Christian community under Ottoman rule.

39. See especially *The Great Church in Captivity* (Cambridge: Cambridge University Press, 1968); and *The Byzantine Theocracy* (Cambridge: Cambridge University Press, 1977).

up early last century. We must recover our Orthodox faith and heritage and proclaim its virtues.

THE CHURCH OF CONSTANTINOPLE AND THE BANE OF NATIONALISM

At this point we must mention the similar treatment accorded our Muslim neighbors. For they, too, have seen their faith dissected and their history disfigured. This is why the Ecumenical Patriarchate is a sponsor of "a dialogue of loving truth" between Muslims and Orthodox Christians. We hope to put behind what is unpleasant while putting forward the best values of humankind. We have a sacred duty, especially in light of our 540 years of coexistence in a predominantly Muslim milieu, to affirm the Christian gospel that we must "love God with all our heart, and love our neighbor as our self." As leaders, we must stand prophetically and work together for tolerance and coexistence among those of different faiths, for the benefit of all. We must set aside our differences and learn to "speak the truth in love," as persons created in the image of the one, true God.

Entire libraries have been written about nationalism. A curious element of most expressions of nationalism is their combination of distant memories with new ideas. In art, this combination of old and new is called "postmodernism," and state-builders are certainly "artists" in the most literal sense of the word. The genesis of nationalism involves selective memory; and, in the case of the Orthodox countries, nationalism has favored past periods of ethnic glory over the combined splendor of Orthodox civilization.

We deeply lament this imbalance. Without the Church, we—particularly within the Orthodox tradition—can never have more than a lopsided, skewed, and incomplete view of who we are. The emphasis on national or ethnic heritage has had the effect of fragmenting the family of our ecumenical civilizations—from Russians and Georgians to Albanians and Romanians. This is particularly disturbing because nationalism is a phenomenon with disastrous consequences. The holy Orthodox Church searched long for a language with which to address nationalism, amid the strife and havoc this new ideology created in the Orthodox lands of Eastern Europe and for much of the nineteenth century. Thus, in 1872, the

Holy Synod issued a definitive condemnation of the sin of phyletism,[40] declaring, "We renounce, censure and condemn racism; that is racial discrimination, ethnic feuds, hatreds and dissensions within the Church of Christ."

Today, more than a century later, nationalism remains the bane of our ecumenical Church. It is time for us to begin to reconcile nationalism and ecumenism. They are not mutually exclusive. That is why the Mother Church has done everything in its power to support, both morally and materially, the reemerging Orthodox churches in Russia and throughout Eastern Europe, especially since the collapse of godless communism. Although these churches are self-governing, they are the daughters of the see of St. Andrew the Apostle. That is why we have spoken out in no uncertain terms against the proselytism by Roman Catholics and Protestants among Orthodox Christians in Ukraine, Slovakia, Romania, and other nations of Eastern Europe—where proselytism occurs as if these lands had never been Christianized.

Indeed, that is why we convened an unprecedented pan-Orthodox council of synods of the heads of the world's patriarchal and autocephalous Orthodox Christians in March of 1992—an unusual display of Christian solidarity and a return to the ecumenism of centuries past. Furthermore, that is why we also convened an assembly of the hierarchs of the Ecumenical Patriarchate in August 1992—some eighty bishops from throughout the world came to the Phanar to discuss the current status of the Great Church. And, finally, that is why the Ecumenical Throne, in cooperation with the other sister Orthodox churches, has been preparing energetically for the convening of the Great and Holy Synod of the entire Orthodox Church—the first such gathering of bishops since the last ecumenical council, which took place at Nicea in 787.

The Ecumenical Patriarchate must play a crucial role in our return to ecumenism. For the Patriarchate, as the first among equals, is the repository of the memory of the "one, holy, catholic, and apostolic Church." Within our walls, Mnemosyne jealously guards the candle of Orthodox Christianity from Lethe; and in that flickering flame lies the promise of redemption. As long as that candle continues to burn, there is the possibility that some day the flame will again pass outside the patriarchal church

---

40. Greek for "nationalism" or "racism."

of St. George and will cast its redeeming light throughout the oikoumene. But that will not happen until lay members of the Orthodox Church—academics, artists, businesspeople, writers, and intellectuals of all ethnicities—also begin to reevaluate the place of their Orthodox heritage in their identity. And in this, the Orthodox Diaspora can surely lead the way—for the Diaspora lives constantly on the borderline of civilization and is forced to reconsider questions of identity all the time.

THE SACRED LEGACY OF THE ECUMENICAL PATRIARCHATE

There are obvious benefits for all of us in this reevaluation; we will undoubtedly end up with a more balanced and more accurate view of our past and our future. Yet the benefits extend far beyond ourselves. If we respect our Greek Orthodox inheritance, others will likely respect it too. We may yet rescue our inheritance—our sacred deposit, or *parakatatheke* (1 Tim. 6.20)—from the oblivion to which it seems to have been doomed in the West. And in Eastern Europe, we have everything to gain by restoring a more ecumenical view. Those countries, just now emerging from decades of totalitarianism, desperately need the help and leadership of the rest of us. They too are the children of the Great Church of Christ, and, if we open our hearts and minds to them in order to include them once again in our oikoumene, then great things will happen. Fragmentation will give way to unity, Orthodox will greet each other as brothers and sisters, and we will echo the words of the Psalms: "Behold how good and how pleasant it is for brothers [and sisters] to dwell together in unity!"

Allow us, by way of conclusion, to reiterate that we do not envision the Ecumenical Patriarchate as another Vatican, nor are we trying to transform it into such. On the contrary, we have stated on many occasions that, even if such an idea were proposed to us, we would reject it as contradictory to the ecclesiology and traditions of the Orthodox Church. The Ecumenical Patriarchate does not desire to become a state. It wishes to remain only a church—a church, however, that is free and respected by all—that is to say, only a religious and spiritual institution teaching, edifying, sharing philanthropic ideals, civilizing, and preaching love in every direction. The Ecumenical Patriarchate is the fullness of the Church that was founded by the God of love, whose peace "surpasses all understanding" (Phil. 4.7). We pursue "what makes for peace" (Rom. 14.19).

We believe that "God is love" (1 John 4.16), and so we are not afraid; for "perfect love casts our fear" (1 John 4.16). Indeed, our philosophy may be succinctly summarized in the renowned words of the Apostle Paul: "Brethren, be watchful in your faith, be courageous, be strong. Let all that you do be done in love" (1 Cor. 16.13–14). This is our faith; this is our hope; and this is our prayer. May the Lord bless you all.

Theological School of Joensuu, June 28, 2003

THEOLOGY AS PRAYER FILLED WITH WONDER

It brings us profound joy to visit this theological school of the holy autonomous Orthodox Church of Finland. As your patriarch and spiritual father, we take the greatest interest in the studies that you are undertaking, and with all our heart we pray that the Holy Spirit will guide and inspire you in your future ministry. At our meeting together today, let us reflect on the meaning of theology. The understanding of the aims and methods of theology is significantly different in the Orthodox Church from what is commonly accepted by Western Christians. In the words of one of the early Desert Fathers, Evagrius of Pontus, "The theologian is the one who prays; and if you pray truly, you are a theologian."[41] This indicates at once that, in the Orthodox tradition, there is an essential connection between theology and prayer. There should never be any separation between doctrine and worship, between dogma and spirituality. All true theology is liturgical and mystical. We are to theologize, as St. Gregory the Theologian insisted, "in the manner of the Fishermen, not in the manner of Aristotle."[42]

This means that theology is not to be regarded as a "science" like, say, geology or astronomy. It is of course true that God has conferred on us a reasoning brain with the capacity for logical argumentation, and we must use this gift of reason to the utmost. In our theological inquiries we are indeed called to pursue the truth with vigorous discipline and a scrupulous respect for the truth. But logical argumentation and critical accuracy are by themselves never sufficient. What is required in theology is personal

---

41. *Chapters on Prayer*, 61. Evagrius lived from 345 to 399.
42. *Homily* XXIII, 12.

commitment to the Christian faith. We should theologize not only with the reason but also with the heart.

St. Gregory Palamas distinguishes three different kinds of theologians. There are, first, those who possess direct experience of the divine energies of the living God—that is, the saints; and they are the only true theologians. There are, in the second place, those who lack this direct experience of God but who nevertheless trust the saints, and they too can be true theologians, so long as they remain faithful to the testimony of the Holy Fathers. Then, third, there are those who lack personal experience and who do not trust the saints; and these are inadequate theologians. This formulation of St. Gregory Palamas may surely serve both as a warning and as an encouragement to us. We may confess in all honesty that we are not saints; for we fall far short of their example. Therefore, we do not belong to the first category of theologians. However, it is possible for all of us to trust the saints; and so, though we are not saints ourselves, we can by God's mercy find a place in the second category of theologians.

Plato insisted that "the beginning of truth is to feel a sense of wonder." Such is the beginning of theology. Without a sense of awe and reverence before the divine truth, we cannot begin to be theologians in the way that St. Gregory the theologian and St. Gregory Palamas envisaged. The theologian is the one who says, in the words of the Psalm of introduction at vespers, "Bless the Lord, O my soul; O Lord my God, You art exceedingly glorious, You are clothed with majesty and honor" (Ps. 103.1). The theologian equally is the one who says, in the words of the great blessing of the waters on the feast of Theophany,[43] "Great are You, Lord, and marvelous are Your works; no words suffice to sing the praise of Your wonders."

Yet let us also recall what happens later, at the culminating moment in that great blessing of the waters, when the celebrant plunges the cross into the waters. For every Christian, and not least for theologians, there can be no blessing from God that does not also involve cross-bearing, no vision of the truth that does not also involve sacrifice, no sharing in divine glory that does not also involve participation in the suffering and anguish of the world. The Crucifixion and the Resurrection go together in the life of the Christian, just as in the life of Christ Himself. The two form a

---

43. On January 6.

single event, an undivided drama. As St. Paul insists (and his words surely apply to all of us): "Dying, and behold, we are alive; sorrowful, yet always rejoicing" (2 Cor. 6.9–10). Such is the creative tension that exists at the heart of all Christian life.

Beloved students of theology, your work here is of incalculable importance for the future of the Church. Make the best possible use of your time at this theological school. Pursue the truth with wonder, gratitude, and joy. Always unite theology with prayer. Theological schools are often restless and unhappy places; may God grant that such is not the case at this school of yours. May it be, on the contrary, a center of peace—of a peace, however, that is not passive but rather dynamic and purposeful. And then, when your studies are completed, go out with courage into the world; go out to share with others what you have learned from your reading and your worship in this school. Be faithful ministers of the mysteries of Christ. May the Holy Spirit give you patience, wisdom, and imaginative vision. May the Holy Trinity—Father, Son, and Holy Spirit—bless you and watch over you, now and always.

Pontifical Oriental Institute, March 6, 2008

LEARNING FROM THE FATHERS IN A MODERN WORLD

It is with great joy that we accepted the gracious invitation of the Pontifical Oriental Institute to deliver the prestigious Donahue Chair Lecture[44] on the occasion of the jubilee celebration of the ninetieth anniversary since the opening of your doors, one year after being founded by Pope Benedict XV. The institute is of course well-known to us personally, but also to the academic world at large, for the research by its renowned faculty in Eastern Church studies and Eastern canon law as well as for its publications, its seminal academic periodicals and monograph series. We were asked on this occasion to speak on the theology that the Orthodox Church would expect from the Pontifical Institute as a service to the contemporary world. In some ways, the historical journey of the Pontifical Oriental Institute itself reflects the gradual openness of this esteemed

---

44. The original title of the lecture was "Theology, Liturgy, and Silence: Fundamental Insights from the Eastern Fathers for the Modern World." This address was part of the celebrations for the ninetieth anniversary of the Pontifical Oriental Institute, where His All Holiness completed his doctoral studies. See Introduction, 3.

institution, which has—especially since the mutual fraternal exchanges and ecumenical openings of Pope John XXIII and Ecumenical Patriarch Athenagoras—searched for ways of serving the unity of the Church as a whole. For this reason, therefore, we have chosen to explore the various principles of theology, as this was developed in the early Eastern, albeit undivided, Church of the Fathers and as it might further shape the theological work of your esteemed institute today for the benefit of the entire Church. In this regard, our aim is to discuss *the role of theology, the rule of prayer*, and *the power of silence* as these inform the ministry of the theologian in the contemporary world.

THE BREADTH OF THEOLOGY

"Speak a word to me, Abba, as to how I may be saved."[45] With these words, people have approached saintly men—and women—through the ages, seeking a word of salvation. What, we might ask today, is the word of salvation, the word that the theology of the Eastern Church, as the theology of the early undivided Church, can bring to the modern world? What is the unique theological word offered by the Eastern Church Fathers to a world that thirsts today for wholeness and healing? From the outset, it should be noted that Patristic theology cannot be reduced to a structured system of truths. Rather, it is the light and grace of the Holy Spirit that gives life to the whole Church and that in turn rejuvenates the entire world. Indeed, separated from the Church and the world, theology proves to be a sterile study of doctrinal formulations rather than a deifying vision of conviction and commitment, one capable of transforming the whole world.

This was certainly the case in Byzantium, where "religious" life encompassed every detail of "secular" life. Theological culture embraced every aspect, manifestation, activity, institution, intuition, and literary achievement of Byzantine society. This was because the Church Fathers were primarily *pastors*, not philosophers. They were concerned first with re-forming the human heart and transforming society, not with refining concepts or resolving controversies. Let us, then, examine some of the

---

45. See *Sayings of the Desert Fathers: The Alphabetical Collection*, ed. B. Ward (London: Mowbrays, 1975), 4 [Anthony, Saying 4].

fundamental aspects of Patristic thought, which should enlighten theology in the modern age, especially as this is developed by faculty and students in an institution of Eastern studies, an institution such as the Pontifical Oriental Institute.

Perhaps the most central theme of Patristic theology is the *dynamic nature* of its doctrine: the doctrine of the Trinity and its Christological doctrine as well as the attendant understanding of the human person and the whole world—all of which are never perceived as autonomous, static realities. This feature has constituted, from the earliest times to the present, both an innate *experience* and a continuous *expectation*. The all-embracing breadth of such writers as St. Symeon the New Theologian and St. Gregory Palamas is part and parcel of this dynamic worldview, sometimes obscured by Byzantium's more dazzling manifestations in, for example, culture and art. Yet the material monuments, manuscripts, and icons of Byzantium point in a most tangible manner to a more intangible spirit. Whether through an intricate analysis of doctrine and the study of the historical life of the Church or through admiration of art forms of perennial value, or even through repetition of liturgical phrases in worship, we constantly discover the same unique vision of a humanity called to know and to become God, as well as of a world transfigured in God and filled with His presence. It is in this context that the Church Fathers dared to expound the doctrine of *theosis*. To quote St. Gregory the Theologian, our fourth-century predecessor on the Ecumenical Throne:

> Admit the origins of your existence. Admit the origins of what is most important of all, your knowledge of God, your hope of the kingdom of heaven, your contemplation of glory. Admit—and now I speak boldly—that you have been made divine.[46]

This positive, open-ended view of humanity and the world implies a continual transcendence of limitations, a vocation to share in life, a vocation made possible in Christ through the Holy Spirit. All theology must interpret and defend this potential communion between God and humanity, communion as experienced by the Apostles and expressed by St. John the Theologian when he wrote of what the disciples "heard, and saw

---

46. Gregory the Theologian, *Oration* XIV, 23–25.

with their eyes, looked at and touched with their hands, concerning the word of life" (1 John 1.1).

Furthermore, it must be remembered that the Church Fathers never perceived theology as a monopoly of professional academics or the official hierarchy. No other age has known as many discussions and controversies—*homoousion* (of the same essence) or *homoiousion* (of a similar essence)? *two* natures in *one* person? *two* wills or *mono*thelitism (one will)? icons or iconoclasm? essence or energies? All levels—episcopal, monastic, and lay—were directly and deeply involved in these theological decisions. There was never any external, juridically defined criterion of truth; orthodoxy was the common responsibility and obligation of all. Naturally, in an un-theological world such as ours, it is difficult to imagine the degree to which religion pervaded society. It is sufficient to recall how Gregory of Nyssa described the unending theological discussions during the Second Ecumenical Council in Constantinople:

> The whole city is full of it: the squares and market places; old-clothesmen and food sellers—they are all busy arguing. If you ask someone to give you change, he philosophizes about the Begotten; if you inquire about the price of bread, you are told that the Father is greater than the Son.[47]

What, then, does this dynamic nature of doctrine imply for the role of theology in the modern world? First of all, it demands an open—indeed, we might add, ecumenical—worldview, whereby we are called to perceive the profound mystery in all people and in all things. There is always much more than meets the eye when we consider human life and the natural environment. We must at all times be prepared to create new openings and to build bridges, ever deepening our relationship with God, with other people, and with creation itself. We must never rest complacent in the ivory towers of either our academic or ecclesiastical institutions.

THE LITURGY OF THE CHURCH

Now, if theology is a communal experience, seeking, as St. Paul tells us, "to make everyone see the plan of the mystery hidden in God" (Eph. 3.9), the Church guarantees the normative continuity from the apostolic

---

47. *On the Deity of the Son and the Spirit*, PG46.557.

era, to the Patristic age, and on through our own time. The Church is most authentically itself, however, when it prays as a worshipping community. The unity and identity of Patristic theology is maintained precisely through the worship of the Church, which expresses its theology in liturgy. This liturgical dimension was the major means by which the Patristic culture and worldview were transmitted to other peoples during the missionary expansion of the Byzantine Church; it also accounted for the survival of the Eastern Church in times of turmoil. It was the aspect of worship, for example, that encouraged—and even served as a means to educate—Eastern Christians during the four hundred years of Ottoman rule as well as, more recently, during persecutions in post-revolutionary Russia. The Church Fathers continue to realize this dynamic symbol of unity and life as they are invoked at each Divine Liturgy.

So liturgy is an essential aspect of Patristic theology. Perhaps more than anything else, liturgy forms the very heart of the Christian Church. In the Eucharist, heaven is reflected on earth and earth is raised to heaven, as Patriarch Germanos of Constantinople[48] writes in the eighth century:

> The Church is an earthly heaven in which the supra-heavenly God dwells and walks. . . . It is prefigured in the patriarchs, foretold by the prophets, founded in the apostles, adorned by the hierarchs, and fulfilled in the martyrs.[49]

As we know, following the Edict of Milan (in 313), the Church acquired, among other things, the freedom to develop its public and external aspects. The effects of this were almost immediately obvious in Church organization, architecture, and, above all, liturgy. Christian worship, formerly the secret matter of a persecuted minority, now became an integral and flourishing part of daily public life. Indeed, particularly from the establishment of Christianity in the early fourth century, New Rome became the center of liturgical synthesis, while the Great Church of Constantinople was respected as a normative standard of theology and worship. This is especially evident in the many canons—for example, in the Council of Trullo (of 692)—regulating liturgical customs. As a direct result of this creativity, the organic development of liturgy never stagnated.

---

48. Germanos (d. 733) served as patriarch from 715–30.

49. *On the Divine Liturgy*, chapter 1.

The liturgy even served as an authority invoked by the Fathers themselves. The powerful liturgical tradition, the numerous liturgical texts, and the unceasing liturgical expressions (for instance, of the *akoimetoi*,[50] who "sleeplessly" performed the practice of prayer) all bear witness to the experience of liturgical prayer as a fundamental criterion of spiritual authority. This approach always distinguished the Eastern Fathers from their Western counterparts. The difference was never formally articulated or widely perceived. However, whereas in the West the gradual development of a juridical source of authority led to an understanding of liturgical rites more as external signs, in Eastern Christianity liturgy was envisioned as an independent, authoritative criterion of faith and ethics.

The Church, therefore, sees in the liturgical tradition an inviolable element of its life. The "rule of prayer" is an essential part of the "rule of faith." Without an appreciation of worship, any understanding of Patristic faith and doctrine is inevitably incomplete. Liturgy is "the melody of theology":[51] The readings, hymns, prayers and services of Byzantium reflect the theological, ecclesiastical, political. and social issues of that era. For it was the common cup of communion that nourished popular *spiritual life* while also nurturing sociological *thought* and political *action*. This is why St. Nicholas Cabasilas describes the liturgy as "the ultimate mystery, beyond which it is impossible to go."[52] And so doctrine is inextricably linked with doxology; theology and worship share the same language. As Metropolitan John of Pergamon writes, the doctrinal insights of the early Fathers are directly attributed to their experience as Eucharistic presidents of local communities:

> The bishops of this period, pastoral theologians such as St. Ignatius of Antioch and above all St Irenaeus and later St. Athanasius, approached the being of God through the experience of the ecclesial community, of ecclesial being . . . [The] Eucharistic experience of the Church guided the Fathers in working out their doctrine of the being of God.[53]

---

50. Greek for "sleepless ones."

51. From a hymn of the Sunday of the Fathers (of the First Ecumenical Council), celebrated on the Sunday before the Feast of Pentecost.

52. *On the Life in Christ*, book 4, 1.

53. See *Being as Communion: Studies in Personhood and the Church* (Crestwood, N.Y.: St. Vladimir's Seminary Press, 1985), 16–17.

This profound sense of community must, therefore, also characterize our theological perception of the world today. This means that no individual can ever exhaust the fullness of truth in isolation from others, outside the communion of saints. With regard to fraternal relations among our sister churches, the two lungs, the Eastern and Western Churches—to adopt the terminology in the exchanges between Pope Paul VI and Ecumenical Patriarch Athenagoras—must breathe in harmony. Neither should assume provocative initiatives, whether unilaterally or universally, in its ministry to God's people. Moreover, the same sense of community implies a responsibility for interfaith openness and dialogue within the wider global reality. Finally, in recent years, we have also learned the painful lesson that we are, all of us, together responsible "for the life of the world" (John 6.51), for the welfare of the poor, and for the well-being of the natural environment.

THE SILENCE OF APOPHATICISM

Finally, Patristic theology cannot be properly understood without an appreciation of its apophatic, or negative, dimension. Apophaticism is normally associated with the fifth-century writings of Dionysius the Areopagite. Yet, already in scripture there are allusions to this dimension, both in the Exodus account of Moses' vision of God and in references to divine light in the Gospel of St. John. Through apophatic theology, the Eastern Fathers affirm the absolute transcendence of God, while at the same time underlining His divine immanence. This ascent of the human intellect toward God may be described as a positive negativity; it is a process of elimination, something resembling the ascetic katharsis[54] of the soul and involving a rejection of all forms of intellectual idolatry.

Of course, classical philosophy and most religions adopt a fundamentally negative approach, inasmuch as they are aware of the awesome transcendence of God. Nevertheless, in Patristic thought apophaticism is not merely an intellectual method of approaching the mystery of God. It is not simply a more effective way of knowing God, through scholastic research. The Fathers continually confess the inadequacy of the human

---

54. The first of three key stages of sanctification underlined by the Greek Fathers: purification, illumination, and deification.

intellect and human language to express the fullness of truth. In the words of St. Basil the Great:

> We know our God through His energies, whereas we do not presume to approach His essence. The energies of God come down to us, while His essence always remains inaccessible.[55]

This distinction between divine essence and divine energies, so eloquently articulated by St. Gregory Palamas in the fourteenth century, communicates the conviction that divine truth is not discovered through the intellect alone; instead, it is disclosed in the human heart, through the Eucharistic community, to the entire world. Ultimately, the awareness of God's transcendence leads to personal encounter with the One who is Unknown. It is the knowledge beyond all knowledge, experienced as divine "ignorance."[56] And so theology transcends all formulations and definitions, being identified rather with a personal and loving relationship with God in the communion of prayer. As Evagrius of Pontus affirms: "If you are a theologian, you pray truly; and if you pray truly, then you are a theologian."[57]

In the final analysis, the Church Fathers are not philosophers of abstract concepts but rather heralds of a mystical theology. For them, the silence of apophatic theology signifies knowledge as communion at its deepest, its most intimate, and its most intense. In the seventh century, St. John Climacus experienced the same truth through asceticism:

> Stillness of body is the understanding of habits and emotions. And silence of the soul is the knowledge of one's thoughts and an inviolable mind. . . . A wise hesychast has no need of words, being enlightened by deeds rather than by words. Such stillness is unceasing worship and waiting upon God.[58]

The ascetic silence of apophaticism imposes on all of us, educational and ecclesiastical institutions alike, a sense of humility before the awesome mystery of God, before the sacred personhood of human beings, and

---

55. *Letter* 234, 1.
56. Cf. Gregory Palamas, *Triads in Defense of the Hesychasts* II, iii, 53.
57. *Chapters on Prayer*, 60.
58. *Ladder of Divine Ascent*, Step 27.

before the beauty of creation. It reminds us that, above and beyond anything that we may strive to appreciate and articulate, the final word always belongs not to us but to God. This is more than simply a reflection of our limited and broken nature. It is, primarily, a calling to gratitude before Him who "so loved the world" (John 3.16) and who promised never to abandon us without the comfort of the Paraclete, who alone "guides us to the fullness of truth" (John 16.13). How can we ever be thankful enough for this generous divine gift?

Venerable administration, esteemed faculty, and beloved students of the Pontifical Oriental Institute, we urge you to serve the theological word by breathing the air of theology and kneeling humbly before the living Creator. Implore God for the renewal of your hearts and minds; invoke His grace for the salvation of every human person, even, and especially, the least of our brothers and sisters (Matt. 25.45); and pray fervently for the transfiguration of the whole world, to the last speck of dust. May God bless you all on this historical ninetieth anniversary!

Opening of the Pauline Symposium, Istanbul, October 11, 2008

THE YEAR OF ST. PAUL

We offer praise and glory to the Trinitarian God for the spiritual banquet that lies before us and that we are blessed officially to open this afternoon following the successful conclusion this morning of a historical synaxis,[59] which has gathered the heads of the Orthodox churches throughout the world in a powerful and symbolical affirmation of our unity in faith and commitment of purpose as hierarchs entrusted with the leadership of our churches in the contemporary world. As we are assembled here at the Ecumenical Patriarchate, we recognize that, truly, "our ministry . . . overflows with many thanksgivings to God" (2 Cor. 9.12).

As we mentioned yesterday, in our address to our venerable brother hierarchs, this synaxis occurs in the unique context of a great anniversary for the Orthodox Church and, indeed, for the entire Christian world. While, according to New Testament scholars, the precise date of the birth

---

59. Referring to the fifth Synaxis of the Heads of the Orthodox Churches, organized by and held at the Ecumenical Patriarchate in Istanbul, October 10–12, 2008.

of St. Paul, the Apostle to the Gentiles, may not be known with any degree of certainty, it is conventionally estimated to be around the year A.D. 8—that is, two thousand years ago. This has led other Christian churches, including the Roman Catholic Church, to dedicate the present calendar year as the Year of St. Paul. In this respect, it was clear that the Orthodox Church, which owes so much to this supreme Apostle, could not do otherwise.

Bearing this obligation in mind, the Ecumenical Patriarchate decided to organize a journey of pilgrimage to certain regions within its canonical confines where St. Paul preached, and fraternally to invite all the other heads of the most holy Orthodox churches, so that together we may honor the infinite labors and sacrifices of St. Paul, all that was endured by him "with far greater labors, far more imprisonments, with countless floggings, and often near death . . . on frequent journeys, in danger from rivers, danger from bandits, danger from [his] own people, danger from Gentiles, danger in the city, danger in the wilderness, danger at sea, danger from false brothers; in toil and hardship, through many sleepless nights, hungry and thirsty, often without food, cold and naked" (2 Cor. 11.23–7).

This is why we deemed it appropriate, in the context of these Pauline celebrations, to organize an international and inter-Christian academic symposium, where select participants—eminent biblical and, indeed, Pauline scholars—from the Orthodox Church as well as from other Christian churches and confessions might address and analyze topics related to various dimensions of St. Paul's life and teaching as we journey in pilgrimage and visit the sacred places where Paul of Tarsus preached and ministered. The final texts of their presentations will be published in a special commemorative volume,[60] which, we hope, will contribute in a humble but substantial way to the field of Pauline studies. It is a great joy, then, to welcome among us this afternoon—and for the remaining part of our time together in spiritual expedition—distinguished theologians from all parts of the world, representing the major Christian confessions, as they prepare to introduce to us diverse aspects of St. Paul's theological message to the nations, inasmuch as he was par excellence the

---

60. See Demetrios Trakatellis and John Chryssavgis (eds.), *In the Footsteps of St. Paul: An Academic Symposium* (Brookline, Mass.: Holy Cross Seminary Press, 2010).

Apostle to the Gentiles. Beloved theologians of the Church, we are at once grateful and indebted to you that you have graciously accepted our invitation to join us and come here, despite your demanding schedules, in order to enrich this extraordinary assembly and exceptional journey. It is our fervent prayer that you will receive, just as you will offer, God's plentiful gifts in abundance.

While St. Paul was not the author of systematic treatises, it is generally acknowledged that there is hardly an area of Christian theology—of pneumatology, christology or ecclesiology, of anthropology or soteriology, indeed of ethics or ecology—for which St. Paul did not sow the seeds in his "bold" proclamation of the gospel. We look forward over the next few days to learning how St. Paul served as apostle and pastor, advocating in this fragile world the hope of the heavenly kingdom. We will also have the opportunity of hearing about the spiritual depth and ecumenical breadth that characterizes the teaching of this ruthless persecutor Saul who was converted to the remarkable preacher Paul. We will be guided through St. Paul's understanding both of the ecclesial dimensions of the gifts of the Holy Spirit and of the never-ending perfection of the "life in Christ." We will be introduced to the profound influence that St. Paul had on the early Fathers of the Church, both Eastern and Western; on our appreciation of the role of the bishop, both in the historical past and in contemporary practice; and also on the notions of race and gender, both in his time and as these bear relevance for in this critical in which we now live. To paraphrase St. Maximus the Confessor, St. Paul truly serves as a "mediator" and bridge, uniting earth and heaven, time and eternity, matter and spirit, male and female, East and West.

IN THE FOOTSTEPS OF ST. PAUL

In order, then, to realize the all-embracing importance and impact of this great Apostle, we have chosen to follow the footsteps of his missionary journeys through key cities of Asia Minor and Greece. Over the next week, we will quite literally be walking and conversing with St. Paul, discerning his traces and discussing his concepts. And so, in scholarly and spiritual fellowship, we will travel together from this City to Smyrna-Izmir (one of the cities along St. Paul's third missionary journey); to Ephesus (where St. Paul met "in the church in the house" of Prisca and

Aquila, those "who risked their necks for his life" [see Rom. 16.3–5]; it is in Ephesus where Paul also preached that "gods made by human hands are no gods at all" [Acts 19.26]); and to Antalya, the ancient Roman port where St. Paul preached the gospel and then set sail to Antioch (see Acts 14.25); to Rhodes, where an entire bay is named after the great Apostle, who landed there toward the middle of the first century; and to Crete, where Paul left Titus, who would serve as that island's first bishop. We can only be in eternal awe of St. Paul's remarkable endurance and perilous travels.

As will undoubtedly become clear from the proceedings of this symposium, the teaching of St. Paul does not simply concern the past; it has, today perhaps more than ever, immediate relevance, relevance for our age and for our world. Indeed, his teaching is extremely significant, chiefly with regard to his emphasis on unity, concord, and harmony in the Church and to the prominence he gives to the dimension of ecumenicity, openness, and freedom. For St. Paul, unity on the one hand and ecumenicity on the other are at once virtues to which we should aspire and gifts from above. Moreover, the concepts of unity and ecumenicity are not simply metaphorical but ontological. They constitute the very fabric and being of the Church's inner life and activity in the world.

St. Paul is justifiably considered the theologian of unity and of freedom alike. For, while he perceived the crucial distinction between unity and uniformity, he also professed the critical value of openness, or freedom, affirming diversity and discerning the joy of Christ in "whatever is true, whatever is honorable, whatever is just, whatever is pure, whatever is pleasing, whatever is commendable, wherever there is excellence and anything worthy of praise" (Phil. 4.8). In its catholicity, the Orthodox Church is truly and profoundly "ecumenical." Nevertheless, this catholicity, or ecumenicity, is not "universal"—either in the etymological sense of the word (from the Latin "tending toward oneness") or in the literal sense of all things being drawn to unilateral homogeneity. This, as we underlined yesterday to our brother bishops during the hierarchal synaxis, is the crucial basis of and essential criterion for Paul's passionate plea for Church unity "in the same mind and purpose" (1 Cor. 1.10). Nevertheless, at the same time, St. Paul prefers to emphasize "conformity" to the body of Christ—"until Christ is formed in you" (Gal. 4.19)—rather than "uniformity" in accordance with certain ethical prescriptions. This is a unity that can be realized only in dialogue and collegiality, not in any universal imposition of opinion or doctrine.

Beloved brothers and sisters in Christ, esteemed theologians of the churches of God, in welcoming you to the Ecumenical Patriarchate and our historical city we convey to you our warmest prayers for a successful and memorable Pauline symposium, and we close with the words of the Apostle to the Gentiles, assuring you, "then, that you are no longer strangers and sojourners, but rather fellow-citizens with the saints and members of the household of God" (Eph. 2.19).

Kadir Has University, Istanbul, November 17, 2009

> The original title of this address and conference was "Contemporary Perceptions of Byzantium." The conference was organized by the Istanbul Studies Center, a newly opened research institute at Kadir Has University.

EXPLORING THE SPIRITUAL TREASURES OF BYZANTIUM

There are many reasons why the modern world would have to be grateful to Byzantium. It is the Byzantine East that preserved the literary works of classical civilization and Roman law, making them available to the Western Renaissance. Plato and Aristotle would simply not have been known without Arabic translations of the high Middle Ages. It was the Byzantine East that Christianized the Slavic north and protected the European south from invasions by the Goths and Visigoths. The Western part of the Roman Empire quickly lost its power and prestige. The silent presence of Byzantium is still more far-reaching. From the forks we use to dine with to the hospitals we depend on for healing and to the academic universities where we pursue advanced knowledge, the legacy of Byzantium has proved a lasting and profound influence.

In fact, after the fifth-century collapse of the Western empire, after which the West entered the period known as the "dark ages," the eastern part of the empire for more than a thousand years continued to be a source of wisdom and a center of culture. Furthermore, the Byzantine currency, the gold *solidus*, or bezant, held its value for seven centuries, making it the most stable currency in history. Even on a social level, the Byzantines built hospitals and rehabilitation centers, dating back to as early as the fifth century; moreover, Byzantine laws forbade the use of torture in legal proceedings. The legacy of Byzantium is apparent not only in these secular and sociopolitical domains; it is still more evident in religious art, spirituality, and doctrine—that is to say, in iconography, monasticism, and theology. It is to these three areas of Byzantine life and thought that we wish to turn your attention in our address today.

HEAVEN ON EARTH: LITURGY AND ART

There is a well-known legend, preserved in the *Russian Primary Chronicle*,[61] about Prince Vladimir of Kiev, who sent a group of envoys throughout the world to ascertain the most authentic religion. He was determined to espouse the faith endorsed by the their findings. His ambassadors traveled to the Bulgars, to Germany, and then to Rome. Finally, they journeyed to Constantinople, where they experienced liturgy in the Great Church of Christ, still known as the Church of Holy Wisdom (or Hagia Sophia). Overwhelmed by the beauty they encountered, they reported:

> We knew not whether we were in heaven or on earth; surely there is no such splendor or beauty anywhere else. We cannot describe it; only this we know, that God dwells there among people. . . . We cannot forget that beauty.

In the ninth century, liturgy at Hagia Sophia would have been magnificent, even by today's standards, reflecting all the splendor and grandeur of the Byzantine Empire. The richness of the ritual, together with the large numbers of clergy and the glory of the music, provided a memorable experience for the visitors. What, then, was the Byzantine church?

The beauty of the icons and the glory of the architecture provided a splendid context for any occasion of worship. When Vladimir's envoys visited Hagia Sophia, icons had already long been established in the city of Constantine. They hadn't always been. What many contemporary Orthodox Christians take for granted, as they enter a church and venerate the icons at the entrance to a church as well as on the iconostasis, or icon

---

61. An early-twelfth-century document, which records the history of the Kievan Rus from around 850 to 1110.

screen, before the altar, is found in seed during the early centuries, although it is more fully and more formally developed in later centuries, notwithstanding periods of turmoil and controversy.

Ecclesiastical writers of the formative Christian centuries were neither immediately nor spontaneously open to the notion of religious images. They were influenced to a greater or lesser degree by ancient Hebrew traditions rather than by Hellenistic notions. And the Old Testament clearly expresses reservation with regard to images of the divine.[62] Moreover, the theological arguments of the opponents of icons were derived not purely from Hebraic sources but even more so from a fear of pagan idolatry and perhaps also from an unduly harsh criticism of Greek philosophical thought.

In fact, however, discoveries from archeological excavations attest to the presence of religious images in the early Christian church well before the fourth century. Didactic and decorative images, narrative and symbolical depictions, were introduced into Christian houses of worship and gathering places, as well as into cemeteries and catacombs, from at least as early as the third century. These images included symbolic representations, such as the fish or the anchor, as well as more developed depictions of the good shepherd or Daniel in the lion's den. For the most part, these images were recollections or interpretations of scripture.

These primitive stages and early seeds of iconography proved as decisive as they did definitive for the development of images in later centuries. The theological implication and doctrinal conviction—later explicitly expressed by St. John of Damascus, the eighth-century champion of sacred images—was that "God Himself was the first to paint and present icons."[63]

THE POWER OF PRAYER: MONASTIC SPIRITUALITY

The historical roots of monasticism lie in scripture. Among the prophets of the Old Testament, Elijah serves as the monastic prototype. In the New Testament, John the Baptist is the preeminent model of ascetic life. Moreover, St. Paul stands as one of its first theological exponents of celibacy. The many and diverse expressions of monastic life were developed

---

62. See Exodus 20.4–23, Leviticus 4.16, 5.8, and 27.15.

63. *On Sacred Images*, book 2, 20.

in Egypt and Syria during the third and fourth centuries, in Palestine and the West during the fifth and sixth centuries, in Asia Minor and Sinai during the seventh through the ninth centuries, and on Mount Athos from the tenth century. From these places, it was transferred to almost everywhere that Orthodox missions expanded through the centuries, with unique and popular expressions developing in the Slavic lands from the fourteenth through the twentieth centuries.

The desert of Egypt was filled with monastics, both men and women, who practiced one of three lifestyles:

the hermit life,
the communal life, and
the middle way, known as the way of the skete.[64]

These three ways are still found and, indeed, continue to flourish on Mount Athos, an entire peninsula in Northern Greece, dedicated to monasticism for the last millennium. Twenty monasteries and numerous sketes and cells adorn the spectacular Athonite mountainside and coast. Also known as the "holy mountain," that peninsula has been the site where many, both known and unknown, have lived holy lives.

Male and female monasteries have traditionally been places of intense prayer and spiritual direction. When a person has dedicated his entire life to the way of prayer, he may also be trusted to offer a word of advice. In fourth-century Constantinople, a monastery was established that came to be known as the brotherhood of the *akoimetoi*, or "sleepless ones." Liturgical worship and contemplative prayer continued without interruption all day and night, as monks prayed ceaselessly, in shifts, for the life of the world. People have always visited such places to discover men and women of prayer and holiness. Monasteries in the Eastern Church are not normally places of scholarship—although many monks and nuns through the centuries were renowned intellectuals and teachers as well as healers of body, mind, and soul.

One of the elders, renowned in more recent years for his spiritual wisdom, who offered such counsel to numerous faithful visitors, was Father

---

64. A small community of four to five monastics.

Paisios (1924–94). A simple yet profound monk, born of pious parents in Cappadocia here in Turkey, Father Paisios was one of those responsible for the rebirth of monasticism on Mount Athos, which was clearly waning—at least from a worldly standpoint of physical resources and monastic population—when we celebrated its millennial anniversary in 1963. After a period of retreat on Mount Sinai, Father Paisios returned to the Holy Mountain, where he directed numerous souls from throughout the world. He would visit my predecessor, Patriarch Dimitrios, when we were privileged to serve as the director of his personal office; we were most impressed by his silence and continued to seek his advice on a personal level.

Like many other saintly monastics, men and women, before him and in our own times, Father Paisios incarnated the words of one of the early Byzantine Fathers, Evagrius of Pontus (346–99), who claimed that "if you are a theologian, then you will pray; and if you pray truly, then you are a theologian."[65] Perhaps the greatest contribution of the monastic way to our contemporary world is its prophetic presence in an age of confusion or ignorance, when people tend to overlook the spiritual dimension of the world. The prayer of monastics sustains the whole world. Their primarily spiritual importance, therefore, becomes social, moral, and even environmental. In the fourth century, the same Evagrius of Pontus defined the monk as "the one who is separated from all and at the same time united to all."[66]

Monasticism thus provides us with a different set of values, an alternative way of living without compromising. It seeks to change the world with silence and humility rather than through power and imposition. It changes the world from within, internally, and not from the outside, externally. In many ways, authentic monasticism proposes a revolutionary worldview, especially in a world where so many people are stuck in established ways that have proved destructive. In many ways, the silent prayer of monastics bears greater influence and impact even on the natural environment than do numerous visible and loud actions that catch our attention. It is no wonder that so many Orthodox saints had a natural and friendly relationship with animals that lived near them.

---

65. *Chapters on Prayer*, 61.
66. *Chapters on Prayer*, 121–25.

THE ECUMENICAL COUNCILS: THE DEVELOPMENT OF DOCTRINE

It was precisely the ecumenical councils of the first eight centuries that finally determined and defined Orthodox doctrine. To this day, these "great" or "ecumenical" councils are accepted by both Eastern and Western churches. All of the earliest councils of the Church, which provided the definitive and formative doctrine of the Christian faith, were held neither in Italy nor in Greece but in Asia Minor. Indeed, all of them were actually held either in or very near the city of Constantinople.

And so, for example, the First Ecumenical Council (Nicea, 325) underlined the divinity of Christ, stressing that Jesus Christ, the incarnate Son of the living God, has one and the same essence as the Father. The Second Ecumenical Council (Constantinople, 381) confirmed the same teaching, declaring divinity also of the Spirit. The "Symbol of Faith," otherwise known as the Creed, was originally defined during these two early councils. It is recited in most of the sacraments but most notably during the baptism of every Orthodox Christian and during each celebration of the Divine Liturgy. The Third Ecumenical Council (Ephesus, 431) proceeded along the same path, affirming the fullness of the humanity of Jesus Christ. The Fourth Ecumenical Council (Chalcedon, 451) proclaimed that this union of the divine and human natures in the person of Christ was "without confusion . . . and without separation." The fullness of the human nature in Jesus Christ was sealed with the teachings of the Fifth Ecumenical Council (Constantinople, 553) and the Sixth Ecumenical Council (Constantinople, 680–81), as well as the Quinisext Council (Constantinople, 692), which insisted on his human will. Finally, the Seventh Ecumenical Council (Nicea, 787) affirmed the use of sacred images as genuine expressions of the Christian faith in the doctrine of the divine Incarnation. This final council was not simply the result of a debate or discussion on the importance of religious art. It is also a clear affirmation of the beauty and sacredness of creation and the natural environment.

What is fascinating and critical, however, about these discussions in Byzantium is that they were never the monopoly of specialists. Ordinary Christians were all involved in theological debates; everyone took sides in ecclesiastical controversies. St. Gregory of Nyssa complained that, during the Second Ecumenical Council, the city of Constantinople was filled with doctrinal discussions; "they were all busy arguing!"[67]

In many ways, it is rightly said that Byzantium is the best-kept secret in the West. Yet, as we have observed, it is not just secular achievements or social advancements that render Byzantium fascinating and formative for our contemporary world. It is—in many ways, above and beyond such invaluable treasures—the cultural, spiritual, and philosophical gifts of Byzantium that are far more impressive, though often unseen and unnoticed. It is these that, as a churchman, we have endeavored to bring to your attention in our response to your theme "Contemporary Perceptions of Byzantium," in order that you might consider their relevance for and impact on our world today.

---

67. *On the Deity of the Son*, in PG46.557B.

5

Messages and Declarations

Messages of the Orthodox Primates, Heads of Autocephalous Orthodox Churches

Ecumenical Patriarchate, March 15, 1992

In the name of the Father, and of the Son, and of the Holy Spirit.

1. Gathered together in the Holy Spirit in consultation at the Phanar, today, the fifteenth day of March 1992, on the Sunday of Orthodoxy, by the initiative and invitation, and under the presidency, of the First among us, the Ecumenical Patriarch Bartholomew, after the expressed will as well of other brother Primates, we, by the mercy and grace of God, the Primates of the local most holy patriarchates and autocephalous and autonomous Orthodox Churches,

> Bartholomew, Archbishop of Constantinople, New Rome and Ecumenical Patriarch
> Parthenios, Pope and Patriarch of Alexandria and all Africa
> Ignatius, Patriarch of Antioch and all the East
> Diodoros, Patriarch of the Holy City of Jerusalem and all Palestine
> Alexei, Patriarch of Moscow and all Russia
> Pavle, Patriarch of Belgrade and all Serbia
> Teoktist, Patriarch of Bucharest and all Romania
> Maxim, Patriarch of Sofia and all Bulgaria
> Elias, Archbishop of Mtskheta and Tiflis and Catholicos—Patriarch of all Georgia (represented by the Ecumenical Patriarch)
> Chrysostomos, Archbishop of Nea Justiniani and all Cyprus (represented by the Patriarch of Alexandria)
> Seraphim, Archbishop of Athens and all Greece

Wasily, Metropolitan of Warsaw and all Poland
Dorotheij, Metropolitan of Prague and all Czechoslovakia
John, Archbishop of Karelia and all Finland

have conferred in brotherly love on matters concerning our one, holy, catholic, and apostolic Orthodox Church and have concelebrated the Holy Eucharist in the Patriarchal Church of the Ecumenical Patriarchate on this Sunday, which for centuries has been dedicated to Orthodoxy. On this occasion, we wish to declare the following:

We offer, from the depths of our hearts, praise in doxology to the Triune God, who deigned us to see one another face to face, to exchange the kiss of peace and love, to partake of the cup of life, and to enjoy the divine gift of pan-Orthodox unity. Conscious of the responsibility that the Lord's providence has placed on our shoulders, as we are shepherds of the Church and spiritual leaders, in humility and love we extend to everyone of goodwill, and especially to our brother bishops and the whole pious body of the Orthodox Church, God's blessing, a kiss of peace, and a "word of exhortation" (Heb. 13.22).

Rejoice, our brethren, in the Lord always! (Phil. 3.1).

Be strong in the Lord and in the strength of his might (Eph. 6.10).

2. The Most Holy Orthodox Church throughout the oikoumene, sojourning in the world and being inevitably affected by the changes taking place therein, finds herself today confronted with particularly severe and urgent problems that she would like to face *as one body*, adhering to St. Paul's observation that "if one member suffers, all suffer together" (1 Cor. 12.26). Moreover, looking into the future of humankind and that of the whole of God's creation in light of our entrance into the third millennium A.D., at a time of rapid spiritual and social changes, the Church, fulfilling her sacred duty, wishes to bear her own witness, giving account "for the hope that is in us" (1 Pet. 3.15) in humility, love, and boldness.

The twentieth century can be considered the century of great achievements in the field of knowledge about the universe and in the attempt to subject creation to the human will. During this century, the strength as well as the weakness of the human being has surfaced. After such achievements, no one doubts any longer that man's domination over his environment does not necessarily lead to happiness and the fullness of life. And so humanity has learned that, apart from God, scientific and technological progress becomes an instrument of the destruction of nature and social life. This is particularly evident after the collapse of the communist system.

We must recognize, alongside this collapse, *the failure of all anthropocentric ideologies*, which have created in the people of the twentieth century a spiritual void and an existential insecurity and led many people to seek salvation in new religious and para-religious movements, sects, or nearly idolatrous attachments to the material values of this world. Every kind of proselytism practiced today is a manifestation of, rather than a solution to, the deep crisis of the contemporary world. The youth of our times have the right to learn that the gospel of Christ and the Orthodox faith offer love instead of hatred, cooperation instead of confrontation, and communion instead of division among individuals and nations.

3. All these call the Orthodox to a deeper spiritual as well as canonical unity. Unfortunately, this unity is often threatened by *schismatic groups* competing with the canonical structure of the Orthodox Church. Having conferred also on this matter, we realized the need that all the local most holy Orthodox churches, being in full solidarity with one another, condemn these schismatic groups and abstain from any kind of communion with them, wherever they may be, "until they return," so that the body of the Orthodox Church might not appear divided on this subject, since "not even the blood of martyrdom can erase the sin of schism" and "to tear the Church asunder is no less an evil than to fall into heresy" (St. John Chrysostom).

4. In this same spirit of concern for the unity of all those who believe in Christ, we have participated in *the ecumenical movement* of our times. This participation was based on the conviction that the Orthodox must contribute to the restoration of unity with all their strength, bearing witness to the one undivided Church of the Apostles, the Fathers, and the ecumenical councils. It was our expectation that, during periods of great difficulties, the Orthodox Church would have had the right to count on the solidarity—which has constantly been declared as the cardinal ideal of this movement—of all those who believe in Christ.

With great affliction and anguish of heart we realize that certain circles inside the *Roman Catholic Church* act absolutely contrary to the spirit of the dialogue of love and truth. We have sincerely participated in ecumenical meetings and bilateral theological dialogues. After the collapse of the atheistic communist regime, by which many of these Orthodox churches were tremendously persecuted and tormented, we had expected brotherly support, or at least understanding of the difficult situation created after fifty or even seventy years of pitiless persecution. This situation in many respects is tragic from the point of view of the economic and pastoral resources of the Orthodox churches concerned.

Instead, to the detriment of the desired journey toward Christian unity, traditional Orthodox countries have been considered "*missionary territories*," while missionary networks have been established in them and proselytism is practiced with all the methods that have been condemned and rejected for decades by all Christians. In particular, we make mention of and condemn the activity, against our Church, of the *Uniates* under the Church of Rome in the Ukraine, Romania, East Slovakia, the Middle East, and elsewhere. This has created a situation incompatible with the spirit of the dialogue of love and truth, which was initiated and promoted by the Christians leaders: namely, the late Pope John XXIII and the late Ecumenical Patriarch Athenagoras I. This has inflicted a most severe wound on this dialogue, a wound difficult to heal. In fact, already this dialogue has been restricted to the discussion of the problem of Uniatism until agreement is reached on this matter.

The same can be said with regard to certain *Protestant fundamentalists*, who are eager "to preach" in Orthodox countries that were under communist control. The consideration of these countries as "*terra missionis*" is unacceptable, since in these countries the gospel has already been preached for many centuries. It is because of their faith in Christ that the faithful of these countries often sacrificed their very lives.

In reference to this subject, we remind all that every form of proselytism—to be distinguished clearly from *evangelization* and *mission*—is absolutely condemned by the Orthodox. Proselytism, practiced in nations already Christian, and in many cases even Orthodox, sometimes through material enticement and sometimes by various forms of violence, poisons relations among Christians and destroys the road toward their unity. Mission, in contrast, carried out in non-Christian countries and among non-Christian peoples, constitutes a sacred duty of the Church, worthy of every assistance. Such Orthodox missionary work is carried out today in Asia and Africa, and it is worthy of every pan-Orthodox and pan-Christian support.

5. Moved by the spirit of reconciliation, the Orthodox Church has participated actively for many decades in the effort to restore *Christian*

unity, which constitutes the express and inviolable command of the Lord (see John 17.21). The participation of the Orthodox Church as a whole in the *World Council of Churches* aims precisely at this. It is for this reason that she does not approve of any tendency to undermine this initial aim for the sake of other interests and expediencies. For the same reason, the Orthodox strongly disapprove of certain recent developments within the ecumenical context, such as the ordination of women to the priesthood and the use of inclusive language in reference to God, which creates serious obstacles to the restoration of unity. In the same spirit of reconciliation we express the hope that the progress made in certain dialogues, such as the dialogue with the Oriental Orthodox (non-Chalcedonians), may lead to favorable results once the remaining obstacles have been overcome.

6. Now, at the end of the second millennium A.D., turning our thoughts more specifically to the general problems of the contemporary world and sharing in the hope but also in the anxieties of humankind, we observe the following:

The rapid progress of technology and the sciences, the means by which the instruments are provided for improving the quality of life and for the relief of pain, misfortune, and illnesses, is unfortunately not always accompanied by an analogous appreciation of spiritual and ethical foundations. As a result, the aforementioned progress is not without serious dangers.

And so, in social life, the accumulation of the privileges we gain through this progress and the power proceeding from it benefits only a segment of humanity. This exacerbates the misfortune of other people and creates an impetus for agitation or even war. The coexistence of such progress with *justice, love, and peace* is the only safe and sure road, so that in the millennium to come, this progress will not be transformed from a blessing into a curse

Tremendous, likewise, are the problems ensuing from this progress— problems for *man's survival as a free person* created in the "image and likeness" of God. The progress of genetics, although capable of making enormous contributions to combating many diseases, is also capable of transforming the human being from a free person into an object directed and controlled by those in power.

Similar, too, are the dangers to the *survival of the natural environment*. The careless and self-indulgent use of material creation by humanity, with the help of scientific and technological progress, has already begun to cause irreparable destruction to the natural environment. The Orthodox Church, unable to remain passive in the face of such destruction, herewith invites all the Orthodox to dedicate the first day of September, the day that marks the beginning of the ecclesiastical year, to the offering of prayers and supplications for the preservation of God's creation and to the adoption of an attitude informed by the Eucharist and the ascetic tradition of the Church.

7. In view of such tremendous possibilities, as well as dangers, for contemporary humanity, the Orthodox Church hails all progress toward reconciliation and unity. In particular, she hails *Europe's journey toward unity* and reminds it that within it live a large number of Orthodox, and it is expected that the Orthodox there will increase in the future. It should not be forgotten that regions of Southern and Eastern Europe have an Orthodox-majority population, which contributes decisively to the cultural formation of European civilization and its spirit. This reality renders our Church a significant factor in the formation of a united Europe and increases her responsibilities.

We are deeply saddened by the *fratricidal confrontations* between Serbs and Croats in Yugoslavia and feel compassion for all its victims. We think that what is required from the ecclesiastical leaders of the Roman Catholic Church and from all of us is particular attention, pastoral responsibility, and wisdom from God, in order that the exploitation of religious sentiment for political and national reasons may be avoided.

Our hearts are also sensitive toward all those peoples in *other continents* who struggle for dignity, freedom, and development in the context of justice. We pray especially for peace and reconciliation in the Middle East, where the Christian faith originated and where people of different faiths coexist.

8. This, in the love of the Lord, we proclaim on the great and holy Sunday of Orthodoxy, urging pious Orthodox Christians throughout the oikoumene to be united around their canonical pastors and calling all those who believe in Christ to *reconciliation and solidarity* in confronting the serious dangers threatening the world in our time.

May the grace of our Lord Jesus Christ and the love of God the Father and the communion of the Holy Spirit be with you all. Amen.

Sunday of Orthodoxy, 1992

Patmos, September 26, 1995

> Blessing and glory and wisdom and thanksgiving and honor and power and might be to our God forever and ever!
>
> Rev. 7.12

1. *Glory, praise, and thanksgiving* we offer to our Triune God for again deeming us, the Primates of the local host holy Orthodox churches, worthy to convene, by His mercy and grace, this time "on the island called Patmos" (Rev. 1.9), in order to celebrate together the completion of 1,900 years since Saint John wrote the sacred book of Revelation, the conclusion of the Church's holy scriptures.

Radiantly solemnizing together and concelebrating before the Lord the sacred commemoration of the holy glorious Apostle and Evangelist John, and partaking of the bread and the cup of our common faith, hope, and love, we wish to direct a message of peace and love to the faithful of our most holy Orthodox Church, to all those who believe in Christ, and to every person of goodwill, so that we might unite with them in listening to "what the Spirit says to the churches" (Rev. 2.11, 17, 29; 3.6, 13, 22) during these critical times.

2. Because *these are critical times indeed*, rendering the responsibility of the Church of Christ somber and multifaceted—her responsibility not only to her own children but also to all of humanity in general and to all of God's creation. The apostasy of man from God and the effort to deify human power and happiness or to transform it into the altar on which everything—human beings and all the rest of material creation—is sacrificed, both prompts and intensifies the crisis, which many characterize as "apocalyptic."

In these times, we believe it is our duty to underscore what *revelation in Christ* means for the progress of humanity as well as for peace and the brotherhood of all peoples. It is the responsibility of the Orthodox Churches to contribute in every way possible to the realization of these principles throughout the world, by becoming bearers and messengers of the spirit and the ethos of the Book of Revelation. Therefore, from this sacred place, sanctified by the Evangelist of love, we make an appeal to all—foremost to those who exercise power on earth and to those who live in regions of conflict and war—for peace and justice for all. To this end, we ourselves as churches are ready to offer our spiritual and moral contribution wherever necessary.

3. Through this appeal, we desire to make clear to all—and especially to all those who deliberately or out of ignorance present an inaccurate or distorted image of the Orthodox Church—that the Orthodox *perception of "nation"* in no way contains any element of aggression or conflict among peoples. Rather, it refers to the particularity of each nation and to its need to maintain and cultivate the wealth of its own tradition. In this way, each one, in concert with others, contributes toward the progress, peace, and reconciliation of all peoples. And so we condemn all nationalistic fanaticism, inasmuch as it is capable of leading to division and hatred among peoples, to the alteration or extinction of other peoples' cultural and religious particularities, and to the repression not only of the sacred right of freedom but also of the dignity of the human person and of minorities everywhere.

4. This message is addressed during a pivotal point in human history, a point that marks *the coming end of the second millennium after Christ and the dawning of the twenty-first century.* The Orthodox Church should not leave this to pass without notice, although certainly she does not ignore that the measuring of time in increments of a thousand years or other units of time is, in essence, a matter of mere convenience. That historical time is measured in reference to Christ calls all those who believe in Christ to note this historical hinge and use it as an opportunity to evaluate the great events during this century that is closing, while discerning the problems and the possibilities of the new century that is dawning.

For these reasons, the Orthodox Church intends to plan *pan-Orthodox celebrations for the jubilee of the year A.D. 2000.* The Church will offer doxology to the Lord of history for all that He has given the Church and His world during this century that is now coming to a close—thereby glorifying God "in all things," in the words of a holy Father of the Church, St. John Chrysostom. In so doing, we are cognizant that His grace, enlightenment, and help will be invoked on the Church and on His people at the beginning of the coming millennium.

5. In recollection, we observe that for the Orthodox Church the closing century has been full of important events. In various lands, Orthodox Christians have suffered cruel and prolonged persecutions. Their martyrdom encouraged the Orthodox to adhere to an ethos of evangelical humility and

of "the endurance and faith of the saints" (Rev. 13.10), to trust in Him who "went out conquering and to conquer" (Rev. 6.2)—to trust in Him with the assurance that, along with the life of the Cross of Christ, comes the experience of the Resurrection. The blood of these known and unknown martyrs connects our Church in a special way with the apostolic age.

6. This experience of martyrdom accompanied the theological witness through which patristic theology was renewed, while the teaching of the Fathers on the world and on humankind, as was well as on the sacraments and the Church, was affirmed. The rediscovery and creative presentation of the teaching of the Greek Fathers of the Church, the "language" and spiritual beauty of icons, the awakening of the missionary conscience, the flourishing of the monastic life, and the rediscovery and appreciation of the spirit of the Desert Fathers in conjunction with a fertile dialogue with the contemporary currents of philosophy and science—all these have made Orthodox theology a living thing and the object of international respect. It is for this reason that we must honor the pioneers of this theological florescence, pioneers who through their diligent endeavors led Orthodox theology to a common witness to the modern world, a witness that transcends racial distinctions and national boundaries.

7. This creative revival of the spirit of the Church Fathers has helped the contemporary theological and ecclesiastical world not only to renew the life of our local churches in general but also to offer to the various organizations of the contemporary ecumenical movement and to *the relative bilateral and multilateral theological dialogues* the witness of "the one holy, catholic, and apostolic Church." The ecumenical movement, whose presence toward the end of this millennium that is now coming to a close has been intense. It has revived sacred hopes among divided Christians, constituted a wide and significant ground of witness, and contributed to the promotion of Orthodox theology. Unfortunately, the crises and deviations observed during the last decades in the bosom of the ecumenical movement impose on the Orthodox Church the need to resist such deviations and to promote the genuine tradition of the Church. We also consider Uniatism and proselytism to be serious obstacles to the progress of our dialogue with the Roman Catholics and Protestants.

8. During these times of rampant secularization, and in view of the spiritual crisis that characterizes the modern world, there is an even greater need to point out and underscore the significance of *the holiness of life.*

The misunderstanding of freedom as permissiveness leads to increased crime and the lack of respect for the freedom of one's neighbor as well as for the sanctity of life; what is more, it leads to the violation of the natural world and to ecological destruction. The Orthodox tradition is the bearer of a spiritual ethos that must be emphasized particularly in our times.

9. This Orthodox experience and witness is offered in humility, fully conscious of our responsibility to the oikoumene, to all persons and peoples without exception, respecting the freedom and particularity of everyone, in obedience to Him who "was slain and by His own blood did ransom men for God from every tribe and tongue and people and nation" (Rev. 5.9). The horizon of Orthodox mission—in spite of temporal difficulties—remains universal, while its direction and expectation remain eschatological.

10. Most especially, with regard to the environmental crisis, which for all of us is crucial and perilous, we reiterate through this present message the vigorous concern of the Orthodox Church for the right use of the environment. Already during our previous meeting at the see of the Ecumenical Patriarchate, we expressed this conviction while recording that, by the initiative of the Ecumenical Patriarchate, conferences related to this issue were organized and September 1 of each year was designated as a day of prayer for the protection of the natural environment. Once again, we affirm that we consider this issue eminently threatening, and we call on all to be vigilant and to take every necessary measure to save and protect God's creation. The Orthodox Church considers humankind to be a steward and not the owner of material creation. This understanding is particularly expressed in the tradition and experience of the ascetic life, in worship, and, above all, in the Eucharist. It is imperative today that we all display love and maintain an ascetic attitude toward nature.

11. And so the meaning and significance of *the Divine Eucharist as the center of the Church and as a criterion for the entire life of the Church* is obvious. All the holy sacraments and the whole of Church life derive from, are centered on, and lead to the Divine Eucharist. Each Divine Liturgy, celebrated under the presidency or in the name of the local canonical bishop, is the axis and criterion of the entire life of the Church; it reveals the deeper and final meaning of the existence of the whole of creation: namely, its communion with the life of the Triune God.

It is, therefore, apparent that, on the one hand, the Divine Eucharist must always be celebrated in the name of the canonical bishop and with his permission, so that it is valid and salvific for the participants. On the other hand, the manner of celebration must be proper to its nature and character as an icon of the Kingdom and as the final meaning of all that exists. It is necessary to point this out because at times serious deviations are observed with regard to the permission given by, and the commemoration of, the canonical bishop in the holy anaphora, while the manner of celebrating the Divine Liturgy and worship occasionally reveals signs of influences alien to the Orthodox tradition.

12. And now, looking forward in faith and hope to the coming millennium, we call all people to prayer and vigilance in view of the grave problems as well as the great possibilities appearing on the horizon. The achievements of science in almost every area, particularly in biology, entail incredible successes but also dangers. The Church cannot remain indifferent to these prospective developments, since the survival of the human person as "the image of God" is at stake.

13. In the field of broader *political changes*, the Orthodox Church remains steadfast to the fundamental principle of noninterference in politics. To be sure, the Church cannot remain indifferent when political decisions affect the very existence of the Orthodox churches, in which case she expects that her position will be heard and taken seriously into account. We consider one such case to be the issue of *the future of the Holy Land*, its holy places and the living community there. This concerns the entire Orthodox Church and the patriarchate of Jerusalem in particular. Any discussion concerning the status quo of the Holy Land, which has been secured by international decisions and conventions over the centuries, should not and cannot take place without the knowledge or the presence of the Orthodox patriarchate of Jerusalem, which has been situated there for centuries.

14. In the broader field of culture, many have expressed the view that the coming century will bring humanity to "a clash of civilizations" in which the religious elements will be dominant. Such a possibility obliges all religious leaders to exercise wisdom, prudence, and courage so that every element of fanaticism and hatred may be eliminated, thereby safeguarding peace in a world that has been tried so severely by war and conflict during the century that is now coming to a close.

15. In a world confronted by all kinds of sects and terrifying interpretations of the book of Revelation, all of us, especially the younger generation, are called to learn and bear witness, in word and deed, that only the love of God, of our fellow human beings, and of God's creation offers meaning and salvation to our lives, even during the most difficult periods of history. The dramatic events depicted therein notwithstanding, the book of Revelation contains in its depth the gospel of Christ, which reveals to us that human sin and demonic destructive forces have been, and will be, defeated by Jesus Christ, the Lord of history, who is "the Alpha and the Omega . . . who is and who was and who is to come, the pantokrator" (Rev. 1.8).

From this sacred island of Patmos, we address this message to you, beloved ones in Christ, embracing you in His name and bringing to you and to all the world the voice of the sacred author of the Apocalypse, a voice of faith, hope, and love:

> Behold, the dwelling of God is with all people. He will be with them, and they shall be his people, and God himself will be with them; he will wipe away every tear from their eyes, and death shall be no more, neither shall there be mourning nor crying nor pain any more, for the former things have passed away. (Rev. 21.3–4)

The grace of our Lord Jesus Christ and the love of God the Father and the communion of the Holy Spirit be with you all.

Jerusalem/Bethlehem, December 25, 1999/January 7, 2000

1. We, by the mercy of God the presiding hierarchs of the holy Orthodox Churches, have convened in a sacred assembly and have concelebrated in the sacred church of the birth of the Lord in Bethlehem today, the twenty-fifth of December 1999/the seventh of January 2000,[1] the Feast of the Nativity according to the flesh of our Lord and God and Savior Jesus Christ. From the divine manger, we address this greeting of love to all our brothers and concelebrants throughout the world and convey God's blessing to all the faithful of the one, holy, catholic, and

---

1. The Patriarchate of Jerusalem retains the "old style" or Julian calendar.

apostolic Orthodox Church, as well as to all those in the world who believe in Christ. Brothers and sisters, rejoice in the Lord always!

2. We praise and glorify our worshipful Triune God, who has set the times and seasons according to His own authority, that He has rendered us worthy to celebrate auspiciously this historic anniversary of the Incarnation of our Lord in the place "where His feet stood" (Ps. 131.7) and where His immeasurable love "bent the heavens and came down" (2 Kings 22.10) for the world's salvation. At the commencement of the third millennium, the Church of Christ which abides in the apostolic and patristic tradition, beholds in awe the ineffable loving kindness of God, who, through the intervention of His love, transforms time from a vehicle of corruption and death to a source of life and incorruption, and from an ordinary measure of calendrical change noted for the human organization affairs to an awesome experience of eternity.

3. According to our Orthodox faith, the incarnation of the Son and Logos of God at a specific time and place signifies above all the sanctification of history and of the world, their sanctification through their transformation into the Kingdom of God. The division of history into "before Christ" and "after Christ" by means of the Divine Incarnation conveys to humanity the message that, from that day, time and history are comprehended and judged no longer by worldly power—whether political, military, or economic, even if such power should prevail for a time—but by the love that characterizes the Kingdom of God, a love that is the primary word in history and the temporal coming of which is signified by the Lord's birth of the ever Virgin Mary and through the Holy Spirit.

4. It is in the light of this truth that we celebrate the Feast of the Birth of our Lord Jesus Christ at this sacred place of its occurrence. We look back at the past millennium of the Church's history with thanksgiving to our Lord and architect of the Church because, according to His word, "the gates of Hades will not prevail against her" (Matt. 6.18). He has safeguarded the Church by the power of the Holy Spirit, despite persecution that has led so far as the shedding of blood. Indeed, throughout her long historical life, the Church has conducted a victorious struggle against manifold enemies. Having nothing to boast of except, in the words of the Apostle Paul, "her weaknesses" (2 Cor. 12.5), she is adorned with the blood of her martyrs and watered "by the streams of tears" of her holy ascetics. And so our Orthodox Church continues to hold up before the

world the Cross of Christ, who is "gentle and humble in heart" (Matt. 11.29), the one who loves all people regardless of race, color, gender, or any other distinction. He loves especially the sinner and the "least of our brethren," whom the powerful of the earth often sacrifice as virtually valueless as they calculate the achievement of their ends.

5. During her two-thousand-year history, the Church of Christ has often been wounded by the failures and sinful conduct of her members, both the shepherds and members of the flock. This has led outsiders, whether looking for a pretext or in good faith, to criticize and even engage in polemics against her holy architect and His precious body "which is the Church" (Col. 1.24). A most tragic expression of this sad reality has been the division of the Christian world, due largely to pride and human weakness. Those who love the Church, and particularly the bishops appointed by God to be guardians of her unity, cannot remain indifferent. The scandal of division, inflicted on us by circumstances and events in the Church's history, stands before us as an open wound. All of us are called to pray unceasingly for healing, to care continuously and to work untiringly for unity.

6. To use again words of the Apostle Paul, "forgetting what lies behind and straining forward to what lies ahead" (Phil. 3.13), we look to the new millennium with trust in the providence, love, and mercy of the all-good God but also with profound awareness of the complexity of the problems and the critical nature of the times and with awareness of the deep agony experienced in the world today. As leaders of the Orthodox Church, which has always been the helper of burdened humanity, we cannot remain indifferent to whatever the new millennium may bring— innovations that, like a two-edged sword, promise solutions to problems and freedom from various evils and yet at the same time portend new dangers not only for the integrity of creation, which is "very good," but also for the very survival of humankind, which is created "in the image and likeness" of God. In this spirit, we confess the incarnate and risen Lord as the Son of God, the only savior of humanity and the whole world, the architect of His holy Church; and we proclaim, as He proclaimed, and as our Holy Fathers taught, the way of repentance as the sole path to salvation for every person in every epoch and circumstance.

7. The present Eucharistic assembly of the presiding hierarchs of the Orthodox churches takes place in Bethlehem, in the Holy Land. Here we

demonstrate our unity and rejoice in receiving the grace of the Lord Jesus Christ, the love of the Heavenly Father, and the communion of the Holy Spirit. This blessed event is an invitation for us to kneel in prayer and to proclaim to all, both near and far, the heavenly message of the angels that sounded during the mystical night of the divine birth of the redeemer: "Glory to God in the highest and on earth peace, goodwill among people" (Luke 2.14). On this occasion and from this sacred place, we appeal to the powerful, to the leaders of the earth, to secure and solidify peace in this region for all people who dwell here and to respect the status quo that has prevailed in the Holy Land for centuries. In peaceful times, the visitation of Christian pilgrims from throughout the world to the Holy Land is truly a special blessing. Such pilgrimages raise the human spirit and renew every conscience in Christ. Through these pilgrimages, we experience and worship, in the words of the Fathers of the Seventh Ecumenical Council, "Him who was here nurtured and manifested and known in the flesh, Christ our God who freed us from deception." Moreover, standing on this holy ground, we perceive with greater depth the theological teaching of our Holy Father Athanasius the Great concerning the incarnate Christ: "For He became human that we may become deified, and He manifested Himself in the flesh that we may obtain knowledge of the invisible Father."

8. Again, from this sacred place and in the same spirit, we invoke the name of the prince of peace, Jesus Christ, and with great love call on all peoples and their leaders to work toward the cessation of war and to solve existing problems through peaceful means, tenaciously promoting and cultivating the spirit of reconciliation. Toward this goal, the Orthodox Church is prepared to contribute by whatever means she possesses, which cannot be of political but rather must be solely of spiritual nature. Religion must cease to be, as it often has been in the past, a pretext for war. It must become an abiding agent of peace and reconciliation. Imbued with this spirit, we look with shared hopes to all the great religions, particularly the monotheistic religions of Christianity, Islam, and Judaism, being ready to build the presuppositions for interreligious dialogue toward the peaceful coexistence of all peoples. By reason of the teaching of the gospels and our sacred tradition, the Orthodox Church rejects hatred toward other faiths and condemns religious fanaticism wherever and whenever it may appear.

9. In addition, from this position and in the name of the Lord Jesus, who "gave Himself for the life and salvation of the world," we affectionately stretch forth a helping hand of compassionate love to all who are persecuted because of their convictions and to all who suffer discrimination of any kind simply because of their physical, social, or cultural differences. The expected increase in the mobility of peoples during the new millennium may create problems of considerable magnitude and will necessitate the peaceful coexistence of peoples of diverse cultures. This development cannot be addressed through policies of assimilation and the leveling of cultural particularities in the crucible of globalization.

It is also necessary to draw the attention of all Christian believers to the appearance of new forms of idolatry—namely, to the apotheosis of violence, the worship of money, and the frenzied pursuit of pleasure. These dehumanizing phenomena foolishly threaten to take the place of the Triune God of love and to take the place of freedom, the notion that each human person is irreplaceable, and the foretaste of the eternal kingdom in communion with God, all which constitute the unique and true meaning of human existence.

10. Guided by a profound sense of pastoral responsibility toward our flock, we feel obliged to condemn the proselytizing by certain Christian confessions and groups in areas where, for centuries, pastoral care has been exercised by the Orthodox Church of Christ. If the principles of Christian ethics, the prevailing ecclesiastical and canonical structures in these regions and mutual respect and understanding on a true Christian level are not taken seriously into consideration, then during the next millennium unpleasant consequences will ensue among the Christians themselves. We hope that these Christian confessions and groups will respect the canonical rights, freedom, and truth of the Orthodox churches wherever they exist in the world.

11. The dawn of the third millennium finds humanity experiencing rapid scientific progress, which, together with technology, promises relief from many diseases and the improvement of the quality of human life. The Church with great joy commends all those efforts. Yet she also takes note of the dangers implicit in the radical interventions in the basic structures and genetic makeup of living beings. Similar risks are involved in any possible disturbance of the balance of the physical environment through irrational and prideful human interference. In the face of such

dangers, we call on all those in appropriate positions to define the true parameters within which science can judiciously operate in order to safeguard the freedom and uniqueness of the human person as well as the integrity of God's creation.

Beyond what has been described above, the great social problems already burdening individuals and nations will become explosive in the new millennium and must be addressed particularly with the help of the affluent nations. These problems include unemployment, hunger, the widening gap between rich and poor, oppressive forms of harsh labor, the commercialization of human life, incurable diseases, and generally the cruel pain that burdens a great part of humanity. The Orthodox Church deems it her obligation to minister above all to today's young people and to help them face the critical problems that concern them. The spiritual cultivation of our young people, their acquired ethos, and their social orientation will in large measure determine the future of human societies and of humanity in general. The inclination toward "the desires of the flesh and the lust of the eyes" (1 John 2.16), the falsely designated "knowledge" of new religions and ideologies, the use of drugs, and the thoughtless deviation from the life with God and into strange lifestyles—all these entail a spirit of corruption and result in the premature withering, both biological and spiritual, of the younger generation. The Church's care, affection, and specific pastoral ministry to children, teens, and older youth will be unceasing and unfailing, according to the example of love set by the Lord Jesus, who blessed them and is their eternal prototype. In this manner, the creativity of the young within the realm of the evangelical faith and the life of the Church will abound with rich fruit for the benefit of the world. For the Church's pastoral care extends to the God-given institution of marriage, which has necessarily always been grounded in the celebration of the holy mystery of Christian matrimony. The source of inspiration, strength, and enlightenment for the solution of the problems indicated here is the light of the gospel and the example of the saints of the Church.

It is also necessary to critique, on the basis of the same spiritual light and the criterion of respect for human rights, the observable international tendencies toward radical restructuring through which the formation of new states is attempted by means either of breaking up or else of unifying existing entities. In such cases, the free consent of the people concerned must be taken into consideration. Neither must their consent be ignored, nor must violence be used. In addition, we reject all tendencies toward racism and phyletism which are a distortion of Orthodox ecclesiology.

12. Brothers and children in the Lord, this sacred place of Bethlehem, an emblem of the world's focused spiritual interest, shines today with the grace of our Triune God and proclaims through us the message of unity, love, peace, and goodwill toward the whole world. The obligation of each Christian—in purity of heart, in humility, and in repentance—is to appropriate this heavenly message as the firstfruits of the new millennium. Let us not be overtaken by sentiments of fear and pessimism. The resounding apostolic *kerygma*[2] is both useful and timely. "Hope does not disappoint us, because God's love has been poured into our hearts through the Holy Spirit which has been given to us" (Rom. 5.5). Christ the Redeemer is the way out of every human impasse; for Christ gives His own peace to the world—as He said, "Peace I leave with you; my peace I give to you" (John 14.27). Christ is the savior of the world and of each one of us. "There is salvation in no one else, for there is no other name under heaven given among human beings by which we must be saved" (Acts 4.12).

The benevolent power of our Holy God in the world overcomes all human weaknesses. "What is impossible for human beings is possible for God" (Luke 18.27). We Orthodox Christians draw our personal rebirth and sanctification from participation in the sacred mystery of the Divine Eucharist, in which we partake of the body and blood of the Lord for the forgiveness of sins and life everlasting. Therefore, in our Eucharistic assembly today, we, together with the whole Orthodox Church, kneel in devotion before the almighty Lord, who shone forth from the manger as the Sun of Righteousness. He has given to the world a supreme standard of life. Through the Cross, He has redeemed us from the bondage of the enemy. He has granted us eternal life through His triumphant resurrection. We believe, hope, and pray that, starting from this sacred place of the earthly birth of the Lord and Redeemer, and always walking toward Him, we will journey into the new millennium, born from above through the Holy Spirit, brothers and children, since "whatever is born of God overcomes the world; and this is the victory that overcomes the world, our faith" (1 John 5.4).

May the grace of our Lord Jesus Christ be with all of you. Amen.

---

2. Greek for "preaching."

The representatives of the Orthodox churches:

The Ecumenical Patriarchate
 John of Pergamon
 Meliton of Philadelphia
The Patriarchate of Alexandria
 Chrysostom of Carthage
 Archimandrite Chrysostom Savatos
The Patriarchate of Antioch
 Meliton of Philadelphia
The Patriarchate of Jerusalem
 Eirenaios of Hierapolis
 Professor George Galitis
The Patriarchate of Russia
 Clement of Kaluga
 Hieromonk Hilarion Alfeev
The Patriarchate of Serbia
 Amphilochios of Mavrovounion
The Patriarchate of Romania
 Cassian of the Lower Danube
 Protopresbyter Constantine Coman
The Church of Cyprus
 Barnabas of Salamis
 Professor Andrew Mitsides
The Church of Greece
 Anthimos of Alexandroupolis
 Professor Vlasios Pheidas
The Church of Poland
 Iakovos of Bialistok and Gdansk
 Protopresbyter Anatolios Szymaniuk
The Church of Albania
 John of Korytsa
 Professor John Lappas
The Church of Czeckoslovakia
 Bishop Simeon
 Presbyter Stefan Sak
The Church of Finland
 John of Pergamon

Ecumenical Patriarchate, December 25, 2000

1. Having gathered with divine cooperation and by kind invitation of the archbishop of the city of Constantine and Ecumenical Patriarch in his see at the Phanar, and having concelebrated unto to the Lord in this historic sacred church of the Wisdom of God in the glorious city of Nicea, where our Fathers were moved by the All Holy Spirit and formulated the unshakeable doctrines of our Orthodox faith, the Primates, by God's mercy, of the most holy Orthodox churches throughout the world, address the Orthodox faithful all over the earth, our Christian brothers and sisters in the whole world, and every person of goodwill, with a blessing from God and an embrace of love and peace. Rejoice in the Lord always, brethren; again we say, rejoice! (see Phil. 4.5).

2. The festivities on the occasion of the sacred jubilee of the two millennia of Church life culminate in our synaxis. Through these festivities, the entire Orthodox Church the world over has offered praise and glory to the Triune God, who, in His boundless love and immeasurable mercy, has deigned that His Son and Word "may dwell among us" (John 1.14) through His incarnation, whereby "we have seen His glory, the glory as of a Father's only Son, full of grace and truth" (John 1.14).

3. In consideration of this great gift, whereby our Lord emptied Himself and, being humbled, assumed within Himself fallen humanity, for our sake becoming "Emmanuel, God with us" (Matt. 1.24), the Church of Christ, as His body extended through the ages, is conscious of its noble mission and profound responsibility within history. It beholds with a sense of awe its course over the last two thousand years as well as the impending challenges of the current age.

4. With respect to its historic course to date, the most holy Orthodox Church of Christ, filled with thanksgiving, exclaims in the words of that Golden-Mouthed Father[3] of the Church: "Glory be to God for all things." From the first day of its life to this very moment, and even "until the Lord comes" (1 Cor. 11.26), the Orthodox Church has lifted His Cross and possessed His grace, which "is perfected in weakness" (2 Cor. 12.9). Being persecuted by all kinds of enemies, it is victorious; and "dying

---

3. Namely, St. John Chrysostom.

daily, behold, it lives!" (2 Cor. 6.9) Calling to mind the Lord's words that "even the gates of Hades shall not prevail against it" (Matt. 16.18), and based on the power of His resurrection (see Phil. 3.10), it is not daunted by those who assault it, no matter how powerful they may be from a worldly perspective. Rather, it agonizes and strives for one thing alone: to transmit and embody faithfully the love of God that was incarnate and revealed in Christ for all people and all times. In this way, the Church and every individual—even the most despised and deserted person in the world—will feel that God is also for their sake "Emmanuel," that it is especially and primarily for their sake that God became human, was crucified, and is risen. And it is for their sake that He granted to the world His body, the Church, in order to gather the scattered (see John 11.52), to reconcile the separated, and to include in its embrace, as if in the embrace of God Himself, all those who "labor and are heavy burdened" (Matt. 11.28), righteous and sinners alike, both poor and wealthy, indeed the whole of creation.

5. When gathered in the Holy Eucharist, the Church realizes and reveals to the world and to history the incorporation of all in Christ, the transcendence of every distinction and contrast, a communion of love wherein "there is neither male nor female, neither Greek nor Jew, circumcised or uncircumcised, barbarian or Scythian, slave or free" (Col. 3.11 and Gal. 3.28). In this way, it presents an image of the Kingdom of God but simultaneously an image of ideal human society and a foretaste of the victory of life over death, of incorruption over corruption, and of love over hatred.

6. Bearing this message of unity and reconciliation as a sacred deposit through the centuries, the Church regards its unity as its primary and greatest concern and benefit. It feels deeply grieved and painfully wounded whenever or for whatever reason—although in its nature it always remains undivided—the seamless garment of the Lord is torn apart and its unity is threatened or fragmented. This is why, in casting our minds back over the past two millennia, we express our pain that, while, during the first thousand years after Christ, His Church experienced a common and undivided tradition, during the next thousand years the Christian world was lamentably divided and fragmented, to the great scandal of the whole world and to the impairment of the message of love and reconciliation, the message the Lord entrusted to us. Without at this

time either seeking or listing the historical causes of this division, we invite everyone to work in a dialogue of truth and love for the unity of those who believe in Christ. We should not spare any pain or labor but should "speak the truth in love" (Eph. 4.15), "without each one looking to his own interests, but to the interests of others" (Phil. 2.4). It is only through a dialogue that is sincere and without ulterior motives, based on the common and undivided tradition of the first millennium after Christ, that we are able to construct the unity that is so deeply desired and needed. And so the proclamation of love and of reconciliation in Christ will be more convincing to the contemporary world. This is what we wish to emphasize with respect to the overall endeavor for the restoration of Christian unity through the "ecumenical movement," in which our Orthodox Church has participated from the outset.

7. Out of concern, then, for the unity of all those who believe in Christ—indeed, agonizing and striving for such unity—we, being entrusted with the leadership of the most holy Orthodox Church, in no way ignore the necessity and obligation to care also for the preservation and increase of unity within our own Orthodox Church. We have received this unity from our Fathers as a unity in the same faith, in a common worship, especially in the holy sacraments, and most especially in the Holy Eucharist, as well as in the communion of saints who bequeathed to us an example and in whose footsteps we may follow. Indeed, it is particularly wonderful that, despite the variety of languages, races, and cultures, this unity pervades the entire body of Orthodoxy, rendering the local holy Orthodox churches a single undivided body—namely, the one, holy, catholic, and apostolic Church of Christ. We humbly recognize this as a gift of the Holy Spirit and safeguard it as the apple of our eye.

8. Those serving in the ministry of ecclesiastical leadership, having been appointed guardians and protectors of this unity, bear a heavy sense of responsibility whenever dangers and divisive tendencies appear in the holy body of Orthodoxy. We have, at previous synaxes[4] such as these, strongly condemned schisms that plague the unity of the most holy Orthodox Church. Once again, to those who for whatever reason have separated from the canonical structure of the Church, we extend the invitation to return. At this present synaxis, we regard it as our duty to remind

---

4. Greek for "gatherings" or "assemblies."

ourselves and one another that in no way should the historically inherited system of autocephalous Orthodox churches provide opportunity or ground for the development of an independence that acts against our unity. For, though we are many local churches, we do not cease to constitute one Church.

9. This reminder is most especially compelling whenever autocephaly is connected to the national identity and peculiarity of peoples. The diversity of nations and cultures is beneficial and blessed by God. Our holy Orthodox Church blesses and sanctifies it. Nevertheless, of its very nature, the Church cannot constitute a vehicle for the facilitation or propagation of political, nationalistic, or racial interests. The condemnation by the Orthodox Church of the heresy of ethno-phyletism at Constantinople in 1872 forever remains of critical importance. Any interference in another canonical jurisdiction through the establishment therein of bishops not belonging to the local church and its canonical shepherds endangers the unity of the Church and contradicts fundamental principles of Orthodox ecclesiology.

10. Every fragmentation of the Church's unity, on the pretext of preserving customs and traditions or supposedly defending authentic Orthodoxy, is equally unacceptable and must be considered condemnable. As the whole life of the Orthodox Church bears witness, diversity in customs in no way prevents eucharistic communion among Orthodox churches, while the preservation of the authentic Orthodox faith is guaranteed through the synodical system which has always been the ultimate criterion on matters of faith in the Church.

11. On this significant and historic occasion, we share these thoughts about the unity of the Church with believers in Christ throughout the world, especially with those who bear the name of Orthodox Christians, inasmuch as we firmly hold that, without unity in faith, worship, and the sanctity of life and unity in the episcopal and canonical structure of the Church, its witness in the contemporary world is in no way feasible.

12. This unity is not a luxury for the Church but rather a constitutive element of its existence and witness in the world. The unity of the Church concerns not only the Church in and of itself but also the unity of all humankind and the whole world. According to St. Maximus the Confessor, the Church is, depicts, and contains, as in seed, all of creation,

because it is the body of Christ, "who fills all in all" (Eph. 1.23). Consequently, in caring and striving for the unity of the Church, we have in mind the deeper human search to transcend various divisions, oppositions, conflicts, and battles. We also recall the human thirst for peace and cooperation as well as the vision of a society where everyone lives in harmony, "bearing with one another in love," in accordance with the apostolic exhortation (see Eph. 4.2). The unity of the Church is offered as a proper example for human unity, a unity that respects particularity among persons and nations in an age of the rapid development of various forms of "globalization."

13. And so we invite all those who believe in Christ to labor tirelessly for the restoration of the shattered unity among Christians, forging dialogues with one another in truth and in love. We urge all those belonging to the holy Orthodox Church to remain united around their canonical bishops, recalling always the divinely inspired words of St. Ignatius of Antioch, the God-Bearer: "Wherever the bishop is, there also is the Church."[5]

14. Once again, we assure everyone that, as responsible shepherds and leaders of the Church of Christ, we are vigilantly caring for its unity and for the fulfillment of its sacred mission m the world and in history. We attentively listen to humanity's anguish and expectations as well as to its fears as we enter the third millennium after Christ. We will do everything in our capacity, by gathering regularly in person or through our representatives, to secure and promote the invaluable unity of the Church of Christ. We will strive to render perceptible and tangible for the entire world the saving reality that, in Christ and through the Church, God is not far from humanity but rather is everywhere present and near everyone; He is Emmanuel, God with us.

15. Finally, embracing everyone, both those afar and those near, in the love of our Lord and God, who was incarnate for the salvation of the world, we pray that His grace and mercy be abundantly showered on all.

At the Phanar, Christmas 2000

Bartholomew of Constantinople
Petros of Alexandria

---

5. See the Letters of Ignatius, *To the Magnesians* vi.i, *To the Smyrnaeans* viii.i–2, and *To the Ephesians* xx.2.

Ignatius of Antioch
Iakovos of Laodiceia (on behalf of the Holy Church of Jerusalem)
Pavle of Belgrade
Teoktist of Bucharest
Maxim of Sofia
Abraham of Siatoura (on behalf of the Holy Church of Georgia)
Vasilios of Trimythous (on behalf of the Holy Church of Cyprus)
Christodoulos of Athens
Sawa of Warsaw
Anastasios of Tirana
Nikolai of the Czech Lands and Slovakia
Ambrose of Oulu (on behalf of the Church of Finland)
Stephanos of Tallinn

Ecumenical Patriarchate, October 12, 2008

In the name of the Father, and of the Son, and of the Holy Spirit.

1. Through the grace of God, the Primates and the representatives of the local Orthodox churches have gathered from October 10 through 12, 2008, in the Phanar, at the invitation and under the presidency of the First among us, Ecumenical Patriarch Bartholomew, on the occasion of the proclamation of this year as the Year of Saint Paul, Apostle to the Nations. We have deliberated in fraternal love on the issues that concern the Orthodox Church and, participating in the festivities of this occasion, we have celebrated together the Holy Eucharist in the most sacred Patriarchal Church of the Ecumenical Throne, today, the twelfth of October 2008, Sunday of the Holy Fathers of the Seventh Ecumenical Council of Nicea. During these days, we have been strengthened by the truth of the gifts of divine providence received by the Apostle to the Nations, the truth that rendered him a superb "chosen vessel" (Acts 9.15) of God and a shining model of apostolic ministry for the body of the Church.

The entire Orthodox Church honors this Apostle during the current year of the Lord, promoting him as an example to its faithful for a contemporary witness of our faith to "those near and those afar" (Eph. 2.17).

2. The Orthodox Church, having the understanding of the authentic interpretation of the teaching of the Apostle to the Nations, in both peaceful and difficult periods of its two-thousand-year history, can and

must promote to the contemporary world the teaching regarding not only the restoration in Christ of the unity of the entire human race but also the universality of His work of redemption, through which all divisions of the world are overcome and the common nature of all human beings is affirmed.

Nevertheless, the faithful promotion of this message of redemption also presupposes that internal conflicts in the Orthodox Church will be overcome through the surrendering of nationalistic, ethnic, and ideological extremisms of the past. Only in this way will the word of Orthodoxy have on the contemporary world the impact that it should.

3. Inspired by the teaching and the work of the Apostle Paul, we underscore, first and foremost, the importance of the duty of mission for the life of the Church and in particular for the ministry of us all, in accordance with the final commandment of the Lord, "You will be my witnesses not only in Jerusalem, but throughout Judea and Samaria, and to the uttermost parts of the earth" (Acts 1.8). The evangelization of God's people, but also of those who do not believe in Christ, is the supreme duty of the Church. This duty must not be fulfilled in an aggressive manner or by various forms of proselytism but with love, humility, and respect for the identity of each individual and for the cultural particularity of each people. All Orthodox churches must contribute to this missionary effort, respecting the canonical order.

4. The Church of Christ today fulfills its ministry in a rapidly developing world, which has now become interconnected through technological advances in communications and transportation. At the same time, however, the degree of alienation, division, and conflict is also increasing. Christians emphasize that the source of this condition is the alienation of humanity from God. No change in social structures or in rules of behavior suffices to heal this condition. The Church consistently points out that sin can be conquered only through cooperation between God and humankind.

5. Under such circumstances, the contemporary witness of Orthodoxy for the ever increasing problems of humanity and of the world becomes imperative, not only in order that Orthodoxy may point out their causes but also that it may directly confront the tragic consequences that follow. The various nationalistic, ethnic, ideological, and religious differences

continuously nurture dangerous confusion in regard not only to the unquestionable ontological unity of the human race but also to humanity's relationship to sacred creation. The sacredness of the human person is compromised by partial claims for the "individual," whereas our relationship toward the rest of sacred creation is subjected to our arbitrary use or abuse of it.

These divisions in the world introduce an unjust inequality among individuals or even among peoples in regard to their enjoyment of the goods of creation. The divisions deprive billions of people of basic goods and cause misery for human beings, leading to mass migration, kindling nationalistic, religious, and social discrimination or conflict, as well as and threatening the cohesion of traditional societies. These consequences are still more abhorrent because they are inextricably linked to the destruction of the natural environment and the entire ecosystem.

6. For the contemporary crisis of this planet, Orthodox Christians share responsibility with other people, whether they are people of faith or not, because they have tolerated or indiscriminately compromised on extreme and erroneous human choices without credibly challenging these choices with the word of faith. Therefore, they also have a major obligation to help overcome the division in the world.

The Christian teaching about the ontological unity between the human race and sacred creation, the unity expressed by the entire mystery of the redemptive work in Christ, constitutes the foundation for interpreting humanity's relationship with God and the world.

7. Efforts to distance religion from social life are the common tendency of many modern states. The principle of a secular state can be preserved; however, it is unacceptable to interpret this principle as requiring the radical marginalization of religion from all spheres of public life.

8. The gap between rich and poor is growing dramatically in the face of the financial crisis, in most cases the result of manic profiteering and corrupt financial activity, which, lacking an anthropological dimension and sensitivity, does not ultimately serve the real needs of humankind. A viable economy is one that combines efficacy with justice and social solidarity.

9. With respect to the issue of the relationship of Christian faith to the natural sciences, the Orthodox Church has avoided pursuing any

ownership of the developing scientific research and it has avoided assuming a position on every scientific question. From the Orthodox perspective, freedom of research constitutes a God-given gift to humanity. While affirming this, however, Orthodoxy at the same time underscores the dangers concealed in certain scientific achievements, the limits of scientific knowledge, and the existence of another "knowledge" that does not immediately fall within the scope of science. This other "knowledge" proves in many ways to be necessary for enjoying the fruits of science and for establishing proper boundaries through the restraint of egocentrism and through respect for the value of the human person.

10. The Orthodox Church believes that technological and economic progress should not lead to the destruction of the environment and the depletion of natural resources. Greed to satisfy material desires leads to the impoverishment of the human soul and of the environment. We must not forget that the natural riches of the earth are not only humanity's property but primarily God's creation: "The earth is the Lord's and the fullness thereof, the world and all who dwell therein" (Ps. 23.1). We ought to remember that not only today's generation but also all future generations are entitled to the natural resources that the Creator has granted us.

11. In firmly supporting every peaceful effort for just solutions to conflicts that arise, we salute the position of the churches of Russia and Georgia and their fraternal cooperation during the period of recent military conflict. The two Churches fulfilled their obligation to the ministry of reconciliation. We hope that their mutual ecclesiastical efforts will help overcome the tragic consequences of military operations and contribute to the swift reconciliation of their peoples.

12. In the ever growing confusion of our times, the institution of family and marriage faces a crisis. In a spirit of understanding the new complex social condition, the Church is obliged to find ways of spiritually supporting and generally encouraging younger, larger families.

We turn our thoughts especially to our young people, in order to call them to participate actively both in the sacramental and sanctifying life as well as in the missionary and social work of the Church, while also referring their problems and their expectations to the Church, inasmuch as they constitute not only its future but also its present.

13. As Primates and the representatives of the most holy Orthodox churches, fully aware of the gravity of the aforementioned problems, and

laboring to confront them directly as "servants of Christ and stewards of God's mysteries" (1 Cor. 4.1), we proclaim from this see of the First Throne among the Churches, and we reaffirm:

i) Our unswerving position and obligation to safeguard the unity of the Orthodox Church in "the faith once for all delivered to the saints" (Jude 3), in the faith of our Fathers, in the common Divine Eucharist, and in the faithful observance of the canonical system of Church governance, as well as to safeguard this unity by settling, in a spirit of love and peace, any problems that arise from time to time in relations among us.

ii) Our desire for the swift healing of every canonical anomaly that has arisen from historical circumstances and pastoral requirements— anomalies such as in the so-called Orthodox Diaspora—and that we may heal them with a view to overcoming every possible influence that is foreign to Orthodox ecclesiology. In this respect, we welcome the proposal by the Ecumenical Patriarchate to convene pan-Orthodox consultations on this subject in the coming year 2009, and we also welcome the continuation of preparations for the Holy and Great Council. In accordance with the standing order and practice of the pan-Orthodox consultations in Rhodes, the Ecumenical Patriarchate will invite all autocephalous churches.

iii) Our desire to continue, despite any difficulties, theological dialogues with other Christians and to continue interreligious dialogues, especially with Judaism and Islam, given that such dialogue constitutes the only way of solving differences among people, especially in a time such as ours, when every kind of division, including division in the name of religion, threatens the peace and hinder unity.

iv) Our support for the initiatives by the Ecumenical Patriarchate, as well as by other Orthodox Churches, for the protection of the natural environment. Today's environmental crisis, which has both spiritual and ethical causes, renders imperative the obligation of the Church to contribute, through the spiritual means at her disposal, to the protection of God's creation from the consequences of human greed. In this regard, we reaffirm the designation of the first of September, the first day of the ecclesiastical year, as a day of special prayers for the protection of God's creation, and we support the introduction of the subject of the natural environment in the catechetical, homiletic, and overall pastoral activity of our churches, in some of which it is already evident.

v) The decision to proceed with the necessary actions in order to form an inter-Orthodox Committee to study issues of bioethics, issues on which the world also waits to learn the position of Orthodoxy.

Addressing these points to the Orthodox people throughout the world and to the entire oikoumene, we pray "again and again" that peace, justice, and God's love may finally prevail in people's lives.

"Glory be to him whose power, working in us, can do infinitely more than we can ask or imagine, glory be to him in the Church and in Christ Jesus" (Eph. 3.20–21).

Bartholomew of Constantinople
Theodore of Alexandria
Ignatius of Antioch
Theophilos of Jerusalem
Alexei of Moscow
Amphilochios of Montenegro (representing the Church of Serbia)
Laurentiu of Transylvania (representing the Church of Romania)
Dometiyan of Vidin (representing the Church of Bulgaria)
Gerasime of Zugdidi (representing the Church of Georgia)
Chrysostomos of Cyprus
Ieronymos of Athens
Jeremiasz of Wroclaw (representing of the Church of Poland)
Anastasios of Tirana
Christopher of the Czech Lands and Slovakia

COMMON DECLARATIONS WITH THE POPE OF ROME

The Vatican, June 29, 1995

Blessed be the God and Father of our Lord Jesus Christ, who has blessed us in Christ with every spiritual blessing.

Eph 1.3

1. We thank God for our brotherly meeting, which has taken place in His name and with the firm intention of obeying His will that His disciples may be one (John 17.21).[6] Our meeting has followed other important

---

6. On the evening of Thursday, June 29, 1995, Pope John Paul II and Ecumenical Patriarch Bartholomew signed a Common Declaration in the Vatican during their last meeting before the Patriarch's departure from Rome. The following is a translation of the Declaration, which was originally written in Italian.

events that have seen our churches declare their desire to relegate the excommunications of the past to oblivion and to begin to reestablish full communion. Our venerable predecessors, Athenagoras I and Paul VI, became pilgrims to Jerusalem in order to meet in the Lord's name, precisely where the Lord, by His death and resurrection, brought forgiveness and salvation to humanity. Subsequently, their meetings at the Phanar and in Rome initiated this new tradition of fraternal visits for the purpose of fostering a true dialogue of charity and truth. This exchange of visits was repeated during the ministry of Patriarch Dimitrios, when the theological dialogue formally commenced. Our newfound brotherhood in the name of the one Lord has led us to frank discussion, a dialogue whereby we seek understanding and unity.

2. This dialogue—through the Joint International Commission—has proved fruitful and made substantial progress. A common sacramental conception of the Church has emerged, been sustained and transmitted in time by apostolic succession. In our churches, apostolic succession is fundamental to the sanctification and unity of the people of God. Considering that in every local church the mystery of divine love is realized and that this is how the Church of Christ manifests its active presence within each of them, the Joint Commission has been able to declare that our churches recognize one another as sister churches, responsible together for safeguarding the one Church of God, in fidelity to the divine plan, and in an altogether special way with regard to unity.

From the bottom of our hearts we thank the Lord of the Church, because the affirmations we have made together not only hasten the way to solving existing difficulties but also enable Catholics and Orthodox to offer a common witness of faith.

3. This is particularly appropriate on the eve of the third millennium, when, two thousand years after the birth of Christ, all Christians are preparing to make an examination of conscience in light of the reality of His proclamation of salvation in history and among people. We will celebrate this great jubilee on our pilgrimage toward full unity and toward that blessed day, which we pray is not far off, when we will be able to share the same bread and the same cup, in the one Eucharist of the Lord.

Let us invite our faithful to make this spiritual pilgrimage together toward the jubilee. Reflection, prayer, dialogue, reciprocal forgiveness, and mutual fraternal love will bring us closer to the Lord and help us to better understand His will for the Church and for humanity.

4. In view of this, we urge our faithful, Catholics and Orthodox alike, to reinforce the spirit of brotherhood that stems from the one baptism and from participation in the sacramental life. In the course of history and in the more recent past, there have been attacks and acts of oppression on both sides. As we prepare, on this occasion, to ask the Lord for His great mercy, we invite all to forgive one another and to express a firm will that a new relationship of brotherhood and active collaboration may be established.

Such a spirit should encourage both Catholics and Orthodox, especially where they live side by side, to a more intense collaboration in cultural, spiritual, pastoral, educational, and social activities. It should encourage them to avoid any temptation toward undue zeal for their own community to the disadvantage of the other. May the good of Christ's Church always prevail! Mutual support and the exchange of gifts can only render pastoral activity more effective and our witness to the gospel, which we desire to proclaim, more transparent.

5. We maintain that a more active and concerted collaboration will also facilitate the Church's influence in promoting peace and justice in situations of political or ethnic conflict. The Christian faith has unprecedented possibilities for solving humanity's tensions and antagonisms.

6. In meeting one another, the Pope of Rome and the Ecumenical Patriarch have prayed for the unity of all Christians. In their prayers, they have included all the baptized faithful, who are incorporated into Christ, and have called for deeper fidelity to His gospel among the various communities.

7. They bear in their heart a concern for all humanity, without any discrimination according to race, color, language, ideology, or religion. Therefore, they encourage dialogue, not only among the Christian churches but also between the various religions and, above all, with those that are monotheistic.

Doubtless, all this represents a contribution to the strengthening of peace in the world, an outcome for which our churches pray constantly. In this spirit, then, we declare, without hesitation, that we are in favor of harmony among peoples, in favor of their collaboration, and especially—and for this, which concerns us most directly, we pray fervently—in favor of the full realization of the European Union without delay. Indeed, we hope that its borders will be extended to the East.

At the same time, we also appeal to everyone to make a determined effort to solve the world's burning environmental problem, in order that we might avoid the great danger that threatens the world today as a result of the abuse of its resources that are God's gift.

May the Lord heal the wounds tormenting humanity today and hear our prayers, as well as those of our faithful, for peace in our churches and in throughout the world.

Pope John Paul II and Ecumenical Patriarch Bartholomew

The Vatican, June 29, 2004

Be watchful, stand firm in your faith, be courageous, be strong. Let all that you do be done in love.

1 Cor 16.13–14

1. In the spirit of faith in Christ and the reciprocal love that unites us, we thank God for this gift of our new meeting that occurs on the Feast of the Holy Apostles Peter and Paul, and witnesses to our firm determination to continue on our way toward full communion with one another in Christ.

2. Many positive steps have marked our common journey, beginning above all with the historical event that we recall today: the embrace of Pope Paul VI and Ecumenical Patriarch Athenagoras I on the Mount of Olives in Jerusalem, on the fifth and sixth of January, 1964. We, their successors, are meeting today in order to commemorate fittingly, before God, that blessed encounter, now part of the history of the Church, faithfully remembering it and its original intent.

3. The embrace, in Jerusalem, of our respective predecessors of venerable memory visibly expressed a hope that dwells in the hearts of all, as the communiqué declared: "With eyes turned to Christ, together with the Father, the archetype and author of unity and of peace, they pray to God that this encounter may be the sign and prelude of things to come for the glory of God and the enlightenment of His faithful people. After so many centuries of silence, they have now met with the desire to do the Lord's

will and to proclaim the ancient truth of His gospel, entrusted to the Church."[7]

4. Unity and peace! The hope kindled by that historic encounter has lit up our journey during these last decades. Aware that the Christian world has suffered the tragedy of separation for centuries, our predecessors and we ourselves have persevered in the "dialogue of charity," our gaze turned to that blessed, shining day on which it will be possible to communicate with the same cup of the precious blood and the holy body of the Lord.[8] The many ecclesial events that have punctuated these past years have placed on firm foundation the commitment to brotherly love —a love that, in learning from past lessons, may be ready to forgive, more inclined to believe in good than in evil, and intent first and foremost on complying with the divine redeemer as well as in being attracted and transformed by Him.[9]

5. Let us thank the Lord for the exemplary gestures of reciprocal love, participation, and sharing that He has granted us to make; among them, it is only right to recall the papal[10] visit to Ecumenical Patriarch Dimitrios in 1979, when the creation of the Joint International Commission for Theological Dialogue between the Roman Catholic Church and all the Orthodox Churches was announced at the Phanar, a further step toward sustaining the "dialogue of truth" with the "dialogue of charity"; Patriarch Dimitrios's visit to Rome in 1987; and our own meeting[11] in Rome on the Feast of Saints Peter and Paul in 1995, when we prayed in St Peter's, despite the painful separation during the celebration of the Eucharistic Liturgy, since we cannot yet drink from the same chalice of the Lord. Then, more recently, there was the meeting in Assisi on the Day of Prayer for Peace in the World, and then the "Common Declaration on Environmental Ethics for the Safeguard of Creation," signed on June 10, 2002, in the context of the Fourth Ecological Symposium, entitled "The Adriatic Sea: a Sea at Risk—Unity of Purpose."

---

7. See the *Common Declaration of Pope Paul VI and Patriarch Athenagoras I, Tomos Agapis* (Vatican–Phanar, 1971), n. 50, 120.

8. See Patriarch Athenagoras I, *Address to Pope Paul VI*, January 5, 1964, in *Tomos Agapis*, n. 48, 109.

9. See Pope Paul VI, *Address to Patriarch Athenagoras I*, January 6, 1964, in *Tomos Agapis*, n. 49, 117.

10. Of Pope John Paul II.

11. Of Pope John Paul II and Patriarch Bartholomew.

6. Despite our firm determination to journey on toward full communion, it would have been unrealistic not to expect obstacles of various kinds: doctrinal, first of all, but also obstacles that are the result of a troubled history. In addition, new problems that have emerged from radical changes in political and social structures have not failed to make themselves felt in relations among the Christian churches. With the return to freedom of Christians in Central and Eastern Europe, old fears have also been reawakened, rendering dialogue more difficult. Nonetheless, St. Paul's exhortation to the Corinthians, "Let all things be done in charity," must always be vibrant among us and between us.

7. The Joint International Commission for Theological Dialogue between the Roman Catholic Church and all the Orthodox Churches, created with so much hope, has marked our progress in recent years. It is still a suitable instrument for studying the ecclesiological and historical problems that lie at the root of our difficulties and for identifying theoretical solutions to them. It is our duty to persevere in the important commitment to reopen that work as soon as possible. In examining the reciprocal initiatives of the offices of Rome and of Constantinople in this regard, we ask the Lord to sustain our determination and to convince everyone of how essential it is to pursue the "dialogue of truth."

8. Our meeting in Rome today also enables us to face certain problems and misunderstandings that have recently surfaced. The long experience of the "dialogue of charity" comes to our aid precisely during these circumstances, so that difficulties may be faced serenely, without slowing or clouding our progress on the journey that we have undertaken toward full communion in Christ.

9. Before a world that is suffering every kind of division and imbalance, today's encounter is also intended as a practical and forceful reminder of the importance that Christians and the churches coexist in peace and harmony, so that, being in agreement, their witness to the message of the gospel may be as credible and as convincing as possible.

10. In the special context of Europe, which is moving in the direction of higher forms of integration and of expansion toward the East of the Continent, we thank the Lord for this positive development and express the hope that, in this new situation, collaboration between Roman Catholics and Orthodox may grow. There are so many challenges to face together if we are to contribute to the good of society: to heal with love the

scourge of terrorism; to instill the hope of peace; to help set aright the multitude of grievous conflicts in order to restore to the European continent the awareness of its Christian roots; to build true dialogue with Islam, since indifference and reciprocal ignorance can only give rise to diffidence and even hatred; to nourish an awareness of the sacred nature of human life; to work to ensure that science does not deny the divine spark that every human being receives with the gift of life; to collaborate so that our earth may not be disfigured and that creation may preserve the beauty with which it was originally endowed by God; but, above all, to proclaim the gospel message with fresh vigor, showing contemporary men and women how the gospel can help them to rediscover themselves and to build a more humane world.

11. Let us pray that the Lord may grant peace to the Church and to the world, and that He may grace our journey toward full communion, with the wisdom of His Spirit, *ut unum in Christo simus* ["so that we may be one in Christ"].

Pope John Paul II and Ecumenical Patriarch Bartholomew

Ecumenical Patriarchate, November 30, 2006

> This is the day that the Lord has made; let us rejoice and be glad in it!
>
> Ps. 117.24

This fraternal encounter, which brings us together, Pope Benedict XVI of Rome and Ecumenical Patriarch Bartholomew I, is God's work and, in a certain sense, His gift. We give thanks to the author of all that is good, who allows us once again, in prayer and in dialogue, to express the joy we feel as brothers and to renew our commitment to move toward full communion. This commitment comes from the Lord's will and from our responsibility as pastors in the Church of Christ. May our meeting be a sign and an encouragement for us to share the same sentiments and the same attitudes of fraternity, cooperation, and communion in charity and truth. The Holy Spirit will help us to prepare the great day of the reestablishment of full unity, whenever and however God wills it. Then we will truly be able to rejoice and be glad.

1. We have recalled with thankfulness the meetings of our venerable predecessors, blessed by the Lord, who showed the world the urgent need

for unity and traced sure paths for attaining it, through dialogue, prayer, and the daily life of the Church. Pope Paul VI and Patriarch Athenagoras I went as pilgrims to Jerusalem, to the very place where Jesus Christ died and rose again for the salvation of the world, and they also met again, here in the Phanar and in Rome. They left us a common declaration, which retains all its value; it emphasizes that true dialogue in charity must sustain and inspire all relations between individuals and between churches, that it "must be rooted in a total fidelity to the one Lord Jesus Christ and in mutual respect for their own traditions."[12] Nor have we forgotten the reciprocal visits of His Holiness Pope John Paul II and His All Holiness Dimitrios I. It was during the visit of Pope John Paul II, his first ecumenical visit, that the creation of the mixed commission for theological dialogue between the Roman Catholic Church and the Orthodox Church was announced. This has brought together our churches in the declared aim of reestablishing full communion.

As for relations between the Church of Rome and the Church of Constantinople, we cannot fail to recall the solemn ecclesial act effacing the memory of the ancient anathemas, which for centuries had shadowed our churches. We have not yet drawn from this act all the positive consequences that can flow from it in our progress towards full unity and to which the Joint Commission is called to make an important contribution. We exhort our faithful to take an active part in this process, through prayer and through significant gestures.

2. At the time of the plenary session of the Joint Commission for Theological Dialogue, which was recently held in Belgrade through the generous hospitality of the Serbian Orthodox Church, we expressed our profound joy at the resumption of the theological dialogue. This had been interrupted for several years because of various difficulties, but now the commission was able to work afresh in a spirit of friendship and cooperation. In treating the topic "Conciliarity and Authority in the Church" at local, regional, and universal levels, the commission undertook a phase of study on the ecclesiological and canonical consequences of the sacramental nature of the Church. This will permit us to address some of the principal questions that are still unresolved. We are committed to offer

---

12. See *Tomos Agapis*, 195.

unceasing support, as in the past, to the work entrusted to this commission, and we accompany its members with our prayers.

3. As pastors, we have first of all reflected on the mission to proclaim the gospel in today's world. This mission, "Go, make disciples of all nations" (Matt. 28.19), is today more timely and necessary than ever, even in traditionally Christian countries. Moreover, we cannot ignore the rise of secularization, relativism, even nihilism, particularly in the Western world. All this calls for a renewed and powerful proclamation of the gospel, adapted to the cultures of our time. Our traditions represent for us a patrimony that must be continually shared, proposed, and interpreted anew. This is why we must strengthen our cooperation and our common witness before the world.

4. We have viewed positively the process that has led to the formation of the European Union. Those engaged in this great project should not fail to take into consideration all aspects of it that affect the inalienable rights of the human person, especially the right of religious freedom, a witness and guarantor of respect for all other freedoms. In every step toward unification, minorities must be protected along with their cultural traditions and the distinguishing features of their religion. In Europe, while remaining open to other religions and to their cultural contributions, we must unite our efforts to preserve Christian roots, traditions, and values, to ensure respect for history, and so to contribute to the European culture of the future and to the quality of human relations at every level. In this context, how could we not evoke the very ancient witnesses and the illustrious Christian heritage of the land in which our meeting is taking place, beginning with what we are told in the Acts of the Apostles concerning the figure of St. Paul, Apostle to the Nations? In this land, the gospel message and the ancient cultural tradition met. This link, which has contributed so much to the Christian heritage that we share, remains timely and in the future will bear more fruit for evangelization and for the cause of our unity.

5. Our concern extends to those parts of today's world where Christians live and to the difficulties they face, particularly poverty, war, and terrorism, but our concern extends equally to various forms of exploitation of the poor, of migrants, women, and children. We are called to work together to promote respect for the rights of every human being, created in the image and likeness of God, and to foster economic, social, and

cultural development. Our theological and ethical traditions can offer a solid basis for a united approach in preaching and action. Above all, we wish to affirm that killing innocent people in God's name is an offence against him and against human dignity. We must all commit ourselves to the renewed service of humanity and to the defense of human life, every human life.

We take profoundly to heart the cause of peace in the Middle East, where our Lord lived, suffered, died, and rose again and where a great multitude of our Christian brethren have lived for centuries. We fervently hope that peace will be reestablished in that region, that respectful coexistence will be strengthened between the different peoples who live there as well as between the churches and the different religions found there. To this end, we encourage the establishment of closer relationships between Christians and of an authentic and honest interreligious dialogue, with a view to combating every form of violence and discrimination.

6. At present, in the face of the great threats to the natural environment, we want to express our concern at the harm, both to humanity and the whole of creation, that can result from economic and technological progress that does not know its limits. As religious leaders, we consider it one of our duties to encourage and to support all efforts made to protect God's creation and to bequeath to future generations a world in which they will be able to live.

7. Finally, our thoughts turn to all of you, the faithful of our two churches throughout the world, bishops, priests, deacons, men and women religious, laymen and laywomen engaged in ecclesial service, as well as all the baptized. In Christ we also greet other Christians, assuring them of our prayers and our openness to dialogue and cooperation. In the words of the Apostle to the Nations, we greet all of you: "Grace to you and peace from God our Father and the Lord Jesus Christ" (2 Cor. 1.2).

Pope Benedict XVI and Ecumenical Patriarch Bartholomew

Reflections on the World Council of Churches

1. This memorandum constitutes the due response of the Ecumenical Patriarchate to the letter of Dr. Konrad Raiser, general secretary of the World Council of Churches, sent to the member churches of the W.C.C.

on the tenth of July, 1993.[13] In that letter, the general secretary raised five fundamental questions pertaining to the nature of the World Council of Churches and its future orientation and asked the member churches to formulate their viewpoint. The initiative was timely, coming precisely after fifty years of fertile, multifaceted, and productive activity, even if this very activity, from time to time and on various occasions, has been the object of reservations, criticism, and disagreement. The forthcoming eighth general assembly, coinciding with the fiftieth anniversary of the World Council of Churches, offers a unique opportunity for an evaluation of the council's work and for a definition of its future orientation. It is with pleasure that the Ecumenical Patriarchate attempts this evaluation, and it is in good faith that it offers an objective formulation of its reflections as well as its vision for the future of an institution so closely bound up with contemporary ecclesiastical reality.

2. In its constitution, the World Council of Churches is defined as a "fellowship of churches," a term suggesting that this institution is primarily an instrument at the disposal of the churches and not of any other organization or movement. As such, it has the objective of assisting the churches in their effort to promote the cause of Christian unity, which is so sought after. It also fosters a productive cooperation among its members, aiming to respond to the manifold problems and needs of the contemporary human person and of all of life.

3. The term *communion*, an ecclesiological expression par excellence, as well as a eucharistic term, which has been used throughout the twentieth century and, particularly—we would even say with a certain emphasis—after the Fifth World Conference of Faith and Order in Santiago de Compostela, probably gives to outsiders a wrong impression of the nature of the relationship and cooperation between churches and confessions within the World Council of Churches. The present reality in the World Council of Churches is, at the very least, a strange one. Within the council, churches coexist and cooperate—and not only churches but also confessions and other Christian entities. Therefore, any definition of the

---

13. The full title of the original text was "Reflections of the Ecumenical Patriarchate on its Understanding and Vision of the World Council of Churches on the Eve of the Third Millennium." It also appeared in *The Ecumenical Review* 48 (1996). The editor is grateful to Dr. Gary Vachicouras, of the Orthodox Institute in Chambésy, for his assistance in supplying this text.

ecclesial character of all its members becomes almost impossible, given that the criteria for membership, criteria based on numbers of faithful, organization, or administration, are neither adequate, sufficiently clear, nor unquestionable in ecclesiological terms. Obviously, we refer here to those Christian entities that originate from or are the products of different historical, ecclesiological, theological, and even cultural traditions and, therefore, cannot be in eucharistic communion with each other and, what is even more difficult, cannot be in communion with churches, such as the Orthodox Church, for which strict and detailed ecclesiological prescriptions apply.

Within the World Council of Churches, churches and confessions constitute a "fellowship" that, according to the same constitution of the council, calls "the churches to the goal of visible unity in one faith and in one eucharistic fellowship expressed in worship and in common life in Christ, and to advance towards that unity in order that the world may believe."[14] This "eucharistic fellowship," we must admit, is not a reality yet, just as everything in the council is in evolution. Nevertheless, after fifty years of fruitful cooperation within the World Council of Churches, its members are obliged to clarify the meaning and the extent of the fellowship they experience in it and to clarify as well as the ecclesiological significance of "koinonia," which is, precisely, the purpose and the aim of the World Council of Churches but not the present reality.

4. Relationships between churches and confessions that cooperate within the council have a distinctive nature and character, which is sufficiently indicated in the Toronto Statement: within the council, churches and confessions reflect together, work together, and walk together, aiming at Christian unity and service to humanity. For this reason, the Ecumenical Patriarchate considers that both the World Council of Churches and the ecumenical movement in general contribute to and serve the ecclesiological meaning of Christian unity—that is, their primary object and raison d'être are the restoration of unity in the Church.

5. The World Council of Churches has been rightly considered as the privileged instrument of the ecumenical movement: It constitutes the forum in which its member churches can freely cooperate, fully defend their own tradition, and develop their multiform ecumenical activities on

---

14. See WCC *Constitution* III, 1.

the ground of their own ecclesial identity, their tradition, and their dogmatic teaching. Experience, however, has shown that, in the past twenty years, bilateral relations between churches and the multiplication of ecumenical and inter-confessional organizations or movements, which serve also the cause of Christian unity, compel the member churches certainly to consider the World Council of Churches as the privileged and yet not the unique or exclusive instrument of the one ecumenical movement.

6. The assertion in the above paragraph certainly prompts the churches to have a new vision of the World Council of Churches as an instrument and coordinating center of the ecumenical movement. It would be desirable, therefore, to ensure, in the foreseeable future, a closer coordination between the World Council of Churches and the regional ecumenical organizations so that any waste in energy, human capital, or material resources may be avoided. It is especially desirable to take into consideration that its is now repeatedly affirmed that all church councils in the world (the World Council, as well as regional and national councils) serve the one and the same ecumenical idea. A closer relationship and cooperation between the World Council of Churches and other councils could—without excluding the degree of internal autonomy that these councils claim for themselves—prove beneficial not only in the promotion of Christian unity but also in the diakonia of its member churches.

7. During its fifty years of existence, the World Council of Churches has increased numerically, counting today approximately three hundred and thirty members. As we have already observed, however,[15] there is little homogeneity among the council's members, with respect not only to theology, ecclesiology, sacraments, tradition, etc., but also to their various stands vis-à-vis problems in contemporary society. This became obvious during recent ecumenical conferences or assemblies of the World Council of Churches. There is no doubt that the readiness of various churches, confessions, and other Christian entities to join the council demonstrates the interest they have in the work undertaken by the council. Nevertheless, in our effort to formulate a new vision for the World Council of Churches, we cannot avoid raising the following question: What, in the coming years, will be the significance of new confessions, small entities, and other ecclesiastical streams adhering to the council—of bodies that

---

15. See above, paragraph 3.

today grow and develop at the expense of historical member churches of the World Council of Churches, and not necessarily only at the expense of the Orthodox? In this regard, the Ecumenical Patriarchate considers that it is necessary to formulate, besides a new vision for the World Council of Churches, some new, clearly theological and ecclesiological criteria for membership.

This is a fundamental request of the Ecumenical Patriarchate, and, we are sure, of all the autocephalous Orthodox churches and, presumably, of many other member churches and churches that have a working relationship with the World Council of Churches—among which one should certainly include the Roman Catholic Church. We consider, therefore, that this should be an immediate priority for the council, whose interest in considering would be to avoid jeopardizing its future, placing itself under question, or rendering itself self-contradictory.

8. As was already observed, the World Council of Churches is an instrument of the ecumenical movement. The space in which it moves and acts is the oikoumene. Nevertheless, the Ecumenical Patriarchate, and the Orthodox Church in general, consider that the technical term "ecumenical movement," which has been used for more than seventy years in Christian circles, should not lose its original meaning. The joint activities of Christians, particularly their encounter with other faiths or ideological streams, certainly take place within the wider framework of oikoumene, and they constitute expressions of the ecumenical movement. But surely they are not its primary purpose. This is why, we believe, this technical term "ecumenical movement" should express the effort aimed at Christian unity only. In this regard, there should be transparency at the level of terminology, so that we may avoid misinterpretations or misunderstandings.

9. The World Council of Churches always, and even before its official founding—namely, when the ecumenical movement was focusing on the interchurch movements of the first decades of our century, with the exception probably of "Faith and Order," which moved and continues to move on a specific theological ground—dealt with a variety of issues directly relating to the life and problems of contemporary society and tried in many ways to find appropriate solutions. This multifaceted and God-pleasing activity of the council was highlighted by the Ecumenical Patriarchate in the message issued in 1973, on the occasion of the twenty-fifth

anniversary of the World Council of Churches. This diakonia of the council was also recognized in 1986 by the Third Preconciliar Pan-Orthodox Conference. Problems in the world today, suffering in war, social injustices, ethnic rivalries, and whatever offends the human person, this very "icon" of God—these offenses compel the council to continue acting, on the basis of common theological presuppositions, in the fields of diakonia, social welfare, justice, peace, defense of human rights, and the protection of the entire God's creation.

10. The Ecumenical Patriarchate, caring also for the spiritual and material growth of the Orthodox churches in Eastern Europe and the Middle East, which were severely tormented for many decades, expresses to the World Council of Churches deep gratitude for its manifold assistance to these churches. As the Orthodox rightly remarked during the consultation about the common vision and understanding of the World Council Churches, which was held last June at the Orthodox Center of Chambésy, the council, even during the difficult times of totalitarian regimes in Central and Eastern Europe, "had begun to speak and act on matters of peace, justice and human rights related to particular conditions in which the local Orthodox churches involved were not free to articulate their position or to affect the situation." The Ecumenical Patriarchate, therefore, believes that the World Council of Churches, in any future programmatic activities beyond the next assembly, should not neglect the field of diakonia, because this particular aspect of its activity translates into action whatever we debate on an academic level and consolidates the fellowship we experience in it.

11. World developments indicate that in the forthcoming millennium churches will be facing difficult situations tending to lead toward deterioration in the relationship between states, nations, races, and religions. This was particularly emphasized by the Orthodox Primates during our recent summit meeting in Patmos, in September 1995. This is why the World Council of Churches should always be vigilant and offer to its member churches every possible assistance in their effort to become agents of peace, stability, and fraternity. In this connection, the Ecumenical Patriarchate wishes to stress that instability, insecurity, and enmity underlie the rise aggressive activity by various sectarian or para-religious groups around the globe. This is why it considers that the combat against this phenomenon, which whets all manner of fundamentalist tendencies and

tensions in inter-Christian and interfaith relations, as well as the combat against the related problem of proselytism should be one of the basic priorities of the council in the years ahead.

12. The Ecumenical Patriarchate always attributes and continues to attribute particular importance to the theological research conducted in the framework of Unit I, particularly within the commission of "Faith and Order," as well as in other programmatic clusters, such as the ones dealing with mission and evangelism. It is a fact that the theological research, even if it has progressed considerably during the last fifty years, was not in a position to bear concrete results able to lead us to Christian unity. Probably because of insurmountable difficulties stemming from the lack of theological and ecclesiological homogeneity of those conversing in the World Council of Churches, fundamental themes, such as holy tradition, ecclesiology, conciliarity, ordained ministry, mysteriology, and particularly the sacraments of baptism and eucharist, have not been adequately advanced. This fact should not discourage us.

For, even if the theological dialogue advances with extremely slow steps, nothing prevents the member churches from envisioning, for the post-Harare period, a World Council of Churches able to ensure a harmonious cooperation of all Christian forces in the moral, social, missionary, and diaconal fields, no matter what their basic doctrinal differences are, just as the Ecumenical Patriarchate was stressing seventy years ago through its very well-known 1920 encyclical. In conclusion, then, we wish to emphasize that one of the visions the Ecumenical Patriarchate has for the World Council of Churches involves the evolution of the council on the grounds of a more rigorous ecclesiological basis and presupposition, as we already mentioned above. This would contribute to the upgrading of its nature and would, at the same time, facilitate the definition of the fellowship experienced within it by its member churches.

The above reflections are submitted by the Ecumenical Patriarchate with great esteem and love in Christ.

At the Phanar, November 30, 1995
Feast of Saint Andrew the Apostle

Index